THE INSIDERS' GUIDE ®
TO
GREATER Charleston

by
Anne Jervey Rhett
and
J. Michael McLaughlin

9 780912 367507

THE INSIDERS' GUIDE ®

Insiders' Guides, Inc.

Published and Distributed by:
The Insiders' Guides®, Inc.
P.O. Box 2057 • Highway 64
Manteo, NC 27954
(919) 473-6100

•

SECOND EDITION
1st printing

•

Copyright ©1993
The Evening Post Publishing
Company

•

Printed in the United States of
America

•

ISBN 0-912367-50-4

The Insiders' Guides®, Inc.

Publisher/Managing Editor
Beth P Storie

President/General Manager
Michael McOwen

Manager/Creative Services
David Haynes

Manager/Distribution
Giles Bissonnette

Fulfillment Coordination
Gina Twiford

Controller
Claudette Forney

•

**A Supplemental
Publication of**

The Post and Courier

Preface

Welcome to the wonders of Greater Charleston! Three counties—Charleston, Berkeley and Dorchester — make up the 2,600 square miles around Charleston proper. Collectively, they are referred to now as the Trident or — by old timers — as the Lowcountry. Although they have some things in common, each county has a unique profile, a different history and a separate agenda for the future.

We begin our exploration of the Trident area in Charleston, and then move out to adjoining areas. Using a standard based on quality and value for, we share our "inside" observations about each county's accommodations, dining, shopping, entertainment, neighborhoods and the like. Then we describe some larger categories such as health care and attractions which pertain to all three. Although we catalog these offerings as a reference service, we also lace the sections with historical reference. Our aim is to give you a realistic overview of what the Trident area *is* because of what it *has been*, all the while leading you to what are some of its brightest and best attributes.

You may come to luxuriate in the indulgences of the city, or perhaps to "stop the world and get off" by taking refuge in the marshes and woodlands of what is — by East Coast standards, at any rate — a last frontier. Then again, the Charleston area may be your new home. In any case, we hope that what you need to become acclimated or to refer to as a resident is contained in these pages. From directions that simplify getting around these parts, to overviews of neighborhoods within your reach, our goal is to help you come to town and stay here.

Welcome to
Greater Charleston!

Acknowledgements

For their input, expertise and assistance in many forms, we thank all who helped with the production of this book — especially Claire Lisle and Frank Rhett, whose diligence resulted in quality research. Some others who went the extra mile include: Mary Jane Bradham; Walt Bonner; Carmel Dodds; Susan Garmany; Mary Graham; Martha Harken; Betsy Howland; Louis and Nancy Jervey; Gerry McCord; Vivian Parker; Marty Pickett; Sanna Prause; Cheshire and Toni Rhett; Heidi Ravenel; C. Wayne Waltz; Liz Tucker of Creative Expeditions; Ms. Meg Lavin at Drayton Hall; the Research Department at the Charleston County Public Library, and Miss Sally Reahard.

We also appreciate the time and information shared by employees of Trident agencies and businesses such as: the South Carolina Wildlife and Marine Resources Department; The Charleston Trident Chamber of Commerce; The Summerville Chamber of Commerce; The Charleston County Park and Recreation Commission; The Charleston County Community Education Program; Arthur Ravenel Junior Real Estate Company; and Joseph P. Riley Real Estate.

About The Authors

Anne Jervey Rhett

Anne Jervey Rhett, a native Charlestonian whose family has been "Inside" Charleston since before the Revolution, is a faculty member at Charleston Day School and a freelance marketing/ public relations consultant. She has taught English at the College of Charleston and worked as Director of Admissions/Public Relations at Ashley Hall School. Anne graduated from the University of South Carolina School of Journalism in 1981 with a master of mass communication degree. As a free-lance journalist, she has covered Spoleto USA Festival for both newspaper and television, and her local interest articles have appeared in national and regional publications. Anne lives away from the bustling crowds, with her husband, daughter, son and two black labs.

J. Michael McLaughlin

J. Michael McLaughlin has been living in and writing about the Lowcountry for the past dozen years. During that time, his interests in history, architecture and the legendary Charleston lifestyle have led him into countless adventures. His writing has found its way into numerous regional and national magazines and his freelance work as an advertising/public relations consultant has captured national marketing awards. Michael was born and raised on a farm in Indiana, but he's quick to point out it was in *southern* Indiana, and "in Charleston, that makes a *big* difference." He graduated from Indiana University in 1967 with a B.S. degree in Business-Journalism — aiming for a Madison Avenue career in advertising. Instead, his first writing job turned out to be in Vietnam where — as a war correspondent — he won a Bronze Star for his coverage of the 101st Airborne Division during the ill-fated Tet Offensive. After a decade back home as an award-winning writer-producer for several Midwestern ad agencies, he joined the writers' colony in Key West, Florida. And that's where he was living when 1979's Hurricane David forced him to evacuate the island — and he discovered Charleston. Since then, he's considered himself "a born again Southerner" — writing about Charleston and the Lowcountry's charming if idiosyncratic ways.

Table of Contents

Charleston Area Overview

SOUTH CAROLINA

Goose
Creek

To Summerville

Cooper
River

Thomas
Island

Hanahan

North
Charleston

Daniel
Island

Wando
River

Ashley
River

Drum
Island

Isle of Palms

Sullivans Island

Charleston

Mt. Pleasant

Stono
River

Charleston Harbor

James Island

Johns Island

Seabrook
Island

Kiawah
Island

Charleston and Surrounds

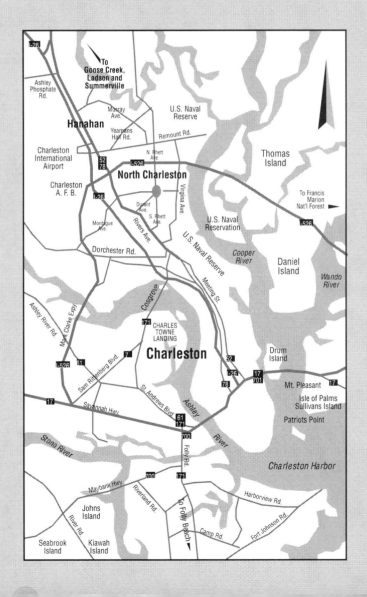

Downtown Charleston

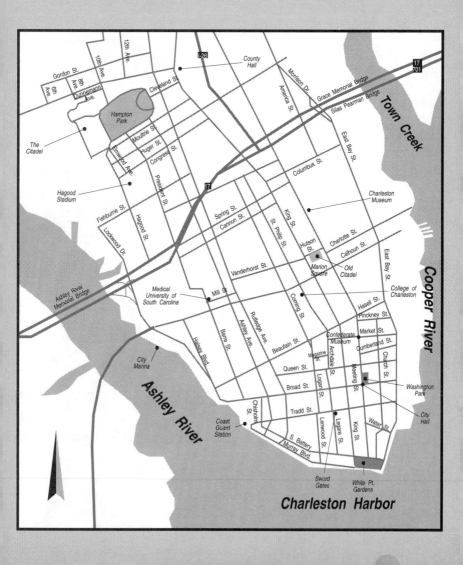

Charleston Harbor

Getting Around
Greater Charleston

Visitors to the Trident area arrive via different modes of transportation, and are faced with challenges unique to each form. For instance, if you fly in, ride the bus or take the train, how are you going to negotiate the trip into town or — worse yet — out to the fringes? Say you came in on a yacht, or you are a passenger on a cruise ship. What next?

American, Delta, USAIR and other airlines fly into the Charleston International Airport with some regularity (see Airports). The task of securing connecting rides from the airport requires little planning as ample cabs, vans and limousines are clustered out front for the taking. The "new" airport (as natives call it, although it is several years old now) is located in North Charleston, off Interstate 26. Passengers can take a limousine or one of the shuttle services to central hotels (see the listing at the bottom of this section). Rates vary but range from $10 to $25 a person. Cabs are the best bet for destinations off the beaten track, unless you would like to rent a car. Of course, if you are in a big hurry and have access to a landing pad, Helicopters Over Charleston (559-1046) is available for charter.

If you are arriving on a bus, the Greyhound Bus terminal (722-7721) is located in Charleston Heights, and is a routine stop for cabs. The Amtrak train station (744-8264) is also in the North area between Rivers and Montague Avenues. Save yourself some possible inconvenience and talk with your travel agent or accommodations contact to arrange a ride ahead of time.

Cruise ship passengers will be docked off Concord Street near — but not in — the restored Historic District. Daytime walking there is fine if you have the stamina and can stand the noise of the traffic, but we suggest cabs or limousines at night for safety and convenience.

Private yachts moor at one of the several marinas in the Trident area. Cabs or rented cars are the best solution unless you are docked at the City Marina, which is centrally located and close to sidewalks. The Ashley Marina, although only blocks away, is not as good for walking because of the fast moving, congested traffic at its entrance; we must note, however, that a walkway has been built into the new portion of the road system and may suit the brave.

You may be traveling in your own car, and need some directions

• *1*

into town. If you are driving north to Charleston, stay on Highway 17 South (which we call Savannah Highway) until you reach West Ashley. Cross the Ashley River Bridge (still on 17 South) and either veer to the right (which becomes Lockwood Boulevard), to head for the Historic District, or slightly to the left (still on 17 South) to reach the northern part of the peninsula or North Charleston, or to cross the Cooper River Bridge to Mt. Pleasant and the East Islands.

If you take a right on Lockwood, you must make a decision at the next stoplight. Are you interested in visiting the medical complexes or the College of Charleston (all of which are visible from Calhoun), shops on King Street or perhaps the Visitors Center? If so, go left and the road will actually curve into and become Calhoun Street. King Street intersects Calhoun first and you can turn right. Or look for the green and white signs that will direct you to the Visitors Bureau on upper Meeting Street, just blocks off Calhoun on the left.

However, if those are not your destinations and you need to reach the southern tip of the peninsula, follow the straight arrow at the stoplight (this will be a continuation of Lockwood), and drive past the City Marina and Rice Mill Building, round the corner by the Coast Guard Station and you will be on Broad Street. Broad eventually dead ends in East Bay Street. Take a right on any intersection street to find addresses "Below Broad"; but, beware: many Charleston streets and alleys

are *one way only*, so look for the signs.

From another approach, driving into Charleston on Highway 17 North, you will cross the older two-lane Grace Memorial Bridge or the newer three-lane Silas Pearman Bridge in its one reversible lane. We recommend driving across Grace as it is a straight shot into town (whereas the Silas Pearman Bridge's lane requires some maneuvering town-side). Likewise, if you are headed in on Interstate 26, stay on the Interstate until it merges with the traffic from the Grace Memorial Bridge. After the first stoplight, take a right at the Rutledge Avenue Exit and follow Rutledge Avenue to Calhoun Street. There, take a left for all above described destinations off the Calhoun route (except the medical facilities, which are located to the right of the intersection). Or, if you are headed for the Southern peninsular, stay on Rutledge Avenue, which will eventually dead end in Murray Boulevard (the Battery).

To reach the in-town marinas or areas west of the Ashley, cross the Grace Memorial Bridge or stay on the Interstate until it becomes The Crosstown (basically an extension of your same highway) until you reach the intersection before the Ashley River Bridge. Go left to reach the marinas or go straight to cross the bridge and be west of the Ashley.

For those of you coming in on I-26, there are two other options to consider if you are headed to areas in North Charleston, west of the Ashley, or east of the Cooper. One choice is to take the Mark Clark

Photo: Janice G. Vermillion

The Charleston peninsula is bordered by two rivers. In the foreground is the WWI Bridge over the Ashley River. In the background dual bridges span the Cooper River.

Expressway (Interstate 526-South) Exit which eventually intersects with 17 South (Savannah Highway); at this point, you will take a left to head toward town or a right to go south to Ravenel or Hollywood. A second choice off the Interstate is to exit right at Cosgrove Avenue (Highway 7), which becomes Sam Rittenberg Boulevard. Sam Rittenberg forks at the Ashley Landing Shopping Center, just after the Orange Grove Road intersection; you may either take Highway 171 (straight ahead) toward the Ashley River Bridge, or stay on Sam Rittenberg Boulevard as it veers to the right. This boulevard is intersected first by Highway 61 and later by Highway 17 South.

If you are heading east of the Cooper and would like to bypass the older bridges, take the Mark Clark Expressway North (which at this time terminates in Mt. Pleasant). You will be amazed by the beautiful scenery, but watch your speedometer as the patrol force tickets offenders with regularity.

With many references to our beautiful bridges, a word of caution is in order: traffic tends to snarl on them and can screech to hour- or hours-long halts. Crossing the old Grace Memorial Bridge, which spans with such style the Cooper River and marshes below, is a thrilling experience until you are stuck immobile on its two lanes. With the main culprits being congestion, never-ending repair work, and accidents, predicting traffic snarls is a roll of the dice. The newer version, with its one lane leading in and the other two leading out of town, is the Silas Pearman Bridge and it suffers the same maladies. The Mark Clark is congested at peak hours, but offers less resistance in terms of road work. The west Ashley Bridges are a better gamble at this time because they are not undergoing extensive repair. However, they are greatly overburdened with the West Islands' traffic and five o'clock is not the best time to take an afternoon drive in that direction.

Another piece of advice: parking on the peninsula is a problem. We have made strides toward managing the situation for the betterment of both residents and tourists, however, with restricted parking hours in residential neighborhoods and parking garages for public use. Avoid costly tickets (starting at $5, and piling up on the windshield with the hours) by parking in a no-limit spot. A list of the parking garages located around the downtown area are listed at the end of this chapter for your convenience:

If you plan to be spending time on the peninsula, consider renting a bicycle by the hour or day as your transportation. Charleston Bicycle Rentals (722-7433) is located at 48 John Street, in close proximity to the Visitors Center. These bikes are the popular "beach cruiser" variety, with comfortable seats and fat wheels. Tandems, approved child seats, adults' and children's helmets, and even guidebooks are available. On Meeting Street, The Bicycle Shoppe (722-8168) also rents single speed cruisers, and sells and repairs bikes.

For short jaunts between the medical complex and the market, consider DASH — clean new buses designed to resemble trolley cars, which shuttle people between the medical complex and the market for $.75 (exact fare is required) from Monday through Friday, 8:00 AM until approximately 6:00 PM. Senior and handicapped citizens pay only $.25 between 9:00 AM and 3:30 PM, and children under six ride free.

Limousine, Taxi and Car Rentals

Ambassador Limousine, 722-7125
Carey Limousine, 723-7601
Jennings Limousine, 853-9726
LowCountry Limousine, 767-7117
Charleston Cab, 747-6111
Yellow Cab, 577-6565
Thrifty Car Rental, 552-7531
Alamo Rent A Car, 767-4117
Avis Rent A Car, 767-7030
Budget Car Rental, 763-3300
Dollar Rent A Car, 760-1112

Lockwood Blvd. and extends to Folly Road. The project was 30 years in the planning and cost $125 million to build.

But now -- at long last -- for those who want a spectacular waterfront view of the peninsula city (with its skyline punctuated by 18th- and 19th-century church spires) there's finally an entrance route that's truly exciting.

You can access the Scarborough Bridge (S.C. Hwy. 30) from Folly Road or Calhoun Street. Eventually -- by December, 1995 -- you'll be able to enter S.C. Hwy. 30 from Hwy. 61 or from I-526 (The Mark Clark Expressway) which circumnavigates the entire Greater Charleston area.

Insiders' Tip

Enterprise Rent A Car, 899-2705
Hertz Rent A Car, 767-4552
National Car Rental, 767-3078

Parking Facilities

Some lots and garages have a flat rate (or maximum charge) per day, while others "keep the meter running" at the hourly rate. Below are listed the major parking facilities in the city.

Charleston County Health Complex Parking Garage
1640 Spaces   720-7050
Hourly Rates: 75 cents/hour
Daily rate: $5/10 hours and $10/24 hours

Charleston Place Garage
400 spaces   724-7419
Hourly rates: 75 cents/hour
$6/night for Charleston Place guests

Concord-Cumberland Garage
651 spaces   724-7387
Hourly rates: 75 cents/hour $4.50 maximum

Cumberland-Meeting Garage
536 spaces   724-7381
Hourly rates: 75 cents/hour
$4.50 maximum

East Bay-Prioleau Garage
Galliard Auditorium Lot
402 spaces   724-7403
 75 cents/hour and $4.50 all day

George-Society Lot
149 spaces   724-7384
Hourly spaces
Hourly rates: 75 cents/hour

George-St. Philip Garage
540 spaces   724-7382
Hourly rates: 75 cents/hour
$4.50 maximum

King-Queen Garage
454 spaces   724-6777
Hourly rates: 75 cents/hour

Liberty Center Garage
327 spaces   722-8232
Hourly rates: 75 cents/hour
$5.00 maximum

Market and Horlbeck
120 spaces   724-7385
75 cents/hour

Medical University Garage
400 spaces   792-4220
Hourly rates: 50 cents/half hour
70 cents/hour

NCNB Place Garage
353 spaces   853-8351
Hourly rates: 75 cents/hour
$4.50 maximum

Rainbow Market Lot
58 spaces   720-3800
Hourly rates: 25 cents/hour
$2.50 maximum

Roper Garage
600 spaces   724-2045
Hourly rates: 35 cents/half hour
$3.00 maximum

St. Francis Xavier Garage
720 spaces   577-1148
Hourly rates: 50 cents/half hour
$5.00 maximum

Visitor Reception & Transportation Center Lots
220 spaces   720-3963
Hourly rates: 75 cents/hour
$4.50 maximum

81 Wentworth Street Garage
513 spaces   724-7383
Hourly rate 75 cents/hour and $4.50 daily

Charleston
History

With cultural roots as diverse as the bounties of her woods and waters, Charleston exists today as a mixed tribute to her early English, Irish, French, Spanish, German, Swiss, Santo Domingan, African, American Indian and Caribbean connections. Located 768 miles from New York City, 590 miles from Miami, and almost 2,500 miles from southern California, Charleston is as cosmopolitan as it is charming.

High temperatures average in the mid-70s, but can peak out in the 100s during the summer. The thermostat sheds an average of just 20 degrees during the cold months, but the humidity — during any season — makes the cold seem colder, the hot seem hotter.

Spring in Charleston, however, more than compensates for the discomfort of other seasons. Days are warm, nights barely chilled and the world appears to be dripping in wisteria and azaleas. This was the Charleston first glimpsed by the early white settlers: English and some Irish colonists who came on ships in the spring of 1670. Historians tell us that these adventurers navigated into the Charleston harbor, past piles of bleached oyster shells at the tip of the peninsula (originally called Oyster Point and, today, White Point Gardens),

East Battery, from a postcard dated 1909.

and then headed up the Ashley River to a high bank they called Albemarle Point. They named their settlement "Charles Town" for King Charles II, sometimes referred to as England's Merry Monarch. (This area is now a museum park called Charles Towne Landing. See our Attractions chapter.)

A decade later, the lure of the pretty shellfish remnants and the safety element of a prominent vantage point drew the Charles Town colonists back to the peninsula, to a new and permanent settlement between the Ashley and Cooper Rivers. British plans — called the "Grand Modell" — were sent over to guide development of 600 prime acres into a proper town.

Both the Spanish and the French were considered early threats, but Charles Towne withstood their advances and became the capital of the Province of Carolina. An aristocratic society evolved, and slipped easily into its Golden Age in the 18th century. Forced to suffer with rumpled dignity the humiliation of two enemy occupations during the Revolutionary and Civil Wars, these colonists resisted bombardment and, as Confederates, rallied to overtake Fort Sumter.

Certainly all was not bleak as the century unfolded. Between the periods of tribulation, the city was renamed "Charleston" and experienced an incredible building boom (look all over town to see Adams-style architecture from this period). Also, the "wagon trade" on upper King Street was an important outgrowth of the cotton and tobacco industries, and preempted the retail stores that make up our present shopping district.

Fire, earthquake, hurricane, yellow fever epidemic and even the boll weevil threatened Charlestonians' health and economic stability during subsequent centuries, but nothing crippled their spirit. Visitors may have observed at dif-

ferent times that our citizens were "too poor to paint"; however, know that most natives were also "too proud to whitewash."

There was a silver lining in that cloud of financial hard times. Those buildings, which our ancestors could not afford to "replace" in the name of "progress" at the turn of this century, escaped the fate of structures in more affluent communities. Today, restored and in an economically stable city, Charleston's collection of historically significant architecture attracts tourists from around the world who contribute to a thriving industry.

Charleston
Shopping

Greater Charleston is peppered with shopping areas — ranging in size from a few city blocks to miles in massive malls. To provide a shopping "tour," we have started on the peninsula and worked our way West of the Ashley. Included are the most exclusive boutiques as well as those offering off-price designer labels. We have described businesses with items of particular interest for our visitors, as well as those frequented by a local clientele. To help you keep your bearings, we have avoided much "skipping around," and have moved block by block or shopping center by shopping center. General area descriptions and occasional street numbers are provided to keep you on course. We hope our guide is a tempting sample of the shopping variety and quality available in

this area; we do encourage you, however, to explore off the beaten track: new and hidden surprises are everywhere!

Although there is not a lot yet to lure shoppers around the **Visitors Center**, the gift shop in the **Charleston Museum**, across the street on Meeting Street, is worth mentioning. Its selection includes jewelry, regional books (for adults and children) and other unique items. Around the block on John Street, a strip of small shops (to eventually be part of an overall development concept called "Camden Station") includes **The African American Gallery** and **John Street Sandwiches** (see the Restaurants chapter). On the first floor of The African American Gallery, the focus is "wearable art" — traditional and contemporary Nigerian clothing for men and women including coats, outfits, akwete cloth, and hats — while the second floor is a gallery with prints, original art and sculpture (See Art Galleries).

From John Street, round the corner to King Street and walk down two blocks to **Marion Square**, a downtown mall at the corner of Calhoun and King streets. This mall is a landmark of sorts in a block that is not a mecca of boutique shopping. The mall itself has spotty vacancies, but includes several fast or fairly fast food restaurants (**Blimpies** submarine sandwiches, **Checkers** pizza, and the **Golden Palace** at this writing). The only big-time fast food establishment on King Street, **Hardees**, monopolizes the front right corner of the mall. In the left corner is **Fast Photo**, a place that produces passport pictures as well as prints, and also processes and sells film.

Across King Street from Marion Square is the downtown **Bookbag**, which carries a wide assortment of paperbacks, magazines and even the *New York Times*. **The Two Step Cafe**, at 363 King, sells baskets of Charleston goodies and has a charming cafe in the back. A few shops down is **The Sportsman's Shop**, in business since 1946 selling quality sports equipment and products. If you are in the market for beautifully crafted doll houses and an extensive inventory of doll furniture, visit **Zeigler's Wood Shed** at 354 King. **Nancy's Boutique** is a small women's shop with fashions for work and play, and is a few doors up from one of our favorites: **Straight Lace**. If there is a little prince or princess in your life, ogle at the display window here — handmade, special-order children's clothing such as smocked or embroidered linen suits, vyella smocked coats, and christening gowns. The off-the-rack clothing and gift selections are charming as well. **The Extra Mile** is a service-oriented, specialty sports shop which sells Nike and other popular brands. **My Sister's Closet** is an upscale clothing boutique, while **Barton's** is an old standby selling candy, cards, gifts, stationary and party supplies (always packed with college students before special holidays).

In the same block, visit **Elza's** to find exquisite ladies' fashions and accessories by designers such as Adolpho, Albert Nippon, DKNY and Anne Klein. The store's name

is synonymous with the best, and the price tags reflect this quality. Elza's annual slashed-price, no-try-on sale is a red star for the calendar: a time when locals bump into everyone they saw last night and the ones they haven't seen in decades. Elza's windows are entertainment in themselves, especially at Spoleto when she captures a bit of drama on her own stage. Parking is available in the back. Next door, at 332 King, is **Bob Ellis** — a shoe store that has been delivering superior service for many years and also has fabulous sales. You will find Donna Karan, Giorgio Armani, Bruno Magli, Pancaldi and other top name brands in hard-to-find sizes.

Max's Men's Store, at 328 King, is a conservative shop with a handsome collection in its display windows. It has been serving its patrons since 1933 and offers trousers by Corbin, coats by Burberry, shirts by Troy Guild, shoes by Bass and much more. Down the street, **Goody Two Shoes** carries children's shoes

that range from good necessities to elegant extravagance. Here you will find children's brands like Enzo, Jumping Jacks and Toddler University. **Wee Ones**, at 322 King, is a shop with a wide seasonal selection of children's clothing and a large selection of headbands, bows and socks, as well as some standbys (like the white christening suit you happen to need in the dead of winter). **Elizabeth Mansfield Specialty Clothing** carries women's lines such as Morton Miles and Oleg Cassini, and is located next door to **Marc Howard**, at 314 King, which features contemporary furnishings, Alessi kitchenware and Ittala glassware, lighting, accessories, a line of gourmet peanuts and even toys. Next door is **Anne's** — a shop that attracts loyal customers because of its contemporary fashions, wardrobe coordination service, bridal department and fashions by names like Catharine Smith and Jane Folgers. **Atlantic Books**, at 310 King, sells rare, out-of-print and otherwise important books, new and used. Authors sometimes have readings here that are open to the public. There is another Atlantic Books on East Bay Street, and between the two they claim to stock a record number of Charleston-oriented books. **Native Son**, purveyors of folk art and gifts, is a welcome addition to King Street. Shop here for an unusual handmade gift and then visit **Croghan's Jewel Box**: a shop that is little in size, but great big in quality. Unobtrusively tucked away behind a small awning and owned by the same family for most of this century, Croghan's carries exquisite jewelry and wonderful gifts for all the important occasions. Ask to see Charleston Rice Beads and sterling silver souvenir spoons. A Croghan's package delivered to your door — sometimes, the smaller the better — is cause for real excitement.

The Bridal House carries attractive formal wear and is located next to **A.J. Davis and Company** — a progressive traditional men's clothing store which is a good source for accessories and sportswear. (Ask about delivery to downtown hotels.) It is located near **M. Dumas and Sons** — the store where Charlestonians have been buying flannel shirts, corduroy pants, jackets, hunting attire, casual wear and the like since 1919.

Across and back up the street a bit, **319 Men** and **319 Collections For Women** are sophisticated designer boutiques. While the men's collection may include clothes by designers such as Hugo Boss, Nicole Miller, Cole Hahn, Trafalgar and ties by XMI, the women's store has sold garments designed by Giorgio Armani, Michi Moon, Emmanuel, Ungaro and Tahari lines. Next door, **319 Sh'Boot** is a chic shoe store which carries lines like Petra, Donald Phiner and Armando Pollini.

Down the street a few steps, at 311 King, **Jack Krawcheck** — with sections for men, women, and students — is another fabled fashion institution. In fact, we have one friend from Columbia whose wife swears he makes the 100-mile drive to buy his socks here. The building itself, with its old brick and small courtyard, smacks of charm, and the designer lines — such as Moschino, Armani, Anya and James Purcell — add to the appeal. **Nice Ice** is a fine jewelry boutique within the store that carries pearls and gold items, as well as sapphire, emerald and ruby jewelry. There is parking in the back for Krawcheck/Nice Ice shoppers.

L'Unique Ltd., an upscale women's boutique (the store's layout itself is even interesting) and **Goin Gallery** (see Arts section) are located at 309 King. **Ellison Shoes**, at 307 King, is another well-respected, top-of-the-line store that carries shoes by designers such as Ferragamo, Arche, Mephisto and Van Eli, and has served generations of Charlestonians.

Affordables, a local chain, can be the below-retail-price solution to a shopper's dilemma. Rather than being known for carrying specific designers, Affordables is known for merchandise that is stylish, functional and — like the name says — "affordable." Women who wear sizes

14 to 24 should shop **Upscale, Inc.**, where "style is not a matter of size." Next door (in a space that was for years a popular men's store, Karl Karesh) is now several businesses under one roof. The group includes **The RSVP Shoppe Ltd.** — a store selling a wide assortment of stationery and invitations; **Larry Jones and Company** — a custom apparel shop; **Public Tailor Shop**; and **Simply Charleston** — a collection of items with that special "Charleston touch," ranging from picture frames and clocks to mailboxes and even hand-worked clothes, most handcrafted by local artisans and exclusive to this store. If you or a man you know needs to rent clothes for a fancy shake, stop in **Formal Wear for Men** (look for the festive storefront windows).

Across King and down Society Street, find **Robinson's Bicycle Shop** at 84 1/2 Society. First opened — at another location — in 1888, Robinson's is a household name to locals and carries such lines as Cannondale, Mongoose, Caloi and Ross. Shop here also for bicycle clothing and accessories. (There is another shop in South Windermere.) On the corner of Society and King, **Stella Nova** is a natural beauty store carrying soaps and cosmetics. Across the street at 289 King, **The Clothes Horse** sells off-price women's and men's casual clothes, with a limited selection of preteen sizes.

Located at 285 King Street, **Charles Kerrison** is another impressive jewelry store with a reputation for carrying superior quality merchandise such as Rolex and Acutron watches. It is also a wonderful source for wedding gifts, and the window displays are simply gorgeous. Down a few doors is **Sarah Anne's Ltd.** — a store that sells what we consider "sophisticated fun" clothing (brands like David Brooks, Sharon Youn, Susan Bristol) as well as loads of accessories for ladies, toys and children's clothing. Half of the fun of Sarah Anne's is being in the middle of all that inventory: upstairs and down, the shop groans with goodies.

Speaking of good things and good taste, **Rangoni** shoe store — at the corner of Wentworth and King — is a retail shop for the Rangoni line. The facility and its merchandise remind us of European boutiques, but without the crowds. In fact, that is one of the overall pleasures of shopping in Charleston: quality and variety in uncrowded settings. **Home**, at 268 King, is a shop selling top quality housewares and cookware. Its dark, wood interior helps create the feel of an historic kitchen house, and it is filled with handsome pots, pans, glasses,

If you are shopping during the Christmas season, *Candyland* and all its trappings decorate a segment of King Street which starts at Wentworth. At all times of the year, note the unusual bricks bearing the names of people who contributed to this brick-laying project that line the street starting at the intersection of King and Wentworth.

Insiders' Tip

tableware, gadgets and the like. **East Bay Gallery** has two locations, 264 King Street and Northcut Shopping Center, and both offer a fascinating cross section of crafts, heirlooms and gifts. Owners John and Margaret Guthrie say their collection represents the work of more than 400 artists (many of whom John knows personally from his years as a potter on the West Coast) from almost every state, and offers the whimsical along with the serenely beautiful (See Art Galleries in our chapter on the Arts).

The Climbing Bear is one of our favorite toy stores — chocked full of the kind of well-made, stimulating, ageless toys we swore we would *only* buy for kids (ah well...). There is a good price range so that birthday or "special" gifts can be purchased here by more folk than the rich-and-famous. **Concepts** is a women's boutique with reasonably priced, for-fun-fashion (there is also a shop in the South Windermere shopping center).

Back up the street on the other side, **Huguley's** — a standby for office supplies as well as cards, gifts and wrapping materials — sells a nice collection of Charleston prints and other Lowcountry items. Growing up in Charleston, we knew this store (and there are several in the area) as "Legerton's" — which represented the same standard of quality at that time that Huguley's does today.

For a blast from the past, don't miss **Woolworth's** next door: an old-timey "five and dime" that sells everything from goldfish to cafe curtains, but is known to the breakfast and lunch crowd for its sit-down-at-the-counter plates and take-out fried chicken.

Winslow and Lewis Consignment Galleries — its front window painted with cheerful morning glories — handles consignment and some new merchandise. Items range from antique and newer furniture to handmade, stuffed animals fashioned from imported angora (See the Antiques chapter). On the corner of Beaufain and King Streets, the **Audubon Shop and Gallery** is another incredible environmentally sensitive toy and nature shop with the benefit of a gallery attached (See Arts chapter). Down King Street, see **Leisure Threads** — an upscale embroidered and silk screened t-shirt company. **Fred** is in this block too, and specializes in classic kitchen basics as well as gourmet housewares (the interior is very minimalistic and could pass for European). **Birds and Ivey** is a garden/coffee and sandwich shop with wonderful outdoor touches (there are also stores on Folly Road and at Kiawah).

At 233 King, **Charleston Collections** is a gift shop that sells an incredible range of "things Charleston": Charleston Chimes, Charleston prints and originals, sea shell lamps and kits to make them, Charleston books and cards, even candies and cookies. Our attention was drawn to the Charleston Doorway Earrings, pins and barrettes, as well as other hand-designed silver jewelry made by local artists. The clerks will ship anywhere, and there are other shops at the Bohicket Marina Village, Kiawah's Straw Market, and the Quadrangle Center in

West Ashley (See Galleries in the Arts chapter). The **Purple Plum Too**, at 231 King (like the other shop at 45 S. Market) sells gifts and collectibles from lines like Chillmark, Lladro, Hummel, Department 56, Precious Moments and David Winters.

Cross the street to shop some of the most exclusive boutiques on King Street: **Charleston Place** is actually a metropolitan mall in the Omni complex, with all the conveniences of climate-controlled shopping in the middle of the downtown shopping district. This is a big plus for guests at the hotel, who simply walk through the lobby and into the shops. If you are not staying there and have a car to park, use the parking garage below the Omni (entered on Hassell Street, which is the first left off King after Wentworth) and avoid the headache of attempted on-street parking. **The Shops**, as they are called, include those fronting King Street: **Spoleto USA Gift Shop**; **Footlocker** (athletic footwear as well as t-shirts, socks and aerobic wear); **Sunglass Hut** (eyewear by Vuarnet, Bucci, Ray-Ban and other), and **Tolberts** (classic clothing, shoes and accessories for women — a complete petite store and a must see for those of us who fit into that category). Inside the Omni find: **Banana Republic** (famous for its safari/travel clothes for men and women, classic and made to last a long time); **Everything But Water** (a specialty shop with trendy water sport wear as well as maternity and mastectomy suits); **Express** (nonrestrictive, French country dressing for women); **The Gap** (unisex play clothes such as jeans and medium priced fun-wear); **Jaegar** (coordinated clothing for women, made in England and including blazers, skirts, walking shorts, and blouses, as well as accessories); **Laura Ashley** (women's and girls' apparel and home furnishings in coordinating stripes, florals and pastel solids); **The Limited** (fun, casual clothing with a European flair); **Dazzles Jew-**

elry (beautiful jewelry at competitive prices); **Gucci** (ties, belts, wallets and accessories); **My Friend's Place** (women's clothes by American designers); **W.H. Smith** (the sundries you forgot to pack as well as an assortment of souvenirs to take home); **Polo Ralph Lauren** (ties, blouses, slacks, skirts, shoes, belts, and socks); **Victoria's Secret** (lingerie, gifts, gowns, robes, and a small selection of underwear for men; see other store in Citadel Mall); **Doubleday Book Shop** (a complete selection of reading materials); **Godiva Chocolatier** (chocolates, ice cream, and gift boxes); **Antiquities** (famous autographs by presidents and sports heroes, as well as engravings, old civil war relics and antique prints); **Brookstone** (games, garden tools, small appliances and other really neat items — all guaranteed for life); **Crabtree and Evelyn** (soaps, powders, lotions and gift baskets); the **Coffee Beanery** (coffee, hot chocolate, coffee beans, mugs and the like); and **The White House** (elegant all-white clothing for women).

Around the corner and still across from the Omni on Market Street, **Charleston Catalog Company's** retail store sells such items as original artwork, one-of-a-kind furniture pieces, hurricane clocks, silverware, windchimes, and glasses decorated with scenes of the Lowcounty by silhouette artist Carew Rice. **The House of Versailles**, at 125 Market, sells 116 women's fragrances — blended in France and manufactured in New York — and some for men as well.

Walk down to Meeting to find a group of retail stores next to The Shops of the Omni Hotel. **Candlelight of Charleston**, at 209 Meeting, features hand-dripped, hand-crafted candles, and offers free demonstrations of the process. **South Eastern Wildlife Exposition Gallery** (see Arts chapter) is also located in this block. **Le Creuset** also has an outlet where you can purchase pieces of this outstanding enamel cast-iron cookware at discount prices. **Camera King** rents camera equipment and sells photography supplies. (Film may be somewhat discounted here.)

Now, head north on Meeting Street and look for Wentworth Street. Take a left by **Reuben's Deli** and find **Futons By Buty**, at 52 Wentworth, which sells those cotton "sleeping systems" that convert from sofas to beds, and range in size from single cot to king. Next door, music aficionados will tune in to **Erwin Music**, selling tapes and compact discs. The store carries (to name a few) jazz, blues, reggae, rock, international, folk, zydeco, cajun, New Orleans R&B, new wave, classic rock, oldies and fusion. If you want something else — not a joke — they do special orders. Owner Gary Erwin, a respected musician in his own right and leader of Charleston's growing jazz-oriented community, hosts WSCI's (89.3 FM) "Blues in the Night," on Friday at 8:00 PM and on Saturday evenings at 10:00 PM. Last in the group, **Carolina Wine and Cheese** specializes in imported and fine domestic wines, cheeses, fresh German bread, coffees and teas.

From Wentworth, walk down

to and take a left on King Street. About two blocks down, at the corner of King and Market, **Christian Michi** — eye catching with its dramatic windows — offers collections for women by fashion designers such as Michael Kors, Comme de Garcon and Romeo Gigli. The shop also sells Chanel cosmetics, perfume and assorted home furnishings. **Le Trend** carries female fashions from Morocco, while Sunny Caribbee — the shop that is an especially terrific

escape during the doldrums of winter — is the source for exotic spices, West Indies art, island crafts and even tropical cookbooks. **Bits of Lace** is an utterly romantic shop with the loveliest of "things intimate," including lingerie, robes and gowns, as well as hair ornaments and perfumes.

American Sterling Galleries, at 195 King, carries a wide variety of obsolete and active sterling flatware and hollowware. Its specialty is hard-to-find patterns, and bridal registry and polishing services are available. **A Zola** may be this block's most unusual and eclectic shop/gallery, changing its theme from month to month (expect the unexpected, from antique chairs to original art, and even gift ideas like designer manure, for the garden aficionado on your list). **RTW** is a boutique for women that carries comfortable, chic clothes by designers such as C. P. Shades, Bluefish and Bryan Emerson. **Joint Venture Consignments**, across the street, is worth a stop if you are in the market for fine jewelry that is pre-owned and on consignment. They also sell safes (a good idea if you value your wearables/stealables) and will even offer to clean your jewelry while you browse. Owners say this store is the only one of its kind in America. In the same block, across the street, **Brittains of Charleston**, at 180 King Street, deserves a gold star for its selection of crystal (by makers such as Baccarat, Orrefors, Lalique and Tiffany), as well as fine china, unique gifts and home furnishings.

Continuing south, **Gibraltar** has an unusual collection of southwestern home decor, including frames, handmade jewelry and other household items. **The Ben Silver Collection** sells more than 800 different blazer buttons, as well as blazers, silk neckties (it claims the distinction of being the nation's leading retailer in striped ties), cashmere sweaters, polo shirts, crests and cuff links. The store stocks buttons and crests representing every college in the U.S. and abroad, and more than 600 fraternal and military schools and organizations. Ben Silver also sells fine luggage and women's blazers, slacks, and skirts. We recommend **The Preservation Society Shop**, in this block, for a nice assortment of gifts ranging from books to works by Lowcountry artists. Across the street, **Cousins** is a sophisticated boutique selling traditional women's clothing and accessories.

At the corner of King and Broad is **Berlin's** — one of Charleston's oldest and nicest stores for men and women. Established in 1883, Berlin's carries brands like Boss, Polo, Johnston-Murphy, Cole-Hahn, Don Sophisticates, Jerry Silverman, and London Fog. Free parking is available across the street on King.

Across Broad Street, the windows of **Historic Charleston Reproductions** are the focal point of the block, with wonderful window displays of lovely furniture, often accented by pretty flowers in the outdoor boxes (see Antiques). There is no shopping to the right on Broad, except **Lakeside Pharmacy** at 141 Broad — which, in addition to pharmaceuticals, sells some gift items and camera equipment — and **Burbage's**, a real corner grocery with what loyal customers say is the best meat in town. (You'll probably see children dashing in and out, running errands or buying treats from Mr. Burbage.) Heading back down Broad toward the Provost, cross Meeting Street at the famous Four Corners of Law and walk to Church Street; take a right and discover several wonderful shops tucked away in an important residential district.

Nobel Dragon, an English style book store and coffee shop, is an oasis for this area. **Small Change** is a consignment store with quality secondhand goods for growing children (a nifty way to snatch up a hand-smocked, nearly-new outfit for nearly-1960s prices). **The Boutique**, next door, sells indulgence items for ladies like scented hand creams and to-die-for negligees, as well as unique wedding gifts and shower presents. **J. Davenport of Charleston**, in the historic former Bank of the United States building, at 100 Church Street, sells fine gifts and decorative accessories such as lamps, pictures, linens and lamps. **Porgy and Bess**, at 91 Church Street, features women's clothing by Adrianna Pappell, David Brooks, Robert Scott, Tanner, Susan Bristol and others, as well as gifts, jewelry and accessories.

Our friends whose hobbies include handwork, say **Cabbage Row Shoppe** is a wonderful source for needlework, canvasses, Paternayan yarn and the like. We also admire the hand-painted gifts, greeting cards, and paper items. A popular shop for stylish formal and semiformal designer dresses, perfect for weddings, graduation ceremonies and also debutante parties, is **Horse Feathers** at 83 Church Street. In addition to fashions, the boutique sells some antiques and antique paintings (see the Antiques chapter).

Moms and significant others have been shopping at **82 Church Street** for generations. The shop sells conservative, traditional clothing for children and is charming in itself. The Charleston Bonnet (puffed with a front top bow and chin tie) as well as hand-smocked dresses from the Smockery are sold here (and made to last as hand-me-downs). A full range of imported and American-made merchandise is available, and the shop's precious display windows are always an escape into fashion innocence.

Don't stop before you find **Stoll's Alley Shop**. Located to the left off Church Street at 10 Stoll's

Photo: The Post and Courier

Charleston Place Shops (Omni).

Alley, in an 18th-century single house, this boutique sells fine clothing for ladies. But that's just the start; those shopping for the bed and bath will find a fabulous selection of all-cotton sheets, monogrammed towels and shower curtains, as well as coordinated accessories and gifts.

Walk up Stoll's Alley to East Bay Street, and take a left heading toward Broad Street. As a shopping district, East Bay has gone full cycle since the 17th century when it was a commercial center. Beginning with major destruction caused by the Civil War and Earthquake of 1886, this segment of town fell into disrepair. Renovation came about in the last decade, and today there are unique shops again lining the street on both sides.

Geiss and Sons Jewelers is located at 116 East Bay Street and sells custom designed fine jewelry and watches such as Rolex, Audemars, Piguet, Bertolucci, Breitling, Tag Heuer, Krieger, and Lemania. Next door, at the corner of Exchange and East Bay, is a very good source for hard spirits and wine — the **Tavern** liquor store.

Around the corner on Broad, is **Utopia** — a boutique selling progressive fashions for men and women, and some art. Cross Broad Street and check both sides of the street for a variety of retail shops on East Bay. **American Originals**, at 153 E. Bay, carries decorative wearables, fine contemporary crafts, gifts and American antiques (see the Antiques chapter). Down Vendue Range, at number thirty, **The Gothic Shop** is worth a stop if you are interested in architectural accents such as gargoyles, columns, statuary and the like. Back on East Bay, **Elegant Options** is a division of **Ruth P. Irvin Interiors**, and offers an outstanding selection of decorative accessories and gifts. If you gravitate toward the eclectic, seek out **Indigo,** which has an inventory ranging from antiques to folk art to international crafts. In this shop, village baskets are nestled next to Shaker boxes, near Edwardian bamboo and old Italian ceramics. Like its twin on King Street, **Atlantic Books** sells used and rare books on all subjects, and prides itself on having the city's most extensive collection of books about the Civil War, Charleston and southern authors.

Across the street, **Charleston Chocolates**, at 190 East Bay Street, sells hand dipped chocolates — like the Charleston Chocolate Truffle — with no additives or preservatives. We love the candy, and are equally fascinated by the decor: windows painted with flowers, ribbons and hearts, a bright mirrored wall and festive wallpaper. At the west corner of East Bay and Cumberland Streets, **Chapter Two Bookstore** has a selection that is exceptional: from splendid photographic studies of the Lowcountry, to the finest hardback books for children. For those who light up while they read or swear by pipe brands like Peterson or Jobi, **The Smoking Lamp** — located between the two bookstores — is a real find. The shop sells cigars, pipes, tobacco, cigarettes, and accessories. Down the street a bit, at 211, is the **Wilton House** which is a wonderful source for unique, traditional home furnishings as well as interesting gift ideas.

As odd as it may seem, we suggest your next stop be a grocery store: yes, the downtown **Harris Teeter**, in the old train station, is interesting in its own right. First-rate basic and gourmet staples aside, you can also pick up beautiful flowers at reasonable prices in the floral department, browse through a large selection of cards, or shop the wine section. Locals also frequent the **Vegetable Bin** next door, a very basic establishment where you can get farm fresh fruit, vegetables and other staples at quite reasonable prices. **The Image Place** is a reliable development service — expect your film to be ready in about an hour. One of our favorite spots for vintage clothing, located around the bend from the Image studio, is **Granny's Goodies**. On the main floor of a lovely home, painted yellow and graced by full piazzas, Granny's Goodies sells wonderful "antique"

clothing — from a kinder, gentler time — as well as collectibles and jewelry.

There is a convenient conglomeration of shops at the corner of East Bay and Inspection Streets, called **Ansonborough Square**. Included in the group are a large **Blockbusters** video rental store; an **Eckerd** drugstore; a **Quick Mail Etc.**, (offering services like FAX, passport, and UPS); **Futon Decor** (which carries futons, frames, screens, covers, pillows and accessories); **Amelia West** (an unusual shop with exquisite gift ideas — from unusual frames and trays, to Wedgewood-look-alike pitchers, fine baby gifts and handpainted tableware); **Bonomo's** (an Italian groceria/gourmet shop); another **Elegant Options With Ruth P. Irvin Interiors**; **Acquisitions** (see Antiques); and **Prints Charming** (a very popular custom picture framing shop, which also sells some nice art); and **earthling**, a spa offering skin care, spa treatments, massage therapy and even Pilates exercise.

After you cross Calhoun Street on East Bay, look for another group of businesses, this one called East Bay Street Shops. There is a **One Hour Martinizing** (also called **East Bay Cleaners**) which may come in handy, and a health food store called **Books, Herbs and Spices**. We like the juice bar upstairs, and enjoy reading the literature about healthy lifestyles.

Take a right on Charlotte Street and head for the water. When you reach Concord Street, you will find **Luden's** — far from the trendy crowds and in close proximity to the action of the real waterfront. Since 1867, Luden's has been selling Charlestonians top-quality clothing, equipment and gear for hunting, fishing and boating.

If you come back out to East Bay Street, and retrace your steps — this time heading south — you will come upon the historic Market Area on your right. Flanked by business-filled, one-way streets (called North and South Market Streets), **The Market** proper has been called one of the oldest shopping malls in the United States. It was built on land that Constitutional signer Charles Cotesworth Pinckney ceded to the city in the 18th century for use as a public market. Consisting of low brick buildings that have survived hurricanes, an earthquake, a tornado, fire and even bombardment during the Civil War, these sheds were used by vendors selling fish, meat and vegetables in days gone by. Now, the **Open Air Market** section, between East Bay and Church Streets, is occupied by local farm-

ers, artisans and international importers selling their wares. Here, the "basket ladies" weave their regional treasures: sweetgrass baskets of all sizes and shapes (see the Arts chapter). The **Center Market**, stretching from Church to Meeting Streets, is a string of specialty shops, boutiques and eateries.

Although you can move in and out of these defined spaces, for descriptive clarity we will make a loop (starting at East Bay on North Market, coming back up South Market) and then shop The Market from the Open Air through Center sections. Our first stop will be the **Rainbow Market**, an unusual cluster of small shops, each with a separate facade but situated within the parameters of two early 19th-century buildings. **Wild Cat** is a store for cat-lovers, where jewelry, mugs, t-shirts and other items pay tribute to the world of cats. **Sea Level** offers nautical gifts and boating accessories such as clocks, barometers, prints, lamps and jewelry, while **Kites Flyin Hi** sells toys for the air. **The Hope Chest** carries beautiful imported, handmade linens for bedrooms and dining rooms. Veera Bradley and Lisa Galimberti linens are leading lines. If you thought the cloth handkerchief was passe, check out The Hope Chest's selection and help save a tree!

Good Scents is a shop that sells fine soaps, lotions and perfume oils such as Penhaligon's of London, as well as Birkenstock footwear. **"Light Be" Charleston Christmas Corner** is open year round selling such seasonal items as Charleston Angels and the Charleston

Santa, German nutcrackers, ornaments and a line of Colonial candles. **Earth Matters** stocks nature-inspired gifts, with themes relating to the environment. **Market Street Munchies** — one of three stores in the area — is a gift basket shop (their baskets are filled with candies, cookies, fruits, nuts and other goodies), while **Charleston Shoreline** specializes in Civil War stamps, prints, and artifacts, and offers a print and document locator service. **Southern Baskets** is a shop selling baskets stuffed with local treats like benne seed cookies, as well its own line called "Southern Ease" — items like Fried Green Tomato Batter. Other interesting shops include **Southern Correspondence**, which sells fine stationery and writing materials, and **Carol J's**, a boutique with ladies' apparel made locally (check out the hand-painted and ultra suede lines). Outside the Rainbow Market proper, is **Round and Round** — a music and poster shop for things nostalgic of the 1950s, and blaring their wares out onto North Market.

Down North Market, past the public parking lot, street-front shops include such stores as **ABC By Lucy**, a custom poster shop where customers can watch the artist at work creating her alphabet designs; **The Pnut Shop of Charleston**, selling nuts, candies, hams, bacon, and other gifts; **Sheila's Shamrocks**, a novelty shop carrying items such as t-shirts and stuffed animals; **Quacker's**, with upscale gifts and accessories such as personalized children's books, stamps, prints, and windchimes; **Fun Thinkers**, a toy store which carries the kind of educational and entertaining toys mom and dad are *glad* the kids like (it is an Official Barney Headquarters!); **Madeline Lingerie**, for lovely intimate apparel; **Gold Showcase**, by R.L. Shogry — a shop with fine jewelry, genuine stones, seaside themes like shell bracelets, and more; **The Mad Hatter**, where hats are made, blocked and finished at discount prices; **Scents Unlimited**, (our editor swears she heads here first before going anywhere else in town) selling versions of European perfume, oils and powders and such special versions as Charleston Tea Olive and St. John's Bay Rum Lyme; a gift shop/ gallery, the **Mole Hole**, which — like the other Mole Hole affiliates in the United States — sells quality items and even a line of soft music (played for the enjoyment of shoppers); and **Savvy of Charleston**, recognizable by its window boxes out front and the affordable, trendy and traditional jewelry inside.

Market Street Sweets, a tempting confection collection of fudge and taffy, also sells Charleston pralines and the like. In this block are also **Sock World** — as the name implies, a shop with socks for babies up to king-sized men; **Photo Express**, set back from the street in a strip of shops, a one-hour film processing service as well as source for photography products, expert service and repairs (with West Ashley and Center Market locations as well); and **Half Moon Outfitters** (which sells outdoor clothes and some equipment, notably by Patagonia). At **Planters Inn**, visit **A Charleston Christmas**, which sells handmade ornaments, pictures, quilts and so forth for the holiday season, and **Objects**, an exquisite gift shop that includes in its inventory reproductions, paintings, porcelains, frames, jewelry, silver and brass pieces.

Walking along Meeting Street, cross over to South Market and visit shops facing this street. **Not Just Country** sells Charleston t-shirts and other gift items, while **Pineapple and Pelicans'** selection includes glass animals, paintings, and — what we think is fun — Olde Tymee Photos (you, dressed in vintage wear, photographed in sepia tones). **Cafe Casuals** is located next to Cafe 99, and has attractive t-shirts. The **Caribbean Expression** sells merchandise ranging from hand-painted t-shirts and hats to children's clothing. **Hog Penny** is an exceptional boutique for men and women, attractive in its decor and carrying such brands as British Khaki, and Bushwacker, while **Black Market Minerals** sells rocks and min-

erals such as onyx from Pakistan and amethyst from Brazil. Civil War buffs may find a souvenir at **Tilly's L.T.D.**, while the fashion conscious will be interested in the reasonable prices and fine quality of women and children's bathrobes and nightgowns at **Gilligan O' Malleys**. For something chic to wear during your leisure hours, try **Resort Works** — an active wear boutique for men, women and children, at the corner of South Market and Church Streets. Next door is **Sea Source**, which — as the name indicates — carries all manner of objects (from mobiles to puzzles to afghans and prints) relating to the sea.

On the opposite corner, the **Linning House Galleries** is a gift shop many locals rely on for special occasion shopping. It carries an extensive inventory ranging from Herend porcelain to Crane stationery, Junior League cookbooks to monogrammed napkins, all arranged in bright, appealing showrooms. Also shop here for adorable children's gifts. To the right on Church Street is **TG's**, a shop full of whimsical gifts. We were amused by the clowns and masks, and liked the toys and antique jewelry. Back on South Market Street, **Elaine's Gift Shop** sells souvenirs, including dolls, pottery, chimes and even miniature glass churches. **The Charleston Nut Place** pulls in shoppers off the street who smell the more than 20 flavors of roasting nuts or just crave the praline pecans. The **Charleston Popcorn Place** sells more popcorn (more than 30 varieties) in more colors and flavors than you imagined existed, while the **Fudge Shops**

Incorporated is the place to find fresh fudge prepared daily. Another **Purple Plum Gifts** is located here as well (see Purple Plum Too on King Street). Turn right on State Street to visit **Lucas Neuhaus Belgian Chocolate** shop. In the back of a row of shops next to A.W. Shucks is **Oops! and Company**, which sells off-price clothing from famous mail-order catalogs like J. Crew. Walk down Artisan's Alley, which connects State and South Market Streets, and where artists show on a regular basis (see Arts Chapter).

To tour historic sections of The Market, called Center Market, start at State Street and work your way toward the Meeting Street end. Basket weavers are usually situated at the junction where **A Touch of Charleston** is nestled. A neat, uncluttered shop which sells and engraves silver items such as flasks and frames, it is also a source for engraved door knockers and the like. **Passing Fancy** sells gift items ranging from oils to colorful stained glass. Shoppers in search of previously owned watches, art, jewelry and the like will enjoy **Flynn's**, while shoppers with children as a focus will want to locate **Designs By Jane** — a shop selling adorable smocked clothes for children as well as appliques, dolls, baby seats and even cradles. In the window may be the Scarlett series of Madame Alexander dolls. **Southern Charm Gifts** is a souvenir shop with such items as Japanese fans, picture frames, ceramic flowers, and jewelry boxes. Looking for a special Christmas ornament? You may find what you want at **Christmas Traditions/Brit-**

ish **Antiques**. **Country Gentleman** and the **Charleston Hat Man**, part of a group of shops clustered behind a quaint facade which appears to be a shuttered house, cater to men and carry carved decoys, decoy boxes, umbrellas, Stetson hats and more. **Gita's Gourmet** is a favorite with us, and we shop here for wine, cheese, specialty items, teas, canned boiled peanuts (don't go home without trying this southern delicacy), as well as soups. Another upscale gift shop is **Lucille Waits Gifts**, where you will find bowls, collectibles (such as the Emmet Kelley Junior series) and a particularly nice selection of pewter. **World of Leather** carries things like belts, bags, buckles, old confederate hats and hairpins. Dolls — even some limited editions — can be procured at **Carroll's of Charleston**, while an interesting collection — including silver and china masks, and earrings — is available at **Quicksilver and Fireflies. At Victorian Delights**, look for merchandise such as fine linen, crystal, tapestry, smokers and even figurines. **The Gold Gallery** is a small shop selling jewelry.

There is another location of **Photo Express** (see the South Market Street description) in the Center Market as well.

Back out on Meeting Street, cross over and walk a half of a block south to the **Gibbes Museum of Art**. The gift shop there is open to the public (with no admission charge) and is one of our favorite shops for unique reproductions and artistic inspiration. On the other side of the street, in the next block, the **Historic Charleston Foundation**

Museum Shop carries such items as books, stationery, jewelry and toys, and offers free viewing of a video on the work that the Foundation does in Charleston (see the chapters on Attractions and Historic Preservation). Now walk back down Meeting Street and take a right on Cumberland. Look for Cumberland Courtyard and visit the **Heritage House** which stocks Charleston reproductions of interior and exterior lighting, Charleston benches, things for gardens, and a complete line of bird feeders.

To head out of town and West Ashley, go back to Meeting, take a right and then a left onto Wentworth Street. Follow Wentworth to its end, and take a right on Lockwood Boulevard. A group of shops on the left in the **Marina Building**, at 3 Lockwood, includes **Timeout**, which sells boating clothing (such as Patagonia, The North Face) and accessories, Vaurnet sunglasses, as well as Mistral sailboards (see the Boating chapter); and the **Armchair Sailor**, which stocks nautical books and maps. For the ultimate in beauty salons with a view, check out **Waves of Charleston**. Patrons watch sailboats race in the Ashley River while their hair is styled, their nails manicured.

West Ashley Shopping

Leaving the Charleston peninsula, you will cross the bridge to the West Ashley area. A popular shopping center on Folly Road is **South Windermere**. It includes shops that front Folly Road, and those on a sort of "second row." There is also a shopping strip bordering the center itself, and those stores have addresses on Windermere Boulevard. Starting at Folly Road and following Windermere Boulevard along the "border," there is **Photo Express**, with a drive-in window; **Spectacles**, an eyeglasses shop; a **Bookbag** bookstore; **Reuter's Music**, selling equipment and even offering guitar lessons; **The Huntington House**, for lights and fixtures; **Louis Tannenbaum**, for more than half a century, one of the premiere men's and women's shops West of the Ashley (quality lines, personal service and an intimate atmosphere — all part of Tannenbaum's appeal); **Robinson's Bicycle Shop**, one of Charleston's oldest —founded in 1888 — and most respected stores, it carries Cannondale, Mongoose, Caloi and Ross bikes, as well as bike clothing and accessories (see the Society Street store downtown as well); **Frames Unlimited**, offering frame work as well as a nice assortment of prints; **The Open House**, a gift shop with elegant paper goods (invitations, cards, stationary, name cards, and gift wrap); **The Weight Watcher Station**; **Nice Touch Baskets**; and **Keep Sakes** (for flowers, balloons and the like). In a row behind the main shopping center is **Hiep-Hoa Laundry**, with drop-off and alteration services; **John's Rod and Reel,** (clothing and equipment for the serious outdoorsman); **Especially Yours,** one of our standbys for unusual gifts and a personal touch — keep an eye out for their sidewalk sales: fabulous bargains;

National Discount Computers; The Learning Center, a tutorial center that also sells educational toys; and **The Country Store**, for plants and other gardening needs.

Up front and visible from Folly Road, see **Rite Aid** drugstore; the **Piggly Wiggly** grocery store (which has a good, very basic take-out deli); **Belks Department Store** (good cosmetic selection and clothes for the whole family); **Woolworth's** (a smaller version of the King Street store); **Mr. Don's Shoes** (which carries shoes for the whole family and ballet attire); **Concepts** (like its twin on King Street, a dress shop with fun, casual clothes for women); **Traditions by Garfield** (gift and jewelry store with A+ window displays — see to believe!); **Radio Shack** (an electronics chain retail store); and **Huguleys** (a small branch of the King Street store, with friendly service and a good selection — for its size — of quality art supplies, books and gifts.

Out Savannah Highway

(Highway 17 South), we recommend **Lyerly's Cleaners**, across from **Krispy Kreme**, a longtime favorite stop for coffee and doughnuts. Next door, hard to miss with its handsome awning and logo, is **By The Yard** — the off-price fabric shop that stylishly dresses many a window in Charleston. The shop also carries distinctive gifts for the home, and the staff offers valuable design suggestions (also visit the other shop in Mt. Pleasant, which is larger and carries some different fabrics). Near the intersection of Magnolia Road and Savannah Highway, see **Consigning Women** — a large shop, with pretty geraniums in planters out front, which sells clothes as well as antiques on consignment.

Down the highway on the left, look — as all the children do — for the Coburg Dairy Cow, reigning over **St. Andrews Shopping Center** from a revolving platform in the front corner. Stores here range from small boutiques to medium-sized department stores, and there are also some business offices. **Phillips Shoes** sells off-price, brand name shoes for the family. **West Ashley Bible Book Store** sells Christian cards, tapes, posters books, plaques and even aids for Sunday School teachers. **Affordables** is an affiliate of the King Street store, **Tuesday Morning** is a bargain shopper's delight, selling close-out items (see shop in Mt. Pleasant, also). **Charmalee Hallmark** sells Hallmark products for all occasions, and **Joli's** is a discount maternity shop across from Marguerite's — a specialty boutique with designer clothes and a focus on wardrobes for the working woman. Don't forget about calling Building Blocks to arrange some quality time-away-from-mom-and-dad for the kids while you shop (see Greater Charleston Child Care and Early Childhood Centers). **Forget-Me-Nots** is a consignment store with a large selection of new and worn children's clothes, across from **Kerrisons** — a department store which has long been an anchor for the center, and still sells clothing, accessories, shoes, perfumes and cosmetics for men, women and children. Little extras such as the gift wrapping service and clerks who remember your name, keep customers regular. **Stein Mart** is the center's upscale, off-price department store with items for the home as well as wearables for men, women and children. There is also a **Rite Aid** drugstore, **Jackson-Ard Optometry** shop, and **Mooney's** barber shop. **Baskin Robbins** ice cream shop is next to **Fox Music House**, one of Charleston's oldest names in the musical instrument business. Fox offers top name equipment as well as sheet music, a variety of music lessons, and tuning, repair and refinishing services.

Across the street, **Kiddin Around** is a boutique consignment store with "gently worn" clothes for children at good prices. **K-Mart** and **Office Max** are farther down the highway, on the left. **Outdoor Outfitters**, in **Ye Olde Towne Shopping Village**, at 1662 Savannah Highway, carries a wonderful range of clothing for the hunter or outdoors person (including 100% cotton sport shirts and shorts, camping equipment, snake-proof boots, and Topsiders). (See Summerville Shopping location, also). Another discount fabric shop of note is **Boone Fabric**, on the left, before the Quadrangle Shopping Center (on the right). In the Quadrangle you will find **Edwin Watts Golf Shop**; **Charleston Collections** (see the King Street location, too); **Morrill's ABC Package Store**; **Nutri System**; **West Ashley Factory Outlet**; **Barett Shoes**; **Smith Family Cleaners**; **Picture This One Hour Photo**; and **S&K Menswear Superstore**. Also, comic book aficionados will enjoy **Chaos** — which deals in comics as well as books.

The next general destination is **Citadel Mall**, located where the Mark Clark Expressway meets Sam Rittenberg Boulevard. This mall has three major department stores — **Belk**, **Sears** and **Dillard's** (formerly Thalhimer's) — as well as more than 100 other shops. The roster reflects a wide selection including family apparel stores, hair stylists, a drugstore, electronic and music stores, card and book stores, fine jewelry stores, women's and men's specialty and accessory shops, maternity shops, shoe stores, a camera shop, a toy store, home furnishing centers, optical centers, a nutrition center and even a dental office. Some of our favorites are **B. Dalton Bookseller** and **Waldenbooks**, complete bookstores that also sell some books on tape; **Casual Corner**, **The Limited** (see the Shops at the Omni as well), and **Paul Harris** — three shops selling contemporary clothing for women; **Victoria's Secret**, a shop for intimate apparel (see the Shops at the Omni); **Pete Banis**, a little shop selling big designer brands such as Via Spiga, Jazz, Unisa, and Studio Paolo (see another location in Mt. Pleasant); **Stride Rite Shoes** for kids; and **Lechters**, for items from cookware to organizers. We enjoy touring the **SCE&G Energy Info Center**, free and fascinating, with answers to a lot of questions about energy conservation.

Across from Citadel Mall are the **West Ashley Shoppes**. Some we frequent are **Pak Mail**; **Rack Room Shoes** (a self-serve outlet price shoe store carrying name brand dress and casual shoes); **Phar-Mor** (a discount store with complete pharmacy as well as video rentals and fast, affordable photo development); **Hammett's Learning World** (a fascinating haunt for creative teachers and parents looking for educational supplies); **People's Computers** (a sales and service oriented business — half of this book was written on one of theirs); and **Pet Emporium** (selling creatures as well as the supplies they require); and **Vans and Stuff Sk8 Shop**, a hub for rollerblade

skating enthusiasts we know (see Mount Pleasant shop as well).

Take a left at the light onto Sam Rittenberg Boulevard, and head for 1840 Sam Rittenberg (on your left) where you will find **Honey Baked Ham**, which sells take-home, spiral-cut hams, quiche, pies, and sandwiches — a great idea for a week at the beach. Also, **Kassis Brothers**, for many years *the* "serious shoe" store on King Street, is now located in this center. Generations of mothers have relied on Kassis to shoe hard-to-fit or growing feet with such brands such as Child Life and Stride Rite. Even adults with orthopedic problems can be fitted at Kassis.

Farther down the road on your left, find **Westwood Plaza**. Here we shop **Workbench** for sophisticated modern furniture; **Waccamaw Linen** for bedroom, bathroom accessories as well as crafts materials; **T.J. Maxx** and **Marshall's** for discount designer items; **Office Depot** for discount office supplies; **Diane's Hallmark** for cards, stationary, calendars, and gift wrap; **Eckerd Drugs**; and **The Wardrobe**, a "gently worn" clothing store run by the Charleston Junior League. There is also a **Blind's Plus**, a large **Blockbuster Video**, and a **Fabric Warehouse**.

Farther down Sam Rittenberg, past **Appel Vision** — an excellent source for fashion eyewear — is **Village Square Center**, where we buy crafts materials at **Rainbow Bay Crafts**. We also like the **Leather Connection**, a factory outlet for men and women's leather goods such as jackets, coats, bike pants, and shirts. **Pecknel Music** sells equipment, instruments and sheet music, and **Fins** is a source for aquariums and fish supplies. Nearby is **Loehmann's**, a sophisticated designer shop for women where the prices are discounted.

The next major shopping center, **Ashley Landing**, is the home of **Condon's**, established in 1897. Condon's carries adorable children's clothes, adult clothing, shoes, gifts and more. (There is also a store in Summerville.) If you or someone you know is in the market for a coat, check the **Burlington Coat Factory** for a wide selection and good prices. The store also carries other clothing, baby items and household goods. **Big Lots**, which sells discounted closeouts, is a good place to buy birthday party favors, stocking stuffers and such.

At **Northbridge Terrace**, across from Ashley Landing on Highway 171, the off-price shoe store **Lottie's** sells men and women's shoes. Women's brands are impressive and vary, and leather dress shoes by Nunn Bush and Stacy Adams are sometimes a draw for men. Around the bend and on the left, at **Orange Grove Plaza**, we recommend **Harbor Records** for a good selection of records, tapes and CDs (check out the stamp program if you are going to be in the area for a while).

To shop along Ashley River Road (also called Highway 61), head toward town on Highway 171 and take a right on Ashley River Road at the third stop light. Look on the left for **Raspberry's Natural Food Store**, at 1331 Ashley River Road, which sells organic produce, vitamins, fresh bread, sandwiches and soups to go, nutrition books, high energy beverages, and cooking ingredients. On the right, see the **Men's Consignment Store** — a store which sells gently worn men's clothes on consignment, and another **Market Street Munchies** (see store in Market area).

To find **Magnolia Park Shopping Center**, cross Sam Rittenberg Boulevard and look for 1901 Ashley River Road. Our favorite shops here are **Southeastern Galleries**; **Lawson Limited**, a shop selling home decorations (terra cotta angels and silver picture frames are quite nice); small accent furniture in traditional mahogany and cherry, ladies apparel (from sportswear to party clothes, some hand-painted and coordinated with handmade jewelry); and **In Good Taste**, a serious gourmet shop which sells kitchen items, herb plants, wines, cheeses, coffees, teas, and gift baskets, and sponsors wine seminars and cooking classes.

Charleston
Restaurants

*E*ating out in restaurants has become popular over the last twenty years in Charleston. With the revitalization of our downtown area and the draw of people to places south, there has been an influx of outstanding new culinary talent and the interest to match. Now, there are establishments and styles to fit most every whim, as well as a true effort to share — and preserve — the traditional fare of the Lowcountry. We have included information and opinions in this chapter that may help you with your selections.

The list is not exhaustive, but gives — we hope — a fair representation of what is available on the peninsula and West Ashley. The code reference guide below should be used to translate which credit cards are accepted, and the price ranges for entrées. We caution that prices, hours, menus and means of payment are subject to change, so if it's an important factor in the restaurant you choose, check ahead.

CREDIT CARDS

AX *(American Express)*
DC *(Diners Club)*
CB *(Carte Blanche)*
MC *(MasterCard)*
D *(Discover)*
V *(Visa)*

Photo: The Post and Courier

Charleston's fishing fleet brings fresh seafood in daily.

PRICE RANGES

Up to $10	$
$11-$15	$$
$16-$20	$$$
$21 & up	$$$$

Restaurants On The Peninsula

ANDOLINI'S

82 Wentworth Street	722-PIES
$	No credit cards

A great place for pizza, assorted beers and calzones, Andolini's looks and feels like the college hangouts of our lost youth. Hours are Tuesday through Thursday, 11:30 AM until 11:00 PM, and Friday and Saturday from 11:30 AM until midnight.

ANSON'S

12 Anson Street	577-0551
$-$$$	Most major credit cards

An elegant restaurant located on Anson Street, less than a block from the Market area, Anson's is as well-appointed as it is deserving of a reputation for fine food and good service. The California/Thai menu includes a decadent cashew-crusted grouper in champagne sauce which should not be missed. Hours are 5:30 PM until 11:00 PM, Sunday through Thursday, and until midnight on Friday and Saturday.

APPLEBEE'S

24 N. Market Street	723-3531
$-$$	AX,MC,V,D

While it is one in a chain of restaurants, Applebee's is worth mentioning because it is a quality establishment — unique in certain ways. Order healthy foods like stir-fry or satisfy a burger craving — it's all on the menu. We can feed the family with Mom's blessing and not exclude any picky eaters at Applebee's. (See West Ashley restaurant too.) Hours are Monday through Thursday, 11:00 AM until midnight; Friday and Saturday, 11:00 AM until 1:00 AM; and Sunday, 11:00 AM until 11:00 PM.

ARIZONA BAR & GRILL

14 Chapel Street	577-5090
$$	Most major credit cards

Arizona's, as the locals call it, is definitely one of the happening waterholes and eateries in the city. Housed in an old train station on the corner of East Bay and Chapel Street (next to the new post office), the decor of the establishment is a whimsical tribute to the wonders of the wild, wild west. Lofty ceilings with gargantuan wooden beams, native American rugs and sculpture reinforce the theme. Diners choose from a wide assortment of unusual Mexican dishes including a rattlesnake appetizer, an artichoke pizza and, of course, the Buffalo Burger. We love the black bean cakes and ribs from the grill. Arizona's is a fun time and the food is part of the entertainment. Food is served from 11:30 AM until 10:00, Monday through Thursday, and until 11:00 PM on Friday and Saturday. Sunday hours are 1:00 PM until 10:00 PM. Dress is nice casual.

A. W. SHUCK'S

70 State Street	723-1151
$-$$	AX, MC, V, DC

More than a decade has passed since Shuck's first opened its doors, and a lot has changed in the market area as a whole — and at Shuck's in particular — since then. What was originally a cozy, popular bar packed with locals has become a bigger, fancier eating establishment where the bar is no longer the only draw. Shuck's features both indoor and outdoor dining. And, oyster connoisseurs will be interested to know that the crustaceans are sold raw or steamed — sky's the limit. Beef, fowl, and all sorts of seafood as well as children's plates are on the menu. A. W. Shuck's is open Sunday through Thursday, 11:30 AM until 10:00 PM, and Friday and Saturday until 11:00 PM.

BJ's Broad Street Cafe
17 Broad Street   722-0559
$ *No credit cards*

BJ's is a weekday haunt for the Broad Street working crowd who prefer ringside seats by the window for people-watching. Buffalo wings, pizza and pocket sandwiches are our favorites, and we have been known to order them as take-out supper over the weekend. BJ's is open Monday through Friday, 7:30 AM until 10 PM, and Saturday from 8:30 AM until 10 PM. It is closed on Sunday.

The Baker's Cafe of Charleston
214 King Street   577-2694
$-$$ *DC, MC, V*

Baker's Cafe is a romantic little gem tucked off in the block below the Omni Complex. Much more than a bakery (although what is baked is delicious), it is a sophisticated but comfortable restaurant. Sunday brunch at Baker's is particularly delightful, with unusual dishes such as Eggs Charleston (with a bed of Canadian snow-crab substituted for the Canadian bacon), mimosas, (made with freshly-squeezed orange juice), and a basket of hot-from-the-oven baked goods. Wine and other spirits are available, and there is wheelchair access. Hours are from 8:00 AM to 3:00 PM, Monday through Friday, and 9:00 AM to 3:00 PM Saturday and Sunday. Dress is nice casual.

Blue Coyote Grille
61 State Street   577-BLUE
$-$$ *Most major credit cards*

Blue Coyote serves what you'd expect at a cowboy/cowgirl hangout — fajitas, quesadillas, fajitas and even ribs and chicken. There is a late night menu and one for the kids (who, by the way, are thoroughly entertained by the wild west setting). Lunch is served from 11:30 AM until 4:00 PM, Monday through Saturday; dinner is served from 4:00 PM until 10:00 PM.

Insiders Like:
Taking in one of the "brown bag" lectures at the Gibbes Museum of Art — for an in-depth view of an exhibit or a chance to personally meet the artist.

Insiders' Tip

BLUE PARROT DOUGHNUT

363 King Street   853-6100
$ No cards

What a find for breakfast on King Street! While you and I sleep, the little elves here huff and puff away from 3:30 AM on to bake delicious muffins, doughnuts and such. They even put on the gourmet coffee (from Two Step Cafe's shop next door) and chill the drinks so that we can enjoy continental from about 7:00 AM on. Blue Parrot closes at 7:00 PM.

THE BLOSSOM CAFE

171 East Bay Street   577-7771
$-$$$ MC, V, AX

The Blossom Cafe is another "see and be seen" place downtown, but offers the bonus of being as affordable or extravagant as your budget allows. There is inside and outside dining, an in-house bakery, a cappuccino bar and extensive menu (same for lunch and dinner) ranging from pastas and seafood entrees to gourmet pizzas from the wood-burning oven. Hours are 11:30 AM until midnight, (pizza until last call) Monday through Thursday, and 11:30 AM until 1:00 AM on Friday and Saturday.

BOCCI'S

Corner of Church & Cumberland   720-2121
$ V, MC, AX, DC

This cozy Northern Italian restaurant keeps them coming back for more calzones, salads, seafood and pasta (topped with a choice of four fabulous sauces). Mozzarella lovers go for the hand-pulled cheese. Our favorite are scallops wrapped in prosciutto. There is a front room view looking out on historic Church Street. Bocci's is open seven days a week, and serves lunch from 11:30 AM until 4:00 PM. Dinner is served from 5:30 PM until 10:00 PM during the week, and until 11:00 PM on weekends.

THE BOOKSTORE CAFE

The Corner of King and   720-8843
Hutson Street
$ No credit cards

Located across the street from the Charleston County Library, The Bookstore Cafe serves breakfast and lunch and sells baked goods and best-sellers (hence the name). Far enough from the madding crowd, this cafe offers some serenity along with its daily specials. Menu items may include fried chicken, meat loaf, soup, salad and even chili. But take home some rhubarb raspberry jam and beer bread. The cafe is open from 7:30 AM until 2:30 PM, Monday through Friday, and from 9:00 AM until 2:00 PM on the weekends.

CAFE 99

99 South Market Street   577-4499
$ V, MC, AX

Cafe 99 is a casual entertainment restaurant, serving lunch and dinner seven days a week starting at 11:30 AM. There is an inside dining room as well as outside dining on the patio. The menu includes buffalo wings, a seafood sampler, pastas, red beans and rice and even (sometimes great deals on) lobster. Entertainment includes live rock and blues on Friday and Saturday nights, as well as a sports bar upstairs. Cafe 99 closes its doors about 2:00 AM.

Photo: The Post and Courier

Market Hall is at the beginning of Market Street, where you'll find some of Charleston's most popular restaurants.

CAFE RAINBOW

282 King Street   853-9777
$ V, MC, D

The outside tables are often occupied at Cafe Rainbow, where young and old stop to read (there is plenty to choose from), sip coffee (imported from the owner's plantation) and eat continental breakfast, light lunch, pastries or ice cream. Hours are 7:00 AM until 11:00 PM, Monday through Thursday, 7:00 AM until midnight on Friday and Saturday, and from 9:00 AM until 6:00 PM on Sunday.

CAROLINA'S

10 Exchange Street   724-3800
$$-$$$$ AX, DC, MC, V

Carolina's is located on the site of old Perditas, a much-respected restaurant of days gone by. There is little in the decor reminiscent of the establishment's roots, as Carolina's is designed for the '90s. There are three main areas: the noisy, see-and-be-seen front dining section, with its showy wine collection (said to be one of the largest in the southeast); a central bar with tables on two sides; and a more secluded, traditional dining room — to the right of the entrance — which, in ambiance, seems a century apart. The menu is expansive, and the style "modern

Carolina" with seafood, veal and lamb being in many instances grilled (not cooked down and swimming in butter like the "old days"). Burgers are a hit as well. Carolina's is open seven days a week, from 5:30 until the crowd goes home. Dress is very nice casual.

CELIA'S PORTA VIA

49 Archdale Street	722-9003
$-$$$	MC, AX, V

Another small Italian jewel in Charleston's restaurant crown, Celia's Porta Via smacks of old world authenticity and charm. Cozy and family-like, the staff and the regulars, as well as the Sicilian cuisine, make this dining experience special. Entertainment around the house piano is sometimes planned, sometimes spontaneous (as when guests burst into song). Don't miss the handmade mozzarella and pastas and a sample bottle from Celia's extensive wine collection. The restaurant is open for lunch from 11:00 AM to 2:30 PM on Monday through Friday, 6:00 PM to 10:30 PM on Monday through Thursday for dinner and 6:00 PM to 11:30 PM on Friday and Saturday. Parking is available, and nice casual dressing is the norm.

CHARLES TOWNE PRINCESS

Charleston City Marina	722-1112
	or (800) 344-4483
$$$	MC, V, D

This cruise offers dinner, dancing and cocktails. A buffet is prepared on ship and includes shrimp, crab, barbecue chicken or fish, red rice or parsley potatoes, corn on the cob, cole slaw, rolls and tea — how Southern can you get?! Boarding is at 7:00 PM, but nights available vary with season. There is a loading ramp and use of a golf cart to accommodate handicapped passengers.

CHEF AND CLEF

102 North Market Street	722-0732
$-$$$	Most major credit cards

Diners come to Chef and Clef for the food and the long hours of live jazz. The restaurant opens every day at 11:30 AM, and serves lunch, dinner and a late night menu until midnight. Its culinary presentation is basic continental with a welcome dash of Creole here and there. Try the reasonably priced and tasty gumbo, pasta primavera, chicken wings, or — our favorite — whiskey chicken. The music starts at 8:00 PM and keeps going until around 2:00 AM (a little sooner on Sunday).

THE COLONY HOUSE

35 Prioleau	723-3424
at the Waterfront Park	
$$-$$$$	Most major credit cards

Housed in an 1814 building across from the pineapple fountain at Waterfront Park, The Colony House has been a Charleston institution for decades. Owners Dayna and Dick Elliott put great emphasis on "local food" as well as "local art." The menu includes fresh seafood, beef and fowl prepared by regional recipes (take, for instance, shrimp and grits topped off with sweet potato pecan pie). If you remember (as we do) this restaurant as a dark "compartmentalized" building, you are in for a pleasant surprise. Recently renovated, the floor plan has been opened up and enlivened with consignment art — from paintings, to wrought iron, to fanciful furniture. The rooftop is open to the public as an observation deck, and the views are exceptional. Lunch is served from 11:30 AM until 3:00 PM, Monday through Saturday; brunch is served from 11:00 AM until 2:00 PM on Sunday. Dinner is served from 5:30 PM until 9;30 PM Sunday through Thursday, and until 10:30 PM on Friday and Saturday.

DOE'S PITA PLUS

334 East Bay Street   *577-3179*
$ *No credit cards*

Doe's offers fresh-baked pita bread for pocket sandwiches, and salads prepared to order (in plain view) while you wait. Although there are a couple of tables and chairs, most people think of "take out" when they think of Doe's. Very popular is what's called "The Tasty Chicken Pocket," which comes bursting at the pita-seams with plums, celery, chicken, green onions, lettuce, tomatoes and alfalfa sprouts. For variety, on the side, sample Doe's ethnic fare such as baba ghannouj, tabouleh, or Lebanese potato salad. Our children love the banana and peanut butter pocket, and do well in the high chair stationed in the rear dining area. Nonalcoholic beverages are sold. Hours are from 8:00 AM until 8:30 PM, Monday through Friday, and on Saturday from 8:00 AM until 5:00 PM. Service on Sunday is from 11:00 AM until 5:00 PM.

EAST BAY TRADING COMPANY

161 East Bay Street   *722-0722*
$$-$$$ *Most major credit cards*

Locals tend to gather in this cavernous space for happy hours, and some stay for dinner. The mood is usually festive, and those who don't fit around the front or back bar proper hang on to the trolley car planted at mid-floor. A glass elevator shuttles guests to dining areas on the second and third floors. Patrons are raving about the beef (servings tend to be large), seafood (try red fish if you like a delicate texture), and sophisticated pasta dishes. Desserts are sinful and worth the mischief. Dinner is served from 5:30 PM until 10:30 PM, Monday through Thursday, 5:30 PM until 11:00 PM on Friday and Saturday, and from 5:00 PM until 9:30 PM on Sunday.

82 QUEEN

82 Queen Street   *723-7591*
$$-$$$ *Most major credit cards*

Exploring the facilities at 82 Queen is an adventure in itself. The grounds include two adjoining 19th-century townhouses, two inside bars (full-service and shot), an outside raw bar (a popular hangout for the after-work crowd), a partially glassed-in romantic gazebo as well as outdoor tables for dining. Seafood, beef, lamb and fowl are specialties. Lunch is served from 11:30 AM until 3:30 PM seven days a week, while dinner is served from 6:00 PM until 10:00 PM, Sunday through Thursday, and from 6:00 PM until 10:30 PM Friday and Saturday.

FANNIE'S DINER

137 Market Street   723-7121
$ MC, V, D

This eatery is a 1950s remake with low key atmosphere. Certainly a blast-from-the-past, complete with black-topped tables (trimmed in chrome, of course) and red booths, this restaurant dishes up homemade soups, burgers, sandwiches, malts and even a blue plate special, 24-hours a day. The juke box looks vintage, but plays CDs. Fannie's is located across from the Omni, and — for obvious reasons — is popular with the college crowd.

FOUR CORNERS CAFE

38 Broad Street   577-0088
$ MC,V,D

The Broad Street crowd and in-the-know locals are loyal customers at Four Corners (cleverly named for the Four Corners of Law at Meeting and King). House specialties include omelets, pancakes, burgers, bacon/lettuce/tomato sandwiches and entrees like prawns in beer batter — very tasty. Outside dining is pleasant, and inside is nice and cool in the hot months. Hours are 7:00 AM until 10:00 PM, Monday through Friday, from 8:00 AM until 10:00 PM on Saturday, and from 8:30 AM until 3:00 PM on Sunday.

THE FRENCH QUARTER

195 East Bay Street   722-1611
Lodge Alley Inn
$-$$$ V, MC, AX

Don't be misled by the name: The French Quarter is not solely a traditional French restaurant, but rather is located in the French Quarter of town, and serves European as well as Lowcountry fare. Under the roof of Lodge Alley Inn, The French Quarter is praised for such Grand Rotisserie favorites as Chateaubriand and Carolina Quail. Its menu and style remind us of the finer American restaurants of yesteryear. Breakfast is served from 7:00 AM until 10:30 AM; lunch is served from 11:30 AM until 2:30 PM; and dinner is served from 6:00 PM until 10:00 PM. Patrons dress nicely.

FUDDRUCKER'S

225 East Bay Street   722-4265
$ V, MC,D, AX

Fuddrucker's, home of "the world's greatest hamburgers" and the wonderful Fudd Mudd Pie, is a good place to go when you want to satisfy that red meat/chocolate craving around meal time. To start with, there is free *parking* (that magic word in the Market area), the children love it, and there is a choice of 1/2 pound or 1/3 pound burgers for different sized appetites. The restaurant is clean and bright, and the service prompt. Hours are 11:00 AM until 11:00 PM, seven days a week.

FULFORD AND EGAN COFFEES AND TEAS

231 Meeting St.   577-4553
$-$$ V, AX, MC, D

This establishment defies conventional definition...is it a restaurant? a specialty shop? an entertainment club? Actually, it's all three rolled into something like what we called "a coffee house" in the 1960s. This is a classy, updated version which carries a wide range of brewing accessories with 200 specialty coffees and teas. Those who wish to sit and sip can enjoy coffee, tea, cappuccino or cafe au lait, while munching on ham and cheese croissants or dessert. Fulford-Egan is a favorite with the college students, who participate in the poetry readings, eat Ben and Jerry's ice cream, and soak up the live music nightly. Hours are from 7 AM until 11:00 PM, seven days a week. Dress is casual.

FULTON FIVE

5 Fulton Street   *853-5555*
$-$$$ *Most major credit cards*

Fulton Five is off the beaten path slightly, and worth the stroll down Fulton Street (just off King). Here is one suggestion: to start with, try the Melanzane (eggplant soup) and an appetizer of field greens and fennel. Move on to linguini mixed with seared tuna, crushed tomatoes and fresh mint, and finally Tuscan roast loin of pork with Rapin and rosemary potatoes. Then, for a light sweet touch, order a lemon sherbet with Campari — the perfect finale. Hours at Fulton Five are Tuesday through Saturday, 11:00 AM until 11:00 PM.

GARIBALDI'S

49 South Market St.   *723-7153*
$$$ *AX, V, MC*

Garibaldi's is a charming Italian restaurant which has survived, apparently without flinching, the continuous ebb and flow of popularity on Market Street. There is service downstairs — with a small bar as well as outside tables — and in the upstairs dining room. Try the outstanding crispy fried flounder when it's offered, and enjoy any of the pastas. We also get weak in the knees over almond coated salmon and crab stuffed grouper — umm, umm, divine. Dinner is served Sunday through Thursday, 6:00 PM until 10:30 PM, and from 6:00 PM until 11:00 PM on Friday and Saturday.

GAULART AND MALICLET FRENCH CAFE

98 Broad Street   *577-9797*
$-$$ *Most major credit cards*

Carved out of what was formerly a long, narrow office with lovely molding, Gaulart and Maliclet is a Parisian-style cafe serving delicious, contemporary French fare (cheese plates, salads and house specials are our mainstay) with Big City speed (hence the restaurant's motto: Fast and French). The owners — French, of course — know what they are doing, and are so pleasant while they are doing it! Their hours vary, but they are open most of every day until 10:00 PM and weekend nights until about midnight. They are closed on Sunday. There is no dress code.

GOODIE HOUSE

168 Calhoun Street	723-8181
$	No credit cards

This little restaurant (recently refurbished) is an old College of Charleston haunt, serving basic breakfast and lunch food — nothing fancy — from the grill. We order soup and a grilled cheese sandwich, and sit at the tiny stools while it's cooked. Expect to see a lot of "regulars" from the campus, and realize that you may stand in line for a seat. Hours are from 7:00 AM until 5:00 PM, Monday through Thursday, and 7:00 AM until 3:30 PM on Friday.

GRANVILLE CAFE

70 1/2 Beaufain Street	853-0120
$	MC,V,AX

A real, honest-to-goodness "neighborhood restaurant," Granville Cafe quickly became a hit with locals. Quaint but not at all "too precious" or contrived, Granville's serves good food (pasta, seafood and the like), with delicious veggies on the side. Hours are from 11:30 AM until 9:00 PM on Monday and Tuesday; until 10:00 PM Wednesday through Saturday; and from 9:30 AM until 9:00 PM on Sunday.

HAAGEN DAZS ICE CREAM SHOPPE

23 S. Market	723-9326
$	No credit cards

An old standard in the gourmet ice cream business, Haagen Dazs rewards the hot and hungry in the market area. This little shop is located on the corner of State and South Market Streets, and is a convenient stop for dessert or a treat if you are in this area. Waist-watchers will be happy to know that this Haagen Dazs now carries frozen yogurt. Hours are 11:00 AM until 11:00 PM during the week, and 11:00 AM until midnight on weekends.

HENRY'S

54 North Market Street	723-4363
$$-$$$	M, V, AX

Henry's has operated at the same location since 1930, but has in recent years changed its focus to entertainment (jazz in particular). Fowl, beef and poultry are still on the menu, and the doors are open from 4:00 PM until 2:00 AM seven days a week. Count on a *large* crowd around the bar most nights.

HYMAN'S SEAFOOD COMPANY

215 Meeting Street	723-0233
$-$$	V, MC, D

A casual dining experience, Hyman's offers reasonably priced seafood which is fresh — check out the whole fish as it is being prepared in full view of the street front window. Upstairs is a raw bar and lounge. We particularly like the fact that Hyman's fries in olive oil, and that seafood can also be ordered either broiled or blackened. Try the okra soup, even if you have always hidden from the vegetable. Open seven days a week, the restaurant serves from 11:00 AM until 11:00 PM, and suggests that patrons park in the Omni Hotel garage.

JACK'S CAFE

41 George Street	723-5237
$	No credit cards

The turnaround at Jack's is fast, and the food as typically American as its no-frills apple or peach cobbler. A loyal crowd of College of Charleston students, professors and alumni, as well as King Street merchants frequent Jack's for its good, old-fashioned burgers (served in plastic baskets) and milkshakes. The value is definitely part of the draw, but so is the vegetable soup (and, in fact, all of the food). People eat in booths, at the counter or around a few tables. Take-out service is available. Hours are 7:00 AM until 3:45 PM, Monday through Friday.

J.J. HOOK'S

| 188 East Bay Street | 853-7292 |
| $-$$$ | AX, D, V, MC |

J.J. Hook's is located in what was once Jilich's — a light, cheerful setting with pickled wood interior and a sense of openness. Seafood is the main attraction, and the atmosphere is casual. Hours are 11:30 AM until 10:30 PM, seven days a week.

JOHNNY ROCKETS

| 41 South Market Street | 723-1700 |
| $ | Most major credit cards |

This may be our favorite diner chain not only because the food is great and the prices are downright alright, but also because the look is so authentically '50's. Nostalgia aside, what could be more fun than to settle into a red booth, surrounded by silver chrome, at a table equipped with its own tiny juke box, and order a soda pop and sandwich plate for less than four dollars? Hours are from 11:00 AM until 11:00 PM, Monday through Thursday, and 11:00 AM until 1:00 AM Friday through Sunday.

KAMINSKY'S MOST EXCELLENT CAFE

| 78 North Market Street | 853-8270 |
| $ | MC,V,AX |

Kaminsky's is an A+ addition to the list of indulge-thyself-peninsula eateries. Handsome brick walls (backdrops for a nice showing of art) and the cafe's intimate size contribute to its appeal. Try an exotic coffee or nonalcoholic drink with your delicious dessert selection, or relax with a beer or glass of wine (the list is international and impressive). Kaminsky's is open seven days a week from 12 noon until 2:00 AM.

KITTY'S FINE FOODS

| 1137 Morrison Drive | 723-0233 |
| $ | No credit cards |

From breakfast through lunch, Kitty's serves the kind of no-nonsense, "home cooking" that many associate with the old south. Fried chicken, flounder, liver pudding and the like are house specialties. Locals know about Kitty's but visitors sometimes miss the location (which is off the beaten path). Expect friendly service and "real food." Hours are Monday through Friday, 6:00 AM until 3:00 PM.

LAFAYETTE BISTRO

| 276 King Street | 723-0014 |
| $$-$$$$ | Most major credit cards |

Situated at the corner of Wentworth and King Streets, Lafayette is an informal French restaurant which seems to pulsate with activity during peak hours. The grill is the focal point, and what comes off of it — from roast chicken au juice, with herbs of Provence, to grilled tuna steak with ginger sauce — is outstanding. An original painting by local artist John Doyle hangs on the back wall and captures the staff's pace at full pitch, with food and orders changing hands across the long bar. Hours are from 11:30 AM until 11:00 PM, Monday through Saturday.

LE MIDI

337 King Street   577-5571
$-$$$ Most major credit cards

Le Midi serves basic French cooking in a subdued and attractive setting. We remember this restaurant when it was still cooled by fans, and consisted of only one room. A friend, transplanted from New Orleans and well-traveled in France, brought us here for "real French food." We fell in love with the Moules a la Mariniere (mussels swimming in secret juices, perfect dipping sauce for French bread) and Flounder Alain (a lightly fried filet in lemony brown sauce, impossible to copy). Luncheon is served from 11:30 AM until 2:00 PM, Monday through Friday, and dinner from 6:00 PM until 10:00 PM Monday through Saturday.

THE LIBRARY AT VENDUE

23 Vendue Range
(in the Vendue Inn)   723-0485
$$$$ AX, MC, V

Located in the Vendue Inn, this restaurant gives the feel of an old English library but has a progressive menu which changes with the availability of fresh ingredients. One can almost make a meal off of the Library's delicious, heavy appetizers. However, seafood, steaks, veal and lamb and accompaniments (offered a la carte) are prepared in

ways that lure us onward. Save room for great desserts. Hours are Monday through Thursday, 6:00 PM until 9:30 PM, and Friday and Saturday from 5:30 PM until 10:00 PM.

LOUIS'S CHARLESTON GRILL

The Omni, 224 King Street   577-4522
$$$-$$$$ Most major credit cards

Although Louis's Charleston Grill is part of the Omni Hotel, it is no ordinary "hotel restaurant." To start with, the establishment has exceptionally handsome dining areas, with warm wood paneling and rich marble floors. We have indulged ourselves in such mellowed settings in New York or Washington — places which have stood the test of time and trend. Actually, this restaurant was just opened in 1989 by Louis Osteen (a man Town and Country magazine has called "one of the most gifted chefs in America"). Esquire put Louis' in the category of "Best New Restaurants of 1990s" and USA Today called it "Hottest New Restaurant of 1990." Dinner is served from 6:00 PM until 11:00 PM seven days a week (with a late night menu served from 11:00 PM until 1:00 AM, Thursday through Saturday. The bar opens at 4:00 PM, and there is jazz nightly after 7:00 PM.

MAGNOLIAS UPTOWN/DOWNSOUTH

185 East Bay Street   577-7771
$$-$$$ V, MC, AX

Magnolias tops the list of hot restaurants on the peninsula. In fact, Travel and Leisure Magazine called it "*the* place in downtown Charleston." This is American cuisine made distinct with its classy southern style. Some of the chef's specialties are shrimp and grits, Clemson blue cheese potato chips (made with the tangy product from our up-country university), and tomato bisque soup dotted with generous lumps of fresh crabmeat. The expansive menu will remind you of its California/Tex-Mex/Cajun inspirations, but the atmosphere is strictly refined, New South. Hours are 11:00 AM until 11:00 PM, Monday through Wednesday; 11:00 AM until 1:00 AM, Thursday through Saturday; and 12:00 PM until 10:00 PM on Sunday.

MARIANNE RESTAURANT

235 Meeting Street   722-7196
$$$-$$$$ AX, DC, MC, V

A French restaurant famous for late night breakfast (served after 10:30 PM), Marianne's is packed after the party. We are fond of the traditional Eggs Benedict, but have friends who would swim laps for Eggs Marianne (which substitutes red snapper for the Canadian bacon). Dinner is a sensation as well, with beef, veal, fowl and seafood being served in a bistro atmosphere. Hours of service are Monday through Saturday, 6:00 PM until 9:30 PM, with a late menu served until 1:30 AM; and Sunday from 5:00 PM until 11:00 PM. Dress is nice casual (although you may see some in black tie, as patrons drift in from other events). There is wheelchair access.

MARINA VARIETY STORE RESTAURANT

City Marina   723-6325
at Lockwood Boulevard
$-$$$ MC, V, AX

Enjoy good food as well as a magnificent view of the Ashley River at what regulars call "the Variety Store." Offering breakfast, lunch and dinner in a very casual setting, the restaurant serves plain, good food. For instance, you can order eggs, bacon and toast for breakfast after church and come back for a tuna salad sandwich and cup of vegetable soup after the noon regatta. If you want to return that night, dinner of fresh fish with red rice and a salad is a distinct possibility. Spirits are available, and children are welcome. Hours are 6:30 AM until 3:00 PM, seven days a week, and 5:00 PM until 9:00 PM every evening except Sunday.

MARKET SQUARE FOOD COURT

170 Church Street   722-4455
$ Credit card policy varies

The Market Square Food Court is the market area's eating mall (into which a few other businesses open). There are tables in the center for dining in, and restaurants — like booths at the fair — ring the enclosed area. For a quick bite and world of choice, you can't beat it. The selection includes ethnic foods, deli items, pizza and much much more.

Insiders Like:
Taking afternoon tea on the mezzanine at the Omni.

Insiders' Tip

McCRADY'S

2 Unity Alley   853-8484
$-$$$ M, V, A, D

McCrady's dark wood and exposed brick interior is the perfect place to meet a friend for drinks or dinner...or both. The fireplace is a draw in the winter, and the cool drinks and relaxing atmosphere make it popular in the warmer months. Like a tavern in the best sense of the word, McCrady's serves wonderful entrees (try the lamb chops) and a fantastic selection of seafood, pastas, vegetables and items a la carte. Open Monday through Saturday. Happy hour is from 4:30 PM until 6:00 PM and dinner is served from 5:30 PM until.

MESA GRILL

32 1/2 North Market Street   723-3770
$-$$ Most major credit cards

For atmosphere and fiery food, Mesa serves up the stuff with a TexMex slant. Salads, burgers, black bean soup, Acapulco shrimp and even baby back ribs give the menu some variety and punch. There is inside and outside dining, made all the more "an experience" by the pervading scent of mesquite fire and taste of "Killer Margaritas." Mesa opens at 11:00 AM every day, and closes at 12:00 , Sunday through Thursday, and at 1:00 AM on Friday and Saturday. There is a Sunday brunch from 11:00 AM until 2:00 PM.

MIKE CALDERS DELI AND PUB

288 King Street   577-0123
$ MC, V, D

Formerly Patrick's, Mike Calders came to town from West Ashley and continues to please its clientele with deli-style food. Such favorites as chef salads, soups and club sandwiches are available. We love the toasted tuna, which comes with Mike's fabulous cole slaw and crunchy pickle. Hours are 10:00 AM until 11:00 PM, Monday through Thursday, and 10:00 AM until midnight on Friday and Saturday.

MISTRAL

99 South Market Street   722-5708
$-$$ AX, D, MC, V

Mistral is a very cozy French bistro that is small and intimate. Dixieland jazz is the live entertainment every Friday and Saturday night. Lunch hours are 11:00 AM until 5:00 PM, Monday through Saturday, and 11:00 AM until 3:00 PM on Sundays. Dinner is served from 5:00 PM until 10:00 PM, Monday through Thursday, and until 11:00 PM on Friday and Saturday. We describe Mistral as casual with understated elegance...a place where you can go light or heavy, salads to seafood. Don't miss the homemade bread!

MOULTRIE TAVERN

18 Vendue Range   723-1862
$$-$$$ Most major credit cards

Located on the site of a tavern founded in 1862, Moultrie Tavern displays 18th- and 19th-century artifacts, and features a menu which includes items with names like "Morris Island Seafood Pie" and "Ham and Shrimp Sumter." We are drawn to an appetizer called "James Island Shrimp Cup" (a combination of shrimp, rice, mushrooms and cream) and "Scallops Secessionville" (sauteed sea scallops in a cream sauce). Open seven days a week, Moultrie tavern serves lunch from 11:30 AM until 2:30 PM, late lunch from 2:30 PM until 4:00 PM, and dinner from 5:30 until 10;00 PM.

NEW TAJ

50 North Market	853-8500
$-$$	MC, V

The New Taj serves Tandoori and Biryani foods, lamb and seafood, vegetable dishes, curries and an assortment of traditional breads (like Roti and Poori). Interesting Indian beers are available. Hours are from 11:00 AM until 3:00 PM for lunch, and 5:00 PM until 11:00 PM for dinner every day.

NÖELLE'S

83 Cumberland Street	723-2843
$$$	D, MC, V

Located in the Nicholas Trott House, built in the 18th century by the same Judge Trott who ordered the hanging of charismatic pirate Stede Bonnet, Noelle's offers a tropical version of Charleston fare. The restaurant is highbrow in setting (note the double fireplaces between dining rooms on both floors), but Caribbean in terms of the relaxed dining experience. Island music sets the mood, and the chef's emphasis is on fresh meats, chicken, seafood and vegetables. Island Pumpkin Fritters and Caribbean Pepperpot (a West Indian specialty of lean beef, pork and tender chicken simmered with Casareep — a vegetable extract from Cassava) are our favorite ethnic selections. We particularly enjoy what comes gratis with each meal: sundry accompaniments, home-made breads and a house salad. Lunch is served from 11:30 AM until 2:00 PM, and dinner is served starting at 6:00 PM every day except Sunday.

NOSH WITH JOSH

217 Meeting Street	577-NOSH
$	V, MC

The only certified kosher eatery and all vegetarian restaurant in the city (according to the management), Nosh with Josh serves Mediterranean dishes and is open from 11:00 AM until 10:00 PM, seven days a week.

OLDE COLONY BAKERY

280 King Street	722-2147
$-$$$$	V, MC

This was our old-fashioned bakery before there were any others to choose from, and we still love it. House specialties include gourmet cookies, cinnamon rolls, benne wafers (about as "Charleston" as you can get), and cream breads. Samples of custom wedding cakes line the showcases and are the only items that fall into top price range. Hours are 8:00 AM until 5:30 PM, Monday through Saturday.

OLDE TOWNE RESTAURANT

229 King Street	723-8170
(across from the Omni)	
$-$$	Most major credit cards

Owners Spiros Fokas and Steve Ferderigos have been serving authentic Greek meals here for 20 years. Their menu includes seafood, salads, Greek chicken and the ever popular Steve's Special: a sampler, good for the gang. Pictures of Greece decorate the walls, and a grill in the front window is a tempting display of chicken being roasted. Hours are Monday through Thursday from 11:00 AM until 10:30 PM, Friday and Saturday from 11:00 AM until 11:00 PM, and on Sunday from 11:00 AM until 10:00 PM (see affiliate restaurants listed under North Charleston and West Towne in this section).

THE PALMETTO CAFE
AT CHARLESTON PLACE

130 Market Street   722-4900
$-$$$ V, MC

This restaurant is part of the Omni complex and serves breakfast, lunch and dinner in a relaxed cafe atmosphere. Our favorite meal is the Jazz Brunch on Sunday. It falls in the $$$ per person category, but is well worth the jingle as the food and live music are tops. The restaurant opens at 6:30 AM and closes at 10:00 PM each day.

PAPILLON

32 Market St.   723-6510
$-$$ MC,V,AX,DC

Once the old Seaman's Chapel, this stylish restaurant, with its open layout and a wood-burning, brick oven, features some very interesting Northern Italian cuisine. Papillon serves homemade pasta dishes, meat and spinach pies, seafood, poultry, lamb and beef entrees and — our favorite — whole wheat pizzas with vegetable and seafood toppings. Hours are from 11:30 AM until 11:00 PM on weeknights and until midnight on the weekend.

PINCKNEY CAFE AND ESPRESSO

18 Pinckney Street   577-0961
$-$$ No credit cards

There's nothing else quite like Pinckney Cafe in Charleston. Sure, we have other restaurants in single houses, and there, too, you can eat out on the porch. But the casual ambiance of Pinckney Cafe is unaffected, and so perfectly suited to relaxed, forget-the-theme-and-let's-eat dining, that everyone feels at home. The menu can be called "new American bistro" as it includes soups, salads, seafood specials and an outrageously delicious black bean burrito. Cappucino is a perfect finale, but we can easily be talked into the bread pudding as well. Pinckney Cafe is open Tuesday through Saturday, with lunch being served from 11:30 AM until 3:00 PM, Tuesday through Thursday, and from 11:30 AM until 2:30 PM, Friday and Saturday. Dinner is served from 6:00 PM until 9:00 PM, Tuesday through Thursday, and 6:00 PM until 10:30 PM on Friday and Saturday.

POOGAN'S PORCH

72 Queen St.   577-2337
$-$$ V, MC, AX

Poogan's Porch is located in a charming old Charleston house where dinner can be enjoyed fireside or outside beneath the stars. Expect casual family dining (including a child's menu) with such Lowcountry favorites as Miss Bertha's she-crab soup, creole, gumbo, seafood specials and even — on the wilder side — rabbit, squirrel and an occasional alligator. Seven days a week lunch is served from 11:30 AM until 2:30 PM, and dinner from 5:30

PM to 10:30 PM. Reservations are recommended for dinner.

PRIMEROSE

332 East Bay Street   723-2954
$-$$$ *Most major credit cards*

A West Coast friend, who travels the world promoting his vineyard's wine, recently commented that Primerose may be his favorite restaurant...anywhere! The Nouvelle American menu offers alfresco dining in a fascinating, basement setting beneath the piazzas of the Primerose House. Our personal favorites from the menu include the crabcakes and walnut crusted grouper with canneli beans and roasted pepper salad. Luncheon is served Monday through Friday, 11:30 AM until 2:00 PM; dinner is served Monday through Thursday, from 6:00 PM until 10:00 PM, and Friday and Saturday from 6:00 PM until 11:00 PM. Sunday brunch hours are 10:30 AM until 2:00 PM.

RESTAURANT MILLION

2 Unity Alley   577-7472
$$$$ *V, MC, AX, DC*

Million is an elegant, formal French restaurant on a quaint alley off East Bay Street. Authentic French haute cuisine is served on tables set with Limoge china in an 18th-century building draped in Aubusson tapestries. Gentlemen patrons always wear coat and tie, and reservations are required. The menu includes five- and six-course, fixed price dinners (appetizer through dessert), as well as dining a la carte. Hours are Monday through Saturday, 6:30 PM until 10:00 PM.

REUBEN'S DOWNTOWN DELICATESSEN

251 Meeting Street   722-6883
$ *No credit cards*

Reuben's is open from 8:00 AM until 4:00 PM every day, serving delicious deli food in a comfortable, cozy setting. You can take out or eat there, and the selection ranges from breakfast foods to a virtual encyclopedia of sandwiches (100 listed, but they'll try anything once). We sometimes call in for sandwiches (we are partial to their Vienna deli meats — a Chicago treat), and specify whole wheat bread, toasted, for a picnic lunch by Colonial Lake. The order comes with a salad-like slaw we love, chips and a pickle...our kind of fun.

ROBERT'S OF CHARLESTON DINNER RESTAURANT

112 N. Market Street   577-7565
(in Planter's Inn)   *or (800) 729-0094*
$$$$ *Most major credit cards*

Elegance, extravagance, entertainment... Robert's packs it all into one evening at one location. A six-course, Prix-Fixe, gourmet meal with unlimited red and white wines is served, while a talented vocalist — usually Chef Robert Dixon himself — sings for your supper. The whole event reminds us of participatory theater, with presentation and delivery so intimate that Robert's guests feel they are part of the action...but, pampered all the while. We consider it two and a half hours of heaven-on-earth, which might start, for example, with the scallop appetizer, then salad, duckling course, fruit sorbet (to clear the palate of its sins and prepare for the next event), beef tenderloin with vegetables and the grand finale: a decadent chocolate desert, hopefully swimming in raspberry sauce. Seating is at 8:00 PM.

SAFFRON

333 East Bay Street	722-5588
$	MC, V, AX, DC

This is a light and airy restaurant, contemporary in design and good for solo ventures as well as joining friends. The space of this pitched roof, modern building is divided into a gourmet product section, a full bakery (we are always seduced by the scent and leave with a loaf of bread) and the dining room — some booths and some tables scattered about. Our favorites are the seafood and spinach salads and pasta dishes, and we always save room for the carrot cake. Hours are 7:00 AM until 10:00 PM, Monday through Saturday, and 8:00 AM until 5:00 PM on Sunday.

SARACEN RESTAURANT

141 East Bay Street	723-6242
$-$$$$	Most major credit cards

When a restaurant's menu changes weekly, we assume that its chef is constantly on the prowl for the best edibles to be found. Such is the case with Saracen. Housed in what was formerly the Farmers and Exchange Bank of 1853, Saracen would be worth the trip for its architectural curiosities alone — the building is said to combine Gothic, Hindu, Moorish and Persian styles. But the French country cuisine is exceptional, too. Consider our lunch of lobster bisque and fish with lemon herb fettucine; or our dinner of sauted duck and melt-away beef tenderloin. Hours are 6:00 PM until 10:00 PM, Monday through Saturday.

SPIRIT OF CHARLESTON DINNER CRUISE

17 Lockwood Drive	722-2628
Charleston City Marina	
$$$$	MC, V, AX, D

Being partial to the water around Charleston, we can think of no better entertainment than to cruise her harbor while dining and dancing aboard a 102 foot boat. The Spirit of Charleston, which serves a four-course prime rib dinner (chicken and vegetarian menu available by prior request) and makes its rounds up and down the waterways, is always a lot of fun. Boarding begins at 6:30 PM, and the cruise is from 7:00 PM until 10:00 PM.

SUSHI HIRO

298 King Street	723-3628
$$	AX, MC, V

Sushi Hiro is a small sushi bar nestled between shops on King Street. In addition to a la carte sushi, there is a varied appetizer menu including tofu salad, chicken tempura and even soft shell crab. Complete dinners range from chicken or beef teriyaki to a combination sushi plate. If you like your seafood unscathed by the flame, this is the downtown place for Japanese delicacies. In addition to stools around the prep station, there are several freestanding tables for those seeking more privacy. Be warned: management does not accept personal checks or welcome tank-top clad patrons. Dinner only is served from 5:00 PM until 10:30 PM.

SWENSEN'S CAFE

57 S. Market Street   *722-1411*
$ *No credit cards*

Swensen's is more than a pick-up-your-cone place; it is a restaurant as well, serving beer and wine to go with homemade soups, sandwiches and the like — usually topped off by one of its delicious ice cream products. We have seen lines for the cool stuff nearly block Swensen's Market Street door; but, never fear: there's another entrance, and plenty of back-up supplies! Hours are Sunday through Thursday, 10:30 AM until 11:00 PM, and on Friday and Saturday, 10:30 AM until midnight.

TASTE OF INDIA

273 King Street   *723-8132*
$-$$ *MC, V, D, AX*

Taste of India serves authentic North Indian food, with a few menu items reflecting Bombay and South Indian cuisine. Natural spices make the difference here in appetizers (for instance, nargisi kabab — deep fried, herbed minced lamb patties), curries, vegetables and even salads. An eight-course lunch buffet is served from 11:30 AM until 3:00 PM, Monday through Saturday. Dinner is served from 5:00 PM until 10:30 PM, Monday through Sunday. Sunday brunch includes 13 courses, and is served from noon until 3:00 PM.

T-BONES GILL AND GRILL

80 North Market Street   *577-2511*
$-$$ *MC, V, AX*

This T-Bones, like its affiliate West Ashley, serves tasty steaks, salads, seafood, and chicken in a casual atmosphere. There is a children's menu with items like peanut butter or cheese sandwiches under $3.00. It is open seven days a week, and serves from 11:00 AM until 11:00 PM (it varies, depending on the season).

TERRIBLE TOM'S

188 Meeting Street   *722-6752*
$ *No credit cards*

Tucked away with the shops in the Old City market, Terrible Tom's is a good place to pick up light breakfast or lunch. The homemade, puff pastries are a treat we enjoy. Not-so-terrible Tom has provided a dozen tables so shoppers can give their tired feet a rest. Hours are 9:00 AM until 4:00 PM, Monday through Thursday, and until 5:00 PM on Saturday and until 4:00 PM on Sunday.

TOMMY CONDON'S IRISH PUB AND RESTAURANT

160 Church Street   *577-3818*
$-$$ *V, MC, AX*

The most authentic Irish Pub in Charleston, Tommy Condon's has Irish sing-alongs on weekends and imported Irish ales every day. The menu is a mixture of Irish and Lowcountry items. There is a covered deck for outside dining, and patrons are welcome from 11:30 AM until 10:00 PM, Monday through Thursday, 11:30 AM until 11:00 Friday and Saturday, and from 11:30 AM until 10:00 PM on Sunday. The bar is open until midnight.

TWO STEPS CAFE

363 King Street   853-6100
$ V,MC

This delightful little cafe is tucked into the back of a gift shop (really they are one and the same) which sells baskets of Charleston goodies, postcards and the like. The cafe corner is bathed in cool, tropical colors and dishes up such treats as fresh fruits, made-from-scratch pitas and other foods unscathed by preservatives. Hours are 9:30 AM until 4:00 PM, Monday through Saturday.

VICKERY'S

15 Beaufain Street   577-5300
$-$$$$ AX,MC,V

Vickery's is located in the Market Corner, across from Celia's, and is as talked about for its unusual bar design as it is for its good food. The original Vickery's is located in Atlanta, and has always gotten good reviews there. Grab a booth or a table, inside or out, and order a burger or a delicious seafood entree. Ask your waiter about the resident pigeon! Hours are 11:30 AM until 2:00 AM, seven days a week.

WILD WING CAFE

36 Market Street   722-9464
$-$$ AX,M,V,D

Wild Wing Cafe is popular with the under-thirty bar crowd, but also draws some of us who have topped out the age group but not the attraction to a good deal and fun time. Wild Wing serves a wonderful platter (of course) of chicken wings dressed in all manner of spices — from the Ginger wing to the Flying Fajita. There are wonderful dips, sandwiches and salads as well as buckets of beer for a table-full of thirsty friends. The bar also serves all manner of bottled beer and spirits as well as nonalcoholic beverages. Hours are 11:00 AM until 2:00 AM every day except Sunday, when the cafe opens at noon.

YOUR PLACE

6 Market Street   722-8360
$ No cards

The fact is, this Your Place may or may not be what you consider to be your "kind" of place; however, many locals (specifically, a lawyer and banker crowd, as well as a tennis coach we know) head over at lunch time to what they consider "a diamond in the rough" for jam-up burgers at no-frills prices. Emphasis here is on the good eats and nothing (absolutely not one thing) fussy. While the exterior resembles an unpainted lobster shack, the interior...well, it's home to some of us. Hours for food are 9:00 AM until 10 PM, Monday through Friday, and 10:00 AM until 4:00 PM on Saturday. Beer is served until midnight.

West Ashley Restaurants

ANNABELLE'S

Citadel Mall   766-5565
$-$$ Most major credit cards

We enjoy the lighthearted atmosphere — trees and umbrella tables as well as cozy booths with high backs — almost as much as the incredibly varied menu at Annabelle's. The chicken salad in an edible shell and stir-fry are two of our favorite entrées. Children love the complimentary crayons and to-be-colored place mats, and look forward to the helium balloons given away as patrons leave. The restaurant is open from 11:30 AM until 10:00 PM, Monday through Thursday, and 11:30 AM until 11:00 PM on Friday and Saturday. Sunday hours are 12 noon until 9:00 PM.

APPLEBEE'S

1859 Sam Rittenberg Boulevard   556-6421
$-$$ *MC, V, AX, D*
This is a family restaurant, as well as a gathering place for the business crowd at happy hour. We like the extensive, reasonably priced menu — standard burgers, a taco and a fried chicken salad, and fajitas being personal favorites. If we are just stopping by for a drink and to watch the game (there are two mounted televisions), we order fried veggies. Sunday's brunch is worth noting: nothing fancy but all that you could want. Hours are Monday through Thursday, 12:30 PM until midnight, Friday and Saturday from 12:30 until 1:00 AM, and Sunday from 12:30 PM until 11:00 PM.

BUDDY'S SEAFOOD

Highway 61 Pierpont   *556-5707*
$$ *MC,V,D*
Buddy's is located West of the Ashley and is a comfortable place for casual dining and local seafood. Lunch and dinner are served Monday through Thursday from 11:00 AM until 9:30 PM on Friday and Saturday, meals are served from 11:00 until 10:00 PM. We enjoy the fried seafood, she-crab soup, catfish stew, shrimp creole and soft shell crabs. Spirits are available.

CALIFORNIA DREAMING RESTAURANT AND BAR

1 Ashley Pointe Drive   *766-1644*
$-$$$ *AX, MC, V*
Every time we go to California Dreaming — by car or boat (to tie up at the dock) — it's an adventure. The kids pretend it's an old fort, and we are mesmerized by the view of the Ashley River and Charleston. The restaurant and the bar do incredible, nonstop business year round with little advertising — just word-of-mouth. The interior is wreathed in flags from 52 states, and divided into two dining levels with seating for 260. The little ones are welcome and can order non-alcoholic drinks (such as a blue concoction called a "Smurf"), as well as food from a special menu. We are crazy about the unusual croissants (flaky puff pastry covered in honey butter) and house salad (topped with eggs, almonds, ham and bacon — almost a meal in itself), and always order the twice-baked potato. All fish is fresh and local, and we also recommend the burgers, ribs, and Mexican dishes. A decadent dessert list includes the fabulous house special, apple walnut cinnamon pie, but we sometimes opt for an ice cream blender drink. Hours are 11:00 AM until 3:00 PM for lunch Sunday through Thursday; dinner is served from 4:30 PM until 10:00 PM those days, and until 11:00 PM on Friday and Saturday. There is continuous service from 11:00 AM until 11:00 PM on Saturday and 10:00 PM on Sunday.

CD's Hot Fish Shop

1660 Hwy. 17   763-7955
$-$$ Most major credit cards

You won't miss CD's on your right when traveling south on 17 (that's Savannah Highway) if you look for the large colorful shellfish appropriately painted on its wall. Just as you would expect, CD's offers fish, shrimp, clams, oysters, scallops and crab and all the beer, wine, whiskey and non-alcoholic drinks you need to wash 'em down. Hours are Monday through Thursday, 11:00 AM until 10:00 PM; Friday from 11:00 AM until 10:30 PM; Saturday, from noon until 10:30 PM; and on Sunday, from noon until 9:00 PM.

Chancy's

1759 Savannah Highway   763-3395
$-$$ V, MC, AX

The parking lot here is always jammed with Chancy regulars who come to drink, watch television sports and have a meal. This restaurant was recently voted in a Charleston *Post and Courier* survey as having the best Shrimp and Buffalo Wings in the area. There is a game room, and food is served from 11:30 AM until 11:00 PM, Monday through Saturday.

Chuck E. Cheese

1610 Sam Rittenberg   763-0663
$ MC, V, D

If you sometimes want to entertain children as well as feed them — and do so under the same roof — you need to know about Chuck E. Cheese. Formerly Showbiz Pizza and now referred to by the costumed mascot's name, this is a pizza place (yes, with beer and wine for the of-age parents) which is inundated with little people...they are "in the balls" (a popular jumping game), on the rides (a quarter a piece) or mesmerized by the electronic animals performing on stage. A far cry from French food by candlelight, this works with kids and the pizza and salad bar are good. The hours are 11:00 AM until 10:00 PM daily.

Emperor's Garden

874 Orleans Road   556-7212
$-$$ M, V

West Ashley gained a popular eatery with the opening of Emperor's Garden. This Chinese restaurant, across from Citadel Mall, prepares Peking Duck (a participatory dish put together, like crepes, at the table) to perfection, and stuffs its egg rolls with substantial portions of real ingredients (no mystery meat or imitation soybean product). Customers come from all over, and children are welcomed. Meals are served seven days a week, from 11:00 AM until 9:00 PM during the weekdays and until 10:00 PM on the weekends.

Gennaro's

851 Savannah Highway   763-0487
$-$$$ Most major credit cards

Gennaro's is a warm and authentic Italian restaurant, with a full Italian menu ranging from veal to pastas, seafood, steaks and even pizza. We have been eating this Eggplant a la Michael and Veal Parmesan for over a decade, and enjoy dining even more now that there is live jazz on Tuesday nights. Hours are Tuesday through Saturday, 11:30 AM until 2:30 PM for lunch, and 4:30 PM until 10:30 PM for dinner.

J. RYAN'S

1901 Ashley River Road   763-4494
$-$$ MC, V, AX

This is a popular lunch spot serving specials every day, with fresh baked bread, a salad and choice of vegetables. Evening dining is casual, and there is a wide selection of seafood and beef. We recently enjoyed delicious steaks cooked to our specifications, and were impressed by the attentive service. Hours are Monday through Thursday, 11:00 AM until 10:00 PM, and Friday and Saturday from 11:00 AM until 10:30 PM.

KENNY ROGERS ROASTERS

1863 Ashley River Road   766-4488
$ No credit cards

A great alternative to fried, this rotisserie chicken is wood-roasted and marinated in natural citrus, herbs and spices. Not only is there less fat in the end, the taste is delicious. We suggest the family dinners with sauces and a couple of hot or cold side dishes for a wonderful take-out supper. Pitas, soups and salads are also good, and — although the restaurant is one of many around the USA — the eatery itself (a wood stack by the door, pots of geraniums in season, and Charleston Green tables outside as well as indoor seating) has a non-chain appeal. Hours are from 11:00 AM until 10:00 PM, Monday through Saturday, and from noon until 9:00 PM on Sunday.

KIM'S KOREAN RESTAURANT

1716 Hwy. 171   571-5100
North Bridge Shopping Center
$$-$$$$ V, MC, AX

Kim's Korean and Japanese Steak and Seafood House, as it is formally described, offers authentic "table show cooking" seven days a week. Not only is this a fun experience, the food is also well prepared and a delight. Take-out is available. Hours are Sunday through Thursday, 5:00 PM until 10:00 PM, and Friday and Saturday from 5:00 PM until 11:00 PM.

KYOTO STEAK HOUSE

1870 Sam Rittenberg Blvd.   571-6025
$ MC, V, AX, D

This Japanese steak and seafood restaurant — part of a chain — rates high on the family entertainment scale because of its hibachi style (table side) preparation and knife-juggling Japanese chefs. Meals include a light soup, salad and entree, and the food is consistently good. If you have never experienced this form of dining, be warned that you may share grill and dining space with strangers. Try the steak and shrimp for a sample of what the hibachi does for turf and surf, or the sushi bar if you like yours "untouched by the flame." Dinner is served seven days a week, from 5:00 PM until 10:00 PM, and "Early Bird Specials" are regularly advertised.

LIBERTY CAFE AND PUB

9 Magnolia Road   571-7255
$-$$ No credit cards

When Liberty Cafe opened its doors, neighbors were right to applaud. Since those days, its reputation has spread and people come from all around (with their families) to eat tasty, affordable food in a cozy cafe setting. Try the *big* burgers or wood-grilled entrees. Hours are 11:00 AM until 10:00 PM, Monday through Thursday, and 11:00 AM until 12 midnight, Friday and Saturday.

MEDITERRANEAN DELICATESSEN & CAFE

90 Folly Road   766-0323
$-$$ MC, V, AX, D

Talk about neighborhood magnets, the Mediterranean Delicatessen & Cafe is a real draw for West Ashley and downtown diners. Not only is the food good and predictable (the menu stays the same and the favorite specials are repeated), but it's just five minutes from the city and parking is no trouble. The atmosphere is very casual, and local photography is displayed. Connoisseurs stock up on wine and imported beer here — there is quite a selection. We are partial to the four-cheese pasta at dinner, but order a pita pocket sandwich with gazpacho soup at lunch time. There is live, low-key entertainment on weekends, and sometimes wine tasting on Monday night. Hours are 7:30 AM until 11:00 AM, Monday through Friday, and until noon on Saturday for breakfast; lunch is served from 11:00 AM until 3:00 PM, Tuesday through Saturday; dinner is served from 6:00 PM until 9:30 PM, Tuesday through Saturday.

MELTING POT

946 Orleans Road   763-4110
$-$$ Most major credit cards

Located just across from the Citadel Mall, Melting Pot is a wonderful source for take-out as well as eat-in Greek and American food. Try a simple Greek salad (big enough to count as lunch) or order the sampler for a crash course in ethnic delights; but, always save room for the outstanding desserts. There is a grocery section as well. Hours are 8:00 AM until 10:00 PM, Monday through Saturday.

PENACHIO'S

2447 Ashley River Road   556-1855
$ V, MC, AX, D

This is a delightful little Italian restaurant specializing in pasta and seafood dinners that include salad and garlic bread. Sunday through Thursday there are specials and our favorite (although it is not Italian) is Chicken Français, prepared in a light cream sauce. Dinner is available from 5:00 to 10:00 Monday through Saturday. Look for the white lights in the trees out front: that's Penachio's.

PIER 61 LTD.

652 St. Andrew's Boulevard   571-7533
$-$$ V, MC, D

Those of us who have been following owner-chef Mike Pappus around for years, now stand in line to eat his delicious specialties at Pier 61. We recommend the seafood — done right and plenty of it — and we're also partial to the chicken salad plate. Mr. Pappus has a full bar, and serves meals the following hours: lunch from 11:30 AM until

2:30 PM, Tuesday through Saturday, and dinner from 5:30 PM until 9:30 PM, Thursday through Saturday.

REEVE'S BAR B QUE

Hwy. 61   763-5798
$ *No credit cards*

Reeve's Bar B Que is located in the Crossroads Centre Shopping Center, and serves tasty Southern food such as ribs, chicken, fried catfish and country-style steak (that means pounded, floured and fried) as well as barbecue and spirits. Hours are from Monday through Saturday, 11 AM until 9:00 PM.

SADIES CAFETERIA

Citadel Mall   571-6700
$ *Most major credit cards*

This is a mall cafeteria with prices that seem like they're out of the back woods. Children's plates (meat and two vegetables) for .99 are hard to beat — even at home. The food here is good and the personnel very kind. Try the eggplant casserole if available. Hours are 11:00 AM until 8:00 PM, Monday through Thursday, and 11:00 AM until 8:30 PM on Friday through Sunday.

ST. ANDREWS CAFETERIA

975 Savannah Highway   556-5333
$ *MC*

When our inner gauge tells us it's time for some "real food" — meat, three straight vegetables, and dessert if you clean your plate — we pack up the family and head for "the cafeteria." Formerly Robertson's Cafeteria, the new management has kept most of the old menu, and the loyal fans keep coming. Lowcountry food like crab casserole, fried shrimp, okra gumbo and even French Huguenot Torte are the reasons why. You may sense that it's just one big, happy, family gathering, but you also will feel welcome. Seven days a week, lunch and dinner are served from 11:00 AM until 8:00 PM.

T-BONES

1668 Highway 171   556-2478
$-$$ *V, MC, AX*

Another vibrant happening spot on the West Side of the River, T-Bones serves a wonderful filet mignon (when you say rare, they take you at your word), as well as fresh gourmet burgers and even seafood. There are photographs of regular customers and Western paraphernalia on the walls, and you can't miss the enormous painting of handsome, renegade cowboys on horseback. We order side veggies (which are sautéed and delicious), and feel comfortable having the kids along. The hours are 11:00 AM until 10:30 PM, weekdays, and on Friday and Saturday until 11:00 PM; Sunday hours are shorter: noon until 10:00 PM.

TROTTER'S RESTAURANT

2008 Savannah Highway   571-1000
(in the Town and Country Inn)
$-$$ *Most major credit cards*

Trotter's Restaurant is a good spot for buffets — that includes breakfast and lunch as well as weekend seafood spreads. We have eaten Sunday brunch and found it to be tasty, with a wide selection of meats, vegetables, and desserts. Others must agree, as there is always a crowd after church. Hours are Monday through Saturday, 6:30 AM until 11:00 AM for breakfast; 11:30 AM until 2:30 PM for lunch; and 5:00 PM until 10:00 PM for dinner. On Sunday, breakfast is served from 7:00 AM until 11:00 PM, and lunch is served from noon until 2:30 PM.

WEST TOWNE

1179 Sam Rittenberg Blvd. 766-2640
$-$$ *V, MC , AX, D*

Founded by the owner of the original Olde Towne restaurant across from the Omni Hotel on King Street (see the listing in the Charleston section, above), West Towne serves Greek food 11:00 AM until 10:00 PM, Monday through Thursday, from 11:00 until 10:30 on Friday and Saturday, and until 9:00 PM on Sunday.

YE OLD FASHIONED CAFE & ICE CREAM

474 Savannah Highway 766-4854
$ *No credit cards*

Open seven days a week and located next to Eckerd, this cafe serves sandwiches, soups and — of course — lots of ice cream. We go to this shop or its affiliate in South Windermere for ice cream cones, and sometimes call ahead for soup and sandwich take-out service (Savannah Highway has a drive-up window, but call first). All their food is delicious, and locals love this place. Hours are 10:00 AM until 11:30 PM, Monday through Thursday, and from 10:00 AM until 12 midnight on Friday and Saturday. Sunday hours are 11:00 AM until midnight.

Charleston
Accommodations

*I*f the Lowcountry knows a thing or two about putting up guests, it's because over 5 million of them visit the Trident area each year. Over the centuries, Southerners have built a reputation for hospitality and they often compete to maintain high standards. Research and experience tell us that Trident visitors arrive with varying expectations, and a large accommodations industry has evolved to meet those needs. We have included in this book what we consider to be good choices in each accommodations category starting with the most intimate Bed and Breakfasts, and working our way through the inns, motels and larger, grander hotels. Like friends in an eclectic gathering, each member of this group has something different to offer and at a different price.

A friendly word of advice is that Charleston attracts droves of visitors year round (there is some attraction nearly every month, with a slight slow down in January), and reservations are strongly recommended. Some hotels and inns will

A view of the city with the Battery in the foreground.

allow guests to keep small pets in the rooms, but this should be cleared before arrival.

Guest Homes and Bed & Breakfasts

One way to feel like an "insider" when you visit Charleston is to spend your visit as a guest in an authentic Charleston house. No matter that you have not received a personalized invitation; you can easily make reservations at one of many Bed and Breakfasts in the area.

The real draw for Bed and Breakfasts (also called B&B's) is that they allow you to temporarily assume native-status with a prime Charleston address. For a fixed price, you enjoy elegant lodging, breakfast and a string of "extras" ranging from cocktails to turn down service (which usually means that your bed linens are folded back, and delicious chocolates and a nightcap left bedside).

There is controversy over what constitutes a bed and breakfast in the strictest sense, and much of the discussion centers on size of the operation and contact with the host family. Some operate as entities in houses that are not private "homes," and some are rental arrangements in primary homes of owners. Obviously, the former operate as businesses in business settings, while the latter operate as businesses in the midst of family routine. Each appeals to a certain traveler, and not another.

Decide which factors are important to you, and call for a detailed brochure. While you have a contact person on the phone, however, ask a few questions to narrow your search. Make certain that you understand what the host or hostess is offering: guest quarters in his or her home? contact with the family? an historically significant setting? close proximity to sight-seeing? basic accommodations at the "right price," without any frills? Clear any particular dietary needs and ask what constitutes breakfast. Is there air-conditioning (very desirable in this climate except during winter), and where is the bath or shower located? Are children or pets welcome, and when do you check in and check out? Are there any curfews, and are guests issued keys? Is there off-street parking?

When choosing a B&B, realize that there are price variations based on location, amenities and various other factors. Bed and breakfasts in the Historic District obviously are the pricey option, but the payoff may be greater than you think. Being able to walk to major sites, stroll along the Battery, and sleep in an antique canopy bed may be advantages warranting the price tag.

If you would prefer that someone else screen the possibilities, consider calling one of two local services that match guests and accommodations. Historic Charleston Bed and Breakfast can be reached by calling (803) 722-6606; Charleston Society Bed and Breakfast's phone number is (803) 723-4948.

Finding the right guest house or B&B to suit your needs and desires can be the start of a long-term relationship. Many proprietors and

Woodlands

formerly Gadsden Manor

Pamper Yourself...
Next Year!

Following extensive alterations, you'll truly feel like a special guest in a grand private home, and experience all the charm of genteel Southern hospitality, in this handsomely restored turn of the century Greek revival mansion. With twenty elegantly furnished rooms, a fashionable restaurant serving such wonderfully prepared food that people come from miles around to experience it, and with a special events setting that makes any corporate meeting, reception, or private function a superb treat that will have people talking for years to come, *Woodlands* will be the place of choice . . .

But, not until the Fall of 1994.

Please call for further information.
329 Old Postern Road, Summerville, SC 29483
Telephone: (803) 875-2600

hosts "entertain" the same guests year after year, and are sometimes booked for months in advance. When contacting these establishments, be sure to ask which forms of payment are accepted; most do not accept credit cards, but will take checks.

Although rates are subject to change, we find the following scale useful and have incorporated it into our descriptions. The $-signs indicate the average rate per night for two adults.

$50 & under	*$*
$51-$75	*$$*
$76-$95	*$$$*
$96-$110	*$$$$*
$110 and up	*$$$$$*

ANN HARPER'S BED & BREAKFAST

56 Smith Street   *723-3947*
$$

An 1870 Charleston single house located near King Street shopping and the College of Charleston, Ann Harper's B&B is furnished with antiques, wicker and reproductions as well as cherished family heirlooms. She rents out one complex guest suite that is air-conditioned, with a double and a single bed as well as separate sitting area with television and bath (complete with one of the deepest tubs you've ever seen). Full breakfast is served — sometimes Ann's famous shrimp and grits — and off-street parking is provided.

ASHLEY INN BED AND BREAKFAST

210 Ashley Ave.   *723-1848*
$$-$$$ *MC, V*

A real taste of Charleston, this home was built around 1835 and is a mansion of sorts by today's standards — seven bedrooms with baths, fireplaces throughout and a lovely garden. Breakfast is served on the piazza, and afternoon tea and sherry are part of the hospitality.

BARKSDALE HOUSE INN

27 George Street   *577-4800*
$$$-$$$$$

This B&B Inn is located in close proximity to King Street shopping and the College of Charleston. In fact, the facility was once a fraternity house. Who would guess that fact today, when the Barksdale House Inn includes ten beautifully appointed rooms — each one different from the other. Half are equipped with fireplaces and whirlpool baths (Oh, what the brothers would have given...). Wine and a nightly turn down service as well as Continental breakfast and free parking are included in the price of the room.

BATTERY CARRIAGE HOUSE

20 South Battery   *775-5575*
$$$$

A wonderful location for starters (these carriage house units overlook the Battery and White Point Gardens), Battery Carriage House rooms are furnished in reproductions, and have private baths and separate heating and air-conditioning controls. Continental breakfast is served each morning, and every effort is made to provide services (such as FAX and copy machines, direct phone lines, speaker phones and message machines) helpful to the business traveler.

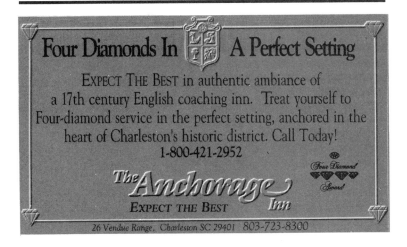
BELVEDERE BED AND BREAKFAST

40 Rutledge Ave.	722-0973
$$$	No cards

The Belvedere gets its name from the interior Adam woodwork, once a part of the 1785 Belvedere Plantation. Oriental rugs and furniture, Continental breakfast and afternoon sherry, as well as a smashing view of Colonial Lake make this mansion special.

BRASINGTON HOUSE BED AND BREAKFAST

328 East Bay Street	722-1274 or
$$$$	800-722-1274

The Brasington House includes four antique-filled rooms in an antebellum residence on East Bay Street. The house is equipped with central heat and air-conditioning. Each room has a private bath and king-size bed, cable television, as well as tea and coffee-making facilities. Complimentary breakfast, wine and liqueurs are included in the room price, as is off-street parking. Mr. Brasington is proud of what he considers to be a true bed and breakfast: a family atmosphere with the extras of an English country inn.

CANNONBORO INN BED & BREAKFAST

184 Ashley Avenue	723-8572
$$$	

Refurnished in 1990, this Bed and Breakfast is decorated with a palate of mauves and pinks complementing the lovely original hardwood floors. The house is furnished with period antiques, and rooms are air-conditioned and equipped with private baths. Complimentary sherry is served each afternoon, and a full English breakfast is served each morning. Off-street parking is provided, and bikes are also available for guests — a nice option in this part of town.

CAPERS-MOTTE HOUSE

69 Church St.	722-2263
$$$-$$$$	

Architecture buffs will be entranced by this Georgian mansion. Built around 1730, the house has Adam mantels and Waterford chandeliers. Rooms are air-conditioned and equipped with private baths. Off-street parking is provided, and breakfast is included in the room rate.

COLONIAL LAKE BED & BREAKFAST
32 Rutledge Ave.   722-6476
$$$$

These two air-conditioned suites are part of an 1852 Victorian house overlooking Colonial Lake — a favorite walking/jogging location in the heart of the city. Guests come and go through a wicker-filled piazza, and — for the duration of their visit — call a spacious, antique-filled room with bath and sitting area "home." Guests eat a wonderful breakfast with the host family.

1837 BED & BREAKFAST/TEA ROOM
126 Wentworth Street   723-7166
$$-$$$

Two artists have restored this historic (c. 1800) house near the College of Charleston and King Street shopping. Six rooms and a brick carriage house are air-conditioned and beautifully decorated. Guests are treated to a full gourmet breakfast and make use of off-street parking. The owners take reservations for afternoon tea in the parlor as well. Rooms have private entrances and baths, refrigerators and televisions. To quote *The New York Times*, it is "a perfect place to unwind."

THE HAYNE HOUSE
30 King Street   577-2633
$$$

Five air-conditioned bedrooms are available in this historic house. Breakfast is Continental, and the house is only a block from the Battery. The Hayne House may be the oldest B&B in town.

KING GEORGE IV INN AND GUESTS
32 George Street   722-7551
No cards

A Federal style house with fireplaces, wide-planked hardwood floors and antiques, and three porches, this inn is conveniently located in the Historic District. There is parking for guests.

KING'S INN
136 Tradd   577-3683
$$$-$$$$

This Bed and Breakfast is the century-old residence of a musician and a photographer, whose artistic talents are evident in their tasteful home. They offer for nightly and longer-term rental a front suite, which is a full apartment, as well as "The Red Room." A Continental breakfast is served to overnight guests, and sherry and fruit are offered in the afternoon. Please call for seasonal rates.

THE KITCHEN HOUSE
126 Tradd Street   577-6362
$$$$-$$$$$

This block of Tradd Street, with its 18th-century homes and gardens, is another in the Historic District. The Kitchen House, built c. 1732 and the home of the Surgeon General of the Continental Army, has free parking and offers guests complimentary full breakfast, sherry and wine. Guests can use the private patio, and rooms are air-conditioned. (*Colonial Homes* and *The New York Times* have raved about this one.)

LOUNDES GROVE INN

266 St. Margaret Street   723-3530
$$$$

On the National Register of Historic Places and built around 1786, Loundes Grove is the only plantation in the city on the Ashley River. The house and grounds, with a spectacular view of the water, is a lush setting for wedding receptions and other festivities. There are six air-conditioned guest rooms with private baths, and an air-conditioned guest cottage for family rentals (with baby-sitting available). As elegant as the facility is, with its pool, Jacuzzi and river dock, it's also quite comfortable. Breakfast is served.

OPUS 11 GEORGE STREET BED & BREAKFAST

11 George Street   722-6606
$$$$-$$$$$

Located near the College of Charleston, Opus 11 George has a full kitchen (with a microwave, of course) telephones, and even a grand piano. The house, built in 1813, was showcased as the Symphony Designer House in 1990, and is filled with family antiques. A full breakfast is available, and cable TV is yours for the watching. If it's cold enough, enjoy the fireplace; or, if it's warm enough, spend some time "being southern" on the piazzas. If you have children and wish to rent separate nursery accommodations and/or a room for a nanny, such is available. Parking is provided.

RUTLEDGE VICTORIAN INN AND GUEST HOUSE

114 Rutledge Avenue   722-7551
$-$$$

This is the kind of guest house that we remember from the old days in Key West, Florida. The atmosphere is R-E-L-A-X-E-D, and the surroundings colorful. Take the exterior, for example: bright, painted Victorian, showcasing a large front porch filled with rocking chairs. Rooms have hardwood floors, 12-foot-high ceilings and fireplaces.

TWENTY-SEVEN STATE STREET BED & BREAKFAST

27 State Street   722-4243
$$$-$$$$$

Joye and Paul Craven own this B&B, built c. 1800. Guests stay in one of the Craven's carriage house suites which include a bedroom,

---

Insiders Like:
Quiet dining AFTER a Spoleto event in an intimate downtown restaurant within walking distance of the performance. (Be sure to make your reservations EARLY, however. Undoubtedly, others will have the same idea.)

Insiders' Tip

living room, kitchenette and private bath. One suite opens into a lovely courtyard, and the other onto the porch. They are furnished with antiques, reproductions and oriental rugs. The Cravens ready the rooms with fresh flowers and fruit, and provide Continental breakfast and a newspaper in the morning. There is free parking and they provide bikes.

TWO MEETING STREET INN
2 Meeting Street   723-7322
$$$$-$$$$$

An elegant 1890 Victorian mansion, Two Meeting Street Inn is located at the intersection of Meeting Street and South Battery across from White Point Gardens. Guests stay in one of nine air-conditioned rooms, each of which has a private bath. Continental breakfast, served in the garden or formal dining room, and afternoon sherry are included in the room rate. Ceiling fans and rocking chairs make the porch an inviting option anytime.

VILLA DE LA FONTAINE
BED & BREAKFAST
138 Wentworth Street   577-7709
$$$-$$$$$

The owners of this columned mansion, with its spacious formal gardens, terrace and fountain, offer four air-conditioned rooms with canopy beds and full breakfast. Restored and furnished with museum-quality pieces, the Villa is a showplace. On-premise parking is available.

BED NO BREAKFAST
16 Halsey St.   723-4450
$-$$

Out of alphabetical order, but not out of the question! Although this listing does not fit the B&B category in the strictest sense, it's a close relation: two large, light, air-conditioned rooms with a private entrance but no eggs-and-grits. Actually, coffee and tea are available in each room as is a refrigerator (which means you can easily do your own Continental breakfast). There is off-street parking, and wonderful sites are within walking distance.

Atmospheric Inns

Inns in Charleston offer some of the same personalized touches that make the B&B's special, but on a larger scale. Most, but not all, operate in modernized facilities either renovated or built specifically for this business. You can usually expect a great deal of charm along with complimentary Continental breakfast, afternoon wine or sherry and evening turn down. What distinguishes one from another is exact location, authenticity of decor, trendy amenities and management style. Prices for double lodging per night change with the seasons, but can be gauged in general by the following scale:

$50 & under	**$**
$51-$75	**$$**
$76-$95	**$$$**
$96-$110	**$$$$**
$110 and up	**$$$$$**

Floating accommodations, just east of Lockwood Marina, Ashley River.

THE ANCHORAGE INN

26 Vendue Range   723-8300 or
                              800-421-2952
$$$$$ Most major credit cards

In close proximity to the waterfront park, this fascinating Four Diamond, luxury inn is the creation of Liz Tucker who also founded and operates Creative Expeditions, one of Charleston's premiere international art and architecture tour services. It was Liz's intention to reflect our ancestors' origins by replicating the ambiance of a 17th-century English seaside inn. Every detail is authentic; period antiques are from her personal collection, and handcrafted reproductions are one-of-a-kind, made specifically for the inn. "Bountiful Breakfast" (in the English tradition, including at least one hot item) is served in the large dining room. Guests enjoy turn down service, and evening tea or "tipple" (the English nightcap) with cookies, rum cake or even syllabub. There are 19 rooms (including two suites), four with Jacuzzi tubs. Ample parking is available.

ANSONBOROUGH INN

21 Hasell Street   723-1655 or
                              800-522-2073
$$$-$$$$$ AX, MC, V

Ansonborough Inn is located at the end of Hasell Street off of East Bay. Thirty-seven suites have been fashioned out of a turn-of-the-century warehouse. Heart of pine exposed beams, measuring 12 feet by 12 feet, and locally made red brick have been incorporated in the rooms to give the inn — even with its magnificent 16- and 18-foot ceilings — a warm feel. The facility's

three floors are laid out around an open center atrium. Suites are equipped with full kitchens, and some have lofts. Guests receive complimentary afternoon wine and can park at no charge. But the most exciting amenity may be breakfast, with homemade sweetbreads — banana, apple-raisin, blueberry — delivered from Airy Hall Plantation. The staff is most helpful with details such as baby-sitting, and will help make golf and tennis reservations.

CHURCH STREET INN

177 Church Street   722-3420 or
                              800-552-3777
$$$$-$$$$$ AX, MC, V

Adjacent to the old City Market, Church Street Inn is in the heart of downtown activity. Management also calls this establishment a "luxury all-suite hotel" because the 31 units are actually nicely appointed one- and two-bedroom townhouse suites. Our friends who recently visited Charleston with children particularly enjoyed staying here and making use of the full kitchen (equipped with everything from linens to the microwave), separate living room and bedroom. The inn offers a grocery shopping and delivery service, and even has a "room service" agreement with some local restaurants. The morning paper and breakfast are delivered to the room or can be enjoyed downstairs. Complimentary sherry is served each afternoon, and a bar is located just off the lobby.

ELLIOTT HOUSE

78 Queen Street   *723-1855*
                                              800-729-1855
$$$$-$$$$$ *AX, MC, V*

Elliott House is located next to 82 Queen Street Bar and Restaurant, and across the street from the Mills House Hotel. This is life as it should be in the refined fast lane: a heated Jacuzzi, afternoon champagne in the courtyard, and breakfast served on a silver service. Guests stay in one of 26 lovely air-conditioned rooms, done to Charleston specifications — complete with the oriental rug and period furniture. Since 82 Queen draws a big (but respectable) crowd, the action for Elliott House guests is just a few strides away. For those who bring the family, baby-sitting service is available.

INDIGO INN

1 Maiden Lane   *577-5900 or*
Meeting/Pinckney 800-845-7639 out-of-state
                              800-922-1340 in-state
$$$-$$$$$ *AX, MC, V*

The Indigo Inn is consistently awarded The Automotive Association of America's Four Diamond Award. It fronts on Meeting Street, across from a charming shopping and restaurant district. With 40 rooms and a private courtyard, the inn is medium-sized and prides itself on impeccable service. Parking is complimentary — another blessing in the heart of the city.

JOHN RUTLEDGE HOUSE INN

116 Broad Street   *723-7999 or*
                                              800-476-9741
$$$$-$$$$$ *AX, MC, V*

Built in 1763 by John Rutledge, a signer of the U.S. Constitution, 116 Broad Street (a designated National Historic Landmark) has been completely restored and transformed, as part of a three-building complex, into a bed and breakfast inn. The National Trust for Historic Preservation named it among the first 32 "Historic Hotels of America" and for good reason. George Washington himself had breakfast here, and was one of many patriots, statesmen and presidents who came to call. Completely restored, the main residence contains original parquet floors, Italian marble mantels and molded plaster ceilings. Rooms have been modernized to include private baths, refrigerators, color televisions and climate controls. Wine and sherry are served in the ballroom, and evening turn down includes chocolates at bedside. Continental breakfast fare and a newspaper are delivered to guests each morning. The inn has earned the American Automotive Association's Four Diamond Award.

KING'S COURTYARD INN

198 King Street   *723-7000,*
                                              800-845-6119
$$$$-$$$$$ *AX, MC, V*

The Kings Courtyard Inn has an interesting history in that the building at 198 King has been used full circle: as an inn (catering to plantation owners and businessmen); private residences; shops; and now guest quarters. Of Greek Revival design, it is nestled between fine antique shops on King Street. Rooms and suites are modernized (all air-conditioned, with private baths) and no two are just alike.

Wine or sherry is provided upon arrival; Continental breakfast and a newspaper are delivered to the room each morning. Breakfast in the courtyards or breakfast room may be arranged at no charge, and guests may even order a full breakfast instead. One of our favorite details is the garden spa, used by guests year round. Cocktails are available in the courtyard bar, and brandy is provided each evening on the first floor.

LODGE ALLEY INN

195 East Bay St.	*722-1611 or*
	800-821-2791 in-state
	800-845-1004 out-of-state
$$$$$	*AX, MC, V*

Lodge Alley is an achievement in balance; with 93 units, it is large in capacity but its rooms maintain that "feel" of an intimate Charleston dwelling. Many a celebrity has checked in to this address because it somehow offers anonymity and class all at once. Imagine yourself in the Lodge Alley setting: robe-wrapped in the comfort of your room, watching flames dance in its fireplace, sipping a drink from your stocked mini-bar and nibbling hors d'oeuvres warmed up in your kitchen. Turn down is complimentary, and — an especially nice touch, from the driver's point of view — parking is on the house as well.

MAISON DU PRE

317 East Bay Street	*723-8691 or*
	800-662-INNS
$$$$$	*AX, MC, V*

There are 13 elegant air-conditioned guest rooms at Maison Du Pre, c. 1904, each with a private bath and furnished with beautiful oriental rugs and appropriate antiques. In the spring and other temperate times in the city, the garden patio — alive with flowers and the therapeutic splash of fountains — is a big draw. In typical Charleston fashion, the piazza is a focal point. The Continental breakfast is complimentary as is the "Lowcountry Tea" (actually wine and hors d'oeuvres, with little tea in sight).

MEETING STREET INN

173 Meeting Street	*723-1882 or*
	800-842-8022
$$$-$$$$	*AX, V, MC, DC*

The front portion of this inn is 140 years old, while the back section is an add-on. A lovely courtyard with a heated Jacuzzi, turn down service and a silver service Continental breakfast are some of the amenities appealing to us. Also, we like the idea of reproduction four-poster rice beds in every room.

MIDDLETON INN

Ashley River Road	*556-0500 or*
	800-543-4774
$$$-$$$$$	*Most major credit cards*

In our estimation, Middleton Inn is the kind of place you can write home about. Situated on the grounds of one of the most beautiful plantations in the world, complete with the nation's oldest landscaped gardens and stunning butterfly lakes, the inn at Middleton Gardens is just 14 miles from Historic Charleston. Guests have access to the nature trails and gardens, and have use of a swimming pool and tennis courts. The facility itself is of national award-winning design, modern in its simplicity, with rooms that have fireplaces as well as European baths. Continental breakfast is served each morning (see the Attractions chapter).

PLANTERS INN

112 North Market Street	722-2345 or
	800-845-7082
$$$$-$$$$$	Most major credit cards

As charming as an antebellum Charleston home, this inn has a European flavor and understated elegance that radiates quality. It came as no surprise to us some years back when Planters Inn captured *Lodging Hospitality Magazine's* first-place award in the guest room category. From four-poster beds to mahogany armoires, authentic Charleston reproductions are showcased in spacious rooms with traditional high ceilings. The inn is located in the Market Area, and is home to the extraordinary Robert's of Charleston Dinner Restaurant.

VENDUE INN

19 Vendue Range	577-7970
	800-845-7900 out-of-state
$$$$-$$$$$	AX, MC, V

Even back ten years, before the recent yuppie trend of exploring-your-own-backyard became *de rigueur*, friends who live out on one of the west islands took mini-vacations by coming into town to "do Charleston" and stay at the Vendue Inn. Small wonder, as the trek is a quick drive and the destination a world apart. When the owners describe the inn's ambiance as "European," they are probably referring to the fact that they work hard to provide an experience that makes the guest feel at home but utterly pampered. Consider such details as fresh cut flowers, fluffy towels, breakfast on the silver service and liqueur with chocolate mints at turn down. The inn has 34 rooms, decorated with 18th-century period furnishings. Vendue West suites have Jacuzzi, marble baths and fireplaces. Complimentary wine and cheese parties — sometimes with chamber music or live jazz — are held each afternoon in The Garden Room. The American Automotive Association has awarded Vendue Inn the Four Diamond Award.

VICTORIA HOUSE INN

208 King Street	720-2944 or
	800-933-5464
$$$$-$$$$$	AX, MC, V

The Victoria House Inn is a 16-room luxury inn done in the Victorian style. Following the standard inn-format of light spirits in the lobby, evening turn down and Continental breakfast, The Victoria is a new addition to the corporate family that includes Kings Courtyard Inn and the John Rutledge House Inn.

Hotels and Motels Downtown and West of the Ashley River

Accommodations in this category are different in ways from the bed and breakfasts or inns, and may offer what you enjoy most. Refer to the following scale to judge prices, and then call for exact quotes (as rates change with seasons):

$50 and under	$
$51-$75	$$
$76-$95	$$$
$96-$110	$$$$
$110 and up	$$$$$

BEST WESTERN INN

1540 Savannah Highway   571-6100
$$ Most major credit cards

This Best Western is only three miles from the peninsula and yet is a very tasteful, affordable option. Continental breakfast is complimentary, and everyone loves the large outdoor pool. We think this is one of the area's good values, particularly since the spacious rooms have been recently refurbished.

BEST WESTERN KING CHARLES INN

237 Meeting Street   723-7451
$$$-$$$$ Most major credit cards

The King Charles Inn has 91 units and is situated next to the shopping district on Meeting Street. Part of the Best Western chain, it is located in the heart of the shopping and restaurant district of Meeting Street. Those of us who drive past on a sweltering Charleston afternoon envy the guests we see frolicking in the second floor outdoor swimming pool. The parking garage is underground and free for guests.

COMFORT INN RIVERVIEW

144 Bee Street   577-2224 or
                    800-221-2222
$-$$$$ Most major credit cards

As part of the Comfort Inn chain, the Riverview establishment offers a string of discounts and other standard features plus its most valuable asset: a view of the Ashley River. It is located just outside the Historic District (but still on the peninsula), and tours are available from the hotel. A fitness room appeals to many travelers, and the outdoor pool with its river view is a big hit with all ages. Continental breakfast is included in the price of the room, and there is no charge for parking.

DAYS INN HISTORIC

155 Meeting Street   722-8411 or
                    800-325-2525
$$-$$$ AX, DC, MC

The 124 units of this Days Inn are air-conditioned and fairly typical of the rooms in this chain. There is a swimming pool and a full-service restaurant and bar. Limited parking on-sight is available. You can not beat the price for the location and standard reliability.

HAMPTON INN HISTORIC DISTRICT

345 Meeting Street   723-4000

$$-$$$ Most major credit cards

There are 171 newly remodeled rooms in this Hampton Inn, conveniently located across from the Visitors Center. One of downtown Charleston's newest inns, the Hampton offers the attractive features of an older, restored building — one mellowed with details like dark wood and recessed windows — decked out in crisp, new furnishings. The courtyard is probably the largest on the peninsula, and its pool is an oasis. Double rooms have two queen-size beds, and an impressive Continental breakfast is part of the deal: muffins, bagels and other breads, as well as cereal and coffee cake. The Lifestyle 50 plan allows two senior citizens to stay for the price of one.

HAMPTON INN-RIVERVIEW HOTEL

11 Ashley Pointe Drive   *556-5200 or*
                              800-HAMPTON
$$-$$$ *Most major credit cards*

Out of the mainstream, the Hampton Inn is located on a road called Ashley Pointe Drive off Albermarle Road. The other landmarks are Ripley Light Marina, across the narrow street, and California Dreaming Restaurant at the end. This is a modern, multistory facility with views of the Ashley River and the outstanding boats docked nearby. Continental breakfast is complimentary.

HAWTHORNE SUITES HOTEL
HISTORIC CHARLESTON

181 Church Street   *577-2644 or*
                        800-527-1133
$$$$-$$$$$ *Most major credit cards*

A relative newcomer to the Market Area, Hawthorne Suites is a comfortable, courtyard hotel consisting of oversized suites. Units have "the Charleston look," and include complete kitchens, separate bedrooms and living rooms. The guest's life is made easy with a complimentary breakfast buffet, and he or she can unwind with on-the-house refreshments at the afternoon reception. For those who enjoy burning the calories they have consumed, there is a fitness center and a heated courtyard whirlpool spa that sits at least 12 comfortably (great for relaxing while gazing at the stars). When energy levels burn down, however, there is always the hotel's VCR tape library to complement the cable television service. Note-

worthy is the fact that 12 suites have complete handicapped access and amenities.

MILLS HOUSE HOTEL

115 Meeting Street   *577-2400*
$$$$$ *Most major credit cards*

Of the city's grand hotels of the Historic District, the Mills probably enjoys the oldest, grandest reputation. Now a Holiday Inn Hotel, it is located on the corner of Meeting and Queen Streets, next door to the imposing white-columned Hibernian Hall (site of many a debutante ball and meeting of the Hibernian Society). Modern in its comforts and antebellum in its decor, the Mills House has always been a favorite with the most affluent travelers. An exquisite courtyard, outdoor pool and deck add a casual side to a proper establishment. The in-house restaurant and bar have been known to draw local patrons as well as the international set. There is live entertainment somewhere on the premises each night, and turn down service is part of the pampering.

HOLIDAY INN RIVERVIEW

301 Savannah Highway   *556-7100 or*
                            800-HOLIDAY
$$$ *Most major credit cards*

This circular hotel is referred to by locals as "The Round Holiday Inn" for obvious reasons. Completely renovated after Hurricane Hugo, on the original West Ashley site, many of the 181 units and four suites have water views. Up top, a restaurant and bar offer panoramic vistas of peninsular Charleston and the meandering Ashley River. The pool area is an outside appendage to the hotel, unusual because of its height and subsequent view.

LANDS INN

2545 Savannah Hwy.   763-8885
(Hwy. 17 South)
$-$$$ V,M,AX

This Lands Inn is out a bit from the city, which makes it more private and relaxing. Speaking of relaxing, there is a private fishing dock for guests, cable TV, and a Continental breakfast in the morning. Rates change with seasons, so call for information.

OMNI HOTEL AT CHARLESTON PLACE

130 Market Street   722-4900 or
                                             800-THE-OMNI
$$$$$ Most major credit cards

In terms of size, the Omni is the granddaddy of Charleston hotels with 443 units sprawling across the second floor of a massive complex in the shopping district. The hotel, with its lounge and reception area, opens into the walkway of a mini-mall that includes such world-class stores as Polo, Laura Ashley, Gucci and Banana Republic. The fitness center and an indoor-outdoor swimming pool are quality amenities, and superb dining is possible right under the roof of Charleston Place.

QUALITY INN HEART OF CHARLESTON

125 Calhoun Street   722-3391 or
                                             800-845-2504
$$-$$$ Most major credit cards

You can't miss the green awning of the Heart of Charleston, located at the corner of Meeting and Calhoun Streets. If you knew this name in years gone by, don't be confused about the location. What was the Holiday Inn is now the Quality Inn Heart of Charleston, and what was the Heart of Charleston is now NCNB Bank (across from the Meeting Street shopping strip). The "new" Heart of Charleston is a multistory building with 126 air-conditioned units and a swimming pool. The Gaillard Auditorium is just down the street, and guests make use of the free parking and courtesy van for downtown travel.

The Battery in Charleston is home to several Bed & Breakfasts.

SHERATON CHARLESTON HOTEL

170 Lockwood Drive   723-3000 or
                            800-325-3535
$$$-$$$$ Most major credit cards

If you are crossing the Ashley River Bridge into Charleston, look to your left to see the towering Sheraton behind riverside Brittlebank Park. There are 350 rooms and suites in this hotel, many with a view of the river. A swimming pool is part of the facility, and tennis courts are an option seldom offered with peninsula accommodations. Abundant parking is available at no charge.

TOWN AND COUNTRY INN

2008 Savannah Highway   571-1000 or
                    800-334-6660 out-of-state
$$ Most major credit cards

What will strike you first about this West Ashley establishment is the electronic billboard out front that gives a running message about the services within. Next, you are likely to be amazed by the fact that this is as much a fitness center as it is a motel. As with one of our favorite French hotels in New York, guests have access to facilities and locals can buy memberships. With an indoor pool, racquetball courts, exercise equipment, a sauna and more, a stay here can qualify as a fitness vacation. Laundry service is an option and, if you are traveling light, efficiencies are available. The restaurant, Trotters, is popular as well (especially with the after-church crowd on Sundays) and runs unusual specials — just check the sign!

Photo: The Post and Courier

As the sun sets in Charleston the city comes to life.

Charleston
Nightlife

When the lights go down, people in greater Charleston do not tuck in. In fact, visitors who seek nighttime entertainment are met with an abundance of choices. If you are interested in listening to live contemporary music, dancing or just making the bar scene, start with the spots we've described below: you won't be bored. There are also a number of conventional movie theaters (and one charming, unconventional theater) in the vicinity. We have listed names and phone numbers, and suggest calling the theaters for titles after checking the *Post and Courier's* movie listings.

Culturally, the area is alive in the evening with artistic expression (see the Arts chapter), and we have gathered some important information to help with finding tickets.

Nightclubs

ARIZONA BAR AND GRILL
14 Chapel Street   577-5090

Locals enjoy southwestern hors d'oeuvres and atmosphere in the bar of this former train station at the corner of East Bay and Chapel streets. Although it is frequented by everyone from college students to visitors, it is definitely a meeting place for the residents (30s and up crowds) as well. The bar at Arizona's is open seven days a week until 1:00 AM or 2:00 AM (see Charleston Restaurants).

ASHLEY'S
170 Lockwood Drive   723-3000

Located in the Sheraton Charleston Hotel, Ashley's is a good place for dancing and cocktails. What we find most appealing is the pool-side happy hour during spring and summer months — true southern living.

BEST FRIEND LOUNGE
115 Meeting Street   577-2400

For a "clubby" atmosphere conducive to sharing an unrushed evening with friends, seek out the Best Friend at The Mills House. A quiet, sophisticated bar, it is open Monday through Friday from 5:00 PM until 2:00 AM, and Saturday from 8:00 PM until 2:00 AM.

BLIND TIGER PUB
36 Broad Street   577-0088

The Blind Tiger is open from 10:00 AM until midnight, Monday through Saturday, and closed on Sunday. If you are looking for atmosphere (specifically British pub),

• 77

escape into this friendly environment with its dark English mahogany walls and cast-iron stools. Order Bass Ale or Guiness Ale, or try a "black and tan" — Bass on bottom, Guiness on top. (Fear not: the beer is chilled appropriately for Charleston, not served lukewarm as is in England.) There is live R&B music on Wednesday night from 6:00 until 10:00 PM, and the weekend crowd gathers around 8:00 or 9:00 PM.

BLUE COYOTE GRILLE
61 State Street   *577-BLUE*
This is the spot downtown for country music and dancing. There is live entertainment and a happy hour from 5:00 until 7:00 PM, and lots of action thereafter. It's a casual kind of place, so come one, come all, and kick up your boots.

CAFE 99
99 South Market Street   *577-4499*
Cafe 99 is one of those places that will catch your eye from the street. First off, the outdoor tables — usually filled with happy revelers — tempt passers-by and remind us that there can be magic beneath those stars. The bar is open seven days a week with live nightly entertainment. Happy hour is from 4:00 PM until 7:00 PM, and patrons enjoy the raw bar and the upstairs sports bar as well (see Charleston Restaurants).

CHARLESTON'S SPORTS PUB AND GRILL
Market Square, Market Street   *577-8887*
Open seven days a week, this is the only large scale sports bar on the peninsula. With 22 televisions, pool and darts, there is never a dull moment. Food is available until midnight.

CHEF AND CLEF RESTAURANT
102 N. Market Street   *722-0732*
There are three floors of live, mellow jazz nightly at the Chef and Clef, and there is also a terrific late night menu to satisfy everyone's munchies. Patrons come for happy hour also, and a good number of college students can be counted on to shut the place down each night (see the Charleston Restaurants chapter).

TOMMY CONDON'S
160 Church Street   *577-3818*
Every day is St. Patty's day at Charleston's only authentic Irish pub. Tommy Condon's has traditional Irish sing-alongs from Thursday through Saturday nights, and serves Irish spirits as well. The layout of the facility makes for a good party flow, and people mix and mingle all around (see the Charleston Restaurants chapter).

CUMBERLAND'S
26 Cumberland Street   *577-9469*
Happy hour here — with its 20-cent buffalo wings and 75-cent draft — is a crowd pleaser. It happens Monday through Saturday, from 5:00 PM until 8:00 PM, and the college crowd rallies to the cause. There is a full-service bar, and live music is on tap Tuesday through Saturday, from 10:00 PM until 2:00 AM.

EAST BAY TRADING COMPANY
161 East Bay Street   722-0722

The full-service bar here has long been a great meeting place for locals. The crowd is a mixture of vintage, and the mood is predictably festive. What with an old trolley car (permanently parked, of course) for entertainment, and plenty of room on the dance floor, the fun comes naturally (see Charleston Restaurants).

EIGHTY-TWO QUEEN STREET
82 Queen Street   723-7591

One of the locals' hangouts, the bar at 82 Queen is narrow, but comfortable enough, and a good place to see friends...almost a thin version of *Cheers*, with a mix of people knowing and not knowing each other's names.

FANNIGAN'S
159 East Bay Street   722-6916
or 723-4477

This is a high energy dance club where everyone gets out on the floor to boogie. A lot of them start off at the happy hour between 5:00 PM and 8:00 PM, Tuesday through Friday, and then rock the night away. Fannigan's is open from 5:00 PM until 2:00 AM Monday through Thursday, until 4:00 AM on Friday, and until 2:00 AM on Saturday.

FULFORD-EGAN
231 Meeting Street   577-4553

An authentic coffeehouse, Fulford-Egan has a mellow atmosphere and serves no alcohol — just coffees, teas and late night desserts. There is live entertainment by local artists nightly, including jazz, blues and folk music, and an occasional poetry reading. College of Charleston students and an assortment of other fans frequent Fulford-Egan, and appreciate the uniqueness of this kind of setting (see the Restaurant chapter).

HENRY'S
54 N. Market Street   723-4363

Henry's used to be known for its "old Charleston" meals and comfortably-worn side bar. Today — under different ownership — it has updated trappings and a new reputation for light food and live jazz. The ambiance is contemporary New Orleans, and a wonderful addition is the second floor — now opened for dancing. There is a happy hour Monday through Friday (see Charleston Restaurants).

HIGH SPIRITS LOUNGE
Holiday Inn Riverview   556-7100

There is certainly nothing misleading in this one's name: located on the top floor of the Holiday Inn, High Spirits has fabulous views of the Charleston harbor and

Insiders Like:
Meeting someone special — to celebrate an occasion or just friendship itself — in the "Best Friends Lounge" at the Mills House.

Insiders' Tip

city lights. There is dancing and a full-service bar. We recommend it as one of the "top spots" for viewing Fourth of July fireworks: totally awesome!

JUKEBOX

4 Vendue Range   723-3431

Located across from the Waterfront Park, Jukebox is all about entertainment and dancing in a '50s atmosphere. A swarm of business men and women flock to the 20-foot, complimentary dinner buffet during happy hour from 5:00 to 8:00 PM, Monday through Friday, and from 7:00 to 8:00 PM on Saturday. The dance floor literally throbs when partners begin matching up and shaking loose. There may be a line at the entrance, and plan to work your way through a crowd inside, too, when your time comes: this is one of *the* spots for the singles crowd.

LOUIS'S CHARLESTON GRILL

The Omni Hotel   577-4522

The bar here draws a regular, local crowd after work and for nightly live jazz. More than offering just a classy, comfortable setting, Louis's Charleston Grill has a reputation for doing things the right way and the bar is no exception — simple, yet elegant. Cocktails are served from 4:00 PM until midnight (see Charleston Restaurants).

MARIANNE

235 Meeting Street   722-7196

In addition to — and sometimes a part of — the dinner set at this exceptional French restaurant, a diverse crowd congregates here to unwind in the piano bar Wednesday through Saturday. You will be impressed with the diversity of the group and with the incredible complexity of food and drink to be had at late hours (see Charleston Restaurants). We stop by for dessert and liqueur in the piano bar after concerts, and splurge calories on the delicious late night breakfast from time to time.

MIKE CALDERS

288 King Street   577-0123

There is live weekday and weekend entertainment at this pub, and College of Charleston students love the fact that it is close to campus. Wide open, with plenty of tables, it stays open until 11:00 PM, Monday through Thursday, and until midnight on Friday and Saturday (see Charleston Restaurants chapter).

MISTRAL

99 South Market Street   722-5708

This romantic restaurant has a full bar with an extended wine list. There is very good, live Dixieland jazz on Fridays and Saturdays. Mistral is closed on Sundays (see Restaurants).

THE MUSIC FARM

525 East Bay Street   853-8989

Popular groups perform here on a regular basis. The college crowd is thick, and there is sometimes a cover charge. Drink specials run every night.

MYSKYN'S TAVERN

5 Faber Street   577-5595

An oldie but goldie —

Myskyn's has been a top biller for years. There is plenty of space for dancing, and live entertainment includes some of the top names in the business. Late night partiers keep on keepin' on here — taking in the sights or playing pool and video games. Myskyn's is located off East Bay Street, and often has a cover charge.

SARACEN
141 East Bay Street   723-6242

If your idea of a relaxing night out is to find a place off the beaten path, where the live music is classical and the setting elegant, Saracen is the stuff of your dreams (see the Charleston Restaurants chapter).

WILD WING CAFE
36 N. Market   722-9464

Crowded with the young (20-something) set at night, Wild Wing Cafe has live entertainment on Wednesday night. Affordable munchies — wings and such — and a full house pulsating with partiers make this a happening place in the Market (see Restaurants).

Movie Theaters

Ashley Landing Cinemas I, II & III
Ashley Landing Mall, 571-2380
Citadel Mall Cinema I-VI
Citadel Mall, 763-7052
Oakbrook Theaters
Oakbrook Shopping Center, 873-1501

Photo: The Post and Courier

There's always plenty of great jazz to be heard at night in Charleston.

Ultravision 1 & 2 Theaters
1812 Sam Rittenberg Blvd., 556-4200

STAGE ONE CINEMA
30 Cumberland Street   *722-1900*
Not your "garden variety" theater; this one shows only alternative films — classics, foreign or by independent film makers — and serves wine and pastries instead of just soda and popcorn.

Concert Information

Gaillard Municipal Auditorium
77 Calhoun Street
Ticket Sales........577-4500
Business Office.....577-7400
King Street Palace
1000 King Street, 723-1075

College of Charleston Entertainment/Arts
Simons Center For The Arts
Theatre Box Office, 792-5604
Sotille Theatre
Box Office, 727-2041
Stern Student Center
792-5726

S.C.A.T. Locations

These locations and phone numbers are outlets for tickets to local concerts and events.
Harbour Records & Tapes
Orange Grove Plaza, 763-0302
McAlister Field House
Ticket Office, 792-5121
Piggly Wiggly
445 Meeting Street, 722-2766
Visitors Center
375 Meeting Street, 853-8000
Monkey Music
320 King Street, 723-7200

Charleston
Neighborhoods

There was a time when died-in-the-wool Charlestonians and informed new arrivals felt that to live in Charleston meant, at the very least, to hang your hat somewhere on the peninsula. If financially possible, you set your sights on the houses "Below Broad," and if not...you crept as close as possible. The undisputed prize was a mansion on the Battery, and all north of that fell into a pecking order.

Today there is still a great market for peninsula real estate. However, thanks to the renovation efforts of our preservation groups,

institutions and individuals, there are more attractive neighborhoods in the city to choose from than ever before and a sprawling Historic District that defies the Broad Street bounds.

Furthermore, the West Ashley area is also an appealing option for homeowners. Just 50 years ago, pockets were still largely undeveloped; one Farmfield resident remembers riding his horse across the Ashley River Bridge to attend (what was then) Gaud School. Pity the man and pity the horse who go that way in the 1990s. The West Ashley we know is

Photo: The Post and Courier

A bird's-eye view of Charleston.

teeming with traffic, neighborhoods and businesses: the banes and blessings of modern suburban life.

Generally speaking, West Ashley has a larger selection of moderately priced houses in desirable neighborhoods than can be found in town. However, the selection is peppered with an assortment of executive homes, plantation houses and other extravagant real estate. In terms of dollars, the most valuable properties are waterfront, marsh-view or situated in the established neighborhoods.

In describing some of Charleston's interesting neighborhoods, we will begin at the southern tip of the peninsula and work our way north, and then west to West Ashley. When possible, we refer to listing prices of houses for sale at press time. These are not true ranges of neighborhood values, but rather random samples which can be used as market indicators. With employment opportunities changing in this community, expect a reflection in the real estate market.

THE PENINSULA

The Peninsula of Charleston is a strip of land flanked by the Ashley and Cooper Rivers. A good portion of this valuable land chunk is divided into neighborhoods collectively referred to as the "Historic District." Outside of this designation but within the category of intriguing real estate, is a neighborhood to the north of Spring Street, near Hampton Park and the Citadel, called Wagener Terrace.

SOUTH OF BROAD

The residences clustered at the southern tip of the Charleston peninsula are among the most exclusive in the Trident area.

Broad Street, a business and legal center of the city, divides the Historic District into what is called "South of Broad" or "Below Broad" and other boroughs to the north. Gracious mansions line such well-traveled streets as Tradd, Legare, lower Church and King, Broad, South Battery, East Bay and Murray Boulevard. Asking prices for large, distinctive houses in this area range from half a million to almost $2 million dollars. Other more modest architectural treasures are found on the same streets or tucked away on charming side streets and alleys. They vary in size, historical value, and condition, and the asking prices reflect those details. You could find a 1,500-square-foot townhouse unit in a 148-year-old house, located Below Broad, close to but without a view of the water, listed at $295,000. Looking for more space? An 81-year-old house Below Broad, with 2,302 square feet, was offered for $398,500. Obviously there is no simple rule for calculation in this market, and your licensed Realtor knows best what is available and what is fair market value.

NORTH OF BROAD

Several clusters of neighborhoods north of Broad Street (between Broad and Calhoun) are considered very desirable.

The **French Quarter** includes the area around Philadelphia Alley, State, Queen, and Chalmers Streets, and is a mixture of commercial and residential zoning. Inns, restaurants, bars, shops and the beloved theatrical entity Footlight Players coexist with busy families in a bustling cosmopolitan atmosphere. For an idea of real estate values in this area of town, consider some examples. A 1,520-square-foot house, historically insignificant, was offered for $275,000. At the same time, there was for sale a 151-year-old, 2,509-square-foot house priced at $505,000. But consider the 4,125-square-foot house nearby tagged at $625,000.

Ansonborough, in recent decades, was considered a "frontier" because there were so many historically significant homes in grievous disrepair for sale at very low prices. Not so today when — for all practical purposes — Ansonborough is "done," and the collective result is a fascinating slice of living history. One of its "newer" houses — just shy of its hundredth birthday — has 1,806 square feet and was priced at $225,000. Around the corner, a 3,000-square-foot plantation-style single house, over 200 years old, was offered for $315,000. Down the block, a 141-year-old 3,390-square-foot house was listed at $615,000.

Wraggsborough includes the blocks between Calhoun and the Charleston Museum. There are a number of restored houses and the closer to East Bay Street, the larger

and more stately the dwellings. Some sample asking prices in this borough include: $219,000 for a 2,200-square-foot two-year-old townhouse; and $825,000 for a 12,000-square-foot, 101-year-old mansion...in need of restoration.

The area around the Medical University, the College of Charleston, Colonial Lake and in between is **Harleston Village**. We found a 13-year-old, 1,280-square-foot house, priced at $189,500. On another street, a 150-year-old, 2,050-square-foot single house was for sale at $225,000. Another 3,700-square-foot single house, dating to 1875, was listed for $349,500. And, with another 424 square feet, a 151-year-old home nearby was priced at $725,000.

Radcliffboro is the area north of Calhoun Street from the medical complexes east to Wraggsborough. Ashley Hall, a school for girls, is a landmark in the neighborhood. There are still some fixer-uppers in these blocks, such as the 100-plus-year-old, 1,400-square-foot house listed at $65,000. We located a renovated 1,600-square-foot, 140-year-old house, for which the owners were asking $173,500. A 136-year-old renovated house with 3,880 square feet was priced at $299,000.

WAGENER TERRACE

The blocks around Hampton Park and The Citadel (South Carolina's military college) constitute what is called Wagener Terrace. The area's many wonderful homes, built in what was considered by early 20th century Charlestonians to be "suburbia," fell out of grace when the crime rates began to rise and life on the edge of town proper became less tranquil. But things are a'changin' again, and there has been a trend — especially with the young, upwardly mobile types — of moving back into this area. Many of the homes facing Hampton Park and those on the Ashley River (including the Loundes Grove Plantation, the restored main house of which is now a Bed and Breakfast) were spectacular in their heyday and have been remodeled or updated recently. The park has been revamped and is a wonderful draw, as is the well-kept campus of The Citadel.

WEST ASHLEY

By the designation "West Ashley" we are referring to the area west of the Charleston peninsula, bordered by the Ashley River and Inland Waterway, stretching to the community of Ravenel. To check out the neighborhoods of West Ashley, start by crossing the Ashley River Bridge and head up Highway 61 (also called Ashley River Road).

MORELAND

This is a rather small subdivision, closest to the Charleston peninsula. Many of the houses have marsh views facing The Citadel and Brittlebank Park. An older neighborhood with large yards, this area has a village feel with an eclectic collection ranging from quaint cottages to larger brick houses. Asking prices start at $60,000, but most houses are priced at more than $100,000.

WESPANNEE

Built up around a beautiful old plantation house on land that is draped in wisteria each spring, this quiet neighborhood is very stable. Just five minutes from town, it is close to mall shopping and public schools. Homes are mostly brick with open yards and winding streets. It is not unusual for houses to list at upwards of $200,000.

CHARLESTOWNE ESTATES I

Charlestowne Estates I is located between the still wooded areas of Charlestowne Landing, and Highway 171 (with a frontage road along Highway 171). Most houses are one-story, brick ranch-style, with large live oaks and some pine trees in the yards. No listing prices are available at this time.

CHARLESTOWNE ESTATES II

This subdivision backs up to the Ashley Landing, with Highways 7 and 171 being its other borders. This is a well-tended, family neighborhood with moderately priced homes. Many are brick and one-story, and most have beautiful azaleas blooming each spring. No listing prices are available at this time.

NORTHBRIDGE

Northbridge is bordered by Highway 7, Orange Grove Road, and

Photo: The Post and Courier

Mounted police patrol the parks and streets of Charleston, adding to its charm.

the Ashley River. Small houses, similar in appearance, are prevalent and list in the high $70,000 range. However, there is a mixture of two-story new and old construction along the river, with some homes just finished.

PARKSHORE I, II, III, IV

The Parkshore family of subdivisions are bordered by Highway 7 and the Ashley River. These are executive homes of newer construction with large lots and some availability. Many have marsh views and some have docks. Residents love the access to a community center with its pool, park and tennis courts. Asking prices begin at around $140,000.

SANDHURST

Across Highway 7, on a high bluff facing the Ashley River, is Sandhurst. Vistas can be outstanding, and the neighborhood garden club produces noteworthy results. Most of the older construction is one- or two-story brick, while some of the newer homes are wood-shingled and of contemporary design. Sandhurst is close to Orange Grove Elementary School and the park. Asking prices begin at around $120,000.

WILMINGTON WOODS

Wilmington Woods is a secluded, well-kept secret off Orange Grove Road. The entire subdivision is clustered on a finger of land which juts out into the marsh of the Ashley River. Most houses fall into executive category, although there are a few smaller homes. Well-kept yards tend to feature camellias, azaleas and large oak trees. This also is within minutes

of the Orange Grove Elementary School and its playground. Asking prices start at around $130,000.

ASHLEY HARBOR

Built around Ashley Hall plantation, Ashley Harbor is a very exclusive, sheltered community enclosed on one side by a brick wall and guarded gates. The other boundaries consist of the Ashley River, along which are deep water docks, and a large lake buffering the community from the Mark Clark Expressway. With rolling lawns and huge old oak trees, Ashley Harbor is a pleasant throwback to the old South. Many houses top the executive category, but some list at $225,000.

MARSH COVE

Off of Highway 61, buffered by an apartment complex, Marsh Cove has resort style, wood shingled houses with high pitched roofs and natural wood porches. Although they blend nicely, there is some variation in style and size. And this is another subdivision where developers seem to have respected the environment by saving natural shrubbery and trees. Current asking prices in Marsh Cove range from around $90,000 to $225,000.

ASHLAND PLANTATION

Nestled behind a smaller subdivision along Highway 61, you enter Ashland Plantation through a New England-style rotary. Most homes here are two and three stories and of executive proportions. This is new construction, of brick and wood. Some waterfront houses face the river, while some face the subdivision's lake. Prices may start around $150,000.

DRAYTON ON THE ASHLEY

Entering from Highway 61, two brick pillars mark the entrance and set the style for this mostly brick subdivision. As you wind through the neighborhood, toward the river, many of the one-story houses are on small lots with one- or two-car garages. Closer to the river, there are tall pine trees and two-story houses of different design and construction. Along the waterfront, similar houses on high lots have views of the Ashley River and the old train trestle. Asking prices in this neighborhood start at around $100,000.

MACLAURA HALL

Of new West Ashley subdivisions, the farthest out on Highway 61 along the Ashley River is MacLaura Hall. These are executive homes, some of which are priced over $300,000. The landscaping reflects a sensitivity to the natural scheme as many original trees and shrubs have been incorporated into the design. There is great variety in architectural styles, and high standards have been maintained throughout. Construction is ongoing, and there are lots available.

SHADOWMOSS

Across Highway 61, with no water boundaries, is Shadowmoss. Designed for country club living, Shadowmoss was laid out around a golf course with room to grow. There is incredible variety in terms of architectural design and asking prices,

including first homes with $60,000-plus price tags, and sprawling houses in the executive range. Residents have community clubs and events, and can make use of the on-site facilities.

ALBEMARLE POINT

Where the Ashley River meets the Inland Waterway, Albemarle Point begins. Porter Gaud School and several large homes with long-time residents are located on the point. The Ripley Light Marina, The Hampton Inn, and the restaurant California Dreaming are also located off Albemarle Road. Although houses seldom become available in this area, the neighborhood is noteworthy for its tranquil beauty and view of the Charleston harbor.

THE CRESCENT

The Crescent is adjacent to Albemarle Point and bordered by Folly Road and the Intracoastal Waterway. Described by someone once as "the country, only five minutes from town," this highly desirable old neighborhood consists of established homes and yards in the upper executive range starting at around $200,000. Generations of children have fed the resident ducks who inhabit the twin lakes, and all age groups take advantage of the quiet streets for walks and bike rides.

WAPPOO HEIGHTS

Wappoo Heights, located across Folly Road from The Crescent, is another well-established and highly desirable neighborhood. A quick stroll from the South Windermere Shopping Center,

Wappoo Heights — like The Crescent — has the advantage of quick access to the city. It is also bordered by the wetlands of the Intracoastal Waterway. There is wide architectural variety, and a family atmosphere. Homes start at around $150,000.

SOUTH WINDERMERE

Bounded by South Windermere Shopping Center, the Coburg Creek and the Intracoastal Waterway, and backing up to Wappoo Heights, South Windermere is a family neighborhood which has soared in popularity with young people in recent years. Houses to date start at listing prices of around $130,000, and range to executive heights in the prestigious blocks of Confederate Circle. St. Andrews Elementary School is within walking distance.

BYRNES DOWNS

One of closest to town yet affordable neighborhoods for first home buyers, Byrnes Downs is bordered by Highway 17 South. It is a quiet neighborhood, with sidewalks and tree-lined streets. A current asking price for a small home here is around $64,000.

WESTWOOD

Westwood is across the street from Byrnes Downs. It is another neighborhood with the All-American feel: neat, modest to nice-sized homes on winding streets, nestled between Blessed Sacrament Church and Highway 17 South.

FARMFIELD

This is a small subdivision bordered by marshes and Coburg Creek, Highway 17 South and Parkwood Estates. The focal point is a beautiful old plantation house and its avenue of oaks. Lots are large and houses are mostly brick and ranch style, some with deep water access. Asking prices range from around $104,000 to $600,000

PARKWOOD ESTATES

Parkwood Estates is a deep subdivision which has layers of homes, the most expensive of which front on Coburg Creek. Hemmed in on all sides by the water, Highway 17 South and Farmfield, Parkwood is secluded and pleasant for families or retirement living (and is used for both). Houses on the market here are starting at around $78,000.

HARRISON ACRES

There are one- and two-story houses scattered throughout Harrison Acres, and most are landlocked. Some are on marsh front lots near an old plantation house (its marker commemorating Eliza Lucas and her planting in 1741 the first indigo seed — a big cash crop for South Carolina). The neighborhood is convenient to BiLo grocery store and Kmart. Although the only houses for sale at the time of our research were listed at around $168,000, less expensive homes can become available.

INDIGO POINT

Across the marsh from Farmfield, bordered by Harrison

Acres and Coburg Creek, Indigo Point is a deep waterfront neighborhood tucked far away from hysterical crowds. Some homes are traditional and built to resemble Charleston mansions, while others are distinctly modern. Current asking prices range from around $175,00 to around $500,000.

EDGEWATER PARK

Edgewater Park is bordered by Coburg Creek and the Intracoastal Waterway. An island at the foot of Wappoo Road, it consists of homes ranging in listing price from around $150,000 to $500,000 on the water. Lots are large and most yards are landscaped with old camellia beds and azaleas. There is access to a private boat landing for property owners.

CAPRI ISLES

An island off Wappoo Road, Capri Isles is bordered by marshes of Coburg Creek and the Intracoastal Waterway. Most lots are marsh fronted, and a few have deep water access. Styles are most often brick, one- or two-story. Listing prices begin at around $112,000.

PARKDALE

Located at the end of Parkdale Road, off of Highway 17, Parkdale has a yacht club with deepwater access for its members. The club itself is an impressive reproduction plantation house with piazzas and a magnificent view. Some houses have been completed, and others are under construction. A current listing is in the $100,000 range.

SYLVAN SHORES I AND II

Sylvan I is the older subdivision, and Sylvan II is in the process of being developed. Both have frontage on vast areas of inland waterway and residents have access to a private boat landing. Listings here begin at around $110,000.

Photo: Ron A. Rocz

Crabbing in the marshes is a favorite Charleston family pastime.

Charleston
Fitness, Participatory Sports and Parks

The warm climate and natural resources of this area make recreation — and keeping physically fit for recreation — a top priority with locals. This chapter deals specifically with some of the things we do for fitness and entertainment, and offers a sampling of the public places designated for fun.

Participatory Sports

Biking

The Coastal Cyclists, an organization of bike riders and racers, can reached by calling 873-8779 or writing P.O. Box 32095, Charleston, South Carolina, 29407. This group plans rides and also is involved in races.

Bowling

TRIANGLE LANES
1963 Savannah Highway   766-0241
(off Mark Clark Expressway)

Located just off the Mark Clark expressway, West of the Ashley, Triangle has automatic scores, trophies, a pro-shop and a lounge. Fees change daily, but the hours are Monday through Thursday, 9:00 AM until 12:00 AM, Friday and Saturday from 9:00 AM until 1:00 AM, and Sunday from 10:00 PM until 12:00 PM.

ASHLEY LANES
1568 Sam Rittenberg Blvd.   766-9061

Rates change at different times of the day, but Ashley Lanes is open from 9:00 AM until 1:30 AM, Monday through Thursday, and from until 2:00 AM on Friday and Saturday. In addition to bowling, there is an amusement center, restaurant, lounge and nursery available.

Camping

There are government-owned, public places for camping in the Charleston area, and the best clearinghouse for this information is the Charleston **County Parks and Recreation Department**, at 762-2172.

There are other private campgrounds with spaces for rent, and some in the immediate area are: **Oak Plantation Campground**, at 3540 Savannah Highway, 766-5936; and **Lake Aire Campground**, at 4359 Savannah Highway in Ravenel, 889-

8373. This campground, set on seven acres of wilderness, has a lake and fishing available. There is also a pool and fitness areas.

For Boy Scout camping information, call **Boy Scouts of America Camping Center**, at 763-0305, or stop by 1025 Sam Rittenberg Boulevard.

Day Camps

Community centers as well as schools and churches operate day camps. For a list of programs run by the county, call Charleston County Parks and Recreation at 762-2172.

Fitness Centers

THE FIRM
77 Wentworth Street   723-3476

The Firm offers weight training and aerobic classes, and sells its own series of videos and workout clothing. This means serious competition for Jane Fonda, and serious (or, as they say, "firm") results for those who persevere. Classes run between 6:30 AM and 8:30 PM, seven days a week. There is a $5 registration fee and the rate is $5 per class or $43 per month for unlimited visits. Baby-sitting is available during some hours.

BODYWORKS HEALTH AND FITNESS
1401 Sam Rittenberg Boulevard   763-6760

Nautilus, free weights and aerobics are offered at this West Ashley center. Body analysis is also available.

DOWNTOWN FITNESS OF CHARLESTON
74 Wentworth Street   577-7262

If you have dreamed of a personal training program, this may be what you're after. Appointments are scheduled between 6:00 AM and 7:00 PM, Monday through Friday, and 8:00 AM and 12:00 PM on Saturday (closed on Saturday during the summer). Fees are $150 per month for 12 visits — each a 60-minute cardiovascular workout using free weights and focusing also on the abdominal section. Showers and a dressing areas are available.

ST. ANDREWS FAMILY RECREATION CENTER
1642 Sam Rittenberg Boulevard   763-3850

St. Andrews is a full-service health fitness facility. The whole family (even the little ones, who play in the nursery) can enjoy aerobics classes, racquetball, squash, indoor swimming, nautilus, free weights, indoor track, life step machines and treadmills. The hours are: Monday through Thursday, 6:00 AM until 9:00 PM; Friday, 6:00 AM until 8:00 PM; Saturday, 9:00 AM until 5:00 PM; and Sunday, 1:00 PM until 6:00 PM. Fees are $5.75 a day per person or $10 a day per family. Annual, three-month, monthly and daily passes are available, and prices vary according to factors such as residence and age.

TOWN AND COUNTRY INN FITNESS CENTER
2008 Savannah Highway   571-1000

Although it is located in a motel complex, this million dollar fitness center is open to the public

A polo match at Boone Hall.

Photo: The Post and Courier

for memberships. For a $50 initiation fee and $25 a month, members can use the Cal-Gym exercise equipment, the life steps, dumbbells, two racquetball courts and a lap pool, as well as showers and a sauna. Family memberships are also available.

WORKOUT EXPRESS

1890 Sam Rittenburg Blvd.   556-2900

This fitness center is for women only, and offers cardiovascular conditioning, aerobic classes, strength training, nutritional programs, circuit training and child care. The hours are Monday, Wednesday, and Friday, 8:00 AM until 9:00 PM; Tuesday and Thursday, 9:00 AM until 9:00 PM; and Saturday, 10:00 AM until 2:00 PM.

Flying

Two airports in the county offer flying lessons. Neither are in Charleston or West Ashley, but both are in close proximity and do fly overhead! For more information,

see East Island and West Island Fitness Sections.

Frisbee Golf

This is a relatively new sport, but Charleston is on top of the fun. Call 724-7327 for more information.

Horseback Riding

MIDDLETON RIDING AND HUNT STABLES

Ashley River Road   556-8137

A premier boarding and lesson facility, Middleton has a dressage arena, cross-country course and lighted ring for evening riding.

Karate

Fred Villari's Schools of Self Defense, located at 21 George Street (call 723-8521) and 1964 Ashley River Road (call 766-4376), are part of an international chain named for Grandmaster Fred Villari — a 10th Degree Black Belt. Self-defense courses in Karate, Tai-Chi, Kung-Fu and Ju-Jitsu are available for all ages.

Polo

There are three polo teams in Charleston — Quimby, Stono Ferry, and Aire Hall — which play matches during both spring and fall seasons. For more information about participation or match schedules, call Stono Ferry at 766-6208.

Roller-Skating

People in this area skate indoors and outdoors, and even have a club — The **Charleston Roll Patrol** — to promote their interest. There is no indoor rink in Charleston or West Ashley, but there are rinks elsewhere in the county (see Fitness in James Island and North Charleston).

Running

The **Charleston Running Club** has monthly meetings the last Tuesday of every month, and has approximately 600 members. The organization publishes a substantial newsletter every other month in booklet form (24-36 pages with results from races, stories, book reviews and a calendar). The club sponsors about a dozen races (and occupies one of the seven seats on the large and successful Cooper River Bridge Run) as well as a summer track series. Members enjoy a party after the Bridge Run and a

picnic in July, as well as discounts to local athletic stores. The membership fee is $10 for an individual and $15 for a family. Call 723-2596 for more information.

Scuba Diving

There is no local dive club in this area, but two shops — one in Charleston and the other in Mt. Pleasant — offer dive trips and serve as gathering spots for people interested in the sport: **The Charleston Scuba**, 35 Lockwood Drive, call 722-1120. Also see Fitness in Mt. Pleasant.

Swimming

For information about public swimming pools and programs, start with the Charleston County Aquatics Coordinator whose office is at **Forest Park Pool**, 780 Playground Road, West of the Ashley (call 723-6473). The **Christian Family Y**, at 21 George Street, also has swimming activities (call 723-6473).

T'aekwon Do

INTERNATIONAL T'AEKWON DO CENTER
1750 Savannah Highway   556-4391

This center offers classes for men, women and children ages five and older who are interested in T'aekwon Do and self-defense. Children can attend a supervised study hall between school and class at the center.

Tennis

An empty tennis court on a pretty day is hard to come by in this area. Call the county Tennis Coordinator at 724-7401 for information about specific locations or reservations at public tennis courts, and about joining tennis leagues.

CHARLESTON TENNIS CENTER
19 Farmfield Avenue   724-7402
These courts are conveniently located West of the Ashley, and are popular with the tennis crowd. Hours are subject to demand but in general are: Monday through Friday, 8:30 AM until 10:00 PM; Saturday from 9:00 AM until 8:00 PM; and Sunday, from 10:00 AM until 7:00 PM. Fees are: $2.00 per resident; $2.50 per out-of-town guest;

and an additional $2.00 per hour light fee for any player at night.

WEST ASHLEY MAYBANK TENNIS CLUB
1880 Houghton Drive   795-6670
This club has both hard and clay courts. New memberships are welcome, and it is open seven days a week.

Volleyball

TRI-COUNTY VOLLEYBALL ASSOCIATION
884-4722
The mission of this association is to support and teach volleyball, and the members go about this goal with a lot of enthusiasm. For an annual fee of $20, members — beginners up to advanced players —

The bandstand at White Point Gardens.

can participate in the Captain's Choice grass tournaments as well as picnics, happy hours and parties. The group sponsors clinics as well as Open Play at different gymnasiums throughout the year, and puts out a newsletter.

Walking

There are beautiful places to walk all around the city and West of the Ashley. One group of organized outdoor walkers, **Hampton Parks Walkers Club**, can be contacted at 724-7336. For those happier with climate control and window shopping, the malls serve as "walking routes."

Leagues

There are leagues for sports ranging from softball to football and soccer to rugby. For more information about children's teams, contact **Youth Sports** at 724-7329. To learn more about teams and competition for adults, call the Adult Sports coordinator at 724-7334.

Community Centers

Charleston County Community Schools provide wonderful opportunities for fitness and fun. For detailed information, write to the Charleston County School District, at The Center, Hutson and Meeting Streets, Charleston, 29402. Also, the **Christian Family Y**, at 21 George Street (call 723-6473), the **YMCA** at 61 Cannon Street (call 577-9622), and the **YWCA**, at 106 Coming Street

(call 722-1644) provide a great deal of opportunity for the community. For example, there are self-enrichment classes, exercise programs and even a swimming team. Membership is open, and it does have its privileges!

Special Events

To learn about the special activities happening in local parks in this area, call The **City of Charleston Recreation Department** at 792-7327.

Parks

The parks we like best are sizeable tracts of land that give the young and old alike a chance to enjoy the great outdoors. We make a distinction between "park" and "playground" because, although the former may include the latter, the park implies more space and characteristics that appeal to children and adults. For more information, call the **Parks and Recreation Department** at 724-7327.

CHARLES TOWNE LANDING
Highway 171   556-4450
Hours: Monday - Sunday 9 AM - 5 PM or 6 PM (in summer)

This is a wonderful park for all ages. There is an animal forest, playground, replica of the ship *Adventure,* a gift shop and even a movie, "Carolina," about the history of the Lowcountry, every hour on the hour. You can rent bikes — ask about the annual bike and vehicle passes...good deals if you are going to be spending time here. Fees are $5 per adult and $2.50 per child, with resident senior citizens admitted free and out-of-town seniors charged $2.50 (see the Attractions chapter).

HAMPTON PARK

55 Cleveland Street   *724-7405*

Located near the Citadel, Hampton Park is a 65-acre park in downtown Charleston with a lake (complete with lots of resident ducks for feeding), grassy areas, a trail for workouts, a bandstand (the site of many an afternoon concert) and even the Police Department's horse stables. A concert series is held here, as is a giant Easter Egg Hunt and the Piccolo Spoleto Finale.

Photo: The Post and Courier

The Battery.

WATERFRONT PARK

Just off East Bay from Cumberland Street to North Adgers Wharf, this is one of the city's newer and most delightful parks. There is a 400-foot pier for viewing harbor activity, and two inviting fountains (in which the young or young-at-heart are allowed to play), as well as lovely grassy areas and swings.

WHITE POINT GARDENS

Located at the tip of the peninsula, White Point Gardens has a beautiful view of the harbor and some of the homes of the Battery. Kids love to climb on the old cannons (and stacked cannon balls) or picnic in the grassy areas. It is often crowded on Sundays when the weather is nice, but is usually pleasant during the work week.

Playgrounds

There are 15 playgrounds in this county, some of which are located downtown and West of the Ashley. For more information about each, contact the coordinator at 724-7332. Some of our favorites are described below:

HAZEL PARKER PLAYGROUND
70 East Bay Street   724-7397

Open from sunup to sundown, this park has playground equipment as well as athletic fields, a tennis court and basketball hoops. You can see Charleston harbor from the grounds, and you are in skipping distance from the Battery.

MARY UTSEY PLAYGROUND
1150 Orange Grove Road   724-7337

We like this playground for its convenient location West of the Ashley and for its shady areas — much appreciated during the many hot months in Charleston.

MOULTRIE PLAYGROUND
41 Ashley Avenue   724-7398

This park was completely renovated a couple of years ago, and has nice equipment for the kids as well as tennis and basketball courts. It is located across from Colonial Lake and is a popular destination for families.

ST. ANDREWS RECREATION COMPLEX
1095 Playground Road   763-3867

This is the headquarters for the St. Andrews Parks and Playground Commission, and up-to-date information on events and activities is available here. There are tennis courts, which are lighted, as well as baseball fields and basketball courts.

Charleston
Worship

*F*or those interested in spirituality or fascinated by antiquity, and for those who pursue both, there are abundant places of worship in the Charleston area. According to our calculations, based on phone calls and the *Post and Courier's* weekly roundup, in the Trident there are nearly 150 religious services each weekend and about 35 active denominations. Some of these groups have a long history here, such as the Episcopalians and the reformed Jews, while others, like participants in Eckankar ("The Religion of the Light and Sound of God"), are relatively new on the scene.

Church history began here in 1682, 14 years after the colony of Charles Towne was founded, with the building of St. Philips Episcopal church on the corner of Broad and Meeting streets. Soon, other denominations built facilities: the Baptists, their early church; the Quakers, their "Friends' Meeting House"; the Presbyterians, their "White Meeting House" (for which Meeting Street was named); and the Huguenots, their "French Church," on upper Church Street.

The congregation at St. Philips grew to such an extent that a larger facility was needed. A new building (said to have been "the handsomest in the country") was built north of Broad Street, and St. Michael's stayed on as a new name in the old location. Actually, the original church on Meeting Street, built of black cypress with a brick foundation, suffered decay and was demolished. The St. Michael's you can visit today has been in existence since 1761 and is the city's oldest intact church building. St. Philips, on the other hand, burned in 1835 and its replacement is the present facility.

As interesting as these details may be, the telling observation about our religious history has to do with the variety of denominations and level of religious tolerance prevalent from the early times. Consider that collected in one city are the oldest Baptist and Catholic churches in the South, and the oldest surviving reform synagogue in the world.

In the pages that follow, we describe some — but by no means all — of the churches and synagogues on the peninsula and west of the Ashley. We attempt to represent the denominations and specific churches or synagogues which publicize their existence, and highlight church facts of historical significance (for more details, see the Attractions chapter). Because hours for services change with seasons, we have only made general reference to morning or evening. Call the church offices for specifics, or check the *Post and Courier's* Saturday listing.

Adventist

CHARLESTON SEVENTH-DAY ADVENTIST CHURCH
2518 Savannah Hwy.   *766-9556*

This West Ashley church meets on Saturdays for Sabbath School and worship service. There is a Bible class also, which meets Wednesday evenings. They have ample parking and are located on Savannah Highway (also called Highway 17 South).

African Methodist Episcopal

EMANUEL AFRICAN METHODIST EPISCOPAL CHURCH
110 Calhoun Street   *722-2561*

This church was established in 1818 and its present building has been in use since 1891. There are two Sunday morning worship services and a Thursday evening service, as well as a Bible study group on Monday. With its large congregation of nearly 1600, the church is active in assisting the Charleston Interfaith Crisis Ministry. The choir presents concerts during the holy seasons, and sermons reflect current and relevant events and are based on scripture.

GREATER ST. LUKE A.M.E. CHURCH
78 Gordon Street   *722-4062*

Greater St. Luke has Sunday services in the morning and evening, as well as Sunday School. A service is also held on Thursday evening. Full-day child care is available Monday through Friday.

Anglican

ST. TIMOTHY'S CHURCH
1900 Parsonage Road   *763-8873*

St. Timothy's is located just

Insiders' Tip

The exact author of the term "Chapel of Ease" may be lost to the mists of time. But when England's House of Commons created the Church Act of 1706, its purpose was very clear....
As distant and primitive as the colonies were at this early date, the Church of England was adamant in wanting to establish itself as the official religion of the New World. Thus, a tax was levied on skins and furs imported from the colonies in order to fund ten parishes with churches and parsonages in the wilderness — getting a jump on any other form of government control in place at the time. In other words, the church of England wanted to make it "easy" for settlers (and wealthy plantation owners) to have access to (and tithe to) the Mother Church. Today it remains an honest question — for whom the "ease" was really intended: The Church of England or the colonists.

off Ashley River Road (also called Highway 61), West Ashley, behind Church Creek Plaza. There are two regular services on Sundays, and the emphasis is on traditional Anglican faith and worship.

Baptist

ASHLEY RIVER BAPTIST CHURCH
1101 Savannah Hwy.   766-5521

The congregation of this very large West Ashley church fills the south side lot as well as many of the spaces in St. Andrews Shopping Center next door. In addition to Sunday School and worship services Sunday morning, there is a church training and worship service in the evening. Bible study is Wednesday night. The church's beautiful cross, covered in live flowers at Easter, is a favorite sight for motorists on Savannah Highway.

CITADEL SQUARE BAPTIST CHURCH
328 Meeting St.   577-3707

Located on Meeting Street near Calhoun, this church faces Marion Square Park. If you cannot attend but would like to experience the service, tune in to Channel 5 for live airing. There are special college and singles programs. All services are interpreted for the deaf.

FIRST BAPTIST CHURCH
61 Church Street   722-3896

First Baptist, the oldest Baptist church in the South, was founded in 1682 and is located in the heart of the residential Historic District. The church was designed by Robert Mills (the first American-born architect) and is one of the

earliest Greek revival buildings in the state. A well-respected school, First Baptist, has its campus on site. There are morning services and Sunday School on Sunday, as well as a Vesper Service in the evening. Wednesday is Family Night, with supper and a prayer service. The concert series features organ recitals and chamber music programs.

NEW TABERNACLE FOURTH BAPTIST
22 Elizabeth Street   722-4374

A stately, large church with a pretty brick facade, New Tabernacle is located on the peninsula just north of Calhoun. Morning service and a morning church school are conducted each Sunday.

NORTHBRIDGE BAPTIST
1160 Sam Rittenberg Blvd.   571-1660

Northbridge is located West of the Ashley and has morning and evening services as well as church school on Sunday. There is a prayer meeting and bible study on Wednesday night.

Baptist Independent

WEST ASHLEY INDEPENDENT
1376 Orange Grove Road   556-5378

On Sundays, there are usually two services, morning and evening, and a morning Bible class. Prayer meetings are held Wednesday nights.

Bible Church

CHARLESTON HARBOR BIBLE CHURCH
524 Arlington Drive   556-1443

This church is located near

Highways 17 South and 7. There are three services on Sundays (morning and evening), as well as one Wednesday evening. The message the church presents is: "Ye must be born again."

Catholic

BLESSED SACRAMENT CATHOLIC
5 St. Teresa Drive   556-0801

The architecture of this West Ashley church is very contemporary, featuring a high vaulted ceiling. Blessed Sacrament holds daily Mass on Monday through Friday and Confessions on Saturday and by appointment. On Saturday and Sunday there is morning and late afternoon Novena and Benediction.

THE CATHEDRAL OF
ST. JOHN THE BAPTIST
120 Broad Street   724-8395
at Legare Street

A focus of Catholicism in the diocese, the Cathedral is an impressive brick building which is in the block with offices and the Bishop's newly restored residence on Broad Street. There are Sunday and weekday Masses, Saturday vigil and confessions on Saturday and by appointment.

SACRED HEART CHURCH
888 King Street   722-2018

Sacred Heart is located at the corner of King and Huger Streets and has Masses on Saturday and Sunday. Confessions are Saturday afternoon. The Charleston Catholic School for the Arts and Sciences is adjacent to the church, and is the only Catholic school on the peninsula.

ST. MARY'S CHURCH
Hasell St.   722-7696
between Meeting and King St.

Being the oldest Catholic church in the state, St. Mary's — established in 1789 — has the Gothic charm of an old world church and an influential membership attracted to its attributes. The church is considered the Mother Church of the Carolinas and Georgia. Masses are held weekdays and twice Sunday, with Confession on Saturday and before masses. There are additional night services during Lent. The congregation supports the Crisis Ministry.

Photo: The Post and Courier

The Charleston skyline has more steeples than skyscrapers.

Traditional Catholic

HOLY FAMILY CHAPEL
1540 Savannah Highway   762-0003

This church follows the traditional Latin Mass, with Confession and Rosary before Mass. As far as we know, this is the only such group meeting in the Charleston area. It currently gathers at the Best Western Inn on Savannah Highway.

Christian

CENTRAL CHRISTIAN CHURCH
1740 Jervey Street   556-4201

Sunday school and worship service are held on Sunday at this West Ashley church, and a prayer meeting is held on Wednesday night. It is located near Orange Grove Road.

Christian Science

FIRST CHURCH OF CHRIST SCIENTIST
137 Moultrie Street   723-3217

There is a Sunday morning service and a Sunday School, as well as a Wednesday evening testimonial meeting at First Church of Christ, Scientist. The Reading Room is located at 1 Liberty Street (near the College of Charleston and King Street), and visitors are welcome. It is open every day except Sunday and holidays.

Church Of Christ

WEST ASHLEY CHURCH OF CHRIST
1744 Sam Rittenberg   769-5876

This church is located in the Windjammer Business Complex.

Bible classes are held Sunday morning and Wednesday evening, and a worship service is slated for Sunday morning and early evening. Video classes in Bible study are offered.

Congregational

CIRCULAR CONGREGATIONAL CHURCH
150 Meeting St.   577-6400

With about 200 members at present, the Circular Congregational Church was organized in 1681. The unique circular brick church at the present site was built in 1891 and gave Meeting Street its name for the "meeting house" that was built to house the congregation. It is credited with establishing the first Sunday School in South Carolina. Service is held on Sunday, with a Monday night study class. Members are involved as a church in such organizations as The Charleston Interfaith Crisis Ministry and Meals Charleston.

Episcopal

CATHEDRAL OF ST. LUKE AND ST. PAUL
126 Coming St.   722-7345

The Episcopal Cathedral of St. Luke and St. Paul is an impressive structure which was begun in 1811, five years after the congregation was formed. Holy Eucharist Rite I and Rite II are performed, and a Sunday School program is offered on the Sabbath.

GRACE EPISCOPAL CHURCH

98 Wentworth Street   *723-4575*

At first glance, Grace Church resembles a white sand drip castle with its spires and external detail. Built in the early 19th century, the church has been completely remodeled recently and the sanctuary and church school classrooms are exquisite. Located in the midst of College of Charleston activity, the Church draws those students and faculty as well as a diverse group of others from all directions. The annual Tea Room, during Spoleto, is a smashing success and generates income which is returned to the community. The church focuses attention on a complete Sunday School program and is involved in many outreach activities. Also outstanding is the music program — a magnet for many serious musicians.

HOLY TRINITY EPISCOPAL CHURCH

95 Folly Road   *766-7871*

Holy Trinity backs up to The Crescent subdivision and draws its congregation from many areas. Church services and Sunday School are held on Sundays, and Tuesday evening is Parish Bible Study. A Holy Eucharist is also performed on Thursday.

OLD ST. ANDREWS PARISH CHURCH

2604 Ashley River Road   *766-1541*

Built and established in 1706, this charming church with its azalea-covered graveyard is one of the treasures of West Ashley. Church school and services are held on Sunday, and a Holy Eucharist service is conducted on Wednesday. A tea room (serving traditional Lowcountry lunch fare — okra soup and the like) is a don't-miss in the spring.

THE EPISCOPAL CHURCH OF THE HOLY COMMUNION

218 Ashley Avenue   *722-2024*

This church has suffered severe hurricane and fire damage in recent years, but you would never know it. Founded in 1848, the impressive facility is in full operation with services every weekday, and three on Sundays.

ST. MICHAEL'S EPISCOPAL CHURCH

Meeting & Broad Streets   *723-0603*

Established in 1761, St. Michael's is Charleston's oldest church. Part of the Four Corners of Law, St. Michael's is frequently visited by tourists who admire the simple but elegant architecture and charm of the walled graveyard. St. Michael's has services on Sunday and a full Sunday School program, as well as a Holy Communion Service on Tuesday and Holy Communion and Healing Service on Thursday. With approximately 850 members, the church supports Meals on Wheels and the Crisis Ministry.

ST. PHILIPS EPISCOPAL CHURCH

142 Church St.   *722-7734*

St. Philips' present building was erected between 1835 and 1838. A handsome church with a pleasant mellowed look, it has an adjoining graveyard as well as one across the street. Services and Sunday School are held on Sunday morning, and on Wednesday Holy Eucharist is performed in the morning and at an evening service which features contemporary music. With about 840 families on the church roster, the church is involved extensively in outreach programs such as: Habitat for Humanity, Crisis Center, mission trips to undeveloped countries, an adoption program in Haiti and many others. Concerts are presented in Holy seasons.

ST. STEPHEN'S EPISCOPAL CHURCH
67 Anson St.   *723-8818*

St. Stephen's is located between Society and George Streets in Ansonborough. A family service is held on Sundays, as is a Sunday School program and adult Bible Study. Architecturally reminiscent of the simple churches of the Caribbean, St. Stephen's is perhaps Charleston's most integrated Episcopal church, with many members active in community volunteer services.

French Protestant

THE FRENCH PROTESTANT (HUGUENOT) CHURCH
Church and Queen Streets   *722-4385*

Established in 1687, this church (built between 1844 and 1845) has one service on Sunday and uses the Huguenot Liturgy of 1737 of Neufchattel and Vallangin — in English. It is the only independent Huguenot church in the United States and holds a special service in French during the spring to honor the French Huguenots who fled France to avoid persecution. There are approximately 450 members, with some "honorary" members who join the congregation periodically to enjoy the unique service. Outreach programs include HELP, My Sister's House and the Confederate Home.

Full Gospel

ABUNDANT LIFE CHURCH
1945 Bee's Ferry Road   *556-0634*

The congregation here describes itself as a "spirit-filled house of worship." In addition to Sunday services, there is a Wednesday night Bible study. Day care is available during the week, and the Christian Academy accepts students in grades K4 through seven.

Greek Orthodox

GREEK ORTHODOX CHURCH OF THE HOLY TRINITY
28 Race Street   *722-2331*

This parish was established more than 80 years ago, and has a diverse and active membership. Of the church's 400 family members, approximately 45% are not of Greek heritage. The church roster includes Protestant and Catholic converts, with some members who are of Russian, Serbian, Rumanian and even Slovak descent. The church building is an outstanding example of Byzantine design, and its award-winning stained glass windows and icons attract artists and other admirers from around the world. A regular morning service is held each Sunday at 11:00 AM (10:00 AM during the summer), and special services are held at other times.

Jehovah's Witness

KINGDOM HALL OF JEHOVAH'S WITNESSES
120 Brigade St.   *723-4790*

Biblical talks — open to the public — are held on Sunday morning. Theocratic Ministry School is conducted on Thursday evenings. Approximately 170 members have been worshipping here for nearly twenty years, and their strongest community outreach is a daily door-to-door ministry. This Kingdom Hall is located in the city, and can be contacted for information about other Jehovah's Witness programs in the area.

Lutheran

CALVARY LUTHERAN CHURCH
Missouri Synod, Hwy. 7   *766-3113*

Calvary is located across from Ashley Landing Mall, West Ashley, and has church school and services on Sunday as well as a worship service on Wednesday evening. It is described as a "Spirit-filled, liturgical church" and offers a prayer counseling service.

ST. ANDREWS LUTHERAN CHURCH
43 Wentworth   *723-2644*

This church was established in 1835 (across from what is now Kerrison's parking lot), and has church school classes as well as a worship service each Sunday. Communion is held the first Sunday of the month.

ST. JOHN'S LUTHERAN CHURCH
Corner Clifford & Archdale   *723-2426*

This historic church was established in 1759 and is located in the same block as Charleston Day School. There are two worship services and church school each Sunday. Holy Communion is offered the first Sunday of the month. Members are involved in outreach programs, and there is a prayer group on Monday night.

ST. MATTHEWS LUTHERAN CHURCH
405 King St.   *723-1611*

Across from the Charleston County Library and Marion Square, Saint Matthew's has church school as well as two Sunday services — the second of which is broadcast on WCSC, 1390 on the AM dial. Holy Communion is offered the first Sunday of the month and on Wednesdays. Many of the approximately 1700 members are involved in such outreach programs as the Franke Home and the Interfaith Crisis Ministry. The building was erected in 1965, after the original (established in 1840) was destroyed by fire.

Methodist

BETHEL UNITED METHODIST CHURCH
57 Pitt St.   *723-4587*

Fronting on Pitt Street and bordered by Calhoun, Bethel United Methodist was established as a congregation in 1797. The church has regular Sunday services and programs as well as a Thursday worship service. There is a handicap ramp and parking spaces.

OLD BETHEL METHODIST CHURCH
222 Calhoun Street   *722-3470*

Old Bethel Methodist was established in 1798, and the present church was erected in 1852. It is a small wooden structure behind a wrought-iron fence. Services are held on Sundays and a Bible study is held Wednesday evening. The congregation includes approximately 214 members.

TRINITY UNITED METHODIST CHURCH
273 Meeting St.   *722-8449*

This is Charleston's oldest Methodist congregation. Visitors will not forget Trinity's remarkable ornate wooden doors. Church school and worship service are held on Sunday, and there is an elevator located at the rear of the church for the physically impaired. Children are intrigued by the creche out front during the Christmas season.

JOHN WESLEY UNITED METHODIST CHURCH
626 Savannah Hwy.   *766-5596*

Established in 1945, this impressive red brick church is the largest Methodist Church in the West Ashley area. Eucharist service is held the first Sunday of the month, and there is a regular Sunday school program. The choir features many concerts (with English handbells) during holy seasons.

Mormon

CHURCH OF JESUS CHRIST OF LATTER DAY SAINTS
1519 Sam Rittenberg Blvd.   *571-2357*

This church is located West of the Ashley and houses two congregations with approximately 3000 members who live in the Trident area. They meet at the Stake Center on Sunday for an education program, the Priesthood meeting, the Relief Society and a sacrament service. Youth services for ages 12-18 are held Tuesday and Wednesday nights and the church is very involved in Boy Scouts.

Nazarene

CHURCH OF THE NAZARENE
Hwy. 61 & Ashley Hall Rd.   *556-1866*

This church has Sunday services, morning and evening, as well as a Christian education program. There is a midweek service on Wednesday as well as teen and children's meetings during the week.

Nondenominational

CHRIST'S CHURCH OF CHARLESTON
172 Rutledge Avenue   *556-2254*

This church meets at Ashley Hall School on Rutledge Avenue. There is a Sunday morning worship service as well as weekly CARE group meetings.

ECKANKAR
849-1734

This nondenominational group was established in 1990 and its approximately 40 members focus on "an individual path to God." Services are held twice a month, with weekly study sessions, but there is no specific place of worship. They describe the religion as one "of the light and sound of God."

Presbyterian

FIRST (SCOTS) PRESBYTERIAN CHURCH
53 Meeting St.   722-8882

Established in 1731, the First (Scots) Presbyterian congregation was formed by immigrants who refused to join the Anglican Church. They nobly gave their church bells to the Confederacy, and have never replaced them. Approximately 1500 members are on the rolls, and some are involved in such outreach programs as the Crisis Ministry. The early service is broadcast on Channel 2.

ST. ANDREWS PRESBYTERIAN CHURCH
712 Wappoo Rd.
766-4262

This church is located across from St. Andrews High School, West Ashley. Church school and service are

held Sunday morning, and there is wheelchair access. A weekday kindergarten is open to children ages three, four and five.

THE SECOND PRESBYTERIAN CHURCH
Meeting Street at Charlotte   723-9237

Second Presbyterian is situated at the back of a long lot fronting Meeting Street. A massive white church (built in 1849) with wonderful facilities, it holds Sunday service and Sunday school. Assistive listening devices are available and there is wheelchair access. A fellowship hour follows the morning worship service. The church works with Habitat for Humanity and Charleston Interfaith Crisis Ministry, as well

Photo: The Post and Courier

St. Philip's Episcopal Church.

as rural missions. There is a weekday kindergarten affiliated with the school.

Synagogues

BRITH SHOLOM BETH ISRAEL ORTHODOX CONGREGATION
182 Rutledge Ave.   *577-6599*

Established in 1854, this synagogue today consists of around 340 families. In addition to services on Friday evening, morning services are held daily. Children in kindergarten through grade eight attend the well-respected affiliate school, Addlestone Hebrew Academy.

KAHAL KADOSH BETH ELOHIM
86 Hasell St.   *723-1090*

This synagogue was organized in 1749, and is believed to be the oldest synagogue in continuous use in the United States. In fact, according to synagogue records, it is the oldest surviving Reform Synagogue in the world. Drop by for a tour during the week, or call the office for more information. Services are held Friday evening and Saturday morning.

SYNAGOGUE EMANUEL CONSERVATIVE CONGREGATION
5 Windsor Dr.   *571-3264*

This synagogue was founded in 1947 and holds services on Friday evenings and Saturday and Sunday mornings. There are also daily morning services. Members are active in the Interfaith Crisis Ministry and other organizations.

Unitarian Universalist

UNITARIAN CHURCH
8 Archdale St.   *723-4617*

The Unitarian Church has a Sunday service and church school, as well as forums held twice a month in the adjoining Gage Hall. There is a coffee house on Friday. Members are involved in such work as the Crisis Ministry and James Island Outreach.

Photo: Janice G. Vermillion

Shrimp boats lined up along Shem Creek in Mt. Pleasant.

Mount Pleasant
History

*P*eople have been drawn to Mt. Pleasant since the 17th century, when the lands east of the Cooper River were wild and uninhabited. It was in 1680 that a large parcel of the land — now Mt. Pleasant — was granted to Florentia O'Sullivan. Eventually houses were built in the area that is called the Old Village by island planters who, over the next century, enjoyed resort life in this peaceful community.

Located several miles down what is now Highway 17 North, Snee Farm was built as the home of Charles Pinckney, who helped frame the Constitution, and was visited by George Washington in 1791.

Mt. Pleasant was incorporated as a town in 1837, and is said to have drawn its acreage from two villages as well as former plantations on Haddrell's Point. Part of this land was once the property of Andrew Hibben, after whom a village street is named.

Just before the Civil War, residents met at Renken's Long Room, near the old ferry wharf, and decided to follow Charleston's lead in advocating secession. Later, during the hard times of Reconstruction, industrious members of this community enjoyed intellectual stimulation from a night school and a debating society.

The local economy was based on farming for about a century, and Mount Pleasant vegetables were reputed to be some of the best in the county. The Old Village was an important linkage to the mainland and to the islands. When mail was transported from the North, down the former King's Highway, it was brought to Haddrell's Point and then carried over to Charleston on ferry boat. Trolley tracks ran from the south end of Pitt Street to Sullivans Island, transporting people and goods across what is now the Intracoastal Waterway.

When a bridge spanning the Cooper River opened in 1929, it changed the profile of Mt. Pleasant forever. Shrimping became an important industry in the 1940s, and the setting of picturesque Shem Creek — with commercial shrimp boats and restaurants enlivening the docks — became a major attraction.

Although some travelers, then and now, just "pass through" Mt. Pleasant on their way to the islands or north, a large percentage make the town at large their destination. Real estate development in this community is fast-paced, but there is an attempt to control its quality and assure a pleasing blend of progress and charm. From the heart of the Old Village, to the new subdivisions off Highway 17 North, through the Francis Marion National Forest — still scarred by the ravages of Hurricane Hugo — up to the old fishing village of McClellanville, Mount Pleasant and the outskirts reflect multilayered serenity which is the beauty and consequence of being part of the Lowcountry.

A Look At McClellanville

No discussion of Mt. Pleasant's outer reaches would be complete without reference to historic St. James Santee Parish, and the charming village of McClellanville. The second oldest parish in the state, St. James Santee was first settled by the French Huguenots in the late 17th century. Later, the English and the Scots arrived as well.

Many important families and chapters in southern history evolved in these woods and waterways. Thomas Lynch and Thomas Lynch, Jr., signers of the Declaration of Independence, lived here. General Francis Marion, "The Swamp Fox," and later Cornwallis set up headquarters in the area. And Rebecca Motte, the Vanderhorst family, Daniel Huger and Gabriel Manigault — all prominent Lowcountry citizens — had plantations or property in St. James parish.

McClellanville, on Jeremy Creek, was part of a tract granted in 1705 to John Whilden, an ancestor of the McClellans. It changed hands several times (a Thomas Lynch having been the owner at one point) before Archibald McClellan bought 1,332 acres in 1850.

McClellan and William Matthews owned much of the area from which the town evolved until R.T. Morrison — the owner of Laurel Hill Plantation (see Mt. Pleasant Accommodations section) — bought Matthew's property. South Santee planters began buying lots, and the village became a summer retreat after the Civil War. Morrison subdivided his portion throughout the 19th century, and gave lots to members of his large family.

For years the people of McClellanville — separated from the rest of the Lowcountry by unpaved roads and an often-flooded causeway — preserved the "village life" concept. There were attempts, however, to make some changes. Sure that his community would enjoy economic prosperity if not so isolated, H. T. Morrison worked to bring modernizations and make the village more accessible. The town was officially incorporated in 1926, and the Cooper River bridge was completed three years later. Enthusiastic about the possibilities, Morrison said: "There is no place of like size to which the Cooper River bridge means as much as it does to McClellanville."

While the bridge and improved road system made the journey north and south easier, but it did not bring the kind of "progress" that could have changed the personality of this town. With lovely homes and shaded streets, McClellanville was a Victorian, storybook village until Hurricane Hugo dealt its blow in 1989. Today, with flowers replanted behind picket fences and reconstruction complete in most areas, McClellanville — although changed — is again a remarkable escape from the pace of the mainstream. (See our Daytrip section for more information on McClellanville.)

Mount Pleasant
Shopping

Mt. Pleasant is a shopper's paradise if you know where to venture. We have reviewed shopping along the two main routes: Coleman Boulevard and Highway 17 North. These are shops with which we are familiar — others exist and more are opening each day, so have fun.

Coleman Boulevard

If you veer to the right when you leave the Cooper River Bridge, you will be driving on Coleman Boulevard. The first shopping center on the left is **Northcutt Plaza**. The stores are grouped into two sections, with separate parking lots. In the first, there is a **Baskin-Robbins**

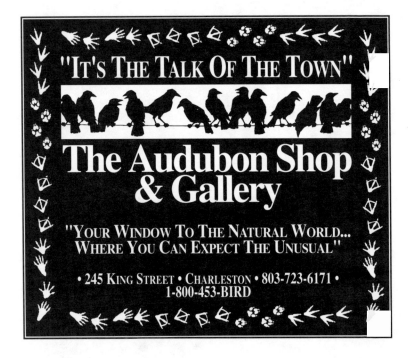

— this one equipped with a drive-up window. **East Bay Gallery** sells unusual selection of items crafted by more than 400 artists around the nation (see King Street shop description). The kids love peeking in the window of **Cookie Bouquet**, which has baskets full of cookies on sticks — an edible way to get the message across. And adults can't resist **Just Cheesecakes**, which sells every conceivable flavor of cheesecake (we warn you, don't walk in unless you plan to indulge because you won't be able to leave without some tasty treat). **'Tis The Season** stocks fun gift items with holiday themes, from Santa Clause to the Easter Bunny. **Uniforms Unique** defies stereotypical, bland uniforms with designer lines for the ladies in white. **The Total Look** is an unusual clothing boutique in that it is also a salon. Our favorite toy store is in this group: **Wonderworks**, a collection of nature and science learning toys, caters to the young and young-at-heart. From a six-foot pinwheel, to a giant Bausch and Lomb telescope or 12-room redwood martin house, these quality nifties are made to amaze and to last. Fashionable kids have their bangs clipped at **Hairbears**, and the selection of hair accessories is good. Next door, tucked into a corner, is **Wallpapers for Mt. Pleasant**, which carries a large selection of in stock wallcoverings at great prices. They feature Waverly patterns in stock, as well as many other name brands. If you are interested in discounted designer fabric and accessories, try **Fabrics, Etc.** which stocks a wide selection and can order others. The

shop has a fabric laminating service, and the staff is qualified to give helpful design advice. **Kid Stuf** carries traditional clothing for preemies to preteens — lots of smocked outfits and coordinated sibling attire. There is also a selection of mother-daughter outfits. **M.J.'s** is a clothing store for men which carries upscale, casual sportswear. Another boutique for women is **Betty Anne's**, which offers eye-catching fashions and lines like Balenciaga of Paris. **Phillips Shoes** (see West Ashley shopping for another store in this chain) sells casual (like Rockport) and dress (like Aigner) shoes for men, women and children.

In the second section of this center, **TCBY Yogurt** offers delicious frozen treats. **Carpentier's Wine and Cheese** sells a nice selection of fine wines, gourmet foods and coffees, and has a deli (see Mt. Pleasant Restaurants). **Pete Banis Shoes** sells upscale lines of shoes for women (see Citadel Mall store), and **Pets N Us** caters to the product needs of all kinds of pets. For designer clothes at a great reduction from the initial cost, try **The Trunk Show** — a consignment shop selling gently worn designer clothing. **Extra Special** is a boutique selling fashionable clothing — from sportswear to mother of the bride — for women in sizes 12 to 52. **The Copper Penny** sells comfortable, fashionable clothes for women. **Pac Mail** (see West Ashley and downtown stores also) ships anything — from art to computers and even furniture — anywhere, and has mailboxes for rent as well as postal services, printing and greeting cards. **Tunes** has a wide selection of CD's and tapes, favorites of our "30-something" crowd. **Polly's Jewelry** is a source for diamonds, gold and watches, and you can have jewelry designed or repaired on the premises (see the other locations in the Shopping chapters of Charleston and North Charleston).

The next grouping, in buildings made to look like a quaint neighborhood of dormer-windowed, columned houses, are **The Shops of Mount Pleasant**. We have brave friends who have rented or bought Roller Blades from **Vans and Stuff Sk8 Shop**, which also sells skateboard equipment. **Fashion Fabrics**, a Bernina dealer, is one of the nicest cloth stores in the area. The shop also sells exquisite sewing accessories such as lace and unusual buttons.

Those who are interested in "things feminine" will find lingerie by such names as Oscar de la Renta, Linda and Felina at **Chantilly Lingerie**. **Jerry Bridges'** photography studio is here as is **Snyders** — custom jewelers who also appraise jewelry and repair watches.

At the **Peach Orchard Plaza**, we shop for health food, teas, cosmetics, and bath products at **The Good Neighbor Health Food** store.

Cross the Shem Creek Bridge to find a small center on the right with **Shem Creek Bike Center**, selling lines like Schwinn, Diamond Back, and BMX. They have bike rentals, clothing and accessories as well. Next door is **Ben Franklin Print and Post** — a full service print and postal shop with reasonable rates.

At 307 Mill Street is **The Pet Vet**: not only a vet, but also a shop catering to all kinds of pet needs and stocking animal greeting cards. Across Coleman Boulevard, on Mill Street, are several shops worth noting. **The Scratch Pad** sells an outstanding assortment of quality paper goods and gorgeous invitations and gifts, while **The Frame Shop** carries prints and frame supplies (with framing service available as well). Stop in **The Common Market** for handsome gifts, or **The Fifth Season** to see its extensive collection — literally rooms and rooms full — of beautiful home accessories (including lamps, rugs, artwork, candles, furniture and heavy brass fixtures). Accessible from Mill Street and Coleman Boulevard is a wonderful cluster of shops at **The Common**. Some of the businesses — each with a distinct facade — open onto the parking lot (visible from the street), but most face the secluded, grassy courtyard or "common." For reading needs, locals shop the **Bookbag**. Four children's shops are especially appealing: **Radical Rags**, fashions for boys and girls, sizes 7 to 14; **Stride Rite**, shoes and socks; **The Ragamuffin**, classic clothes for infants and children; and **Hollipops**, a top-of-the-line shop featuring the most exclusive toy lines (such as Briar, Gund, and Brio) and allowing "hands on" inspection by children.

Facing the courtyard, shops include **The Crystal Hutch**, with crystal gifts and collectibles; **Once Upon A Time** (see the Antiques chapter); **Museum Collections**, charming reproductions from such places as Williamsburg, Winterthur, Historic Charleston, Monticello, Historic Newport, Smithsonian, Historic Savannah, Old Salem, and the Henry Ford Museum; **Eden's Garden Shop**, from bird baths to planters, objects to enhance the garden; **Kids Kuts**, for children's hair cuts and styling; **The Country Bumpkin**, a gift shop with lovely Christmas ornaments, handmade jewelry, hair accessories and even craft classes; **The Batter's Box**, selling sports cards; **The Picture Show**, a collection of market samples, statues, replicas and museum sketches (wood-carver Jim Doss demonstrates his craft here on the weekends); **Flotsam and Jetsam**, art objects such as wreathes made by the owner from things that wash up on our beaches, as well as baskets made by Seminole Indians and other unique crafts. In Suite M, **Konsignment Kollection** is an upscale resale shop for men, women and children. Inventory includes career, casual, sports and "after five" wear for men and women, and clothes for infants to preteens.

At the bend of Coleman Boulevard, stop by **Mrs. Capper's Plants-N-Things**. Her green thumb shows through in what she sells for the garden as well as her house plants, and every year — just before spring — she comes up with the planters and garden objects everyone wants.

Heading off to the right, sidetrack on an excursion into the **Old Village**. The first stop is **Growing Children** and **Victoria's** on Hibben Street. These are consignment shops under the same roof, selling gently worn clothes. The former carries sizes infant through 20 for boys and infant through preteen for girls. The garments are often smocked, and sometimes are brands like Paper White. Victoria's carries clothing for the mother-to-be.

On Pitt Street, in the heart of the village, see **Tomorrow's Treasures** for unusual consignment antiques including furniture, linens, china and some jewelry, and **Complements** for stained glass and similar treasures. Don't miss the **Pitt Street Pharmacy** for a soda and sandwich from its old fashioned soda fountain — this is a real, deliver-your-order-to-your-door operation, where everyone is treated like family.

Back out on Coleman Boulevard, **Randy's Hobby Shop** sells kites and other equipment for hobby building. On the left, in **Moultrie Shopping Center**, see **Tuesday Morning** — a store that sells closeouts — and **Heath Farms Fresh Produce** (put your name on *the list* for shelled lima beans, and try the lemon chewies, sourdough bread or some boiled peanuts for the road).

Across the street and down a few blocks on the right (where Coleman Boulevard turns into Ben Sawyer Boulevard), see **Royall Hardware** — an impressive facility with practically everything imaginable for maintaining houses and yards — and **Hadrell's Point Tackle and Supply**, which sells the right equipment for crabbing and sport fishing — surf, jetty, reef, blue water and even coastal.

There is a **Belk** department store and an **Eckerd** drugstore in the **Sea Island Shopping Center**, as well as **Memory Lane Card and Gift Shop**, a shop with interesting cards, gifts and prints.

Our favorite island wear spot for fun, casual clothing is **Sailsports** — a shop that also is a mecca for windsurfing enthusiasts. Down the street at 1460 Ben Sawyer Boulevard, situated in a large, barn-like building, **Pages Thieves Market** is a must for those who enjoy browsing in secondhand/antique furniture shops. Don't miss the old wagon and flock of feathered friends out back — children are intrigued.

The Bypass — Highway 17 North

Following the bypass off the Cooper River Bridge, the first shopping center is **Village Pointe**. There is an **Affordables** with women's apparel (see the other Affordables in the Charleston Shopping chapter); the **Little Professor Book Center**, Mt. Pleasant's source for a wide selection of books, including children's books, newspapers and magazines (gift wrapping is complimentary); **Concepts**, a boutique for juniors and women carrying lines like Ivy, Chu and Lauren Ember; **Cindy's Closet**, clothes for infant through preteen girls, and up to size seven boys; **Cinnamon Tree**, a gift shop selling candles, sachets, collectibles (like David Winter cottages); a particularly civilized **Harris Teeter** grocery store; **Eckerd Drug**; and the new location of **Gwynn's**. This expansive store, formerly located in the Moultrie Shopping Center, has departments for men, women, children, shoes and

gifts — all top flight and in great taste.

Across Houston Northcutt Boulevard, **Patriots Plaza** has a variety of businesses including some of our picks: **Diane's Hallmark**, with cards, wrapping products and other Hallmark merchandise; **Green Lion Gifts**, an exceptional gift shop that carries Ms. Noah's Animals, beautiful dolls and jewelry, as well as engraved sterling silver and pewter items; a **Bookbag**; **The Magic Shop**, with magic trick supplies as well as great gag gifts; **Loy Harn Jewelers**, a small but unique shop, with services of a jewelry repair specialist; the **Mount Pleasant Factory Outlet**, brand name women's clothing at outlet prices; **Carolina Outdoors**, a shop that clothes men and women elegantly for fun outside; and **Alterman's Color Lab**, a photography studio/processing business run by professionals who produce quality work.

Heading north on Highway 17 South, you will see **East Cooper Plaza** on the right. Among the businesses, there are a branch of **Huguley's** for office supplies and attractive gifts (see Charleston Shopping); an **Eckerd** drugstore; a **Piggly Wiggly** grocery store that has family-pleasing, take out dinners; a **Wal-Mart** discount store; and **Stagecoach**, which sells men's and women's conservative, casual clothing.

On the left, see **Lafayette Village** and **Replay Sports Consignment** — a shop that specializes in racket stringing and club gripping. In the same group, **Jean's Bridal and Formal Wear** carries good lines of wedding attire and accessories for the bridal family, as well as formal dresses for very dressy occasions.

The **Fairmont Center**, on the right, is home to a very large **Danco**, a Scandinavian furniture store, **Kitchens By Design**, and **Nostalgia Antiques** (see the Antiques chapter). Next door, in the **Anna Knapp Plaza**, check out **Easy Rider Bikes** for brands like Earth Cruiser, Bolle and Nishiki. If you want information about the local biking scene or just advice on getting started, these are the people to see.

Skatell's Manufacturing Jewelers is located on the left, at 1036 Johnnie Dodds Boulevard, and sells a lovely selection of jewelry. Skatell's can also make jewelry to your specifications.

On the right again, **Crickentree Village** is a collection of shops and businesses such as **The Match Box**, a reasonably priced gift shop with candles, holiday ornaments, baby gifts and more; **Hewson's Cabbage Patch**, a maternity shop with clothes so fashionable the non-expecting crowd looks twice; and **Chuck Campbell's Wallpapers and Window Blinds**, a discount store with a huge selection and fair prices. (We love the easy-to-see displays and big, take-home samples.)

Across the highway, **Havens Picture Frames** (1070 Johnny Dodds Boulevard) is a popular spot for custom framing or custom frame-it-yourself. (If you have never framed anything, fear not: the employees are very helpful.)

Around the bend in the highway, at 1460 Highway 17 North,

Abide A While Nursery and Garden Center is set back on the left — acres of gorgeous flowers, plants, trees and herbs, as well as an exceptional assortment of vessels in which to grow them. There are bird baths, bird houses and an assortment of fertilizers and insect deterrents. Take one of their little shopper's wagons and wander about making selections; better yet, find one of the Donaldsons — the owners who have been in this business for years — and get some professional advice.

Across the highway is **Wando Crossing** — a relatively new center which includes a **Lowe's** hardware store and a **TJ Maxx**.

Golf enthusiasts should visit **The Golf Shack Corp**. This shop was honored as one of "America's 100 Best Golf Shops" in 1991 and has a complete selection of irons, woods, wedges, putters, clothes and accessories, as well as a full-service repair department.

Heading north toward Awendaw and McClellanville, you cannot help but notice the Basket Ladies who sell their wares from displays on the side of the road (see the African-American Heritage chapter). Look also for **A.B. McConnel General Merchandise** — a quaint, old-fashioned one-stop shop selling the essentials — and **Laurel Hill Plantation**, a charming bed and breakfast which also sells antiques, folk art and gifts.

At the turnoff for McClellanville, see **Bull's Bay Supply** — a large, attractive new True Value hardware and lumber center.

Mount Pleasant
Restaurants

*F*rom Creole to Italian, health-food to junk food, there is an abundance of restaurants in Mt. Pleasant to suit. Here, we highlight some of our favorites, whether they fall into that category for their food, atmosphere, staff, or all of those qualities combined. Remember, this list is not exhaustive, and if we've left your favorite out, let us know! Maybe we just haven't found it yet, but will be pleased to do so and will include them in our updated book.

Although prices change, use this scale as a guide to the cost of entrées at restaurants in the Mt. Pleasant area:

Under $10	$
$10-$15	$$
$16-$20	$$$
$21 and up	$$$$

Happy eating!

ACME Bar and Grill
413 Coleman Blvd.   884-1949
$ M, V, AX

ACME serves tasty pub food in a small, intimate setting. Look for the tiny lights around the deck on Coleman Boulevard, and grab a table outside or in the main room. Hours are 11:00 AM until 3:00 PM, for lunch, and 5:00 PM until 10:00 PM for dinner, Monday through Saturday. Sunday hours are noon until 4:00 PM.

Alex's Restaurant
506 Coleman Boulevard   884-9125
$ MC, V

Open 24 hours a day, this Alex's is a popular spot for breakfast on the way to the beach or a late night meal on the way home. Recently, the Sunday lunch crowd is thick as well. The new facility is large and attractive, and we like to order standard eggs and bacon — you can't miss.

Backstage Deli
900 Houston Northcutt Blvd.   881-7814
$ MC, V, AX, D

Positioned in front of the Northcutt shopping center, this deli is a good spot for sandwiches, salads and homemade soups. Beer and wine as well as limited hard liquor are available, and the crowd tends to span the ages. Hours are 11:00 AM until 9:00 PM, Monday through Wednesday, 11:00 AM until 10:00 PM, Thursday and Saturday, and 11:00 AM until 8:00 PM on Sunday.

Bailey's Seafood and Spirits
410 Mill Street   856-9376
$-$$ MC, V, D

Bailey's, with its great views of Shem Creek, offers a full menu with an emphasis on seafood. Crabs (boiled or fried), shrimp and lobster tails are our favorites. Hours are 11:00 AM until 4:00 PM, Monday through Friday, for lunch, and 9:00 AM until 2:00 PM, on Saturday and Sunday, for brunch. Dinner is served Monday through Thursday, 5:00 PM until 10:00 PM, and until 11:00 PM on Friday and Saturday. The lounge has a Happy Hour from 4:00 PM until 6:00 PM.

CAPTAIN GUILD'S CAFE
101 Pitt Street   884-7009
$-$$ *V, MC, AX*

One of our favorites for lunch or dinner, Captain Guild's Cafe ranks high for an atmosphere that is charming and food that is delicious. Nestled in the heart of the Old Village of Mt. Pleasant, the cafe is picture perfect — just what you expect in a residential village where all but a few hints of commercialism are kept at bay. There are tables on the sidewalk for dining as well as indoor seating. The chalkboard menu lists the day's specials — things like chicken or shrimp salad, spinach salad, stuffed baked potato, shrimp fritters, corn fritters — and the list goes on. Our favorites for dinner include leg of lamb, duck and fresh fish. Lunch is served from 11:30 AM until 2:30 PM, and dinner from 6:00 AM until 10:00 PM, Tuesday through Saturday. Sunday brunch is available from 10:00 AM until 2:00 PM.

CARPENTIER'S FINE WINE AND CHEESE
Northcutt Plaza   884-9386
$ *MC, V, D*

Insiders know about the deli at Carpenter's — a gourmet's delight. Choose from meats and European breads and cheeses, homemade pate, as well as daily specials. The distinctive aroma of roasted coffee and store-baked cookies and pastries fills the air. There is a limited selection of imported beer and fine wines, and a few, small tables for dining. Hours are 9:00 AM until 6:00 PM.

CATCH AND COW
508 Mill Street   884-8103
$$$ *MC, V, AX*

The Catch and Cow features, as one might expect, prime seafood and prime beef cooked to perfection. Owned by John and Angie Avinger, locals who understand the Southern formula for good times and good food (see Shem Creek Bar and Grill, next door, and The One Eyed Parrot and Banana Cabana, on the Isle of Palms — three other Avinger achievements), Catch and Cow offers great views to go with the food.

CHARLESTON CHICKEN
Anna Knapp Plaza
1039 Johnnie Dodds Boulevard   881-8646
$-$$ *V, MC*

Described by the owner as "fine dining to go," Charleston Chicken is a wonderful alternative to standing over the hot stove. You still provide the atmosphere and get the credit from your family or a larger crowd when you pick up marinated rotisserie chicken (which comes with two side dishes and a choice of delicious corn bread or biscuit), side dishes (like our favorite: squash casserole), salads and even baked goods. There is a special catering menu that includes gourmet items for special occasions. Charleston Chicken is open Monday through Friday, 11:00 AM until 8:30 PM, and Saturday, from 12:00 noon until 7:00 PM.

COMMON SEASON

The Common, 217 Lucas Street   881-0770
$-$$$ MC, V, D

There is something warm and cozy about the Common Season — maybe it is the unpainted wood interior, or maybe the regulars who pack the place for lunch and dinner. Located on the "common," in the shopping area of that name, the chef whips up wonderful, local delicacies such as shad roe and gumbo with a sort of California twist. The menu is expansive, and is best described as American cuisine. Those who knew this restaurant/bar as The Common Ground, will find the new establishment still casual but with the option of a formal (white tablecloth) dining room as well. The retail shop opens at 10:00 AM and sells homemade desserts, cheeses, pickles and relishes, and even meats. Hours for lunch are 11:30 AM until 3:00 PM, Monday through Saturday, and for dinner, 5:30 PM through 9:00 PM, Tuesday through Saturday.

THE CRAB POT

10024 Highway 17 North,   887-3156
McClellanville
$-$$ MC, V

Charlestonians sometimes make the 30-minute drive to McClellanville just to eat at The Crabpot. We believe — and we are not alone — that there are no oysters in the world to compare with those pulled from these waters. The Crabpot prepares them and the other seafood it serves the way we like it: plain and simple. Such is the ambiance of the place, so don't dress up, but do come hungry. The menu features such Lowcountry items as crab cakes, shrimp creole, sauteed shrimp and grits, clam strips, seafood chowder and crab dip, as well as fried chicken, hamburgers and salads. Hours are Tuesday through Saturday from 11:30 AM until 10:00 PM, Monday from 11:30 AM until 3:00 PM, and Sunday from 11:30 AM until 3:00 PM.

EAST SIDE BAKERY

Crickentree Village   881-1260
$ No credit cards

East Side serves homemade pastries to eat in or take out, and some delicious and healthy lunch items (salads and sandwiches). Continental breakfast is served from 7:00 AM until 10:`30 AM, Monday through Friday, and lunch is served from 11:00 AM until 3:00 PM, Monday through Friday.

FISH AND SHRIMP HOUSE

409 Coleman Boulevard   884-0880
$ V, MC

This is a good place for fast service Chinese food. Although you can dine in, we generally order Moo Goo Gai Pan or fried fish (in a light tempera-like batter) to go. The restaurant is open from 11:30 AM until 9:00 PM, Monday through Friday, and 11:00 AM until 10:00 PM on Saturday.

FONDUELY YOURS

853 Coleman Boulevard   849-6859
$$ AX, DC, MC, V

It is safe to say that Fonduely Yours is one-of-a-kind in this area. As the name suggests, this restaurant specializes in fondues. Try cheese, vegetable, seafood, teriyaki sirloin, and — even chocolate for dessert. The food is tasty, and the whole concept is lots of fun. Dinner is served Sunday through Thursday from 5:30 PM until 10:30 PM, and Friday and Saturday from 5:30 PM until 11:00 PM.

GOURMET BLEND

354 West Coleman Blvd.   849-8949
$ No credit cards

For a delightful treat, try Gourmet Blend which serves salads (sometimes shrimp), sandwiches, muffins and the like as well as a large selection of fresh brewed coffees and teas. One exciting plus is that Gourmet Blend has a drive through window. Hours are Monday through Friday, 6:00 AM until 5:00 PM; Saturday from 7:00 AM until 4:00 PM; and on Sunday from 7:30 AM until 1:30 PM.

HUCK FIN'S RESTAURANT

130 Mill Street   849-8824
$$$ Most credit cards

Huck Fin's serves seafood caught by their own boat, and has beef on the menu as well. There is outside dining, and a menu for the kids. Hours are 11:00 AM until 2:00 AM.

JAY'S DELI

Patriot's Plaza   884-7579
$ MC, V, AX

This is a great place to grab a deli sandwich, or sample one of the daily specials. The atmosphere is casual, and the prices are reasonable. Try our favorite sandwich; mozzarella cheese, cream cheese, peppers, tomatoes, sprouts and onions — grilled and delicious.

JIMMY LOU'S

819 Coleman Boulevard   884-5052
$$-$$$ V, MC, D

This is one of Mt. Pleasant's more stylish restaurants. The seafood is fresh and a jazz pianist entertains on weekends. A diverse assort-

---

Insiders Like:
Beaufort Stew (sausage, corn-on-the-cob and shrimp all cooked together).

Insiders' Tip

ment of house specialties includes oven roasted duckling, filet mignon, blackened tile and rainbow trout. Hours are Tuesday through Friday, 5:30 PM until 10:30, and Saturday from 5:30 PM until 11 PM.

JOSIE JOE'S
1313 Shrimp Boat Lane   881-8671
$-$$ V, MC, AX

Josie Joe's has become quite an evening destination for the singles set, but also a restaurant with appeal for all age groups. The menu is free running — from prime rib, to pasta, to fried creek shrimp — and everything comes with a salad, potato or rice and a vegetable. Blue plate specials include items like southern fried catfish, fried veal cutlet over gravy and grilled ham and turkey sandwich, and the salad bar stretches to eternity. Lunch is served from 11:30 AM until 3:30 PM, and dinner is served from 4:30 PM until 10:30 PM every day.

LA TASHA'S CREOLE RESTAURANT
626 Coleman Boulevard   884-0770
$$ V, MC

For a creole meal like from the kitchen of our cajun friends who live around New Iberia, Louisiana, come — dressed casually — to La Tasha's. Order creole shrimp, egg rolls, etouffé, or jambalaya: in short, whatever is being served that night. There is a huge cooler of beer in the back of the restaurant, and big portions of whatever you choose to eat. Plan to settle in, eat well and have some fun. Lunch is from 11:00 AM until 2:00 PM., Monday through Friday, and only dinner is served on Saturday, from 5:00 PM until 10:00 PM.

LOCKLEAR'S
427 Coleman Boulevard   884-3346
$-$$ AX, D, DC, MC, V

It did not surprise us when we heard that Locklear's was voted best value for local seafood in a recent poll. We've known that secret for years, but also rate the chicken salad plate as top of the line. Lunch is served Monday through Saturday from 11:30 AM until 2:30 PM, and dinner on Monday through Thursday from 5:30 to 10 PM, and on Friday and Saturday until 11:00 PM. Sunday hours are from 12 noon to 9:00 PM.

MELVIN'S SOUTHERN BARBECUE
925 Houston Northcutt Blvd.   881-0549
$ V, MC, AX

The delicious barbecue, cole slaw, onion rings, hamburgers and (even!) vegetables at Melvin's make it a good bet for a quick meal. The prices are quite reasonable, too. The restaurant is open from 10:30 AM until 9:30 PM every day.

PAGODA CHINESE RESTAURANT
Fairmont Plaza   884-8665
1035 Johnnie Dodds Blvd.
$ MC, V, AX, D

When the craving for Hunan, Szechuan or Cantonese food has us scampering for our chop sticks, Pagoda is one of our choices. Each order is individually cooked, and the servings are large. We are crazy about the chicken cashew — big chunks of the bird, loaded with nuts — and think the egg rolls have real substance. Hours are 11:30 AM until 3:00 PM for lunch, and 5:00 PM until 9:30 PM for dinner, seven days a week.

PORTABELLO'S

Northcutt Plaza   881-7733
$$ MC, V, AX

Mount Pleasant's Italian restaurant, Portabello serves wonderful homemade pasta and is a casual dining experience. Hours are Monday through Saturday, 11:00 AM until 3:00 PM, for lunch, and Monday through Friday, 5:00 PM until 10:00 PM and Friday and Saturday, 5:00 PM until 11:00 PM for dinner.

R.B.'S SEAFOOD RESTAURANT AND RAW BAR

On Shem Creek   881-0466
$-$$$ AX, V, MC

Another casual spot where diners get the view of the creek, R.B.'s serves oysters, scallops, fish and shrimp as well as landlubber fare like hamburgers. Lunch is served from 11:30 AM until 4:30 PM, and dinner from 4:30 PM until 10:30 PM daily.

RONNIE'S

I Shrimp Boat Lane   884-4074
$$ AX, MC, V

Ronnie's is an upscale restaurant on the creek, where specialties include local seafood as well as Maine lobsters and king crabs. The kids love to watch those crustaceans swim in the giant tank, and adults park themselves, if possible, at a table next to the window for a view of the shrimp boats. Dinner is served Monday through Saturday, from 5:00 PM until 10:30 PM, and on Sunday from 12 noon until 9:00 PM.

SHEM CREEK BAR & GRILL

508 Mill Street   884-8102
$$-$$$ MC, V

To experience eating out the way the locals do it, go to Shem Creek Bar and Grill (affectionately dubbed just "Shem Creek" by the regulars) and find yourself surrounded by them. The menu has something for everyone — from hamburgers to grilled seafood specials — and the raw bar is always a temptation. In the warmer months, it is *the* hangout for an extended boating set who arrive on power boats. There is casual dining inside and outside, with views of the creek from most seating. Lunch is served from 11:30 AM until 4:00 PM, dinner from 4:00 PM until 10:30 PM, Sunday through Thursday, and 4:00 PM until 12:00 AM on Friday and Saturday.

SKOOGIE'S

826 Coleman Boulevard   884-0172
$ No credit cards

For quick deli food and terrific milkshakes, we stop at Skoogie's. Our all-time favorite is a Skoogie hot dog — the best around. It's open from 10:30 AM until 8:00 PM every day, and is especially crowded on good beach days.

SUPPER AT STACK'S

Corner of Venning and Pitt   884-7009
$$$$ V, MC, AX

If "supper" sounds extremely light and unexceptional, then learn a new connotation for the word as it applies to this restaurant in the Old Village. Supper at Stack's fixed menu is a delightful four-course meal including soup, salad, beef or fish and a choice of dessert. The setting is a charming old house, completely refurbished, and patrons dress in very nice casual clothing. Spirits are available, and reservations are necessary. Dinner is served Tuesday through Saturday from 6:00 PM until 10:00 PM.

THE TRAWLER SEAFOOD RESTAURANT

Highway 17 North,   *884-2560*
along Shem Creek
$-$$ *AX, DC, MC, V*

Locals and visitors have been returning to The Trawler for 23 years. Open seven days a week in a handsome new facility, the restaurant is known for its seafood platters. In recent years, veal and lamb have become best-sellers as well. We are old fans of the crab dip, and also call during the "r months" (months with the letter "r" are generally those when oysters can be picked from local beds) to find out about roasted oyster specials. The serving hours are 11 AM until 11 PM, Monday through Saturday, and noon to 9:30 PM on Sunday.

VILLAGE CAFE

415 Mill Street   *884-8095*
$-$$$ *V, MC, AX*

For a meal of American Nouvelle cuisine at a cafe which, from the outside, looks like someone's grandmother's quaint,

brick cottage, make reservations at the Village Cafe. Beef, veal, chicken and shellfish are prepared in unusual but delicious ways to make for a memorable dining experience. Lunch is served from 11:00 AM until 3:00 PM, Monday through Saturday. Dinner is available from 5:30 PM until 10:00 PM weekdays, and until 10:30 PM on Friday and Saturday.

THE WRECK OF RICHARD AND CHARLENE

106 Haddrell Point   *884-0052*
$-$$ *No credit cards*

Tucked between Magwood and Wando Seafood Companies, look for the two flags but no sign to find The Wreck. The restaurant is unpretentious, and you can arrive via your own boat if you don't mind crawling around docks to disembark. You may dine on the deck or screened-in porch if you like to feel "right out there," and please try the shrimp and grits for breakfast or the lightly fried scallops thereafter — you will never be able to leave the Lowcountry again. Portions come as either "Richard's size" (large) or "Charlene's size" (not as large, but plenty), so order according to your appetite. Beer and wine are available, and hours are 8:00 AM until 10:00 PM, and from 11:30 AM until 9:30 PM on Sunday.

Mount Pleasant
Accommodations

*P*eople enjoy staying in Mt. Pleasant for a variety of reasons including its inherent beauty and proximity to the beaches and town. Whether you prefer to stay in a family's bed and breakfast, an inn, or a motel, there is an option in Mt. Pleasant.

Remember that prices change with seasons, and that you should call ahead to make reservations and get answers for such questions as: Can the pets come too? (Some establishments allow them, some do not.) Are children welcome? (This can be an issue at some Bed and Breakfasts.) What, if any, are the curfews?

We have listed some good accommodations choices below, and suggest using the following scale to estimate costs per night for two adults:

$50 and under	$
$51-$75	$$
$76-$95	$$$
$96-$110	$$$$
$110 and up	$$$$$

CHARLESTON EAST BED & BREAKFAST

1031 Tall Pine Road   *884-8208*
$-$$$$ *Some take major credit cards*

This service is a clearing house for Bed and Breakfasts in Mt. Pleasant and on the islands. You tell the coordinator what you want in terms of basic accommodations as well as the frills — air-conditioning, golf and tennis privileges, a pool and so forth — and she matches you with accommodations. Extended stays can be arranged, but pets are not allowed. Most Bed and Breakfasts represented by this service fall between the $-$$$$ range, and some of them take credit cards. Obviously, you also need to ask about the cost and method of payment when you make your reservations.

COMFORT INN

310 Highway 17 By-Pass   *884-5853*
or 1-800-221-2222
$$ *Most major credit cards*

This motel has more extras than you might imagine, and is a good value. Complimentary breakfast and a daily paper start the day off right, while an exercise room with a whirlpool, a sauna and equipment allow you to stay fit or wind down at the end of the day. There is free Show Time movie service as well as laundry facilities for taking care of the beach sand in your shorts.

DAYS INN-PATRIOT'S POINT

261 Highway 17 By-Pass   *881-1800*
$$ *AX, DC, MC, V*

One of our favorite things about this Days Inn is the pool area

— medium-sized and sheltered by mature shrubbery. All rooms are air-conditioned and the restaurant is a plus in our book for early risers who like to be close to that first cup of coffee. In our estimation, this is another good value in accommodations.

GUILD'S INN BED AND BREAKFAST
101 Pitt Street   881-0510
$$-$$$$ V, MC, AX

There are six bedrooms in the lovingly restored Guilds Inn, each beautiful and typically "Old Village." Every room has a private bath, and Continental breakfast is complimentary. Guests enjoy the charm of this unique residential area where walking is a popular pastime.

HAMPTON INN
255 Johnnie Dodds Boulevard
881-3300
$-$$ Most major credit cards

This is a 121-room hotel with inside hallways (rather than the outside breezeways that characterize motels). There is no charge for local calls, and children stay free. Continental breakfast is "on the house," and nonsmoking rooms are available.

HOLIDAY INN
Highway 17 Bypass   884-6000
$$-$$$ Most major credit cards

This elegant, full-service hotel has views of the harbor and is only minutes away from the city. Rooms are furnished with period reproductions, and a concierge level provides additional service and convenience. There is a fitness center with a sauna, as well as a seasonal pool.

MASTERS ECONOMY INN

300 Wingo Way   *884-2814*
$ *Most major credit cards*

This is a bargain in terms of proximity to the city and islands (three and seven miles, respectively) and offers some extras such as a pool, cable television and free phone calls. There is a lounge and restaurant on site, and Continental breakfast is served each morning. Efficiencies are also available.

RAMADA INN

301 Highway 17 Bypass   *884-1411*
at Mathis Ferry
$$ *Most major credit cards*

The Ramada Inn has been recently remodeled — 224 rooms with everything down to the bedspreads brand new. There is a nice view of a little lake and a pool for swimming. Although there is no restaurant in the facility, there are many nearby.

SHEM CREEK INN

1409 Shrimp Boat Lane   *881-1000*
$$$-$$$$$ *MC, V, AX*

With views of the shrimp boats moving in and out of docks and the sun sparkling off miles of marsh, Shem Creek Inn is fun for both children and adults. Each of the 50 rooms has a private balcony, and king-sized rooms have garden-sized tubs. There is convenient parking under the building, and Continental breakfast is served each morning. All of the Shem Creek nightlife goes on in close proximity to the inn, and boat dockage is available.

Mount Pleasant
Nightlife

Although Mt. Pleasant is a family-oriented community, there is plenty of excitement for the grown-ups when the stars come out. We have described some of the bars that are popular with locals, and also the movie theaters.

ACME BAR AND GRILL
413 Coleman Blvd.   *884-1949*

ACME is a cozy, neighborhood pub with an inviting interior and a nice deck (protected from Coleman Boulevard by trees and festive little white lights). Hours are 11:00 AM until 2:00 AM, Monday through Saturday, and until 4:00 PM on Sunday.

BAILEY'S
410 Mill Street   *856-9376*

Bailey's has a Happy Hour from 4:00 PM until 7:00 PM. There is a dessert case on display for those who crave nighttime sweets. It is open 10:00 PM, Sunday through Thursday, and 11:00 PM on Friday and Saturday.

BEE'S KNEES
802 Coleman Blvd.   *881-6187*

The Bee's Knees is a large pool hall which has the feel of a Las Vegas casino. With regulation pool tables and a snack bar, it is open from 4:00 PM until 2:00 AM.

BLUE'S BAR AND GRILL
1039 Johnnie Dodds Boulevard   *881-1858*

Blue's likes to be compared to television's famous "Cheers" bar in that it is casual and very friendly, attracting lots of locals. There is a daily happy hour until 7:00 PM, and general hours are 11:30 AM until 2:00 AM, seven days a week. Entertainment is featured once or twice a month — maybe a band playing Jimmy Buffet music or a comedy act. In the interim, three televisions are running to catch the latest in sports events, and the patrons ... well, everybody knows their na-a-ames!

FONDUELY YOURS
853 Coleman Boulevard   *849-6859*

This restaurant has a nice side bar which is open from 4:00 PM until 10:30 PM, Sunday through Thursday, and 4:00 PM until 11:00 PM Friday and Saturday. A lot of people come to hear the live entertainment on Fridays and Saturdays, and there are regulars for the happy hour from 4:00 PM until 7:00 PM every day of the week.

HUCK FIN'S
130 Mill Street   *849-8824*

This is a nice spot for an afternoon drink. We particularly like the downstairs bar — it feels like being underneath someone's beach house, but with all the setups for a good time. Happy hour is from 4:00 PM until 7:00 PM, and the bar stays open until 2:00 AM (with food served until 1:00 AM).

JIMMY LOU'S
819 Coleman Boulevard   *884-5052*

A sophisticated group knows about Jimmy Lou's, and frequents the bar which is open every day but Sunday and Monday. There is a weekend jazz pianist, and the cozy atmosphere tends to draw a contented group. When having dinner at Jimmy Lou's, we often step in here first for a drink and then wander back through for the music before we head home. Hours are from 5:30 PM to 10:00 PM, Tuesday through Friday, and until 11:00 PM on Saturday.

JOSIE JOES
1313 Shrimp Boat Lane   *881-8671*

Josie Joes is a flashy nightspot and restaurant at the harbor end of Shem Creek. As a bar, it is known for happy crowds who spill out onto the deck in nice weather and enjoy the complimentary buffet between 5:00 PM and 7:00 PM, Monday through Friday.

SHEM CREEK BAR AND GRILL
508 Mill Street   *884-8102*

High on the list of nighttime destinations, Shem Creek (as the locals call it) is one of the most popular watering holes in the area. It certainly has some great things going for it — namely, the bar dockside, the raw bar inside and the characters who make it their home-away-from-home. The mood is usually upbeat, and the munchies are delicious.

SPORTS
816 Johnnie Dodds Boulevard   *881-6157*

Obvious from its name, Sports is that kind of bar and is one of the most popular with young people. There are golf games, a pool table and wide screen televisions for optimum viewing possibilities. Happy hour features bar brands for $1.50, mixed drinks for $2.50, and pitchers of beer for $5. The menu includes delicious sports-watching snacks like macho nachos, and the kitchen is open late.

Insiders Like:
A sunset oyster roast along some Lowcountry creek on any crisp winter's evening.

Insiders' Tip

RB's

97 Church Street *881-0466*

RB's is another low-key, unpretentious bar where old friends file into booths, sit at the bar or enjoy outside seating on the creek. We always order plates of onion rings, and like the fact that we can hear each other. RB's is open from 11:00 AM until at least 10:30 PM, seven days a week.

THE TRAWLER

Hwy. 17 North, *884-2560*
along Shem Creek

Live entertainment and a raw bar make The Trawler a nice place to come for a drink and some relaxation. The whole facility has had a facelift and is quite contemporary and handsome. The hours are 11:30 AM until 11:00 PM, Monday through Saturday, and from noon until 9:30 PM on Sunday.

Movie Theaters

MT. PLEASANT CINEMA 1, 2 AND 3
1001 Johnnie Dodds Boulevard *884-3614*

Mount Pleasant
Neighborhoods

*B*ecause Mt. Pleasant is one of the fastest growing communities in Charleston county, there are many fine neighborhoods to explore. After crossing the Cooper River Bridge, you will have the option of heading straight across the overpass, on 17 North — toward McClellanville and Georgetown — or off to the right, following the signs to the islands. When possible, we have included some general prices or price ranges, gleaned from available asking prices at the time of this research. A piece of insider advice is this: the market here fluctuates, and pricing becomes dated quickly. Use our numbers only as guides, and rely on newspaper ads and licensed Realtors for up-to-the-moment market trends.

HARBOR WATCH

Just off Highway 17 North, Harbor Watch has two- and three-story homes, some with old Charleston porches. These are executive homes with newly landscaped yards, in close proximity to the Cooper River bridges. Some have views of the bridges, tidal creek and harbor. Homes start at around $229,000 and go up to at least $495,000.

MOLASSES CREEK

Surrounded by an eight-foot privacy fence made attractive with landscaping, this subdivision has large, two-story brick and wooden homes. Some of the houses are on the marsh, and lots tend to be of very manageable size. Many houses fall in the range of $190,000 to $500,000, with marsh views and water frontage costing more.

HOBCAW

A large, established subdivision, Hobcaw has homes in many executive price ranges and is popular with longtime residents as well as young people with children. Proximity to the Hobcaw Yacht Club, with its outdoor swimming pool and other facilities, is an appealing option. Some houses are on the water, and these tend to be the priciest. Prices include those falling in the range of $129,900 to $300,000.

HERON POINT

Down Mathis Ferry Road, protected from the road by an eight-foot, privacy fence, is Heron Point. These one- and two-story homes are wood and brick, with small yards. There are some vacant lots on the water, near the point on Hobcaw Creek. The new Mt. Pleasant Library — probably the most technologically up-to-date facility of its kind in the Trident area — is located nearby. There are some houses in the $169,900 to $250,000 range.

SOMERSET POINT

On the left, farther down Mathis Ferry Road, Somerset Point is a subdivision with large lots and old trees. A winding road leads toward Hobcaw Creek. Most of the Somerset homes are brick. The turnover is this area is low. A home may be found for $169,000, but the prices go upward.

POINT PLEASANT

A very well-kept residential area with many two-story houses on manageable lots, Point Pleasant is home to many young, upwardly mobile families. The houses tend to have lovely hardwood floors, fireplaces, molding and other appealing extras. Homes are listed from $129,000 to about $335,000.

WAKENDAW LAKES

This is a large and winding subdivision, with one- and two-story brick and wood homes. Some are on the marsh or lakes, and others are on Hobcaw Creek, while most line the streets inland. Wakendaw Lakes is another area that has experienced an influx of young, successful families. Although houses have been on the market for $79,000, the asking price can be twice or triple that according to size and proximity to marsh or water.

CANDLEWOOD, COOPERS LANDING, COOPER'S POINT AND GLENN LAKE

To find these small subdivisions, drive underneath the access to Wando Terminal and take a left on Whipple Road at Wando High School. Homes tend to be smaller but well cared for in these newly developed subdivisions. There are homes in these areas that range from $80,000 to $110,000 asking price.

HOBCAW CREEK PLANTATION

Taking a left onto Long Point Road, heading toward the Wando Terminal, Hobcaw Creek Plantation is on the left. This is a beautifully landscaped area with natural gum and pine trees throughout. The impressive, wrought iron street lights and small lakes add interest to the streets. Some houses — very large and stately — are on deep water, while many are on closely positioned, small lots in the interior. Most houses are two- or three-story traditional, and some new construction is underway. The tennis courts, swimming pool and playground are nice amenities. We found real estate here in the $169,000 to $648,000 range.

HIDDEN COVE

Farther down Long Point Road, next to the Wando Terminal, is Hidden Cove. The homes here are situated on large lots, with space between them. Most are two-story, although there are some smaller houses. There are impressive homes on deep water, and new houses are being built. Available lots still have natural growth and there is a good selection. There have been homes ranging in asking price from $116,450 to $149,000.

LONG POINT

Long Point is located at the other end of Long Point Road, almost to Highway 17 North. Beautiful views of the marsh are one of Long Point's best features. These nice, newly constructed homes are nestled amidst gum and pine trees. There is a soccer field and tennis and basketball courts as well as Palmetto County Park nearby. Asking prices for homes range from $86,000 to $365,000 and up.

SNEE FARM

Long Point Road intersects Highway 17 North at Snee Farm. Located on an historic site, this is a large development with a country club atmosphere. The golf course and tennis facilities as well as the Clubhouse are much in demand, and homes range from one-story Spanish architecture to two-story executive mansions. Pretty, old oaks and gum trees soften the skyline and enhance a very attractive neighborhood. Asking prices here start around $65,900 and go up to at least $465,000.

ROMAIN RETREAT

Many homes at Romain Retreat were destroyed by Hurricane Hugo, but those that have been rebuilt are in many cases more spectacular. The views of Cape Romain are wonderful, and some residents commute to work in Charleston or Georgetown. Interior lots start at about $45,000 and homes are often priced in the $250,000 range.

CROWN POINT

Heading toward town, one finds Crown Point — tucked away behind a black, wrought iron fence. Many homes are two-story, wooden, and some have privacy fences. There is a man-made lake which enhances the setting. Prices are in the range of $121,500 to $152,000 and up.

RAVENS RUN

Houses in this subdivision are situated on large lots, and tend to be very large and impressive. There is construction underway, and a sense of privacy is provided by the security fence and manned gate. Asking prices can be between $245,000 and $365,000.

QUAIL HOLLOW

These houses tend to be one-story residences with two car garages. There is a fence separating the subdivision from the road. Asking prices begin around $95,000.

SWEET GRASS

Two-story homes in this area are on small but attractive lots. There are small lakes throughout, and a low turnover of houses. Expect to find houses in the mid-$90,000 to low $100,000 range.

HIDDEN LAKES

The large central lake here gives this subdivision its name. Many homes are two-story, brick Colonial, and some houses have small docks. The large lots have old oaks and pines, and there is a good bit of new construction. Residents make use of the community tennis court and swimming pool. Prices start around $159,000 and go up to at least $222,000.

CASSINA PLANTATION

To date, Cassina has no paved roads but beautiful homes on large lots. Real estate starts at about $200,000 and goes up to $400,000-plus homes.

OAK HAVEN PLANTATION

True to its name, this area has outstanding oak trees as well as gum trees and a few ponds. The homes already built are one- and two-story, and are situated on medium-sized lots. There are community tennis courts, and a wooden security fence along the highway. Lots are for sale and construction is still underway. Homes with asking prices of $85,000 are neighbors to homes in the $190,000 and up range.

HARBORGATE SHORES

Homes here are one-story for the most part, and are 10 to 20 years old. Located across the street is Whiteside Elementary School, and closer to the marsh is Fiddler's Marsh. Asking prices are often in the $75,000 to $80,000 range.

FIDDLER'S MARSH

There is an interesting selection of homes in this exclusive, new subdivision. Most are built off the ground (a good feature in the event of a hurricane), and many have a nice, marsh view. The small pond and community dock, with a lovely gazebo, provide an aesthetic quality which residents appreciate. There are vacant lots available. Prices average about $149,000 for houses and in the $29,000 to $65,000 range for lots.

NORTH POINTE

Back out on Ben Sawyer Boulevard, heading toward the islands, North Pointe is located on the left — across the street from Pages Thieves Market, and behind the BiLo. These one- and two-story homes are built around an attractive oak grove, which is a focal point for the area.

SIMMONS POINTE

Across and down Ben Sawyer Boulevard, on the right, Simmons Pointe is a new subdivision with condominiums and houses looking out at Simmons Bay. Beautiful fountains and ponds with small bridges add to the charm of the development. Almost all of the single family homes and condos have spectacular views of the Intracoastal Waterway and Sullivans Island. There are houses that fall into the $130,000 to $225,000 range.

FOX POND

Fox Pond is a handsome, up-scale patio-home community off Center Street. The houses have similar facades and floor plans, most with nice screened porches. There are many children in this neighborhood, and privacy fences divide many property lines. Asking prices here start around $79,900 and up.

Photo: The Post and Courier

Captain Peter C. Lewis house, 206 Live Oak Drive, circa 1855.

PIRATE'S COVE

Buffered from the street by trees and fences, these two-story wooden patio homes are close to each other and to Mt. Pleasant Academy — a desirable pubic school. There are also some single family homes overlooking the waterway in the rear of the subdivision. Asking prices for these homes range from $82,600 to $139,000.

THE OLD VILLAGE

Judging from the prices of homes — particularly those on the water — and our personal opinion, this is one of the most desirable neighborhoods in the Trident Area. Many of the antebellum homes are situated on large lots, while others are clustered along the tree-lined streets to form a unique "village" setting. Many houses were built in this century — some in this decade — and only a very few available lots remain. Although certainly a real estate target for young, affluent professionals, the Old Village has retained much of the unpretentious, casual elegance for which it was known in the first part of this century. Small homes may start with asking prices in the $150,000 range, with most larger homes falling into the $300,000 to $600,000 range.

SHEMWOOD I

This established subdivision is located along Shem Creek, and has many one-story ranch homes as well as two-story homes along the river. Attractive yards are well maintained, and most homes have two-car garages. Homes here are priced around $110,000 and up (with prices doubling for waterfront and large square footage).

SHEMWOOD II

Off the Old Georgetown Highway (Business 526), Shemwood II is a quiet subdivision with one- and two-story brick and wood homes that border Shem Creek. Several houses are on the marsh with rolling lawns and pretty landscaping. Very much a family-oriented neighborhood, there is a secluded community park popular with the young. Asking prices range from around $88,900 to $120,000.

MILLWOOD

After crossing Shem Creek, the first right is Pelzer Drive — an appealing, road with beautiful, established homes and yards that are dotted with magnolia and oak trees. Some of these residences are on deep water with docks. Asking prices start around $179,900, and — for waterfront property — around $350,000.

COOPER ESTATES

Millwood spills into Cooper Estates. There are many styles of houses and a good price range in Cooper Estates. Some of the homes are on the water and most line the curved streets of the subdivision. Yards are kept nicely, and a shopping center is nearby. Homes here are advertised from $90,000 to $155,000.

CREEKSIDE

Another waterfront community, this one off Highway 17 North, Creekside is also home to the

Charleston Tennis Club. Residents have access to this sports facility with its tennis courts and swimming pool, and live in executive homes — most two-story and handsomely individual. Some homes have a nice view of Shem Creek. Asking prices range from about $169,000 to $425,000.

BAYVIEW

With views of Shem Creek and Charleston Harbor, Bayview is close to the Cooper River bridges and just off Coleman Boulevard. Homes in the best spots can carry asking price tags in the $450,000 range, whereas a house on the interior may be priced at $98,500.

THE GROVES

Closer to the bridge, between Coleman Boulevard and Highway 17 North, The Groves consists of mostly one- or one and a half-story, brick homes. This is an established,

Photo: The Post and Courier

Storm damage in McClellanville from Hurricane Hugo.

family neighborhood, with a nice park for the children and some quiet streets for bike rides and strolls. There is a good selection of houses in the $120-$150,000 range.

McClellanville Neighborhoods

For a detailed description of this little town, see the History chapter of this section. There are those who live here and commute to Charleston or Georgetown for work. It is also a second home community to some residents. McClellanville is rebounding nicely from its Hurricane Hugo ordeal, and those with foresight may find this an excellent time to wiggle into that community. Prices range from $100,000 to $350,000.

Mount Pleasant
Fitness, Participatory Sports and Parks

There are many indoor facilities and outdoor settings for recreational activities in Mt. Pleasant. The Wando Community School offers courses ranging from aerobic exercise to Tai Chi to ballroom dancing. Call 849-2829 for current course descriptions. Public parks allow visitors to take advantage of the lovely setting that is Mt. Pleasant, and an energetic population supports a wide range of athletic activity. For information about leagues and organized sports, call 884-2528.

Participatory Sports

Camping

BUCK HALL
McClellanville   887-3257

There are 15 sites here, located in the National Forest — just over two miles past Awendaw. Call

for information about availability.

CAPERS ISLAND
Capers Island   762-5000

This 2,000-acre barrier island can only be reached by boat, but is well worth the effort of securing a ride. The state's only primitive beachfront camping area, Capers is without any facilities and camping here is absolutely "in the rough" (which is exactly like plenty of people want it). It is protected under the Heritage Trust Program and managed by the state's department of Wildlife and Marine Resources. Contact the Division of Marine Resources at Fort Johnson, on James Island, for a permit.

Canoe Paddling

Contact the Lowcountry Paddlers, at 883-9883, to find out about membership in this organization. Meetings the third Monday of every month at Murray-LaSaine Elementary School are open to anyone interested. Guest speakers talk about their experiences outdoors as well as conservation issues and upcoming trips. The Charleston County Parks and Recreation Commission can also help with a list of Community School courses in paddling (call 762-2172).

Fitness Centers

LIFEQUEST

Moultrie Shopping Center,   *849-1414*
Coleman Boulevard

Lifequest is a locally owned, state-of-the-art fitness center. The facility is sparkling clean and attractive, with a seven-layer, antibacterial, aerobics floor, 11,000 pounds of free weights, a dumbbell section, circuit training machines (of Lifequest's own design), and 24 pieces of cardiovascular equipment (including steps, bikes and treadmills), as well as a self-defense studio. Tanning beds and massage therapy are available at an extra cost. Included in the membership fee is child care for children four months and older. Membership fees are $50 per month or $550 annually (paid up front).

EAST COOPER HEALTH AND FITNESS

910 Johnnie Dodds Boulevard   *884-2120*

This health club has free weights, Nautilus and cardiovascular equipment as well as aerobics classes. There are five racquetball courts. Memberships range from $384 to $660 annually, or $10 per visit. Hours are from 5:30 AM until 10:00 PM, Monday through Thursday, 5:30 AM until 9:00 PM on Friday, 9:00 AM until 7:00 PM on Saturday, and 9:00 AM until 9:00 PM on Sunday. Child care is available much of the time.

Flying

PALMETTO AIR

700 Airport Road   *884-8914*

For primary flight instruction East of the Cooper, talk to the instructors at Palmetto Air. They also offer sight-seeing flights over Charleston for those of us who are not yet ready to earn our wings.

Putt-Putt

CLASSIC GOLF

1528 Ben Sawyer Boulevard   *881-9614*

Classic Golf has two 18-hole courses and is a great place for a child's birthday party. The adult fee is $4.50 per game, and children under 10 years old are charged $2.25 per game. Hours vary with the seasons.

SAND DOLLAR MINI GOLF

1405 Ben Sawyer Boulevard   *884-0320*

With animal obstacles, this course is especially fun for children. Birthday parties are encouraged and there are special group rates. Sand Dollar is closed from December to February, and stays open March through Labor day, from 10:00 AM until 10:00 PM. Game prices are $3.00 per adult, and $1.50 for children age 12 and under.

Scuba Diving

AQUA VENTURES
426 Coleman Boulevard   *884-1500*

Open Monday through Saturday, from 10:00 AM until 6:00 PM, Aqua Ventures sells equipment like Day-Core and Tabata. Four-week diving classes as well as weekend dive trips and local offshore charters are offered.

Swimming

CHARLESTON TENNIS CLUB
790 Creekside   *884-6111*

This club features a six-lane pool as well as a baby pool for the little ones. There is also a tennis center and organized programs for adults and juniors.

PALMETTO ISLANDS COUNTY PARK
444 Needlerush Parkway   *884-0832*

The outdoor swimming hole at Palmetto Islands County Park is open the months of April, September and October from 10:00 AM until 6:00 PM, May through August, from 10:00 AM until 7:00 PM, and from November through March, from 10:00 AM until 5:00 PM.

RICHARD JONES RECREATION COMPLEX
391 Egypt Road   *884-2528*

There is a six-lane, indoor swimming pool at the Richard Jones Complex, and swimming lessons are available. Membership costs $5 for Mt. Pleasant residents. Call for nonresident membership information.

SNEE FARM COUNTRY CLUB
Highway 17 North   *884-8571*

Three swimming pools are available in the Snee Farm Country Club. From mid-May to mid-September, members and their guests can enjoy a large Junior Olympic-sized pool, an enclosed adults-only pool, or a wading pool for the little ones. Lifeguards are on duty during regular pool hours, and there is a Snee Farm Swim Team.

Tennis

There are public as well as private tennis courts in Mt. Pleasant. Call 884-2528 for information about public facilities, and for information about private clubs, contact the following:

CHARLESTON TENNIS CLUB AND PRO SHOP
790 Creekside Drive   *884-6111*

There are 12 lighted courts at this club, which hosts a pro tennis event in May. Members enjoy use of lockers and a lounge, as well as a six-lane swimming pool. There is an active adult and junior program as well. The initiation fee for resident membership is $500, with $40 monthly dues. There are no court fees.

SNEE FARM COUNTRY CLUB
Highway 17 North   *884-8571*

There are 14 tennis courts with lights for evening play at Snee Farm, available to members only. Four of these are clay and 10 are hard courts. Snee Farm also has an 18-hole, championship golf course and Junior Olympic swimming pool.

Contact membership secretary Barbara Ann Sims for more information.

Parks and Recreational Centers

ALHAMBRA PARK
Middle Street   *884-2528*

This simple yet lovely park is wide open, with free public admission from sunup to sundown. It offers a scenic view of the Charleston harbor, as well as a nice lawn. The selection of playground equipment — swings, slides, climbing toys and a merry-go-round — keep the children busy. For picnics, there are several tables under the shade of the big oaks.

BOONE HALL PLANTATION

Boone Hall was originally a cotton plantation of more than 17,000 acres. Today, it still has some of the most impressive moss-draped oaks in the South — trees that were planted in 1743. Visitors receive a guided tour of the mansion's first floor. Adults are charged $6.00 and children $2.00 for admission. There is a restaurant that serves Lowcountry dishes to plantation visitors (see Daytrips section).

PALMETTO ISLAND COUNTY PARK
$1 per person

This family-oriented nature facility is set in heavily wooded areas with a two-acre pond and one-mile canoe trail. There is a very well planned playground as well as picnic sites and boat docks. It is a perfect place to jog, walk, bike, rent a pedal boat or a canoe. The swimming hole is popular in the warm months. Charge is $1.00 per person.

PATRIOTS POINT
40 Patriots Point Road   *884-2727*

This is the "World's Largest Naval and Maritime Museum", and is home to the World War II aircraft carrier Yorktown. There are five ships to explore, as well as a gift shop for souvenirs. Admission charge for adults is $8.00, and for children, $4.00, with no charge for those under seven (see Attractions section).

RICHARD L. JONES RECREATION COMPLEX
391 Egypt Road   *884-2528*

Opened in March 1991, this large, modern building provides a facility for scheduled recreation programs, a gymnasium, a six-lane pool and an activity room. Membership for Mt. Pleasant residents is $5, and there is a $20 fee for tee-ball, softball, basketball, baseball and soccer. Crafts classes, CPR classes, swimming lessons and gymnastics camps (half-day and full-day) are offered.

Mount Pleasant
Worship

There are churches of many denominations in Mt. Pleasant, and some are nearly as old as the original settlements. We have described a sampling of the congregations that gather regularly and are visible in the community. Check the Sunday religion section in the *Post and Courier* for current activities and special programs at these churches, as well as information about other places of worship.

African Methodist Episcopal

FRIENDSHIP A.M.E. CHURCH
Royal Avenue   *884-6748*

Friendship A.M.E. is located on the edge of the Old Village. There is a Sunday School program and worship service on Sunday mornings, as well as an early church service some Sundays. A bible study followed by a prayer meeting is slated for Wednesday evenings.

GREATER GOODWILL
A.M.E. CHURCH
2818 N. Hwy. 17   *884-0903*

Sunday school and a worship service are held Sunday mornings. Prayer meeting is conducted on Thursday evening as well, and visitors are always welcome.

OLIVE BRANCH A.M.E. CHURCH
1734 N. Hwy. 17   *884-5130*

Olive Branch has approximately 1,400 members, and meets on Sunday for morning Sunday School as well as late morning worship service. There is an evangelistic service on Thursday evenings, and services are aired by WPAL radio on Sunday morning.

ZION A.M.E. CHURCH
12 Miles Awendaw   *884-7468*

This church was founded in 1908 in Awendaw, and today has a congregation of about 88 members. There is a Sunday School program as well as church service on Sunday morning and a bible study on Thursday evening.

Adventists

MT. PLEASANT
SEVENTH-DAY ADVENTIST
142 Hibben Street   *881-6244*
(corner of Hibben and Church Streets)

Another Old Village church, this congregation meets for Sabbath celebration every Saturday morning. A study session is held late morning as well.

Baptist

EAST COOPER BAPTIST CHURCH
950 Whipple Road   *884-0694*

Established in 1974, East Cooper Baptist Church has church school classes as well as three worship services during the day and one early evening service on Sunday. A nursery is provided for all services. Pre-taped sermons are aired on Sunday morning on WYFH FM radio. Cell groups meet on Wednesday evenings, and this congregation of approximately 1,200 supports Interfaith Crisis Ministry, Pregnancy Center and ECCO (East Cooper Community Outreach).

FIRST BAPTIST CHURCH OF MT. PLEASANT
681 McCants Drive   *884-8521*

This church, located on the outskirts of the Old Village, was established in 1917. There are approximately 1,500 members in the congregation. Two morning and one evening service, as well as a Sunday School program take place on the Sabbath. There is an evening broadcast on WOKE radio, and a midweek evening service. The church has a very active Christian youth ministry, and a school for toddlers through sixth grade.

LONG POINT BAPTIST CHURCH
Long Point Road   *884-6997*

Established in 1985, Long Point Baptist Church has approximately 175 members. There is a morning worship service on Sunday as well as a Sunday School program. Teen Talk meets on Tuesday evenings, and there is a Praise Meeting on Wednesday. The congregation sponsors a food pantry and participates in programs for the homeless as well as the Interfaith Crisis Ministry.

Bible

GRACE BIBLE CHURCH
1570 Mathis Ferry Road   *884-7074*

There is both a Sunday morning Sunday School and a worship service at Grace Bible Church. There is also a Sunday evening service.

Catholic

CHRIST OUR KING CATHOLIC CHURCH
1122 Russell Drive   *884-5587*

This large parish counts about 1,434 families as members. There is a late afternoon Mass on Saturday, as well as two morning, one midday and one evening Mass on Sunday. The congregation participates in such organizations as Knights of Columbus and St. Vincent de Paul Society, and has very active youth and elderly ministries. Christ Our King has been involved in ECCO (East Cooper Community Outreach) since it was formed in 1990. There is an affiliated school—Christ Our King-Stella Maris — which has a fine reputation in the community.

Church of God

MT. PLEASANT CHURCH OF GOD
1332 Erckman Drive   *881-4710*

This church has been in existence for 15 years and has a congregation of 50 members. There is a church school and worship service Sunday morning, and a Bible Study on Wednesday evening.

Community

SEACOAST CHRISTIAN COMMUNITY CHURCH
750 Long Point Road   881-2100

Established in April of 1988, this congregation has approximately 400 members. There are two Sunday morning services, as well as a Wednesday evening service. This interdenominational congregation is involved in Habitat for Humanity and Interfaith Crisis Ministry, and supports Bethany Christian Services.

Episcopal

CHRIST EPISCOPAL CHURCH
2304 N. Hwy. 17   884-9090

This historic church was one of ten parishes created in 1706 as part of the "Church Assembly Act" and was established as a church in 1708. Today, the church has both a Holy Eucharist Rite I and a Rite II service early Sunday morning, and a Rite I service again at the late morning service. There are also fellowship and Christian education programs on Sunday morning, and on Wednesday, a Holy Eucharist Rite I service in the morning as well as a Rite II service in the afternoon. This congregation of approximately 271 people supports ECCO (East Cooper Community Outreach), Meals on Wheels, Windwood Farms Home For Boys and Interfaith Crisis Ministry, and is a meeting place for

Alcoholics Anonymous. It gives monetary support to Episcopalian seminaries as well.

ST. ANDREW'S EPISCOPAL CHURCH
440 Whilden Street   884-6169

Established as a Chapel of Ease to Christ Church in 1835, St. Andrew's became a parish in 1954. Today, there are approximately 1,750 members. Rite I and Rite II services are performed early Sunday morning, followed by a Sunday School program and a late morning service. On Wednesday, there is a morning Holy Eucharist and Healing service, and an early evening Holy Eucharist service with contemporary music, followed by supper and then a Bethany Service. The congregation is involved in many outreach programs, and the church is headquarters for some including a medical clinic on Tuesday and Thursday evenings and local Meals on Wheels.

Holiness

GARDEN OF PRAYER PENTECOSTAL HOLINESS CHURCH
2537 Hwy. 17 North By-Pass   884-1616

There is a morning Sunday School, as well as midday and evening worship services on Sunday. On Monday, there is a Consecration Service followed by a Bible Study. Evening worship is held also on Tuesday and Friday evenings. Transportation available and can be arranged by calling the office for details.

Jehovah's Witness

KINGDOM HALL OF JEHOVAH'S WITNESSES
1142 Dingle Road   881-0606

This Kingdom Hall has public talks on Sunday morning. It supports a daily door-to-door mission of the Jehovah's Witnesses.

Lutheran

ST. PAUL'S LUTHERAN CHURCH
604 Pitt Street   884-3107

Established in 1884, St. Paul's Lutheran Church — in the Old Village — has approximately 530 members. Two services are held on Sunday mornings, and there are weekday services during the Holy Season. The church supports Crisis Ministry, Lutheran Social Services, Meals on Wheels, My Sister's House and Florence Crittendon Home. It is a meeting place for Alcoholics Anonymous, and operates a much needed service of picking up day-old bakery goods and distributing them to shelters and food distribution centers.

Methodist

HIBBEN UNITED METHODIST CHURCH
690 Coleman Boulevard   884-9761

Established in 1901, Hibben United Methodist Church has 1,200 members. Following an early morning worship service is Sunday School and then a late morning worship service. The congregations supports ECHO (East Cooper Community Outreach) and the Interfaith Crisis Ministry.

Presbyterian

HERITAGE PRESBYTERIAN CHURCH U.S.A.
2125 N. Hwy. 17   881-0967

This church held its first service on July 1, 1984, and today has a congregation of approximately 125 families. Early service on Sunday morning is informal and followed by a Sunday School and Fellowship. A late morning service is also conducted on Sunday. Community outreach includes involvement in Habitat for Humanity, Alcoholics Anonymous meetings, Boy Scout meetings, and the Interfaith Crisis Ministry.

MT. PLEASANT PRESBYTERIAN CHURCH
302 Hibben Street   884-4612

This lovely church in the Old Village was established in 1827. It holds Sunday morning church school and two worship services. There is a fellowship supper on Tuesday evenings. The congregation includes 1,400 members, and supports Habitat for Humanity, Crisis Ministry, Meals on Wheels, PALS (Aids Hospice Program), ECCO and People Against Rape. In fact, half of the yearly budget is spent on people in need outside the parish.

East Islands
History

Sullivans Island

The captain of the *Carolina*, the ship that brought the first English settlers to this area, was Florence O'Sullivan, for whom Sullivans Island is named. He was a member of the provincial parliament, and held the deed to much land east of the Cooper River.

In the early days, Sullivans Island was covered with pine trees and was used as a strategic point of defense for Lowcountry settlers. In 1706, the Spanish-French fleet lost footing after a battle at the west end of the island. Here, also, the naval and land forces of Sir Peter Parker were set back in what has been called "the most decisive battle of the American Revolution."

Moultrie is a name connected in many ways with Lowcountry history. General Moultrie rescued the patriots' battle flag here and, 100 years later, Federal commander Major Robert Anderson moved his forces from Fort Moultrie to Fort Sumter where The War Between the States began. Osceola, a Seminole Indian chief, was held prisoner at Fort Moultrie until his death, and is buried outside the fort. Edgar Allan Poe was stationed at Fort Moultrie, and later wrote an island-inspired story: "The Gold Bug."

Charlestonians began building summer residences on Sullivans in the 19th century to escape the heat of the city. As recently as the early part of this century, moving to "the island" meant packing up all of the household essentials and making the break for several months. Eventually a school and a few shops made year round living possible.

Today, many "islanders" are full-time, and Sullivans is a favored residential area. Development has been monitored so that there is precious little commercial activity and a relatively subdued lifestyle. Although there are still a few empty lots, courtesy of Hurricane Hugo, much of the island has been rebuilt — sometimes, "grander" than she was before.

The Isle Of Palms

In the early years, Sullivans Islanders ventured over to the next island, the Isle of Palms, for boat picnics or to fish and shrimp the waters. By the late 19th century, some visitors were regulars who came by water or the railroad bridge. Records from 1941 indicate that there were only 25 year round residents. Several years later, owner J.C.

Long started selling small vacation homes on his island and, over the next three decades, growth was steady. As the pavilion became an entertainment mecca, so did the Isle of Palms' reputation for fun and games. Surfers discovered the waves in the 1960s, and the young flocked to "the strip" to strut their baked bodies by day, and dance from club to club by night.

By the end of the 1970s, the undeveloped point of Isle of Palms became Wild Dunes: a self-contained, planned resort community.

Today, many residents are full-time inhabitants who live in the scattered neighborhoods or at Wild Dunes. There is a steady stream of short-time visitors also, people who come out to enjoy vacation rentals or just a day's or evening's entertainment.

Photo: The Post and Courier

A large number of boats damaged by Hurricane Hugo are piled together in Wild Dunes Yacht Yard on Isle of Palms.

East Islands
Shopping

While most people shop on the mainland, Sullivans Island has two convenience stores and an open-air produce stand. On the Isle of Palms, there are several established shopping strips (one with a grocery store which carries a little bit of everything — including some good wines and gourmet items).

Sullivans Island

ISLAND BOY MARKET AND CAFE
Middle Street, Sullivans

Across from the playground, the Island Boy Market and Cafe is an open-air vendor that sells produce and other edibles (we're hooked on the Hawaiian shaved ices!). Upstairs, the owners serve cafe fare.

GRUBER'S WISHING WELL
2019 Middle Street   883-3838

"The Wishing Well," as Sullivans Islanders call it, is open seven days a week. It carries beer and wine as well as drugstore items.

Isle Of Palms

WAVE TRADE
1012 Ocean Boulevard   886-9878

This retail store is located on the Isle of Palms. Selling casual beach clothes, surfing accessories and equipment, Wave Trade is a good place to shop for surfing clothes, wet suits and also surf boards.

THE PAVILION SHOPS

This modern, streamlined strip of shops, restaurants and businesses — across from the beach on Ocean Boulevard — includes some old and some new to the Isle of Palms.

MCKEVLIN'S
1001-B Ocean Boulevard   886-8912

McKevlin's has been around since surfing made its debut on the island. Expect to wipe your sandy feet in the bucket outside the front door and come in to admire the boogie and surf boards as well as accessories displayed everywhere. Morey and Maxx'd Out are two of the popular brand names McKevlin's carries.

ISLAND CENTER

The first "shopping center" on the island, Island Center, located on Palm Boulevard, covers the basics and then some. Anchored by a Red and White Grocery Store and the Isle of Palms Hardware Store, the center also has some specialty shops and businesses.

ISLAND VIDEO
886-5127

Since many of us count video-watching in our definition of recreation, it is worth noting that this video store offers free membership with video rentals. Out-of-town customers may rent videos with a credit card (MasterCard or Visa) imprint, and may select from current movies or classics.

ISLAND CARDS AND GIFTS
886-8253

This shop is also known as "Just for Grins." Inventory includes Hallmark products as well as island gifts and memorabilia.

OCEAN PARK PLAZA
Palm Boulevard   722-2615

Ocean Park is the Isle of Palms' newest, most comprehensive shopping plaza. Included in the Plazza are: Simmons Seafood Market (which sells the same fresh seafood the other Simmons sells on Ben Sawyer Boulevard — a long-time favorite of locals); Panache (with gifts, stained glass and home furnishings); Pier Ice Cream (generous cones and many flavors); the Island Pharmacy (the only one on both islands); Beach Town (with children's and adult's beachwear and beach necessities like towels, flip-flops and the like).

East Islands
Restaurants

*P*atrons often expect tropical fare when dining on the islands, and these restaurants offer that — with a twist of old Charleston — and more. Prices and hours vary slightly with seasons, but the following scale is offered as a guide for entrée prices:

Under $10	$
$10-$15	$$
$16-$20	$$$
$21-and up	$$$$

SULLIVANS
2019 Middle Street   883-3222
$-$$ V, MC

A favorite with the islanders and others in-the-know, Sullivans is a family restaurant with affordable, good food. Not fancy, Sullivans is just what the regulars want: a place where they can order delicious, traditional specials like shrimp and grits or seafood casserole with two vegetables and a dessert — all for less than $6. Daily hours are 11:00 AM until 2:00 PM for lunch, and — every day but Sunday — 5:00 PM until 9:00 PM for dinner.

STATION 22
2205 Middle Street   883-3355
$-$$ MC, V, AX, D

Casual, but not flip-flops and a t-shirt, Station 22 offers variety in the menu and island history on the walls (which showcase dozens of photographs of Sullivans Island). Try the beef filet or seafood specials, served with delicious Island Boy Bread, and save room for Uncle William's Brownie Fudge Pie. Hours are 5:00 PM until 10:00 PM, Monday through Thursday, and until 10:30 PM on Saturday and Sunday.

THE SEA BISCUIT CAFE
21 J.C. Long Boulevard   886-4079
$ No credit cards

This one is a petite charmer — complete with a tiny front porch, substantial side porch (for dining) and fabulous island fare. The Sea Biscuit, tucked away on one of Isle of Palms' less chaotic streets, serves breakfast or brunch with the house specialty: fabulous biscuits, of course. Try shrimp and gravy with grits and eggs, seafood omelettes, quiche and even Eggs Benedict. We drink gallons of the special house tea, and watch our children devour the best pancake (a Mickey Mouse look-alike) we've tasted. Hours are Tuesday through Friday, 6:30 AM until 2:30 PM, and Saturday and Sunday, 7:30 AM until 1:00 PM.

THE PALMS RESTAURANT
1010 Ocean Boulevard   886-6986
$ V, MC

The Palms is an older seafood restaurant that serves no-nonsense, seafood plates at reasonable prices. With a casual atmosphere, it attracts many locals who come for traditional breakfast or a full meal — like fried shrimp and the fixin's. The kids can order from a separate menu, and everyone enjoys the entertainment at nights. Hours are Monday through Friday, 6:00 AM until 11:00 PM, and Saturday and Sunday, 7:00 AM until 11:00 PM.

HEARTS OF PALM RESTAURANT

1009-A Ocean Boulevard 886-9661
$-$$ No credit cards

The menu at Hearts of Palm, on the Isle of Palms, is a tempting assortment of healthy foods. In addition to vegetable entrées and omelettes, there is chicken parmigiana, tuna salad plate and pasta salad, as well as hamburgers. The restaurant is open from 7:00 AM until 2:30 PM, every day but Tuesday, and from 5:00 PM until the crowd thins on Friday and Saturday for dinner.

ONE EYED PARROT

1130 Ocean Boulevard 886-4360
$$-$$$ Most major credit cards

The One Eyed Parrot is a fun restaurant with good food, served ocean side on the Isle of Palms. Captain John Avinger and his wife Angie have been successful restaurateurs in this area for years — they also own Shem Creek Bar and Grill — and stamp a winning sense of style on their businesses. The Parrot's menu includes various versions of shrimp, scallops, oysters, dolphin, and tuna, a Bimini stew (a tomato-based seafood and sausage dish) as well as steamed oysters in season. Seafood aside, there is Caribbean chicken (baked and fried), steak, salads and pasta specials. Hours are 11:30 AM until midnight, seven days a week.

DOUBLES PIZZA

1101 Ocean Boulevard 886-4241
$ No credit cards

Doubles serves what its full name suggests and also submarine sandwiches, for dining in or carry-out. Hours are 11:00 AM until 10:00 PM, Monday through Thursday and Sunday, and 11:00 AM until 12 midnight on Friday and Saturday.

LONG ISLAND CAFE

1515 Palm Boulevard   *886-8809*
$-$$ *Most major credit cards*

Long Island Cafe became a local favorite soon after its doors opened, and still has a loyal following. The cafe's lightly breaded seafood and snapper with deviled crab are traditional favorites, while a cheddar, ham and apple omelette puts a new twist on brunch. A nice selection of soups, salads and sandwiches is also available. The restaurant is open for lunch Monday through Saturday, 11:30 AM until 2:30 PM, and for Sunday brunch from 11:00 AM until 2:00 PM. Dinner is served on Monday, Wednesday, Thursday, Friday and Saturday from 6:00 PM until 9:00 PM.

TRADEWINDS RESTAURANT

41st Avenue   *886-5678*
$-$$ *AX, V, MC, D*

Tradewinds serves traditional Lowcountry fare, some of which is caught by Tradewinds' own boats. In addition to the Chef's Special, there are entrées like Lowcountry shrimp and pasta dishes, fried and broiled seafood and a breast of chicken, all of which are served with homemade bread. There are different hours during the high and low seasons. During the summer, hours are 5:30 PM until 9:30 PM, Monday through Thursday, and until 10:00 PM on Friday and Saturday. During the winter, hours are scaled back to 9:00 PM during the week but still 10:00 PM on the weekends. Sundays, from Memorial Day until Labor Day, breakfast and lunch are served from 9:00 AM until 2:00 PM; dinner is served from 5:30 PM until 9:30 PM.

THE LINKS RESTAURANT

Wild Dunes   *886-6000*
$-$$ *MC, V, AX, D*

The Links — part of the Wild Dunes resort scene — serves contemporary Lowcountry cuisine such as crab cakes, fried fish, and a mixed grill as well as a filet of duck with orange sauce. Hours are 11:30 AM until 2:30 PM for lunch, and 6:00 PM until 9:00 PM for dinner, seven days a week.

East Islands
Accommodations

Sullivans Island and the Isle of Palms are popular vacation destinations and are covered with rental property. With no hotel, motel, condominium or resort development, Sullivans has less to offer in terms of overnight rental but has a lovely assortment of old and new island homes for rent in weekly increments. On the Isle of Palms, in addition to weekly house rentals, a major resort and two large complexes offer flexibility in length of stay. Also, Bed and Breakfast arrangements are sometimes available in island homes.

We have listed some good accommodations choices below, and suggest using the following scale to estimate costs per night for two adults:

$50 and under	$
$51-$75	$$
$76-$95	$$$
$96-$110	$$$$
$110 and up	$$$$$

BEACH ACCOMMODATIONS
1204 Palm Blvd.   886-8600 or
                         803-533-1343
$$-$$$$$ V, MC

Beach Accommodations is an agency which handles private homes, villas and Sea Cabins for daily or weekly rentals on the Isle of Palms, Sullivans Island and Wild Dunes. One- to three-bedroom villas and three- to seven-bedroom homes are available in all locations. We find the staff to be particularly courteous and friendly.

EAST SIDE BED AND BREAKFAST
1031 Tall Pine Road   884-8208
$-$$$$ Some take major credit cards

This clearinghouse is the source for Bed and Breakfasts on the islands. The coordinator will match your special wants and needs — ranging from air conditioning to tennis or golf privileges — with available accommodations. Breakfast is served at participating homes, but the pets must stay at home. Most of the Bed and Breakfasts fall between the $-$$$$ range and take major credit cards.

OCEAN INN APARTMENTS
100 Palm Boulevard   886-4687
$$-$$$ AX, MC, V

With beautiful ocean views, these completely furnished — down to the linens and dishes — air-conditioned apartments have bedrooms, a living room and a kitchen. There is a phone, cable television, HBO and laundry facilities to make your stay a real home-away-from-home. For those less inclined to swim in the sea or who enjoy a "clear dip" after the beach, there is a swimming pool. Rentals are available by the day or week.

SEA CABINS

1300 Ocean Front Boulevard   *886-8144 or*
800-845-2546
$$$-$$$$$ *MC, V*

These cabins are available by the week or night (with a two-night minimum), and prices vary according to season, night of the week and view. For instance, second floor accommodations on the weekend are the most expensive option. Units are equipped with kitchenettes, and guests enjoy the use of the pool and tennis facilities.

WILD DUNES RESORT

Isle of Palms   *886-6000 or*
800-845-8880
$$$-$$$$$ *AX, MC, V*

Rental possibilities at Wild Dunes include two- and three-bedroom villas located by the ocean, golf courses, tennis courts or lagoon. Golf is a big attraction, with The Links — designed by Tom Fazio and ranked as a top course by Golf Magazine — and the Harbor Course, with holes along the Intracoastal Waterway. There are Har-Tru tennis courts for day and night play, and tennis clinics and lessons are available. Of course the sandy beach is beautiful, and there are many activities for families. Pets are not allowed at Wild Dunes, but the resort will recommend local kennels.

East Islands
Nightlife

Although the islands east of the Cooper River are basically family beaches, there are several notable watering holes nestled behind the dunes. A word of warning: Don't let the casual setting lull you into ignoring the Open Container Law (in other words, don't stroll outside with an unsealed alcoholic beverage).

BANANA CABANA

Below the One Eyed Parrot,   886-4360
1130 Ocean Palm Boulevard

Happy Hour is Monday through Friday, from 5:00 PM until 7:00 PM at the Banana Cabana, but the bar is open seven days a week. On the beach at the Isle of Palms, the Banana Cabana has a volleyball net and putting green as well as lots of cool, refreshing libations and munchies.

BERT'S BAR

2213-B Middle Street   883-9646

Many years ago, Bert's was Sullivans Island's pharmacy and soda fountain. Gone are the ammonia cokes and grilled cheese sandwiches — blues and rock 'n' roll is what Bert's whips up these days. The kitchen does serve burgers, soups and salads between 11:30 AM and 4:00 PM, and even has a Friday Fish Fry from 5:00 PM until 8:00 PM

that draws a steady group of "island characters." There is a cover charge for the live entertainment on Friday and Saturday, and it is generally a noisy, boisterous good time.

DUNLEVEY'S

Sullivans Island   883-9646

A welcome watering hole for the island, Dunlevey's is a pub that draws the locals as well as visitors. Bill Dunlevey is usually on hand, and makes one and all feel welcome. Hours are 11:45 AM until 1:00 AM or 2:00 AM, depending on the crowd. On Sunday, it is open from noon until 1:00 AM .

MARKER 116 LOUNGE AT TRADEWINDS RESTAURANT

41st Avenue   886-5678

The lounge at the Tradewinds is a real find and a well-kept secret. Featuring live entertainment on the weekends, the Tradewinds has indoor and outdoor seating to make the most of an incredible, unobstructed view up the Waterway. Hours vary but a rule of thumb is: Monday through Thursday, 5:00 PM until 10:00 PM and until 11:00 PM. On Saturday and Sunday, food is served continuously from 10:00 AM until 11:00 PM.

STATION 22

2205 Middle Street   *883-3355*

A handsome, comfortable bar — its walls adorned with wonderful old pictures of early days on the island — Station 22 has been a local favorite since it opened some years back. We have experienced quiet evenings here as well as those late nights when the jukebox (said to be one of the best in town) was cranked loud and revelers "cut a rug" where there was none. A charming train encircles the bar proper, and bartenders blow its whistle when the time is right. Hours are 5:00 PM until 10:00 PM, Monday through Thursday, and until 10:30 PM on Friday and Saturday.

WINDJAMMER

1008 Ocean Boulevard   *886-8596*

The Windjammer has been the Big Deal in entertainment on the Isle of Palms for decades. We remember kids heading out to dance the "Dying Cockroach" at "the 'Jammer," back before surfing came into its own...that long ago. The facility is new (since Hurricane Hugo) and high on stilts these days. But the intensity of action is the same: Monday through Saturday, doors are open from 11:30 AM until 2:00 AM, and from 12 noon until 2:00 AM on Sunday. Live bands play Thursday, Friday and Saturday, and there is a cover charge. Happy Hour is 5:00 PM until 7:00 PM, Monday through Friday. Patrons must be at least 21 years old to enter after 8:00 PM.

East Island
Neighborhoods

Sullivans Island, Isle of Palms, Wild Dunes, and Goat Island — with their beautiful vistas, laid-back atmosphere and impressive public school district — are all popular residential areas East of the Cooper River.

There are no official "subdivisions" on Sullivans Island; rather, the location of property is described by proximity to the water or landmarks — for instance, "front beach" or "near Ft. Moultrie." Such is also the case with the Isle of Palms, with the exception of Wild Dunes.

Just 15 miles from Charleston proper, Wild Dunes is a separate community at the end of the Isle of Palms. Wild Dunes has conference facilities, vacation rentals and villa accommodations, as well as homes and homesites for sale. Across from the Isle of Palms is Goat Island, accessible only by boat.

Sullivans Island, the Isle of Palms and Wild Dunes have inviting, sandy beaches and access to the creeks on the back of the islands. In some cases, renovation after Hurricane Hugo has enhanced real estate. Bigger and better houses, built high on stilts to avoid future water damage, dot all three islands. And, there are many old-style summer homes that add charm and history to island life.

Goat Island is strictly residential — a small, sparsely populated island with houses tucked amid native vegetation. Most property owners have docks on the waterway and enjoy the fact that they are completely removed from the mainstream.

In the recent market, houses on Sullivans Island ranged from $159,900 for a classic two-bedroom, 1,200-square-foot house on the main road, to $985,000 for a 167-year-old, renovated, 2,600-square-foot house (with a separate guest house) on front beach.

Isle of Palms houses range in cost from $117,000 for a 1,200-

square-foot ranch house in the middle of the island, to $1,350,000 for a front beach, 5,000-square-foot home with exquisite views and four bedrooms.

Wild Dunes prices at the time of our research included $67,000 for a 1,600-square-foot, three-bedroom furnished house on the third row, $825,000 for a 3,800-square-foot, three-bedroom house with a pool and dock, on the Intracoastal Waterway, or $950,000 for a 3,800-square-foot house on front beach.

Although Goat Island houses and lots are not often on the market, we found one — an architect's furnished, two-bedroom, 1,100-square-foot retreat — with an asking price of $129,900. To live on Goat Island, one must be willing to travel by personal commuter boat to the Isle of Palms (across the Intracoastal Waterway), perhaps an inconvenience for active families on a daily basis, but the ultimate "escape" for those who have the time.

East Islands
Fitness, Participatory Sports and Parks

The most obvious recreational attraction on Sullivans Island and the Isle of Palms is the beach — miles and miles of exceptional sands and sea. Except in the coldest months of the year, expect to see windsurfers, swimmers, walkers, runners, kite-flyers, bocchi ball players and just plain sun-worshipers out on Sullivans. Much of the same action as well as a dedicated surfing crowd brings the Isle of Palms to life year round. A Recreation Center on this island provides a full range of organized activities for young and old, and the Wild Dunes resort provides additional opportunities — including a complimentary children's recreational program — for its residents and guests.

Participatory Sports

Aerobics

ISLE OF PALMS PARK AND RECREATION DEPARTMENT
24-28th Avenue   *886-8294*
Classes are offered for adults (and there is even a class tailored to the needs of senior citizens).

Baseball

ISLE OF PALMS PARK AND RECREATION DEPARTMENT
24-28th Avenue   *886-8294*
There is a Dixie Minor League, an adult league and a church league (the less expensive option).

Basketball

ISLE OF PALMS PARK AND RECREATION DEPARTMENT
24-28th Avenue   *886-8294*
Basketball courts are located across from the Isle of Palms Park and are open to the public. This facility has two outdoor lighted courts, available until 10:00 PM, and one indoor court. There are youth and adult basketball teams organized by the recreation department.

SULLIVANS ISLAND PARK
Middle Street   *883-3198 (Town Hall)*
The lighted court at Sullivans Island Park is open to the public until 11:00 PM. A fairly steady flow of regulars and people looking for a pick-up game keeps the action in the hoops.

Gymnastics

ISLE OF PALMS PARK AND RECREATION DEPARTMENT
24-28th Avenue   *886-8294*

Regular classes are offered for children ages three and older, and for two through four-year-olds in the fall and spring. There is a fee for each monthly session.

Soccer

ISLE OF PALMS PARK AND RECREATION DEPARTMENT
24-28th Avenue   *886-8294*

There are teams for children ages five through ten, and a nominal charge for participation.

Softball

ISLE OF PALMS PARK AND RECREATION DEPARTMENT
24-28th Avenue   *886-8294*

Youth and adult teams, which play in a league, are organized by the department. Information about church leagues is also available by calling the number listed above.

Tennis

ISLE OF PALMS PARK AND RECREATION DEPARTMENT
24-28th Avenue   *886-8294*

Two hard courts are located across the street from the Isle of Palms Playground. They are lighted until 10:00 PM, and open seven days a week.

SULLIVANS ISLAND PARK
Middle Street   *883-3198 (Town Hall)*

There are two lighted public courts as well as a practice wall — enclosed by a fence — at the island park. The courts open at sunup and may be used until 11:00 PM.

Wild Dunes

ISLE OF PALMS
886-6000

There are 16 Har-Tru tennis courts as well as a stadium court for tournaments and a practice court. Eight of those courts are lighted, and non-guests can play on a space available basis.

Volleyball

ISLE OF PALMS PARK AND RECREATION DEPARTMENT
24-28th Avenue   *886-8294*

Coed adult teams play volleyball in January and February. There is a nominal charge for participation.

Parks and Recreation Centers

SULLIVANS ISLAND TOWN HALL
Middle Street   *883-3198*

Although there is no official recreation department on Sullivans Island, one member of the Town Council serves as Head of Recreation. The island has a nice park at "The Mound" (constructed by the military during World War II) on Middle Street with a bandstand, basketball and tennis courts, and children's wooden play equipment in a fenced-in "tot lot."

ISLE OF PALMS PARK AND
RECREATION DEPARTMENT

24-28th Avenue   *886-8294*

This comprehensive facility includes a big playground (complete with separate equipment and areas for different ages), volleyball court, athletic fields (for soccer, football and kickball), baseball fields, tennis and basketball courts and a center with night basketball courts, tumbling equipment, ping-pong tables and more. There are even sheltered tables and grills for picnics. The department sponsors special programs — like a summer day camp, youth dances, and a senior citizens group — as well as events such as kite flying day and sand sculpting contests. The park is open from sunup to sundown; the recreation building is open from 9:30 AM until 6:30 PM, Monday through Friday, and from 12:30 PM until 6:30 PM on Saturday.

East Islands
Worship

*H*ouses of worship on the East Islands are accustomed to having beach vacationers as visitors. The atmosphere at these houses of worship is casual and welcoming.

Baptist

ISLE OF PALMS BAPTIST CHURCH
24th Avenue   *886-6762*

Isle of Palms Baptist Church was founded in 1958 and has a congregation of approximately 119 members. There is a Bible study and worship service Sunday morning, as well as a service in the evening. Members are involved in outreach programs such as the Lowcountry Crisis Pregnancy Center and Bethany Christian Services.

SULLIVANS ISLAND BAPTIST CHURCH
1753 Central Avenue   *883-3601*

Established in 1948, Sullivans Island Baptist now has 220 members. There is a church school program followed by a service on Sunday, and a family night on Wednesday. The congregation is involved in outreach programs such as local Baptist mission work with migrant workers and Habitat for Humanity.

Catholic

STELLA MARIS CATHOLIC CHURCH
12004 Middle Street   *883-3108*

With its delicate steeple and open sanctuary, Stella Maris is situated at what locals call "the quiet end" of Sullivans Island. The original church was built in 1846, but has existed at the present site since 1867. Its 601 families constitute a membership that is involved in programs like the Soup Kitchen, ECCO, and the Inner Island Ministerial Committee. Mass is held every morning, and a Vigil is conducted on Saturday afternoon. Two services are conducted Sunday morning, and there is also a Mass that evening. Reconciliation is offered daily before Mass, on Saturday afternoon, or by appointment.

Episcopal

CHURCH OF THE HOLY CROSS
2520 Middle Street   *883-3586*

One of the buildings that retained its facade and charm through the perils of Hurricane Hugo, Church of the Holy Cross has an early church service followed by a family worship service, Sunday School and a late morning Rite I service. It was founded in 1907 and has around 434 members. The church is very much family-oriented, evidenced visibly by its large covered picnic area for church gatherings and a nice play yard for the children. Members participate in more than 30 outreach ministries including: Campus Crusade for Christ, Meals on Wheels, Crisis Ministry and the Soup Kitchen.

Lutheran

ST. MARK'S LUTHERAN
300 Palm Boulevard   *886-8557*

St. Marks has a congregation of 180 members, and has been located on Isle of Palms since 1953. Church school and a service are conducted on Sunday, and Alcoholics Anonymous groups meet here regularly. Plans for a child care program are in the making.

Methodist

FIRST UNITED METHODIST CHURCH
12 21st Avenue   *886-6610*

First United Methodist was established on the Isle of Palms in 1950 and today has approximately 430 members. A service is held on Sunday morning, and members volunteer in missions, the Shelter for the Homeless, as well as the James Island Rural Mission.

Presbyterian

SUNRISE PRESBYTERIAN CHURCH
3222 Middle Street   *883-3888*

Located on Sullivans Island with incredible views of the Breech Inlet and ocean beyond, this church, established in 1955, now meets in a beautiful, new sanctuary. Church school is followed by a late morning service on Sunday, and there is a Wednesday night education program as well. Approximately 475 members participate in outreach programs such as Crisis Ministry, ECCO, My Sister's House and Habitat for Humanity.

West Islands History

James Island

The Cusabo Indians, whose name has been translated as Coosawhatchie River People, lived here as long as four centuries ago and left their mark ahead of the white settlers. It was probably the Kiawah tribe who blazed the trail — along which they met to sign treaties and smoke peace pipes — from the Stono River to the beach. This path became King's Highway, an important road for the European settlers.

James Island was called Boone's Island in early records, named for the colony's agent, Joseph Boone. Around 1671, James Town, the second settlement in South Carolina, was officially established on one of this island's creek banks. Later, plantations were built as was a summer retreat for plantation owners: the village of Secessionville. It is believed that the first shots of the Civil War were fired from the island's Fort Johnson onto Fort Sumter in 1861.

By 1866, all but a handful of dwellings — from stately plantations to ginmills and barns — had been destroyed by the war. The island was for many years afterward a farming community where cotton and, later, vegetables were the cash crops. Today, there are many businesses and residential areas covering this once sparsely populated land. Residents are enthusiastic about the partially completed connector, which will channel traffic directly to the peninsula and initiate the next chapter of James Island's history.

Folly Beach

It is believed that the Bohicket tribe of Cusabo Indians summered on Folly in the 17th century. During the Civil War, at both ends of the island there were Union batteries with thousands of men. For many years after the war, Folly Beach was described as a "tent city" because of the many temporary dwellings used for shelter. More permanent houses were built at the turn of the century, and George Gershwin stayed in one during the 1920s while he was writing *Porgy and Bess*.

It was a pier and pavilion that probably put Folly on the map. Big names like Tommy Dorsey, Artie Shaw, Harry James, Guy Lombardo and Vaughn Monroe and the Ink Spots played at Folly's "Atlantic Boardwalk" in the 1930s.

Around 1936, when the jail was literally a cage in the marsh and

Photo: The Post and Courier

Enjoy the quiet beaches of Kiawah Island.

the toll road was just paved, a township form of government was established. Fire destroyed the boardwalk in 1957 but it was reopened in 1960 as the Ocean Plaza. Over the next decade, Folly became a mecca for surfers. Drawn to the sizeable waves, they congregated around the pier. Again in 1977 fire destroyed this landmark, and eight years later a multistory Holiday Inn went up in its place.

Hurricane Hugo scrambled homes and businesses on this island as well, but, with the hurricane's debris hauled off and Sunset Point, the island's first subdivision, under construction, the focus today is positive.

John's Island

Cusabo Indians also inhabited John's Island before the British arrived. By 1695, there were perhaps 14 white families farming the land which was also home to wild animals like buffalo, wolves and cougars. With the plantation system came the development of Legarevill — a summer village, with homes built by plantation owners.

Wadmalaw Island and Rockville

As on other islands, the plantation system was in place on Wadmalaw by the 1700s. Plantation owners here also built summer houses, nestled together in what became the village of Rockville. Legend has it that Rockville was named for the ore deposits that once projected (but were removed during Federal occupation) from the bluff of the waterfront. There are records from as early as the 18th century describing a 496-acre plantation known as the "Rocks" — part of which is included in present-day Rockville — and another, west of the public road named Rockland. Because Federal gunboats were raiding waterways during the Civil War, the Confederate government ordered residents inland for safety. Although most southerners had trouble paying taxes during these hard years, many did keep their property, and some of the homes now on the National Register of Historic Places still belong to descendants of the people who built them. An annual regatta, which began as a race between cousins in the late 19th century, still draws massive crowds and transforms a tranquil zone into a pulsating party.

Kiawah

Kiawah Island was home to the Kiawah Indians as early as the 16th century. Europeans arrived in 1688, when the island was granted to Captain George Rayner by the Lords Proprietors of the Carolina Colony. The Vanderhorst family later owned and grew cotton, indigo and other crops on the island for 180 years. During the Revolutionary War, British troops occupied the island, and Union troops raised their flag for two years during the Civil War. When the dust of war settled, the Vanderhorsts resumed farming but lost their battle to the boll weevil in 1914. The island was used as a hunting and fishing retreat between 1952 and 1974 when it was owned by C.C. Royal of Aiken. Old-timers still talk about the profit he turned in 1974 when he sold the island — land he purchased for $50,000 — to The Kiawah Island Company, a Kuwait Investment Company's subsidiary, for $17.4 million. The real business news story came, however, in 1988, when it changed hands again: this time, for $105 million.

Seabrook

In 1666, British subject Lt. Col. Robert Sanford arrived on Seabrook as an explorer in royal service to King Charles. The island was claimed for the Crown, and enjoyed by many owners before becoming the property of wealthy plantation owner, William Seabrook. In 1972, developers began planning the residential community that Seabrook is today. Sixteen years later, the island became incorporated as the Town of Seabrook.

West Islands
Shopping

There was a time when the locals had to come to Charleston proper for purchases, but those days are past. There are interesting places to shop in shopping centers and mini-malls on the islands west of the Ashley.

AFFORDABLES BY LOWELLS
Merchant Village   795-4695

Follow Folly Road to find another store in the Affordable's group. This store seems to carry a particularly good selection of career and after-hours clothing — all at off-prices. If your size is not in stock, there is a good chance that the staff can locate what you need at one of the other Affordables in the area.

ISLAND CENTER

This retail complex is located at 3714 Bohicket Road, three miles from the Kiawah-Seabrook gates, and includes stores with items ranging from home furnishings to groceries. Within the center is **The Design Center** — a group of shops and services relating to interior design. The concept is that together they provide one-stop-shopping for the home.

ISLAND CENTER SUPERMARKET

The supermarket includes a hot food bar and bakery, as well as all the essentials you would expect.

ISLAND CENTER LIQUORS
768-9165

Island Center Liquors carries more than 200 varieties of domestic and imported wine and champagne — from French to Australian. The liquor selection is impressive also, and there is a complete array of cordials.

ISLAND DIPPER
763-2328

A good place to buy a frozen yogurt or ice cream cone (or even a hot dog), the Island Dipper is open Monday through Thursday, from 11:00 AM until 8:00 PM, and 11:00 AM until 9:00 PM, on Friday and Saturday.

IRVIN MEADOWS AND CO., INC.
768-5519

This interior design shop sells furnishings, wallpaper and accents. It is part of the family of shops in the Design Center (see above). The Design Center also includes the following:

MCCANTS GLASS AND MIRROR
768-009

This is a good source for glass, mirrors, cultured marble and closet systems.

PALMETTO TILE DISTRIBUTORS
768-200
Out of Columbia, Palmetto carries a wide assortment of tiles and marble.

FURNITURE GALLERY
768-1001
This is a full-scale furniture store selling bedroom, living room, and dining room furniture as well as accessories, lamps, rugs and more.

AUDIO WAREHOUSE
768-2001
This business sells custom designed audio and video systems.

ARNIE HUME FLOOR
768-5519
Arnie Hume Floor stocks wonderful flooring products.

SOUTHERN LIGHTING SHOWROOM
768-4045
Our last stop in The Design Center, this is an interior and exterior lighting showroom.

KIAWAH-SEABROOK SEAFOOD
3966 Bohicket Road   768-0753
In a place like the Lowcountry, seafood is on the minds of many of the people much of the time. If you are like us — when we vacation we make a beeline to the grocer to check out what the natives are catching, harvesting or growing — you will want to see the array of fresh seafood for sale. This shop is one of the nicest around, and is located about two miles before the Kiawah turnoff. It carries excellent, fresh seafood as well as condiments. There is even a full service carry-out if your cravings get the best of you!

THE SHOPS OF BOHICKET MARINA VILLAGE
This shopping strip is located at Bohicket Marina Village, between the entrances to Kiawah and Seabrook Islands. For more information, call 768-1280.

ASHLEY NICOLE'S
768-9434
This shop features children's toys and t-shirts, candy, Charleston prints and other collectibles.

CHARLESTON COLLECTIONS
768-9101
This shop is one of four gift shops in a local chain, featuring many items that capture the flavor of the Lowcountry.

ISLAND SPIRITS
768-9751
Open six days a week, this shop carries a nice selection of both imported and domestic wines and spirits.

ISLAND STYLE
768-1757
This shop carries resort wear for men and women's casual dressing, as well as a fashionable collection of swimwear. There is also a shop in the Kiawah Straw Market.

LAUGHING DOLPHIN
768-7483
If you are looking for that perfect antique, piece of original art, unusual screen or maybe just some special stationery, stop by the Laughing Dolphin. They also offer design service.

SHIP'S STORE
768-3467

This shop reminds us of the old-fashioned general store at the beach where we summered as children — a place that had a little of everything. You will find fishing information, beach umbrellas, toys, hardware and household items, nonprescription drugs, film and blank videotape, and even Pawleys Island Hammocks.

VILLAGE TRADER
768-1222

This is possibly the largest shop around these West Island resorts. In addition to distinctive gifts and collectibles — such as gourmet baskets, glassware, pottery and sculpture — Village Trader carries designer and name brand clothing with such labels as Chaps/Ralph Lauren, Panama Jack, Outlander, Maria/Kim, Sportif and Duckhead.

VIDEO LIBRARY
768-0874

For VCR-VHS rentals and top-rated movies, come to this store, which stays open seven days a week. It also carries a line of books-on-tape.

THE GENERAL STORE
Beachwalker Drive at Kiawah's Gate 768-9541

This store *is* a general store, carrying essential and frivolous groceries, beer and wine, deli goods, beach supplies, fuel, the daily newspaper and even laundry service. You can't miss it as you drive in the gate: a one-stop shop on your right.

THE STRAW MARKET

Kiawah's "shopping strip" is an attractive group of resort-oriented shops. Fine clothes, jewelry, gifts and even ice cream are in the offerings.

BIRDS AND IVY
768-3121

A lovely garden shop, like the other two Birds and Ivy, this is a wonderful source for garden accents and the like. There seems to be a real effort to stock things that seem natural to the surroundings (in this case, the laid back but sophisticated island life).

CHARLESTON COLLECTIONS
768-7487

This gift shop, like its affiliates around Charleston, carries a wide selection of cards, gifts, books and gourmet foods. This is a good place to find the crafts of Lowcountry artisans — things like sweetgrass baskets, shell lamps and even fine art prints.

ISLAND STYLE
768-1166

Men and women both find resort clothing and accessories (even sandals and hats) for casual wear at this boutique. There is also a boutique in the Bohicket Marina Village.

KIAWAH KIDS
768-2341

Children love to take home clothes or other items that remind them of a vacation. Kiawah Kids carries funwear featuring an animated window display of "Bears at the Beach" in sizes infant to pre-teen, as well as beach toys, games and gifts.

THE KIAWAH SHOP
768-1284

This shop sells Kiawah logo apparel and gifts. There is a nice selection of cards (and the stamps with which to mail them!) as well as t-shirts, sweats, golf shirts, sweaters and jackets.

OBSESSIONS
768-7483

The jewelry in Obsessions' cases is exclusive designer merchandise. There is a selection of gold and silver, and many are adorned with precious stones — from diamonds to onyx. Obsessions is now located inside Sea Island Interiors, Kiawah's grande dame of interior design.

SCOOPER'S
768-2121

We always agree to an ice cream break, especially if the frozen treat is Haagen Dazs. Choose from Scooper's cups, cones, shakes

or specialty ice cream bars. If you are "going lighter," try a frozen yogurt or fruit juice bar.

THE STRAW MARKET CONFECTIONERY
768-4466

This is the place that can satisfy a sweet tooth. The Straw Market Confectionery sells cotton candy, homemade fudge, popcorn, caramel corn, sno-kones, tropical ices, lemonade and limeade.

319 BEACH
768-7400

For a wide range of fashion — from clothes you wear in the city to swimsuits that wow them by the pool — visit 319 Beach. The shop carries some nice designer separates as well.

TREASURES
768-6705

Treasures is a "collectibles" shop, with a lovely collection of pewter, crystal, Mark Hopkins sculpture, glass figurines and more. They also stock Crabtree and Evelyn as well as a nice selection of soft, New Age tapes and CDs.

West Islands
Restaurants

*P*eople come from all over the greater Charleston area to dine at some of the West Island restaurants. Whether you're looking for a quick deli sandwich or an elegant evening dining experience, you'll find it.

While prices vary with seasons in a resort area, the following scale should be helpful as a guide for restaurants west of the Ashley River. The dollar symbols denote what you can expect to pay per entrée:

Under $10	$
$10-$15	$$
$16-$20	$$$
$21 & up	$$$$

ALANO'S
The Shops of Bohicket   768-2424
Bohicket Marina Village, between the
entrances to Kiawah and Seabrook Islands
$-$$$ No credit cards

If you are looking for a pizza and want free delivery to the west island resorts, this is the place. Alano's has good pizzas — made fresh daily, in three sizes, with a choice of 15 fresh toppings — in addition to hoagies and salads. Hours are noon until 10:00 PM during the week, and noon until 11:00 PM on weekends.

ANGLEFISH RESTAURANT
520 Folly Road (Merchant Village)   762-4722
$-$$ MC, V, AX

Located in the Merchant Village shopping center, Angelfish has a bright and high-tech atmosphere. The menu is innovative and reflects the bounty of our local seafood and produce. Patrons enjoy shrimp stirfry, grouper, salmon cakes, grilled shrimp, dijon fried flounder and even shrimp potato cakes. There is an assortment of pasta dishes, vegetarian entrées, quiche, omelettes and salads, as well as a pita pizza with three cheeses and even an artichoke egg roll. Lunch is served from 11:30 AM until 3:00 PM, Monday through Friday. Dinner hours are from 6:00 PM until 9:30 PM, Monday through Thursday, and from 6:00 PM until 10:00 PM, Friday and Saturday.

ATHEN'S GREEK RESTAURANT
325 Folly Road   795-0957
(Crosscreek Shopping Center)
$-$$$$ MC, V

The line moves quickly at Athens, but there is usually a crowd eager to dine at this Greek restaurant. Specialties include Greek chicken, spanakopita, lemon chicken soup, Greek salad with feta cheese, and baklava. A full range of spirits is available. It is open seven days a week, and hours are from 11:00 AM until 10:00 PM from Monday through Thursday, from 11:00 AM until 10:30 PM on Friday and Saturday, and from 5:00 PM until 9:30 PM on Sunday.

BUBBA'S FAMILY RESTAURANT

3775 Maybank Highway 559-2755
$-$$ V, MC, D

 Bubba's is located in the large, unnamed shopping center at the intersection of Maybank Highway and Bohicket Road. The menu includes standard lunch fare (burgers, sandwiches, hot and cold plates) as well as seafood, pasta and other heavy entrées in the evening. There are items for the children as well, and the atmosphere is family charged. Bubba's is open from 11:00 AM until 9:00 PM, Monday through Thursday, and until 10:00 PM on Friday and Saturday. Breakfast is served some Saturdays and Sundays.

BUSHY'S FOLLY RIVER SEAFOOD

Wheelhouse Lounge and Bar 588-2890
2 Folly Road
$-$$$ AX, MC, V

 The menu at Bushy's includes chopped sirloin, chicken, prime rib and steak, but we think of seafood at Bushy's: blackened red fish, fresh grouper and salmon or the fisherman's platter with the works. There is a children's menu as well. Bushy's is open from 5:00 PM until 10:00 PM, seven days a week.

CAFE SUZANNE

4 Center Street   588-2121
Folly Beach
$-$$$ No cards

 Certainly this is the place if you are looking for a fresh, roman-

tic spot on Folly. The emphasis on "fresh" characterizes the food and even the herbs and flowers that owner Suzanne Corwell grows. There are usually four or five kinds of fish as well as scallops, duck breast and even grilled tenderloin on the menu. Dine by candlelight or sit at the nice little bar and enjoy a cool beer or wine with your ocean breeze (the Atlantic is just across the street). Hours for lunch are 11:00 AM until 2:00 PM, Thursday through Saturday; dinner hours are Monday through Saturday from 5:30 PM until 10:00 PM; and on Sunday, brunch is served from 9:00 AM until 3:00 PM.

CAPPY'S SEAFOOD

2408 Maybank Highway 559-3552
$$-$$$$ AX, MC, V

 We like to go by boat to Cappy's, and enjoy the fresh seafood and view of the Stono River. Shrimp, scallops and fish are fresh, and spirits are available. Lunch is served from 11:30 AM until 2:30 PM, Monday through Friday, and until 3:00 PM on Saturday. Dinner is served from 5:00 PM until 10:00 PM, every evening except Sunday, when service ends at 9:00 PM.

CAROLINA WILDLIFE

861 Folly Road, James Island 795-1001
$-$$$ Most credit cards

 As you might guess, the interesting menu items here have to do with the wilder side... or at least a version of the original. Try seafood sausages, duck, fowl and game. This is Lowcountry cuisine with a dash of new American (all done without any gaudy flash). Hours for lunch are 11:30 AM until 2:00 PM, Wednesday through Sunday, and dinner or drinks at the bar from 5:30 PM until, seven days a week.

THE CHARLESTON CRAB HOUSE

145 Wappoo Creek Drive   795-1963
$-$$ V, MC, AX, D

Located on the Intracoastal Waterway, the Charleston Crab House is open for lunch from 11:30 AM until 2:30 PM, and dinner from 3:30 PM through 10:00 PM, seven days a week. The restaurant specializes in steamed garlic crabs (cooked until they are red, and put before you for what locals call a "crab crack"), and has a raw bar as well as outside tables for dining close to the water. We enjoy arriving by boat and mooring at the restaurant's dock. No reservations are necessary.

DRAGON GATE CHINESE RESTAURANT

1739 Maybank Highway   795-3398
$ Most major credit cards

The Dragon Gate, located in the James Island Shopping Center, serves authentic Chinese food. There is a full bar, and a lunch buffet special. Hours are Sunday through Thursday, from 11:30 AM until 10:00 PM, and Friday and Saturday from 11:30 AM until 11:00 PM.

EASTERBY'S

1977 Maybank Hwy.   762-4890
$-$$$

Easterby's serves steaks, seafood, and barbecue. There is a children's menu, and the hours are 11:00 AM until 10:00 PM, Monday through Thursday, and until 11:00 PM on Friday and Saturday.

FISH AND SHRIMP HOUSE

967 Folly Road   795-0885
$ No credit cards

This fast service, Chinese restaurant serves standard oriental fare as well as fried seafood and chicken at reasonable prices. It is one of several Fish and Shrimp Houses in the area, each one slightly different from the other. Try the fried rice — very nice. The restaurant opens at 11:30 AM and closes at 9:00 PM, Monday through Thursday, and at 10:00 PM on Friday and Saturday.

THE GALLEY CAFE

The Shops of Bohicket   768-1807
Bohicket Marina Village, between the
entrances to Kiawah and Seabrook Islands
$ AX, MC, V, D

We have enjoyed delightful soups, sandwiches and salads here during fishing tournaments, and felt very much part of the action. Our choice is a seat out on the deck where we can enjoy the view and the luncheon. Gourmet items are also for sale, and beer and wine are available. Hours are Monday through Saturday, 9:00 AM until 11:00 PM, and Sunday from 9:00 AM until 10:00 PM.

GENERAL STORE DELI

Kiawah Island   768-9541
$ All major credit cards

For a quick pick-up breakfast or lunch, try this deli. The bakery items are fresh, and what we really like best is the fried chicken and enormous fries. Hours are 6:30 AM until 11:00 PM, Monday through Friday, and 7:00 PM until 11:00 PM, Saturday and Sunday.

GILLIGANS STEAMER AND RAW BAR

160 Main Road   766-2244
$-$$ V, MC, AX, D

Gilligans has a great family atmosphere and delicious steamed seafood. Seafood also comes fried, and steaks and chicken are also on the menu. Two veggies, a choice of salad or slaw and hush puppies round out each meal. Crayons are available so the kids can draw while they wait. Dress for everyone is casual. Hours are 11:30 until 10:00 PM, Monday through Saturday, and 11:30 AM until 9:00 PM on Sunday.

GOLD BUDDHA CHINESE RESTAURANT

325 Folly Road   762-1999
$ V, AX, MC

There is a daily — seven days a week — lunch buffet at Golden Buddha. Broccoli chicken and moo goo gai pan are our favorites, but all the classic Chinese specialties are on the menu. Cocktails are available, and dress is very casual. Hours are Sunday through Thursday from 11:30 AM until 10:00 PM, and Friday and Saturday from 11:30 AM until 11:00 PM.

HERON PARK GRILL

Night Heron Park   768-6440
Kiawah Island
$-$$$ Most credit cards

Heron Park Grill's menu includes unusual pizzas — with toppings like grilled tuna, Greek olives and artichokes — as well as short ribs and chutney sauce, roasted eggplant and marinated shrimp. It is open Sunday through Thursday, from 5:30 PM until 9:30 PM, and until 10:00 PM on Friday and Saturday.

THE JASMINE PORCH

Kiawah Island Inn   768-2121
$$-$$$$ Most major credit cards

Views of the Atlantic Ocean, framed by lovely, live oaks, are a big part of the experience at The Jasmine Porch. We have been great fans of the Sunday buffet for years, and bring the children to see the vast array of delicious foods and impressive ice sculpture. Seafood as well as Continental items are house specialties. Gentlemen wear jackets in the evening. Hours are daily 7:00 AM until 11:00 AM for breakfast, 11:30 AM until 2:30 PM for lunch, 2:30 PM until 5:00 PM for late lunch, and 6:00 PM until 10:00 PM for dinner.

JONAH'S

Straw Market   768-2121 ext. 2020
Kiawah Island
$-$$$ MC, V, D

Whether dining inside or out, this is a nice and casual place to unwind in a comfortable, family atmosphere. The soups are homemade and the burgers are the real thing. The menu also includes fresh fish, other seafood, baby back ribs, chicken and steaks. A full complement of cocktails, wine and beer is available. The hours are 11:30 AM until 9:00 PM daily.

MELVIN'S SOUTHERN BARBECUE

538 Folly Road   762-0511
$ MC, V

Melvin's has delicious barbecue, hamburgers, onion rings, cole slaw and the fixin's for a complete Southern picnic. There is a dining room, or orders may be carried out.

Hours are Monday through Saturday from 11:00 AM until 10:00 PM, and Sunday from 12:00 noon until 9:00 PM.

OCEAN ONE — AT HOLIDAY INN

1 Center Street   588-6464
$-$$ *Most major credit cards*

Seafood and steaks are on the menu at this oceanfront restaurant and lounge on Folly Beach. Call about Early Bird Specials such as baked stuffed flounder, prime rib, fried or broiled shrimp, Southern fried chicken and crab cakes. Breakfast and lunch are served from 7:00 AM until 2:00 PM, and dinner from 5:30 PM until 10:00 PM.

THE PRIVATEER RESTAURANT

The Shops of Bohicket   768-1290
Bohicket Marina Village
$-$$$ *Most major credit cards*

With its "sophisticated casual" atmosphere, The Privateer serves delicious, gourmet seafood and other entrées that appeal to the landlubber as well. Outstanding shrimp and scallop dishes, seafood pastas, broiled pink snapper, as well as tempting veal and steaks are part of the menu. There is an all-you-can-eat entrée each night, and special items for children are included on the regular menu. The views are lovely, and we try to arrive in time to watch sunset. Hours are from 5:00 PM until 11:00 PM.

STONO CAFE

2008 Wappoo Drive   762-4478
$-$$$ *M, V*

With a laid-back, "tropical" atmosphere, Stono Cafe is on James Island — just ten minutes from town — but seems like one of those restaurant in the Florida Keys: dedicated to serving fresh seafood without a lot of fuss. Oysters are something Stono does well that you can't always get on the panhandle. Also, pastas, homemade soups and vegetarian dishes are on the menu. Hours are 5:30 PM until 10:00 PM, Monday through Saturday, and Sunday brunch from 9:00 AM until 1:00 PM.

West Islands
Accommodations

Visitors interested in the islands west of Charleston will find a range of accommodations, including a comfortable Bed and Breakfast, an oceanfront, high-rise hotel, and exclusive resort communities as well as old-style beach houses available for rent. Much about the decision-making process is a matter of style, but certain basic questions should be addressed concerning each option: Is there a crib for my baby? Can my small pet stay with me? What is included in the room price or rental, and what is not? Use the scale below to gauge rates, but remember that rates vary with seasons and demand — call and you may be pleasantly surprised.

Use our $-symbol scale below to get an average idea of what you can expect to pay per room/night for two adults:

$50 and under	*$*
$51-$75	*$$*
$76-$95	*$$$*
$96-$110	*$$$$*
$110 and up	*$$$$$*

HOLLIDAY INN OF FOLLY BEACH

114 & 116 West Ashley Avenue   588-2191
$-$$$$ MC, V

Not to be confused with the high-rise of a similar name, this "two L" Holliday Inn is an independent motel that has been around for years. Its large swimming pool and expansive deck are attractive features.

HOLIDAY INN

1 Center Street   588-6464 or
     800-HOLIDAY
$$$-$$$$ *Most major credit cards*

The only oceanfront hotel, restaurant and bar in this part of the Lowcountry, the Holiday Inn's rooms provide beautiful views at Folly Beach. A nice touch are private balconies, which make wave-watching all the nicer. There is a pool for those who do not dip in the salt water, as well as a game room for inside entertainment.

KIAWAH ISLAND RESORT

P.O. Box 12357,   768-2121 or
Charleston, 29422-2357   800-654-2924
$$$-$$$$$ *Most major credit cards*

Called by *Vogue* magazine, "South Carolina's joy of a resort isle," Kiawah Island is a 10,000-acre, semitropical island with rental options galore. Choose from 300 villas, cottages, private homes or stay at the 150-room Kiawah Island Inn. There are actually two resort areas, or "villages," within walking or biking distance of island shopping and dining. Villas and cottages are fully equipped and have up to four bedrooms, while homes for rent in adjacent residential areas have as many as seven bedrooms and elaborate extras. Plan to swim, bike, shell, boat, fish and explore the many nature trails that encircle the island. According to *Golf* magazine, Kiawah — site of the 1991 Ryder Cup Matches — is one of the best golf resorts in America. Kiawah's tennis program, with state-of-the art facilities at two centers, ranks high as well.

SEABROOK RESORT

1002 Landfall Way,   *768-1000 or*
Seabrook Island 29455   *800-845-2475*

This resort offers one-, two- and three-bedroom villas — some in the maritime forest, others overlooking the sea — for family vacations in an island, residential setting. Seabrook has two championship golf courses and a tennis complex, as well as the area's only resort equestrian center. Swimmers choose between the pools and a beautiful stretch of the Atlantic Ocean. We have jogged Seabrook beach and nearly kept pace with dolphin swimming parallel to the shore — it is just that tranquil. Kids love old-fashioned fun like puppet shows, finger painting and ice cream making, while their parents relish a little time alone.

West Islands
Nightlife

*N*ighttime activity on the islands west of the Ashley River is often located on or near the water, in settings that are attractive but casual. Most night spots are part of restaurants, and some — with docks — cater to the boat crowd.

ATLANTIC ROOM/SPUTNIKS
Holiday Inn Folly Beach   588-6464
Facing Folly Beach proper, the Atlantic Room opens at 12:00 PM and closes at 6:00 PM Monday through Friday, and from 11:00 AM until 6:00 PM on Saturday and Sunday. Sputniks opens when Atlantic Room closes, and stays open until about 2:00 AM. Hotel guests as well as a crowd of locals enjoy the ocean view.

CAPPY'S
Highway 700, Johns Island   559-3552
The bar at Cappy's is a popular stop for boaters, who enjoy pulling up to the dock. It is open from 11:30 AM until 10:00 PM daily.

THE CHARLESTON CRAB HOUSE
Foot of Wappoo Creek Bridge   795-1963
This is a popular spot on the Intracoastal Waterway, with tables dockside and space for mooring boats. There is live entertainment on weekends, and a Happy Hour from 4:30 PM until 6:30 PM, Monday through Friday.

THE SAND DOLLAR
7 Center Street, Folly Beach   588-9498
Definitely a young or young-at-heart kind of place, The Sand Dollar features live music at the beach. Blues and rock 'n' roll is standard fare, and the hours are from 12 noon to 2:00 AM Monday through Saturday, and from 1:00 PM until 2:00 AM on Sunday. There is no cover charge, but you must purchase a membership for $1 and cool your heels for 24 hours while it's activated.

SUNDANCER'S
Kiawah   768-2121
This is a seasonal bar, open

only in the spring and summer, but it is one of our favorite settings for wave watching. We know it is really not "nightlife," since it closes in the afternoon, but we think a drink here is a good way of *leading up* to the night! Talk about pretending to be a million miles from any place stuffy — this upstairs lounge is up top with the birds, overlooking the ocean and buzzing with the sound of blenders endlessly whipping up those tropical drinks. Hours are from 11:00 AM until 8:00 PM.

THE SUNSET LOUNGE
The Privateer   *768-1290*
Open year round, the Sunset Lounge features live entertainment on the second floor of the Privateer Restaurant at Bohicket Marina. We like to watch the sun set over Bohicket Creek, and enjoy the music and dancing later on. The crowd is a sophisticated mix of the yachting and resort sets, and the mood is generally way upbeat. Hours are 4:30 PM until 2:00 AM, seven days a week.

TOPSIDER LOUNGE
Kiawah   *768-2121*
The Topsider is open from 5:00 PM until midnight or 1:00 AM, seven days a week. There is live entertainment on weekends, and the attire is typical "resort" — casual but nice.

Movie Theaters

JAMES ISLAND CINEMA THEATRE
795-9499

Photo: Ron A. Rocz

A solitary island sunset.

West Islands
Neighborhoods

The islands west of the Ashley River, connected by a series of bridges, are a diverse and intriguing group. Densely populated James Island has spectacular views of Charleston's harbor and peninsula, and is home to many who work throughout the Trident area. Low-key Folly Beach is a casual, year round island community with one new 168-lot subdivision, Sunset Point. Real estate offerings includes front beach, marsh, river and in-land houses and lots. Much of Johns Island is still rural, although a main road, Bohicket, has been widened in part near the resorts — literally "paving the way" for development. Kiawah and Seabrook resorts are technically part of Johns Island, and are prestigious, year round residential communities. Wadmalaw Island includes a mixture of farm land, deep water property, and the charming village of Rockville.

James Island

COUNTRY CLUB I

Having crossed the Wappoo Bridge, on Folly Road, one is on James Island. Take a left at the traffic light to enter Country Club I — an older, executive development with beautiful houses and well-kept lawns. Our research unearthed ask-

ing prices for houses that started at $165,000. When they come on the market, most houses are listed at twice that figure with those on the waterway commanding more. The club, pool and golf course are wonderful assets, and the proximity to the peninsula is a plus.

RIVERLAND TERRACE

By taking a right at the traffic light (instead of the Country Club's left) one may head for Riverland Terrace on the right off Maybank Highway. Riverland Terrace, an established neighborhood, is a large conglomeration of sizes, styles and prices. There are interesting "handyman possibilities" as well as extraordinary turnkey dwellings throughout. Young people have been drawn to this area in recent years because of its tranquility and — in some instances — relative affordability. Houses on the waterway, when available, are listed upwards of $600,000, while smaller houses in the middle of the neighborhood can be purchased for less than $100,000.

COUNTRY CLUB II

Back out on Folly Road, the next important subdivision is Country Club II. Take a left at the stop light before the Exxon (just after the plantation, visible from the road) and across from Captain D's Seafood restaurant. This country club is another desirable area, with executive homes and established landscaping. Some homes here are less expensive than in Country Club I, but the real estate is in equal demand. At the time of our research, there were no houses on the mar-

ket, but they become available from time to time and are worth investigating.

BATTERY POINT AND LAWTON BLUFF

Harbor View Road is a left turn off Folly Road, heading away from town. Two established subdivisions along James Island Creek are Battery Point and Lawton Bluff. Houses here are currently listed at between $70,000 and $160,000, but command higher prices on the water.

LAKESHORE COMMONS

There are lakes on either side of this subdivision. Houses tend to be newer and attractive, usually made of wood with an island-resort look. Asking prices start in the low $100,000s.

STILES POINT PLANTATION

Houses in this newer subdivision are a mixture of brick and wood, two-, three- and four-story dwellings. List prices to date start at $130,000 and go up into the $300,000s for waterfront homes.

CLEARVIEW

Harborview Road dead ends into Ft. Johnson Road. Take a left to explore subdivisions beginning with Clearview. With well-kept, established landscaping, pretty trees and nice ponds, this is a desirable area. There is much harbor frontage, and some homes have docks. Recent listings include a range from $89,000 to $390,000.

DELLWOOD AND EASTWOOD

These two subdivisions, on

the left off Ft. Johnson Road, are adjoining and both are attractive. Eastwood is newer, but both have houses listed in the $100,000 to $200,000 range.

FT. JOHNSON ESTATES

Heading back toward Harborview Road (still on Ft. Johnson Road) look for Ft. Johnson Estates on the left. This is another established neighborhood, with one- and two-story houses and nurtured yards. Some houses have long docks, and there is access to community tennis courts and a swimming pool. Views of Morris Island and the marsh are beautiful. There are a few new homes and lots for sale. One house we ran across was listed at $165,000. Others list from $90,000 to $200,000.

PARROT CREEK

There is much to see in Parrot Creek. These newer houses and lots are large and beautifully landscaped, some fronting on deep water or marsh. Comprised of mostly two-story homes on half-acre lots, Parrot Creek offers architectural variety and desirable extras (such as wide porches to catch those prevailing breezes). Recent listing prices range from $137,000 to $385,000.

HARBOR WOODS

Harbor Woods is a large subdivision with three areas — Harbor Woods, Harbor Woods II and III — and an assortment of brick and wood houses, landscaped by established shrubbery. There is no water access, but homes are solid and there is no new development. We found listings here for between $85,000 and $200,000.

BAY VIEW FARMS

Across from James Island High School, Bay View Farms is buffered from the road by woods and marked by tabby gates. One- and two-story houses on small, attractive lots are situated in this neighborhood, which is punctuated by small ponds. Recently, a lot was listed here for $44,000.

STONEFIELD

To reach Stonefield, take a left on Sessionville Road. These elevated, streamlined houses are clustered together, and the subdivision includes several cul-de-sacs. The area is surrounded by woods and backs up to the marsh. Asking prices range from $70,000 to $130,000 for water views.

SEASIDE PLANTATION

Seaside Plantation is a lovely area with duck-inhabited lakes and

Insiders Like:
Driving down old Bohicket Road toward Kiawah Island — under the spreading canopy of live oak trees — in the filtered light of an afternoon sun.

Insiders' Tip

fabulous views of Morris Island and Folly Beach. Homes and some docks have been built on approximately one-third of the lots. Architecture tends to be contemporary — wood and brick, two- and three-story houses built above flood levels. At this writing, lots are available from $63,000 to $85,000.

FOLLY BEACH

Coming from Sessionville Road, take a left on Folly Road and follow it to Folly Beach. Real estate on this island ranges from dilapidated, rental property to impressive, modern primary residences. Most homes fall somewhere in the middle. **Sunset Point**, an attractive new subdivision under development, will offer more uniformity at its end of the island. A house with a water view on Folly, at this writing, is offered at an asking price of $129,000. A more elaborate option on beach front is priced at $285,000. The new development, Sunset Point, is divided into six sections;

some are a block from the beach, while others front the marsh and deep water of Folly River. Sites, averaging a quarter acre, start at $21,900, and the average house price is $125,000.

Johns Island

Bordered by the Intracoastal Waterway, Church Creek, the Bohicket, Stono and Kiawah Rivers, Johns Island includes a vast amount of land — much of which is still very rural. Large farms and deep water property are available on the island, as well as homes in subdivisions that are in the beginning stages of development. The most well-known developments in the island's mailing area are two resort communities: **Kiawah** and **Seabrook**. Separated from Johns Island by water, these islands are entities in their own right.

HEADQUARTERS

Coming from the peninsula across the Wappoo Bridge, take a right at the first traffic light. This is Maybank Highway (at first, on James Island) which crosses the Stono River and comes into Johns Island. Headquarters is the first development on the right, and is a marsh island. Marsh views are impressive and homes are large and attractive. Recent listings ranged from $115,000 for a townhouse to $215,000 for a home with water views.

CHURCHHILL LANDING

Take a right on Main Road at the intersection of Main and Maybank and look for Churchhill Landing on the left. This neighborhood has large two- and three-story houses designed around the beautiful oaks, pines and magnolias. There are some vacant lots along the river, and houses with docks along Church Creek Flats. Lots are available from $15,000 to $40,000.

GIFT PLANTATION

Back on Main Road, see Chisolm Road on the left. A few miles down Chisolm, Gift Plantation is located on the right. There are numerous waterfront lots, some with wooded areas, bordering the marshes of the Intracoastal Waterway. As of this writing, there is only one house built (priced at $189,000) and lots ranging in asking price from $30,000 to $110,000.

CHISOLM GREEN

Chisolm Green is located several miles down from Gift Plantation, still on Chisolm Road. This subdivision has houses with large yards (one is even home to a horse) and notable architectural variety. There are views of the waterway and marsh as well. We found a listing for $295,000 here, but understand that homes in the $150,000 come on the market occasionally.

ROYAL OAK

Follow Main Road until it be-

comes Bohicket Road (which leads to Kiawah and Seabrook), take a left on Edenvale, and drive to River Road. At River Road, turn left and see Royal Oak Road with Appapula Creek on the right. Roads are not paved, and houses are scattered about to take advantage of the creek views. A few have docks on the creek, and porches on which to enjoy the tranquil country setting. Homes are priced up to $495,000, and lots range from $40,000 to $150,000.

KIAWAH

Head back up River Road until it intersects with Bohicket. Bohicket runs out to the resorts, of which Kiawah is the first on the left. Some of the nation's most interesting resort architecture can be found at Kiawah. While the houses unobtrusively blend into the environment, they are by no means uniform. Palatial residences with creative use of glass and materials make the most of spectacular views — from ocean to lagoon — and there is a consistency in landscaping throughout. A variety of wildlife abounds, and residents are often avid "watchers." Residents can enjoy the use of athletic facilities and the beach, as well as participate in structured social activities. Kiawah also has a very active vacation rental program, which contributes to the "resort flavor." Condos and patio-

type homes start around $100,000, but most properties run over $200,000. We know of 3,000-square-foot homes being offered for $485,000 to $700,000, while the top of the market recently included a $1.6 million price tag for a 5,900-square-foot home on deep water. Vanderhorst Plantation is a strictly residential area of very upscale homes under development at Kiawah, and front beach lots here are priced in the $600,000 range.

SEABROOK

Seabrook is Kiawah's "next-door neighbor." While it is smaller and actually an incorporated town, Seabrook is similar in terms of being an upscale island community with a wide assortment of real estate options and amenities. Seabrook appeals to the equestrian set as it has a well-maintained stable and aesthetically pleasing trail and beach rides. Golf, tennis and swimming are popular here as well, and there is a clear retirement and year round living focus. Prices are somewhat less expensive than on Kiawah, with condominiums starting around $50,000. Our research turned up an interesting selection of single family homes in the $300,000 to $690,000 range, while there was also a contemporary beach front home, with 3,400 square feet, offered for $950,000.

West Islands
Fitness, Participatory Sports and Parks

The west islands are a Lowcountry paradise, and opportunities for recreation are bountiful. From camping to participatory sports, there is something for everyone.

Participatory Sports

Camping

JAMES ISLAND COUNTY PARK
795-7275

There are 128 camping sites at this magnificent park. Campers can spend the night in tents or in recreational vehicles — most sites are equipped with full water, sewer and electricity hookups. The cost ranges from $12.96 to $19.44 per night (depending on residential status, special exemptions and so forth), and the setting is unbeatable.

OAK PLANTATION
Johns Island 766-5936

There are 352 sites at this campground, located on Johns Island — away from the hectic crowds. There are laundry facilities, a play-ground, a swimming pool and a fresh water lake for fishing.

Fitness

Charleston County's Community School programs offer a wide range of classes at nominal cost. For more information, contact **James Island Community School**, at 762-2793, or **St. Johns Community School**, at 559-6400. In the private sector, contact:

ISLAND FITNESS STUDIO
1001 Landfall Way 768-4000 or
768-4004

Island Fitness is located on Seabrook Island above the Village Market. It offers classes in aerobics, yoga, strength training and senior fitness.

Flying

CHARLESTON EXECUTIVE AVIATION
Executive Airport 559-2401
2700 Fort Trenholm Road

This company offers flying lessons at beginning and advanced levels and a charter service, offering a variety of plane sizes. Helicopters of Charleston also operates out of this airport and can be reached at 1-800-264-8550.

Horseback Riding

BRICKHOUSE PLANTATION
EQUESTRIAN CENTER
2669 Hamilton Road, Johns Island   559-2867

Ponies are the specialty at Brickhouse. Lessons, boarding and showing are also offered, and there is a summer camp as well.

SEABROOK ISLAND
EQUESTRIAN CENTER
Seabrook Island   768-7541

This center is located at Seabrook, but is open to the public. Private lessons, trail rides into the undeveloped portions of the island's woods and marshes, rides on the beach in the summer, and boarding are available.

SEA HORSE STABLES
1487 Brownswood Road   559-3327
Johns Island

Sea Horse offers dressage, instruction, boarding and training. No rentals are available, however.

STONO STABLES
5304 Stono Ferry Course   763-0566
Hollywood, S.C.

Stono Stables offers lessons, boarding and sales. Staff members are involved in polo, and this is a good source for information about that sport.

STONO RIVER RIDING
AND BOARDING STABLE
2962 Hut Road, Johns Island   559-0773

This established riding school specializes in racing and training, and has horses for sale. There is dressage and a cross country course, as well as a wonderful facility for children's birthday parties out by the barn — hayride and all. The owners welcome visitors, and children regularly "drop by" to feed a favorite pony a carrot.

Jazzercize

JAMES ISLAND
PRESBYTERIAN CHURCH
1632 Fort Johnson Road   762-2491
at Folly Road

This class is taught by a certified instructor, and enrollment is continuous. The cost for eight classes is $22, or one class for $4. Baby-sitting is available for 50 cents per child.

Kayaking

JAMES ISLAND COUNTY PARK

Classes are offered in sea kayaking and canoeing at James Island County Park. Call 795-7275 for more information.

Skating

HOT WHEELS SKATE CENTER, INC.
1523 Folly Road   795-7982

Even the little ones can skate here in clamp-on skates. This is a very popular place for birthday parties, and it is often booked for weeks. There is a snack bar for light refreshments.

Swimming

JAMES ISLAND RECREATION COMPLEX
1088 Quail Drive, James Island   720-3806

There are lifeguards at this outdoor pool, which is slated to be open in the summer months (June through August). Water fitness classes and swimming lessons are planned for the mornings, and free swimming in the afternoon.

Tennis

HERBERT TENNIS
1349 Sea Aire Drive   *795-0278*

This private club is open from sunup to sundown. The courts are made of asphalt, and paddle tennis is also available. Annual single memberships and family memberships are available.

WEST ASHLEY MAYBANK TENNIS CLUB
1880 Houghton Drive   *795-6670*

This private club, located on James Island, has both hard and clay courts. New annual memberships are $150, and the club is open 24 hours a day, seven days a week. Members may bring guests.

KIAWAH
Kiawah Island   *768-2121*

Kiawah has two separate, highly acclaimed tennis centers, with hard and clay courts. Lessons are offered with a pro instructor or the tennis director, and courts are available on a space available basis. Hours are 8:00 AM until 6:30 PM,

off-season, and from 8:00 AM until 8:00 PM during the summer.

SEABROOK RESORT
Seabrook Island   *768-1000 or 1-845-2475*

Only club members and overnight resort guests may play on Seabrook courts. There are 24 courts and instruction is available to those with access.

Parks

Three of Charleston's four major parks are located on the West Islands. For an excellent, 47-page publication describing in detail the many courses and resources available at these facilities, contact the **Charleston County Park and Recreation Commission** at 762-2172.

BEACHWALKER PARK
Kiawah Island   *No phone available*

This park is located on a nice beach with beach chair and umbrella rentals, as well as a snack bar. Parking is $3 per car, and all 150 spots are often filled early. There are lifeguards, outdoor showers and rest rooms.

Insiders Like:
Turning out for the casting call and becoming an "extra" in some Charleston-made movies or TV shows — which are produced quite frequently.

Insiders' Tip

FOLLY BEACH COUNTY PARK

West Ashley Avenue on Folly Beach   762-2172

At the tip of Folly Beach, this county park is a easy, family-oriented beach destination. Enjoy the sand and waves, or bring along binoculars for viewing feathered friends in the marsh or en route to nearby Bird Key. In addition to beach chair and umbrellas rentals, there is a snack bar and gift shop. A shelter with natural gas, oyster roasting pit and barbecue cookers is also available.

JAMES ISLAND COUNTY PARK

861 Riverland Drive   795-7275

This incredible, 643-acre park offers biking, nature trails, an elaborate playground, pedal boats, 16 acres of lagoons, a Spray-Play area, fishing and crabbing dock, cane pole fishing and picnic areas. There are 10 vacation cottages, camping sites and four picnic shelters that can accommodate 100 or more people each.

West Islands
Worship

There are numerous options for worship on the islands west of the Ashley. As in other communities of the Trident area, some churches were founded centuries ago while others are relatively new entities.

Baptist

FIRST BAPTIST OF JOHNS ISLAND
3483 Maybank Highway   559-0367

First Baptist of Johns Island formed as a congregation in 1932, and now has a membership of 835. On Sunday, there is a morning Bible study followed by a worship service, evening church training, and another worship service. The midweek prayer service is held on Wednesday evening. The congregation is involved in such outreach projects as Crisis Ministry, work at the homeless shelter, and in nursing homes.

FOLLY BEACH BAPTIST CHURCH
77 Center Street   588-9414

This church serves Folly Beach, and has Bible School as well as a worship service on Sunday. There is a Wednesday evening meeting, and special outings for the children throughout the year. Established in 1939, the church now has approximately 100 members and assists others in the community with a Food Closet and financial assistance for necessities.

FT. JOHNSON BAPTIST CHURCH
1473 Camp Road   795-3232

On Sunday, there are two worship services — morning and evening — as well as Sunday School. On Wednesday evening, mission organizations meet and then have a prayer service.

CALVARY BAPTIST CHURCH
942 Folly Rd.   762-1718

Calvary was founded in 1983 and has about 100 members. The church body is "young" and family-oriented, with the average member being between the ages of 25 and 45. There are services and church school Sunday morning, as well as a service Sunday night and Wednesday evening. Outreach projects include a Crisis Closet and the Crisis Pregnancy Center.

Independent Baptist

VICTORY BAPTIST CHURCH
335 Woodland Shores Road   795-8229

The Sunday services are in the morning and evening, and there is a morning Sunday School program as well. On Wednesday, a prayer service is conducted in the evening.

Catholic

CHURCH OF THE NATIVITY

1061 Folly Road   795-3821

Nativity was established in the 1950s, and today serves a congregation of approximately 1,000 families. On Saturday, Confessions are heard in the afternoon and Mass is conducted in the evening. There are three services on Sunday. Church members are involved in the Crisis Ministry as well as Habitat for Humanity.

HOLY SPIRIT CATHOLIC CHURCH

2545 Bohicket Road   559-0353

This church serves Johns, Kiawah, Seabrook and Wadmalaw Islands. There is a Saturday afternoon vigil as well as Confession. Mass is held two times Sunday morning.

OUR LADY OF GOOD COUNSEL

Corner of Center and   795-3821
East Indian Streets

Our Lady of Good Counsel serves the residents of Folly Beach with morning Mass, seven days a week. On Saturday, there is also an afternoon Vigil Mass. This small church has its own pastor, but relies on Church of the Nativity (see Nativity phone number listed above) for general office assistance.

Episcopal

ST. JAMES EPISCOPAL CHURCH

1872 Camp Road   795-1623

This church was founded in 1730, and now has about 1,500 members in its congregation. It holds services on Sunday, including early morning Holy Communion and late morning prayer and sermon. Members support Crisis Ministry, Episcopal Foreign Missions, My Sister's House, James Island Outreach and James Island Senior Citizens Center.

ST. JOHNS EPISCOPAL CHURCH

3673 Maybank Highway   559-9560
Johns Island

Founded in 1734, Saint Johns has a congregation of about 700 members. There is an early and mid-morning service on Sunday, as well as Christian education for all ages. The midweek Bible Study is held Wednesday night. Church members are involved in a variety of outreach projects such as: Trident Literacy; making "ditty bags" for rural missions; The Third Thursday Lunch — Communion, lunch and fellowship, targeted at those age 50 and older, but open to the community; and The Soup Kitchen (specifically, canning farming members' tomatoes for use by the Soup Kitchen).

THE CHURCH OF OUR SAVIOR

4416 Bohicket Road   768-2046

The Church of Our Savior has early morning Holy Eucharist on Sunday, and a coffee hour following the service. Located just outside the gates of Kiawah and

Seabrook resorts, it is convenient for those residents as well as resort visitors.

Full Gospel

LIVING WORD CHURCH
1566 Folly Road   *795-7732*

On Sunday this church has Children's Church as well as a morning worship service. There is also a Wednesday evening service.

Lutheran

MARTIN LUTHER LUTHERAN CHURCH
1605 Harbor View Road   *795-4855*

Established in 1961, this church has a membership of approximately 783. In addition to two Sunday services and Sunday School, there is an evening Bible study. A midweek Bible study is held Wednesday night. The church sponsors a Boy Scout and two Girl Scout troops, as well as outreach projects within the community.

Nondenominational

JAMES ISLAND CHRISTIAN CHURCH
12 Sawgrass Road   *795-9449*

There is a morning service and church school on Sunday morning. On Wednesday evening, a supper is followed by a praise singing and testimony.

United Methodist

FOLLY BEACH UNITED METHODIST
118 W. Indian Avenue   *588-9174*

This small church of approximately 130 members has a morning service as well as church school on Sunday. Members help the needy in the community with such projects as holiday dinners, and describe themselves as "very friendly."

EPWORTH UNITED METHODIST
1540 Camp Road   *795-3722*

Epworth has approximately 325 members. Both church school and worship service are held on Sunday morning. The congregation volunteers with the Interfaith Crisis Ministry, and the church serves as a meeting center for four Alcoholics Anonymous groups.

Presbyterian

HARBOR VIEW PRESBYTERIAN CHURCH
900 Harbor View Road   *795-4072*

Harbor View Presbyterian has a Sunday morning worship service, followed by a coffee fellowship and Sunday School for all ages. The Youth Fellowship meets on Sunday evenings.

Insiders Like:
Listening to gospel music sung by African-American church choirs at special candlelight concerts held in Drayton Hall.

Insiders' Tip

JAMES ISLAND
PRESBYTERIAN CHURCH

Corner Ft. Johnson and Folly Roads   795-3111

This historic church was founded in 1706. On Sunday there is a church school program and a morning worship service.

JOHNS ISLAND
PRESBYTERIAN CHURCH

2550 Bohicket Road   559-9380

Johns Island Presbyterian was founded in 1710. Assembly, Sunday School and two worship services are conducted each Sabbath.

Inside
North Charleston

The following chapter represents a departure from the usual
Insider format. The reason has a great
deal to do with the way North
Charleston evolved...and how this
third largest municipality in South
Carolina (estimated population,
70,000) has witnessed unprec-
edented growth in just the past few
years.

As the City of Charleston out-
grew the natural boundaries of the
peninsula, urban development
spread to the area (now North
Charleston) as early as the turn of
the century. But the separate municipality known as North Charleston has only been officially incorporated as a city since 1972.

The geographical area of
North Charleston actually crosses
the borders of Charleston,
Dorchester and Berkeley counties.
Clearly, the urban sprawl has blurred
those lines in many more ways —
culturally, socially and economically.

Many aspects of life in North
Charleston overlap with listings and
services described elsewhere in various chapters of this book. (See, for
example, our chapters on Spectator
Sports, Schools, Child Care, Media,
Medical Care and the Military.)
Other aspects of the North Charleston life-style are linked more closely

with neighboring Summerville, and
are handled as part of that city's
overview or in a combined linking
section we call "The North Area,"
meaning that section where North
Charleston/Summerville and Berkeley and Dorchester counties
tend to blur into one another, especially when it comes to services
shared by residents. (See the chapters on the History of Summerville,
North Area Neighborhoods, North
Area Parks and North Area Worship.)

Categories exclusive to the
North Charleston area, however, are
as follows:

We'll look at the history of the
area from fossils to its nuclear submarines. Then we'll look at closely-
related Dorchester County — and
some historic sites found there. We'll
also review neighboring Berkeley
County and some of its interesting
sites.

We'll briefly profile some of
North Charleston's longtime businesses and introduce some of the
newer ones that are adding to the
area's growing reputation as an industrial center.

We'll explore the North
Charleston dining options — checking out some of the favorite family
restaurants and some more exotic

spots as well.

We'll review the major shopping centers that cater to the growing north area population and we'll look at some of the accommodations for families and business travelers along 1-26 through the heart of North Charleston.

Then, in combined chapters (where city borders are less meaningful than county lines), we'll look at some of the new neighborhoods springing up the north area.

Finally, we'll list some of the major houses of worship attracting congregations from all over the north area.

PROFESSIONAL PROFILE
MAYOR BOBBY KINARD

Welcome to the Hub of the Low Country.

North Charleston is a young, vibrant and growing city. In only 20 years we have grown from a little over 21,000 people since incorporation in 1972 to a present population of 72,000. The City is now the 3rd largest in South Carolina. North Charleston's multi-purpose coliseum was completed in 1992, making it the largest in the state. This facility will attract top name entertainment and a variety of activities ranging from ice shows to sporting events. The Coliseum, resorts, beaches and historic Charleston are easily accessible from the many quality hotels in North Charleston via the new Mark Clark Expressway. Whether for business or pleasure, our hotels offer meeting facilities with all the amenities needed for your next trip. You can reach North Charleston by way of interstate highways, AMTRAK and the international airport. The City of North Charleston has numerous shopping areas and is the leading city in South Carolina in retail sales. If you are traveling through the South Carolina Low Country, I hope you will select our city as a place to stay and visit.

**For further information on North Charleston call:
(803) 554-5700, Ext. 504.**

North Charleston
History

According to the Smithsonian Institute, a giant condor — a prehistoric bird — left its bones on land now being used (appropriately enough) as the U.S. Air Force Base. And 19th-century industrial mining done in what is now North Charleston unearthed a stone hatchet, a few arrowheads, and human bones which, upon analysis, became evidence that Stone Age man lived in the area thousands of years ago. Though only a municipality since 1972, the area of North Charleston has seen a lot of history pass its way.

Shortly after the first English colonists put ashore and established Charles Towne in 1670, lands in the north area were granted, sold and resold again. Early on, deer skins, pitch, tar and turpentine from the north area's abundant pine trees became an important part of the Lowcountry's economy.

By the time of the American Revolution, there were probably 60 plantations in the north area successfully raising rice and indigo. Regular ferry service was available on the Ashley and Cooper Rivers — so the distance to Charles Towne was easily conquered. However, largely because the plow didn't come into general use here before 1810 and planters neither used fertilizer nor rotated their crops, the soil in the north area was quickly played out. In fact, it was of little use for agriculture after the Revolution.

Things took an upward turn for the north area in 1830 with the coming of the railroad. In fact, it was the destruction of these tracks and trains that had the greatest impact on Charleston during the Civil War.

Phosphates (used in making fertilizer) were discovered and mined along the Ashley River after the Civil War — and that gave employment to thousands of freedmen during Reconstruction. These freedmen became landowners and formed churches and burial societies that are still in evidence today. Phosphate mining soon gave way to booming fertilizer plants. These and successful lumber companies provided employment, company housing, and (at last) the basis for a diversified economy not completely tied to downtown Charleston.

The north area experienced a brief setback with the Great Earthquake of 1886 since its land mass was at the epicenter of the disturbance (at a point near what is now I-26 and Deer Park).

The one great catalyst for

change in the north area was the coming of the U.S. Navy Yard in the early 1900s. Suddenly land values soared, drainage plans were drawn up, and roads were built.

The words "North" and "Charleston" were first put together in 1912, according to Ruth W. Cupp, a *News and Courier* writer who compiled a warm, memory-filled history of the area in 1988. It was the name given to a vast land development plan which included 3,000 residential lots for housing "the labor force of the future."

Although the ambitious "North Charleston" real estate development went into foreclosure during the Great Depression, the inertia for a separate municipality continued to build momentum. Workers from the Navy Yard started a Savings & Loan Association — one of the first in the country. Then, West Virginia Pulp and Paper Company broke ground for a new plant in the area. Things started looking up. In fact, in that company's honor one of the north area streets was renamed "Virginia." Not far away, an old Indian path that had been widened and straightened was named "Rivers Avenue" for a local kid who became a U.S. Congressman.

With the coming of World War II, thousands of newcomers settled in the north area as the Navy Yard provided employment in three shifts, 24 hours a day.

Private industry and residential communities multiplied quickly after the war. Aviation traffic increased, an interstate highway was built, and the natural growing pains of a burgeoning city began to call for more political autonomy. The various factions and communities grafted themselves together and formed the City of North Charleston on July 12, 1972. Sworn in as the first Mayor was John E. Bourne who served the city for 18 years.

In 1990, Robert (Bobby) Kinard was elected Mayor of North Charleston. Today, the city is growing at a faster rate than at any time in its history. North Charleston's second mayoral administration is anxious to be rid of the city's old image of being a small, mostly military town on the outskirts of Charleston. Instead, North Charleston is building an identity all its own.

Residents can take justifiable pride in the fact that the population center for Greater Charleston (the Trident area) is in North Charleston. Smart businesses and industries are noticing that in greater numbers every day.

The greatest symbol of this renewed civic spirit is the new North Charleston Coliseum (see Arts) which opened in 1993. This is South Carolina's largest indoor facility — seating nearly 14,000 people. The Coliseum is home to both professional hockey and Big South Division I basketball teams. And it brings North Charleston into focus as a destination for major shows and entertainment attractions of all kinds.

There's no question that the decision of the Base Closure Commission — the loss of the Navy Base and the Naval Shipyard (see Military) — will impact North Charleston heavily. But it's also true that those changes aren't going to be immediate. And the actions of the Trident Chamber of Commerce, the BEST Committee (a group of civic and political leaders "Building Economic Solutions Together"), and the federal government's special compensatory programs are bound and determined to soften the anticipated economic blow. As we go to press, major new industries are presently exploring the north area — bringing the promise of new jobs and newfound economic security. In other words, North Charleston will continue to be a real "land of opportunity" here in the heart of the Lowcountry.

Photo: The Post and Courier

Mayor Bobby Kinard assists former city councilman "Zip" Zipperer in the cutting of the six-foot-long birthday cake.

Park Circle in North Charleston.

Photo: The Post and Courier

Dorchester County
History

*D*riving through the rapidly growing development so evident in Dorchester County today, it may be difficult to picture the role this countryside once played in the longer, historic Lowcountry saga.

Acreage was being granted to settlers in what is now Dorchester County just a few years after the initial landing at Charles Towne in 1670. The first planters were mostly Englishmen favored by the Crown — which was anxious to see English settlements do well in the New World. Indeed, some of the plantations created from these early land grants flourished in this area for nearly 200 years.

It was in Dorchester County that the legion of Lt. Col. "Light Horse Harry" Lee was posted after their Revolutionary battle at Eutaw Springs. Col. Lee, who was the father of Gen. Robert E. Lee, was encamped at a plantation called "The Villa" not far from Summerville when he wrote:

"The first day's march brought these detachments to the country settled by the original emigrants into Carolina. The scene was both new and delightful. Vestiges, though clouded by war, everywhere appeared of the wealth and taste of the inhabitants. Spacious edifices, rich and elegant gardens with luxuriant and extensive rice plantations were to be seen on all sides...."

The plantation era in Dorchester County came to an abrupt end with the Civil War. Burned out plantations quickly deteriorated due to the area's desperate poverty during the last half of the 19th century. The charred ruins and run-down old houses were extremely vulnerable to the Earthquake of 1886 — which hit Dorchester County particularly hard. As a result, many of the old planter families left the area, never to return.

Today, Dorchester County is in a dead heat with Berkeley County for the title "Fastest Growing County in South Carolina." Its population has increased 82 percent since 1970. Summerville is the most urbanized area in the county; St. George is the county seat.

The city limits of Summerville actually cross over into Berkeley County, but the majority of the city is claimed by Dorchester County. Summerville, "Flower town in the Pines," is addressed in the section called "Inside Summerville."

Dorchester County
Historic Sites

THE FRANCIS BEIDLER FOREST
Route 1, Harleyville   (803) 462-2150

The 5,820-acre Francis Beidler Forest deep within South Carolina's Four Holes Swamp may sound like a strange kind of tourist attraction. But it contains the world's largest remaining stand of bald cypress and tupelo gum trees — anywhere. And it offers the visitor — who takes the time to go there — an adventure that is...otherworldly.

In the heart of this verdant sanctuary, the ancient groves of bald cypress stretch upward into the sky — towering over still, clear pools and blackwater streams. Many of these towering forest giants are more than 1,000 years old and seem to stand there as if silently mocking time.

The tupelo trees, swamp black gum, and water ash add pattern, texture, and shadows to the green cathedral walls. And in this setting, time itself seems to stand still. Here, you are exploring one of the last remnants of the great swamp forests that once laced the southern coastal plain at the dawn of time.

The Visitors' Center is the gateway to this sanctuary. In comfortable surroundings, you may view a slide program and see other pictures and displays which help you understand and appreciate the swamp and its inhabitants. Members of the staff are on hand to meet you and help answer questions about the forest and its operations. (The building is barrier-free to handicapped persons.)

The Francis Beidler Forest is named for the lumberman-conservationist who preserved this area — saved it from the logging operations which destroyed the vast majority of areas like this in the first decades of this century. He allowed much of his timberland to remain standing while taxes, interest, hurricanes, and insects took their toll.

Beidler died in 1924, but his family continued to preserve large areas within Four Holes Swamp until the late 1960s when the estate was being liquidated. Local conservationists, led by members of the National Audubon Society and The Nature Conservancy, raised funds of nearly $1.5 million to protect the property from logging. The first purchase saved 3,415 acres; more acreage has been added since then.

OLD FORT DORCHESTER STATE PARK
Hwy 642, off Old Trolley Road
Dorchester County

Here is an interesting stop for history buffs and nature lovers. Fort Dorchester was an early English fortification built in 1757 on the banks of the Ashley River. Soon a little village sprang up nearby (also known as Dorchester). During the Revolutionary War, several skirmishes took place here and, today, a few tabby walls of the 18th century fort remain along with the crumbling tower of the small community's church.

The small state-run park is manned by a forest ranger only, but you'll find interesting archaeological displays of colonial life there and it makes for a romantic idyll — perfect for a spring picnic or a fall nature-walk.

Take the four-lane Dorchester Road through the Oakbrook section past Old Trolley Road. About 500 yards down Highway 642 is the park entrance. It's open daily except Tuesday and Wednesday. Admission is free.

Berkeley County
History

*J*ust to the north of Charleston County is the fastest growing county in all of South Carolina, Berkeley County. Industrial investment in the early 1980s totaled more than $1.7 billion. The greatest concentration of population and of residential and commercial development has been in the southern portion of the county and in the vicinity of Moncks Corner.

Berkeley County's main town is Goose Greek (1990 Census figures show the population to be 24,692). Next largest is Hanahan (population 13,176). Moncks Corner ranks third (with a population of 5,607).

Industrial development is concentrated along Highway 52 above Goose Creek and on the island formed by the Cooper River, Black River and its tributary branches.

Much of the northern portion of Berkeley County is cultivated farmland. Most of the eastern portion and large areas of the western portion are in pine forest — one of the county's most distinctive features.

In fact, lumbering became Berkeley County's main industry in the late 19th and early 20th centuries. But the coming of the Great Depression in the 1930s left the timber companies financially troubled. They petitioned the U.S. government to buy some of their holdings to establish a national forest reserve, and the 245,000-acre Francis Marion National Forest was established by (FDR's) Presidential proclamation in 1936.

Not only was this vast timberland once farmed for its hardwood and pines, it was once the battleground where General Francis Marion, "The Swamp Fox," engaged Col. Banastre Tarleton's British troops during the Revolutionary War. Today, the Francis Marion National Forest is still recovering from the ravages of Hurricane Hugo in 1989, but there are (limited) campgrounds, hiking and biking trails, plus picnic areas for visitors. To get to the Forest, take Highway 52 north to Highway 402. Exit Highway 402 on Highway 171, turn on Highway 125 and look for signs to the Witherbee Ranger Station. For more information, you can also call the U.S. Forest Service at (803) 336-3248.

In addition to its wooded wonders, Berkeley County is a fisherman's paradise. Anglers come here from all over the United States to fish for Berkeley County's catfish and legendary striped bass. The area boasts numerous varieties of crappie, bream, white bass, and the ever-popular large mouth bass, too.

The Lakes and Rivers

Two man-made lakes, Marion and Moultrie, bring thousands of visitors to Berkeley County each year. Here, they have a choice of water sports to enjoy — besides fishing — which includes skiing, scuba diving, sailing, hydro sliding and swimming.

Additional water recreation opportunities can be found on the Cooper, Santee and Wando Rivers, as well as the Black River Reservoir. The Cooper River offers a water passage through the history of the Lowcountry — along the same route used by the earliest settlers (and the Native Americans who hunted and fished here before them). To travel up the Cooper is to journey past historic sites, early churches, and great plantation homes with their once-flourishing rice fields — now hosting an abundance of wildlife in a remarkably picturesque habitat.

Berkeley County Attractions

BERKELEY COUNTY HISTORICAL SOCIETY MUSEUM

950 Stoney Landing   899-5101
Moncks Corner

On the grounds of the Old Santee Canal State Park in Moncks Corner, 30 miles outside Charleston, is a museum specifically dedicated to one of South Carolina's oldest and most fascinating areas, Berkeley County. Its focus is on the cultural history of the county, with the area's natural history included. Exhibits reflecting various periods include the Stone Age, the American Revolution, plantation culture, the industrial Colonial society of the 18th century, life-styles of the early 1900s, early medical practitioners, and the formation of the Francis Marion National Forest.

Visitors will see exhibits from the riches and finery of the great plantations to the simple life-style of the postwar farmers. They'll see artifacts from the Huguenot settlements of the 17th century to the mammoth rural electrification project of the 1940s. The museum also sponsors a Living History series with workshops and educational programs for people of all ages.

Membership in the society is available at a number of levels. Admission is charged. Museum hours are 9:00 AM to 5:00 PM, Monday through Saturday; and 1:00 to 5:00 PM on Sunday. The museum is closed on Thanksgiving and Christmas.

CYPRESS GARDENS

Located 8 miles south of   553-0515
Moncks Corner, off Highway 52

From the earliest days of the first European settlers in the Lowcountry, the cypress forests were considered to be mysterious, dangerous places — best left to the native Indians. They were, for the most part, impenetrable to all but the most adventurous trappers and hunters. After all, it was from deep in the maze of these swamp forests that Francis Marion, "The Swamp Fox," foiled the British and emerged as one of the greatest heroes of the Revolutionary War.

The forest at Cypress Gardens is typical of the Lowcountry swamp forest (Hugo notwithstanding). But it has been altered to combine the mystery and beauty of the natural swamp with the horticultural splendor of azalea and camellia blossoms — as only the Lowcountry can produce them.

The gardens now occupy 250 acres of the original Dean Hall (rice) Plantation on the Cooper River which was developed in the mid-18th century. Records show that by 1842, Dean Hall was supporting a population of more than 500 people. The rice grown in the rich soil reclaimed from swamp could yield enormous crops.

Vital to successful rice growing is an abundant source of fresh water — to flow into the fields at such times when the tidal river water might be brackish (too salty). These fresh water "reserves" were built in the swamps from an elaborate network of ditches and dikes. The lake here at Cypress Gardens is one of those — created from a natural swamp whose waters were held captive in "reserve."

After the Civil War, this agricultural system collapsed completely. Most of Dean Hall reverted to wilderness and the lake at Cypress Gardens was left to grow wild. In 1927, Benjamin R. Kittredge, then the owner of Dean Hall, conceived the idea of using this setting

for a garden of brilliant azaleas. The mirrorlike blackwater lake was cleared of debris and undergrowth and opened for the passage of small boats. About 200 men were employed for the project and they worked several years. Literally thousands of plants were set out; azaleas, narcissus, daffodils and daphne odora. Later, camellias were added — more than 300 varieties.

In 1963, Cypress Gardens was donated to the City of Charleston and the property is now operated by an independent board and Charleston's City Council.

Visitors are advised to explore the gardens both by boat and by foot path — and see it from two separate perspectives. Our favorite time to visit is in the early spring when tree buds are still chartreuse and the new golden pollen falls on the black waters and floats in swirling, yellow streaks — like liquid marble. The trip by row boat takes about half-an-hour or so, and you'll see remarkable reflections of color and enjoy the sense of peaceful tranquility.

Horticulturists will find literature there explaining some of the rare varieties as well as the native trees and plants.

The spectacular flower bloom at Cypress Gardens comes, of course, in the spring. Starting in late February and all through March and April, you're guaranteed a delightful show. Camellias bloom around Thanksgiving and on through the winter months.

Admission for adults (during spring bloom) is $6; senior

citizens, $5; children (ages six through 12), $2; and children under six are free.

Take I-26 to the Moncks Corner/Goose Creek off ramp (Exit 208). Follow Highway 52 north and look for highway signs to Cypress Gardens a few miles past Goose Creek.

OLD SANTEE CANAL STATE PARK

900 Stony Landing Road   *899-5200*
Moncks Corner

The period after the American Revolution saw tremendous growth in the South Carolina "up country." As more settlers moved inland from the coastal areas, they found more fertile lands and soon thereafter had a pressing need for a cost-effective way to get these crops back to coastal markets. Until 1800, these goods had to be shipped overland by wagon, floated down the state's (relatively short) rivers, or sent by ship up and down the coast to Charleston. None of these routes was safe, inexpensive or reliable.

Early on the area's business and political leaders recognized the need for a new transportation system — if they were going to compete against rival seaports. They decided on building an inland waterway.

Construction began in 1793 and more than 700 laborers worked for over seven years with picks and shovels as their primary tools. When it was done, the finished canal was 22 miles long, 30 feet wide and 5½ feet deep — finished at a staggering cost of $650,000. Boats and barges laden with cotton and other goods could be pulled down the canal by mules and horses using a 10-foot wide towpath running along both sides. The lock system was designed to raise a boat 34 feet through three locks, then fall 69 feet through seven more locks — between the Santee and Cooper Rivers.

Operations for the canal went smoothly for the first 16 years and this "crowning achievement of engineering and economic development" even started to show a profit. Its peak year was 1830 when a total of 700 barges and boats used the inland waterway. But in 1840, the growing railway system was extended all the way from Charleston to Columbia rendering the canal obsolete for all practical purposes. By 1850, the South Carolina General Assembly revoked its charter at the request of the shareholders.

Today, most of the canal lies beneath the waters of Lake Moultrie. Only the upper portions of the waterway can now be seen — where boats once entered the headwaters of the Cooper River at Biggin Creek. This is the setting for Old Santee Canal State Park.

The park's Interpretive Center ties together the canal's history and its natural environment. Displays there reach back in time to 4,000 B.C. with early hand tools and examples of the life that flourished here 30 million years ago. You'll find a model of the canal, an operating canal lock, and other displays concerning the history of the area.

Visitors can canoe the waters of Biggin Creek and the old canal or hike the 2-1/2 miles of board-walks and trails reaching into the heart of this natural world. The park is accessible by water — as well as by land. There's a permanent floating dock at the Tail Race Canal available to boaters. Winter hours are 9:00 AM to 5:00 PM. Summer hours are 9:00 AM to 6:00 PM. There is no admission price, but a parking fee is charged; $3 for cars and motorcycles, and $15 for multi-passenger vans and mini-buses.

RICE HOPE PLANTATION INN

206 Rice Hope Drive   *761-4832 or*
Moncks Corner   *800-569-4038*

One fine Berkeley County getaway place — popular with locals and area visitors is actually a bed and breakfast in a beautiful plantation setting. Set among old live oaks on a bluff overlooking the Cooper River, locals like to come here for business meetings, seminars, and special occasions — like garden weddings. There's tennis and a fishing pier, too. Rice Hope Plantation Inn offers lunch and dinner (for non-staying guests) with reservations. Call Doris Kasprak for serving hours and directions.

Historic Sites In Berkeley County

ST. JAMES GOOSE CREEK CHURCH
Hwy. 52 (Old State Road), Goose Creek

Just off Hwy. 52 near Goose Creek — and partially hidden in the thick new growth replacing the pine forest lost to Hugo — is one of the best preserved and most interesting churches in the Lowcountry.

Built during the years 1708 to 1719, this little Chapel of Ease is considered by many to be one of the most beautiful and architecturally sophisticated rural Anglican churches in Colonial America.

Outside the building on the pediment above the entrance is a rare and significant feature; note the figure of a pelican tearing at her breast to feed her hungry young. It is the symbol of the Society for The Propagation of the Gospel in Foreign Parts, which was organized in England in 1701 to send missionaries to Carolina.

Inside, over the altar (in fact, above it — in what is definitely a political statement) is the Royal Coat of Arms for King George I. The ultimate authority of England was thus clearly stated. On the other hand, simply because the Royal Arms were so displayed, this church was spared by marauding British soldiers during the American Revolution.

This church is not usually open to the public. But respectful devotees and architectural researchers might be lucky enough to find a caretaker on site and be granted a brief peek inside.

BIGGIN CHURCH RUINS
Hwy. 402, 3 miles north of Moncks Corner

Called Biggin Church after nearby Biggin Creek, this was the church designated for St. Johns Parish in 1712. The original church burned in a forest fire in 1715. This building — now in ruins — was begun in 1756. Because it was built on high, strategically important ground, the British stored gun powder there during the Revolution. When they retreated, the church was burned.

It was rebuilt soon after the war, but partially destroyed again in the Civil War. Another forest fire swept through the area and completed the destruction in 1890. Today, only two substantial walls remain — along with the small cemetery which contains markers from the 18th century to the present. Call 889-7396 for more information.

STRAWBERRY CHAPEL
West Branch, Cooper River
St. Johns Parish
Berkeley County

Built in 1725, this "chapel of ease" was built to serve those planter families and parishioners who could not attend the more distant Biggin Church near Moncks Corner. This one was purely for convenience — only for baptisms and burials — and lacked the parochial rights of a Rector and an endowment. Originally, services here would have been held on major church holidays only. However, 100 years after it was built, Strawberry Chapel became the replacement for the ill-fated Biggin Church (described above).

Strawberry Chapel is the site of one of the Lowcountry's most spine-chilling (supposedly true) legends. In the late 18th century, a seven-year-old little girl, Catherine Chicken, was tied to one of the tombstones in the churchyard by a wicked schoolmaster who was boarding the child. He left her there all night — and she was res-

cued at dawn by a faithful family servant. The schoolmaster was driven out of the area by an outraged citizenry, but poor little Catherine's face was disfigured on one side for the rest of her life by the trauma of her night spent in Strawberry Chapel churchyard. To visit Strawberry Chapel, call 889-7396 for more information.

MEPKIN ABBEY
HC 69, Box 800   *761-8509*
Moncks Corner

Since 1949, the scenic and peaceful land that was once a famous Cooper River rice plantation — dating back to the 1700s — has been a place of indescribable peace and quiet. It is the (Cistercian-Trappist) Catholic monastery named Mepkin Abbey. Its name, "Mepkin," is Indian — meaning serene and lovely.

The 600-acre plantation has been witness to a great deal of history since the English first arrived here in the Lowcountry. The land was acquired by the patriot Henry Laurens, President of the Continental Congress (1777-1778), before the American Revolution. Laurens was born at Charles Towne in 1724 and died at Mepkin Plantation in 1792. He is buried on the property alongside other members of his family.

The plantation passed down through time and various owners until it was purchased in 1936 by Henry R. Luce, the Time-Life publishing magnate and his wife, Clare Boothe Luce, the noted playwright and Congresswoman. The property was their private retreat until 1949 when they donated a major portion of it to the Cistercian-Trappist monks of Gethsemani Abbey in Kentucky. Soon afterward, a group of monks arrived and began building the monastery as it is today.

The quiet monastic brotherhood observes a strict religious lifestyle of prayer, worship and work. They engage in egg farming as a means of maintaining their livelihood. Hospitality is basic to the monastic tradition, and many visitors come to Mepkin Abbey during the course of the year. Visiting hours are 9:00 AM to 4:40 PM daily.

Very limited accommodations are available for private spiritual retreats (for both men and women). For serious retreatants, Mepkin Abbey can be profoundly rewarding. Interaction with the monks, however, is limited — as each one carries out a daily work program according to the needs of the monastic community. Still, there is ample time for private prayer, religious study and other suitable reading consistent with the rather austere monastic life-style. Arrangements can be made for retreatants to be met at Charleston's airport, the Greyhound bus station in Charleston or Moncks Corner, or the Amtrak depot in North Charleston.

To visit Mepkin Abbey by car, drive northeast out of Moncks Corner on U.S. 52 (Hwy. 17-A). You'll cross a high bridge over the Tail Race Canal (also called Dennis Bishop Bridge). A short distance beyond (3/10 mile), turn right on a ramp-approach onto Route 402 and go two miles until you reach a boat landing/recreation area called Rembert Dennis. Look for a tiny bridge (named Wadboo) and a sign to Mepkin Abbey there. Just across Wadboo Bridge, turn right on River Road. Follow that for six miles to Mepkin's clearly-marked entrance. Drive down the old oak-lined lane to the log Reception Center where a Guestmaster will meet you when you ring the big bell.

North Charleston
Industry

Several important companies have called North Charleston home for many years. Others are relative newcomers—attracted to the large, trained labor force in the area. Among those that are helping the area to become known as an industrial center are the following companies.

ALUMAX OF SOUTH CAROLINA
Hwy. 52 and Mt. Holly Road   572-3700
Goose Creek
This is one of the Lowcountry's major employers — with a 1993 labor force of more than 627 people.

BERKELEY ELECTRIC CO-OP
Hwy. 52 North   761-8200
Moncks Corner
This is a major electric utility in the north area — employing 190 people.

ROBERT BOSCH CORPORATION
8101 Dorchester Road   760-7000
North Charleston
One of the area's largest manufacturers, Bosch has more than 1,750 employees. They produce fuel injector and braking systems for the automobile industry.

COBURG DAIRY
5000 Lacross Road   554-4870
Coburg is the largest independent dairy in South Carolina — processing milk from local farms in its 100,000-square-foot, state-of-the-art plant located in North Charleston. Coburg markets a complete line of traditional dairy products, "light" dairy products and other dairy and beverage items. The company has been in business more than 70 years.

DUPONT
Busy Park and Cypress   797-9000
Garden Road
Moncks Corner
Clearly one of the area's major employers — this plant manufactures textile fibers, dacron and polyester.

DYNAPOWER/STRATOPOWER
Cross County Road   760-5700
Dynapower/Stratopower is a precision manufacturing company recently relocated to North Charleston from Watertown, New York. It is a unit of General Signal Corporation, a FORTUNE 500 company, based in Stamford, Connecticut. Dynapower/Stratopower manufacturers hydraulic power units for heavy machinery and farm equipment plus hydraulic power units

for the aerospace and defense industries. The move has added 200 new jobs to the North Charleston economy.

EVANS RULE COMPANY

6555 Fain Street   *797-2500*

Evans Rule, a division of the L.S. Starrett Company, is a leading manufacturer of steel measuring tapes and other hand tools. The main manufacturing plant is in North Charleston and there are assembly facilities in Puerto Rico and Canada. The company was founded in 1948 and manufactured its first product in Newark, N.J. In 1958, manufacturing moved to Elizabeth, N.J., and began Charleston operations in 1972.

GATES RUBBER COMPANY

1 Belt Drive   *761-8100*
Moncks Corner

This north area manufacturer produces automotive belts and hoses.

GENERAL DYNAMICS

2040 Bushy Park Road   *863-3101*
Goose Creek

This division of the major American manufacturer produces heavy steel fabrication and employs more than 600 workers.

GENERAL GRAPHICS

3325 Ashley-Phosphate   *767-3398*
Road, Suite 204

General Graphics Printing and Distribution Facility serves as a full-service printing and warehousing firm supporting the CIGNA companies by producing, storing and distributing printed materials.

The CIGNA companies are leading providers of insurance, health care employee benefits, pension and investment management and related financial services to business and individuals worldwide.

HUNTER MANUFACTURING COMPANY

5806 Campbell   *747-3646*
Hanahan

Here is a north area manufacturer creating children's dresses — with an employee roster of 190 people.

JW ALUMINUM

435 Old Mt. Holly Road   *572-1100*
Goose Creek

This company, located in the Goose Creek area, fabricates aluminum sheet and foil products. The current employee force is 280 people.

LOCKHEED MISSILES AND SPACE COMPANY, INC.

Leadbank Road   *764-2000*
Goose Creek

This division of Lockheed does guided missile assembly and testing. Their employee list is 170 at this time.

M. D. T. HOSPITAL DIAGNOSTICS

7371-B Spartan Blvd.   *522-8652*

In North Charleston since 1971, M.D.T. Diagnostics manufactures medical and dental equipment.

MILES, INC.

1530 Bushy Park Road   *553-8600*
Goose Creek

This employer — with 600

workers — manufacturers dyes and organic pigments.

PIGGLY WIGGLY CAROLINA
4401 Daley Avenue   554-9880

This giant food store chain, started in 1947, now has more than 500 employees at their North Charleston warehouse facility.

R. M. ENGINEERED PRODUCTS
4845 O'Hear Avenue   744-6261

An Intertech Group company, R. M. Engineered Products has been in Charleston since 1985 — making elastic seals, molds, rubber parts and expansion joints. They currently have 830 employees.

WESTVACO CORPORATION
Virginia Avenue, N. Charleston   745-3000

For nearly 70 years, Westvaco has been an integral part of the South Carolina business community. Their arrival was considered a bold move in the uncertain 1920s and '30s when the technology of using southern pine trees for making paper products was revolutionary. Now Westvaco Corporation ranks in the top half of the FOR-TUNE 500 listing, with 15,000 employees working in nearly 50 cities around the world. South Carolina is home to four of the company's 10 division headquarters; a wholly-owned subsidiary (Westvaco Development Corporation), a computer center, a forest science laboratory and a corporate research center. Westvaco's North Charleston operation began in 1937. The company recently launched a $42 million capital improvement project designed to further enhance their competitive strength in the world market. Today, the North Charleston mill is Westvaco's largest center in the state. Here, three large paper machines produce 2,200 tons of premium unbleached paper and paperboard products daily.

WETTERAU FOOD DISTRIBUTION GROUP
2001 Mabeline Road,   797-6700
Charleston Heights
2955 Ashley Phosphate Road   552-5330

Since 1970, Wetterau has been distributing food items and general merchandise from their North Charleston location.

North Charleston
Restaurants

*T*he north area has some of the Lowcountry's oldest and best-loved restaurants — longtime survivors in a crowded marketplace are always proven winners. And because the north area is a busy crossroads for so many business types and vacation travelers, the dining spots are interesting, varied and generally reasonable, too. Here are some of our favorites.

Although prices change, use this scale as a guide to the cost of entrées at restaurants in the North Charleston area:

Under $10	$
$10-$15	$$
$16-$20	$$$
$21 and up	$$$$

APPLEBEE'S

7818 Rivers Avenue   *577-8137*
North Charleston
$ - $$ *Most major credit cards*

Here is North Charleston's version of this popular restaurant chain. Other locations include 1859 Sam Rittenburg, 24 N. Market Street, and 88 Old Trolley Road in Summerville. Their standard menu is varied and includes some low-calorie and heart-smart choices, as well. Service is fast and friendly. Their Saturday and Sunday brunch, from 11:00 AM to 3:00 PM is especially nice. Gathering Hour is 4:00 to 7:00 PM, and 10:00 PM to closing.

THE ATRIUM

7401 Northwoods Blvd.   *572-2200*
$ - $$$ *Most major credit cards*

This restaurant is part of the North Charleston's Best Western Inn. Their breakfast and lunch buffet is popular with business types working in the north area. Their regular menus feature Lowcountry fare — including fresh seafood. Dinner hours are 5:00 to 10:00 PM daily.

BINH MINH

7685 Northwoods Blvd.   *569-2844*
$ - $$ *MC, V, D*

For something different, authentic and really delicious, try Vietnamese cuisine. This popular spot is just outside Northwoods Mall. The atmosphere is very casual, and the interesting food has become a local favorite. It's a relatively small place, so call for reservations early — especially on weekends. Hours are 5:30 to 10:00 PM Tuesday through Saturday.

CRACKER BARREL

7351 Mazyck Road   *553-4232*
North Charleston
$ - $$ *Most major credit cards*

This is another chain restaurant popular with many travelers.

Located just off I-26 at Ashley Phosphate, this one is easily visible from the interstate. It's convenient to business folk working in North Charleston and Northwoods Mall shoppers, too. The fare is country-style cooking — for breakfast, lunch, and dinner; plus there's a curio shop that's always fun for browsing. Hours are 6:00 AM to 10:00 PM, Sunday through Thursday; and 6:00 AM to 11:00 PM on Friday and Saturday.

DOCK RESTAURANT
Off Hwy. 52   761-8080
Moncks Corner
$ - $$ Most major credit cards

Right on the picturesque Tail Race canal, this restaurant has been around since 1959 — a local favorite. They serve catfish, fresh seafood, chicken and steaks. Hours are 11:00 AM to 9:30 PM daily.

GENNARO'S TRATTORIA
8500 Dorchester Road   760-9875
North Charleston
$ - $$ Most major credit cards

For lunch or dinner, this is North Charleston's version of the popular Gennaro's on Savannah Hwy., west Ashley. Their highly rated (by Italians who should know) entrees and live entertainment (nightly) make every visit an occasion. Lunch hours are 11:30 AM to 2:30 PM; dinner is from 4:30 to 10:00 PM. They're closed on Mondays.

NOISY OYSTER
7571 Rivers Avenue   824-1000
$ - $$ Most major credit cards

This is one of the area's newest seafood restaurants — albeit a somewhat inland one. Their catch is always fresh and served in a relaxed and friendly setting. Daily lunch is 11:00 AM to 4:00 PM; dinner is from 4:00 to 9:00 PM Sunday through Tuesday; and they stay open until 11:00 PM on Friday and Saturday.

TOM PORTARO'S
5600 Rivers Avenue   747-1128
$-$$ Most major credit cards

This popular Italian restaurant is one of the oldest eating establishments in the Lowcountry. They've been at it since 1960 — serving all your favorite traditional Italian dishes. Mike Portaro says any of their veal dishes is a special winner; they do veal like nobody else. They're open from 5:00 to 9:45 PM, Monday through Thursday, and they stay open till 10:00 PM on Friday and Saturday.

PRESTON'S STEAK HOUSE
6258 Rivers Avenue   747-1528
$ - $$ Most major credit cards

Look here for Texas-style aged beef — served in a super casual, hang-loose atmosphere. This is a popular spot with locals and those with hearty appetites. Hours are 11:30 AM to 10:00 PM, Monday through Friday. On Saturday, they open at 4:00 PM; they're closed on Sunday.

DOE'S PITA PLUS
5134 N. Rhett Ave.   745-0026
$ No credit cards

At last! Fast food that's really good for you. Recently opened in their new North Charleston location is this pita restaurant — an offshoot of the popular East Bay

Street spot in Ansonborough Square. They serve vegetarian and white-meat pocket sandwiches in homemade pita bread. All the fillings are low or no fat; nothing is fried. Eat in or take out. Cuisine is Middle Eastern or traditional with a twist. Hours are 11:00 AM to 2:30 PM Monday through Friday, and 11:00 AM to 5:00 PM Saturday.

CAREY HILLIARD'S RESTAURANT

6601 Rivers Avenue   797-5561
$ Most major credit cards

Here's a full-service restaurant for the whole family. They've been here 15 years now and their seafood is the specialty of the house. Incidentally, there's a Carey Hilliard's at 1734 Sam Rittenberg Blvd., too. Their phone is 571-1325. Hours of operation are from 11:00 AM to midnight daily.

RUBY TUESDAY RESTAURANT

Northwoods Mall   553-1285
$-$$ All major credit cards

Ruby's is a favorite with the young professional crowd — especially their 4:00 to 8:00 PM Happy Hour every weekday. They serve a widely varied menu with everything from ribs to blackened seafood. Also available are seven kinds of burgers and an all-you-can-eat salad bar that won't quit. They've been around for almost ten years. Hours are Monday through Thursday, 11:00 AM to 11:00 PM; Friday and Saturday, 11:00 AM to midnight; and Sunday 11:00 AM to 10:00 PM.

NORTH TOWNE GREEK RESTAURANT

2093 Eagle Landing Blvd.   863-1001
$-$$ All major credit cards

Insiders (official and otherwise) have always loved the ethnic charm and great food at Olde Towne Restaurant on King Street in downtown Charleston. Recently, the owners have offered a new place in the north area — with the same great food. Check out their seafood and steaks, but as far as we're concerned, you can't beat their famous Greek chicken. They're open 11:00 AM to 10:00 PM on weekdays; and from 11:00 AM to 11:00 PM Friday and Saturday.

OLIVE GARDEN ITALIAN RESTAURANT

2156 Northwoods Blvd.   764-0200
$-$$ All major credit cards

Opened three years ago across from Northwoods Mall, this Olive Garden is very popular with locals and business people. They offer seasonal specials along with their traditional Italian cuisine and they're famous for serving their huge family-style salads with the soft bread sticks that always hit the spot. Business folks appreciate their "to go" service on busy office days. They're open from 11:00 AM to 10:00 PM, Sunday through Thursday. Friday and Saturday, they're open from 11:00 AM to 11:00 PM.

ORIENTAL CUISINE

5900 Rivers Avenue   747-9812
$ All major credit cards

This Rivers Avenue spot is a favorite with business types every day for lunch and families enjoy the evening hours there. Our favorites are the Emperor's Chicken and the Pressed Duck. From 11:00 AM to 3:00 PM Monday through Friday, they serve a plentiful lunch buffet. From 3:00 to 5:00 PM they offer several combination specials. From 5:00 to 9:30 PM, the dinner buffet is presented.

THE HAVEN
RADISSON INN AIRPORT

I-26 & E. Aviation Avenue   744-2501
$-$$ All major credit cards

Hard to believe, but the Sheraton has been there — just off I-26 — for 18 years. It is a handy meeting place for downtowners and local business types who are carpooling to Columbia or other parts north. And so, the early bird breakfast is a hit. The Haven has a great lunch buffet and it's open at night, too. We like their Friday night flounder special. Hours are from 6:30 AM to 2:00 PM and from 5:30 to 10:00 PM.

KEY WEST BAR & GRILL

7242 Northside Drive   572-3663
(I-26 & Ashley Phosphate)
$-$$ All major credit cards

Here's a laid-back, South Florida-styled spot that's really popular with young professionals and the North Charleston in-crowd. Their elaborate seafood/salad bar is complete down to the caviar and crackers. Seafood is their specialty, but the prime rib is tops, too. Dress is casual, the mood is fun. Hours are Monday through Saturday, 4:00 to 10:30 PM; and Sunday, 4:30 to 9:30 PM.

PICCADILLY CLASSIC
AMERICAN COOKING

Charles Towne Square   747-5813
$ All major credit cards

Here's another old-timer that's a favorite with locals. In fact, most of North Charleston's City Hall can be found here for lunch on weekdays. It's a cafeteria with everything you're looking for — including their own seafood gumbo (Louisiana style). They're open daily from 11:00 AM to 8:30 PM.

CHATFIELD'S LOUNGE
AND PARKSIDE RESTAURANT

Marriott Hotel, 4770 Marriott Drive   747-1900
$-$$ All major credit cards

Another popular and handy business address is the Marriott with its Chatfield's Lounge and Parkside Restaurant. They open for the early-bird fliers at 6:30 AM with a giant breakfast buffet. Lunch is served from 11:00 AM till 2:00 PM. Dinner is served from 5:00 to 10:30 PM with nightly specials. On weekends, the Marriott's Parkside doesn't open until 7:00 PM. All major cards are accepted, but no personal checks.

Photo: Ron Anton Rocz

Basket ladies working their craft.

North Charleston
Shopping

The north area has several major shopping malls in addition to the myriad of smaller convenience stores and strip-mall shopping venues. Because North Charleston has no real downtown section per se, the major shopping malls offer the area's most popular and convenient shopping opportunities.

CHARLES TOWNE SQUARE MALL
I-26 at Montague Avenue,   554-7945
North Charleston

This was Greater Charleston's first big covered mall — built in the 1970s — with major retail anchors, a variety of interesting specialty shops, clothing and shoe stores galore, and even fun places to eat. Today, all that's still true. The location is still the most convenient for many north area neighborhoods near I-26 and the Navy base. And the architectural style, reminiscent of historic downtown Charleston, makes it a relaxed, pleasant place to shop, too.

The major anchors are J.C. Penney and Montgomery Ward (the only such stores in the area). A third anchor, Service Merchandise has arrived to keep some 50 other stores company. You'll find Radio Shack, Endicott Shoes, Music Land, Footlocker, General Nutrition and Exposure 60, a handy one-hour pho-

tographic service known for high quality work, among them. One unusual spot that is truly interesting for browsing is CSA Galleries. Not only do they have nice gifts and collectibles, but they also offer the largest collection of Confederate art we've seen in the area. You'll find suitable-for-framing Charleston art — including the popular ghost prints — as well. And, you won't even have to go elsewhere for the frames as they will gladly, and expertly, do the job for you on-site.

We're always snagged at Waldenbooks and at Huguley's, too. And, if you find yourself in the mall with insufficient cash, you can go to Charleston-New York Gold Exchange and sell off some of your gold, silver or diamonds. They offer in-house appraisals and even buy scrap metals. While you're in the jewelry mood, check out Barry's Jewelry. They are a full-service shop offering not only a fine selection of diamonds and other gemstones, but also the expertise to repair your treasured pieces on-site — even the same day if you're in a hurry. They also design custom pieces and can make appraisals.

There are fast food outlets in the mall if you're shopping on the run, and there's a service desk for quick reference and additional help if you need it. Mall hours are 10:00 AM to 9:00 PM, Monday through Saturday, and 1:00 to 6:00 PM on Sunday.

FESTIVAL CENTER

5101 Ashley Phosphate Road   North Charleston

This, one of the area's newest shopping centers, was considerably slowed by Hurricane Hugo, but it's now back in action — better than ever. The major anchors are Piggly Wiggly, Hamrick's, and Waccamaw Linen. There's also a Levi Special store and Old Mill Clothing. There's a Radio Shack and some handy convenience stores (a barber shop, Causey's, a dry cleaner and a Pak Mail store), a State Farm agent and Players' Place Billiards, a popular place with locals. So one stop accomplishes a great deal. Pizza Hut is here for convenient eating, too. Hours are 10:00 AM to 6:00 PM, Monday through Saturday; and Sunday 1:00 to 6:00 PM.

NORTH RIVERS MARKET

7800 Rivers Avenue   North Charleston

Located just across Hwy. 52 from Northwoods Mall is North River's Market, anchored by a TJ Maxx and a Marshall's for discount shoppers. Here, you can find the latest fashions and accessories for everyone in the family at direct-from-the-factory prices up to 70% off. The giant Toys 'R Us is always a hit with the kids. And there's a Phar-Mor handy for everything from aspirin to potato chips. Check out Rack Room shoe store and Opti-World, too. Herman's Sporting Goods gives Dad something to do while Mom shops the shoe stores. Hours are 10:00 AM to 9:00 PM, Monday through Saturday; and Sunday noon to 6:00 PM.

NORTHWOODS MALL

Rivers Avenue   North Charleston

This is one of the Lowcountry's largest and most complete shopping malls. It's anchored by Belk and the new Dillard's which replaced Thalhimer's in this market. There's also a big Sears store with an automotive center and a financial network center. There are no less than 15 shoe stores to choose from here, and a wide variety of specialty shops and boutiques. If you're hungry, there's Sadie's Cafeteria or Ruby Tuesday for a quick bite between stores. Family events and community oriented activities are frequently held here. Mall hours are from 10:00 AM to 9:00 PM, Monday through Saturday; and from 1:00 to 6:00 on Sunday.

North Charleston
Accommodations

When the business and industrial boom in North Charleston really took off in the '60s and '70s, a number of major hotel/motel chains built new accommodations along the I-26 corridor coming into Charleston. Now, not only are these accommodations located in the very heart of the Lowcountry's population density, but they all have easy access to the airport and convenient Hwy. 526 (the Mark Clark Expressway).

Business travelers with appointments in the north area and vacationers (unable to secure lodging downtown) may want to choose from these options along I-26 — only a short distance from Charleston. This chapter tells you some of the signs to look for.

To give estimated weekday costs for two persons staying overnight at these accommodations, we've provided the following scale:

$50 and under	$
$51 - $75	$$
$76 - $95	$$$
$96 - $110	$$$$
$111 and up	$$$$$

AIRPORT TRAVELODGE
4620 Dorchester Road 747-7500 or
800-255-3050
$ - $$ All major credit cards
Here's an option with 104

units—some are suites with Jacuzzis, others are king executive rooms with microwaves and refrigerators. You'll find free airport and base shuttle service, HBO cable TV, VCR rentals, and complimentary hors d'oeuvres served in the lounge from 4:00 to 8:00 PM. They have free local calls, FAX and copy service, too.

QUALITY SUITES
5225 North Arco Lane 747-7300 or
I-26 at Montague Ave. 800-228-5151
$$-$$$ All major credit cards
Just off the Interstate, these 168 upscale suites have become very popular with business folk who need a little more room and with larger families wanting togetherness without being crowded. Suites sleep four to six comfortably and all have a living room, bedroom and bath. Each unit has two cable TVs with a VCR and wet bar. You can choose king or double beds. Some suites have whirlpool baths. Their health club features a pool, hot tub and exercise machines. There's no restaurant on site, but a full breakfast is included and cocktail hour (from 5:00 to 8:00 PM) includes complimentary hors d'oeuvres.

COMFORT INN

5055 N. Arco Lane   554-6485 or
                                  800-221-2222
$$ All major credit cards

Here you'll find 122 rooms with cable TV and free HBO. No-smoking rooms are available. A free continental breakfast is served and on-site amenities include a health club with a whirlpool, sauna and exercise equipment. Discounts are offered to seniors, families and AAA members. Comfort Inn has another location in downtown Charleston at 144 Bee Street near the MUSC and the VA medical complexes.

RADISSON INN, CHARLESTON AIRPORT

5991 Rivers Avenue   744-2501 or
(I-26 & East Aviation Avenue)   800-333-3333
$$ All major credit cards

This is a beautifully appointed inn located only minutes from downtown Charleston's historic area and nearby shopping malls. There's a large atrium with skylights and lush plantings around an indoor pool, whirlpool, sauna and exercise room. Their on-site restaurant and lounge features live entertainment. They offer free airport shuttle service, daily newspapers, and premium cable TV.

RAMADA INN AIRPORT

2934 W. Montague Avenue   744-8281 or
                                  800-272-6232
$-$$ All major credit cards

Again, just off I-26, you'll see a Ramada Inn at Exit 213 or the "West Montague" exit. This Ramada has 155 rooms with a choice of king or double beds. There's a restaurant and a lounge on-site plus an

outdoor pool. Room service is offered from 5:00 to 10:00 PM.

THE RESIDENCE INN

7645 Northwoods Blvd.   572-5757 or
                                  800-331-3131
$$$ - $$$$ All major credit cards

This all-suite luxury facility offers three types of accommodations; with one queen bed, with two doubles (side by side), and their penthouse suite has one queen bed with bath downstairs and another queen bed and bath upstairs in a loft. All suites have full kitchens and sitting rooms. Complimentary breakfast is served daily and a hospitality hour with free hors d'oeuvres is offered on Monday through Thursday afternoons. The Inn features a restaurant courier service (like room service) from seven of the area's best restaurants. And there's free airport transportation at any time. Rates vary according to length of stay.

CHARLESTON MARRIOTT

4770 Marriott Drive   747-1900 or
(I-26 at Montague Avenue)   800-228-9290
$$$ All major credit cards

Look for this full-service high-rise hotel which is a major crossroads for business travelers in the north area. It has 300 rooms with king and double beds — including "parlor" suites, a hospitality suite and meeting and convention rooms. Amenities include an indoor-outdoor pool with a health club that features hydrotherapy and exercise equipment. You'll find a gift shop, restaurant and lounge plus room service and free parking. There is also a concierge floor with free continental breakfast provided daily. Limousine service is available to downtown Charleston and the airport three times daily.

THE NORTHWOODS ATRIUM INN - A BEST WESTERN
7401 Northwoods Blvd.   *572-2200 or 800-292-4772*
$$ *All major credit cards*

Conveniently located on I-26, this facility features a tropical atrium setting with an inviting indoor pool, whirlpool, sauna, atrium restaurant and lounge plus room service. Sports facilities include volleyball, basketball, exercise room, outdoor pool and sun deck. Here, you're within walking distance to Northwoods Mall — the Lowcountry's largest shopping enclave. Complimentary airport shuttle service is offered.

HAMPTON INN AIRPORT
4701 Arco Lane   *554-7154 or 800-426-7866*
$$ *All major credit cards*

Here's another offering from the major national chains that's always popular with business travelers and vacationers alike. This one has 125 rooms — with one double bed, two double beds, or one king bed; and their king suites offer one king bed with an extra pull-out double. Both smoking and nonsmoking rooms are available. A complimentary breakfast buffet is served from 6:00 to 10:00 AM daily. Airport transportation is provided.

HOLIDAY INN INTERNATIONAL
I-26 & Aviation Avenue   *744-1621 or 800-HOLIDAY*
$$$

This major chain hotel has 260 rooms with a choice of king or double beds (and there's one on-site suite). Their in-house meeting and banquet rooms attract many business travelers, plus there's a restaurant and lounge included. Sports facilities include tennis courts, a swimming pool, and a health club with Jacuzzi and sauna. Complimentary airport transportation is available.

HO JO INN BY HOWARD JOHNSON
I-26 and Dorchester Road   *554-4140*
$-$$ *All major credit cards*

For inbound Charleston traffic, you'll see a large "message" sign on your left — flashing latest headlines, temperature readings and coming area events. This multistory (former) Howard Johnson hotel — is now a Ho Jo Inn. Their 131 rooms have been recently refurbished for economy travelers. All rooms have basic cable TV with both double and king beds available. A restaurant is just next door.

North Area
Neighborhoods

Charleston County Neighborhoods — North

Greater Charleston's north area abounds with new and affordable neighborhoods — especially for the first time buyer. Several major developers have entered the tricounty market over the past few years with a variety of new housing options. You'll note a concentration of new neighborhoods in Dorchester and Berkeley counties where tax rates can be lower than in Charleston County.

Because of the pending base closures, a great deal of the real estate in the north area is likely to be affected. This period of transition for North Charleston (and the entire Trident area) may result in a temporary housing glut — a chance for newcomers to find a great deal.

We've organized some of these north area neighborhoods by county — which will largely define which school districts and tax rates are involved.

HEMMINGWOOD

This is a West Ashley neighborhood that could be called "north" by some standards because it's just off Hwy. 526 with easy access to North Charleston jobs. It is a Squires Homes project — now complete — which sold in the $70,000 range. Look here for resales. From Charleston, take Hwy. 61 north. Turn right on Dogwood, then left into Castlereagh.

NORTHPOINTE

This neighborhood is minutes away from the north area military bases and prices there start in the mid-$60s. From I-26, take Montague Ave. west, turn right on Dorchester Road, then right at the first light onto Scarsdale Road, and right (again) onto Napoleon. Look for the model home on your right.

VILLAGE GREEN

Although technically West Ashley, this neighborhood is just off the new Mark Clark Expressway (Hwy. 526) which makes it close to all north area jobs. This John Crosland neighborhood off Hwy. 61 features two different areas; River Oaks with prices in the mid-$70s, and Willow Oaks with homes in the low $100s.

Dorchester County Neighborhoods

Dorchester County's phenomenal growth during the 1980s

created nothing short of a real estate boom for the area. The decade's 41.4% population increase made Dorchester County the hottest market for home buyers in the whole state.

Summerville was the main beneficiary of this growth. Both moderate and reasonably priced neighborhoods in and around the town sprang up like mushrooms — no doubt inspired by Summerville's quaint shopping and its charming historic district with Victorian summer houses and brilliant azalea gardens. (See Inside Summerville.)

ASHBOROUGH ON THE LAKE

Off Dorchester Road and on the headwaters of the Ashley River, these two-story traditional homes from the Squires Homes, Inc. builders start at about $115,000. Located on the outskirts of Summerville, you're near good schools and shopping here. From Dorchester Road, turn on Nantucket in to Ashborough and turn right on Mayfield. Their model home is on your left.

BRANDYMILL

This John Crosland neighborhood in Summerville features a private swim and tennis club and is just across the street (Old Trolley Road) from the new YMCA with its year round planned activities — good for growing families. Prices here are in the $90,000 range.

COOSAW CREEK

This private, upscale country club community from Greenwood Development Co. is close to Summerville schools, shopping and all major north area highways. Residents here have access to first-class private amenities including their 18-hole Arthur Hills golf course. Turn right off Ashley Phosphate Road.

CRICHTON PARISH

In the popular Oakbrook section of Summerville is another Squires community: these traditional homes range in the $60s. Take Dorchester to Old Trolley Road and turn left on Travelers Blvd., then left onto Parish-Parc Drive. A furnished model home is on your right.

MILL CREEK

Look at these Squires homes in the new Windsor Hill development. Prices start in the $60s here. From I-26, turn left on Ashley Phosphate Road, then right into Windsor Hill Plantation. Once inside, turn right onto William Moultrie and look for the furnished model on your right.

RICEFIELD

This is a new neighborhood within Windsor Hill from Ryland Homes with houses in the $70s to $90s range. From I-26, turn off Ashley Phosphate before Dorchester Road; then turn into Plantation Blvd. and look for the model home. Also within Windsor Hill is the planned Ryland neighborhood of Indigo Ridge with homes priced in the $60s.

SUMMERVILLE ON THE ASHLEY

This brand new offering from Ryland Homes is right on the picturesque Ashley River in a heavily wooded area near Summerville. Prices range in the low $80s. Take Hwy. 61 to Bacons Bridge Road and look for the signs between Bacons Bridge and Dorchester Road.

SUMMERVILLE PLACE

This John Crosland neighborhood in the Summerville area features homes from the mid-$60s on up. Take the College Park exit off I-26 and turn left. Follow College Park onto Ladson Road and turn right at the first light.

WOODINGTON

Theses Squires homes in the River Oaks community begin in the mid-$80,000 range. From I-26, turn west on Ashley Phosphate Road, continue to Dorchester Road past Festival Center, and go across the intersection into River Oaks. Follow the road to the end and turn right onto Wynnfield. Look for the model home

Berkeley County Neighborhoods

Berkeley County has witnessed a virtual explosion in suburban housing in the last decade. Since 1980, more than 7,200 new homes have been built. Many of them are in planned neighborhoods devel-oped by major builders who — by virtue of their volume buying and scale of operation — can offer a lot of house for your buying dollar.

Berkeley County's proximity to the Charleston area military bases makes it a natural choice for many young military families. These (frequently transient) families tend to network well among themselves to help make a transition to a new area smoother and easier for the family.

CADBURY

This is a neighborhood in the fast-growing Crowfield Plantation neighborhood of Goose Creek offered by the John Crosland Co. Prices here are in the low $90s and residents share Crowfield's amenities like pools, mini-parks, tennis and the 18-hole golf and country club.

DEVON FOREST

This neighborhood features traditional homes from Ryland, ranging from the $70s to the $90s, and is conveniently located directly across the street from Alumax, near Crowfield Plantation. Take College Park to Crowfield Blvd. to Hwy. 176 and turn left.

GREENWICH HALL

Greenwich Hall is located in Goose Creek's Plantation North

Insiders Like:
Taking an all-day picnic to the Spoleto Finale Concert at Middleton Place; frisbee all afternoon and listening to great music under the stars well into the night.

Insiders' Tip

area. These are Squires-built homes which sold in the mid-to-low $60s, but the development phase is now sold-out. Resales are likely in this neighborhood popular with military personnel prone to transfers. Take Hwy. 52 to Goose Creek, turn left on Hwy. 176, then left at Plantation North's entrance. Once inside, turn right onto Alcester Road.

PEMBROKE

This is the Ryland offering within Crowfield Plantation with all of Crowfield's amenities included. These traditional homes start at $110,000 and go up. Once inside Crowfield, turn left on Centennial and look for the Ryland model.

STONEHURST
(CROWFIELD PLANTATION)

The giant Crowfield Plantation development has numerous neighborhoods built by different developers. This is a Squires offering with houses starting in the upper $60,000 price range. Take Hwy. 52 to Goose Creek, turn left on Gainsborough, then right on Centennial and right (again) on Lowndes Road to the model home.

North Area
Fitness, Participatory Sports and Parks

As a part of the north area's housing boom, many of the developers have built fitness/jogging trails and exercise centers as an integral part of their neighborhood amenities. So, it's not unusual for residents to have some kind of fitness facility right in their own community. Even some of the more progressive new companies joining the north area's industrial complex have in-house fitness programs to help keep employees fit, healthy and on the job.

This chapter deals with some of the other fitness and recreational outlets in the north area — including a list of municipally-owned parks and community centers.

Participatory Sports

Bowling

BRUNSWICK SANDPIPER BOWL
3291 Ashley Phosphate Road   552-8530
North Charleston

This large-scale bowling complex has 32 fully-automated lanes, a snack bar, billiard room, electronic game room and a lounge. Take I-26 to Ashley Phosphate Road and turn left at the light; look for their sign on the left after the third light. They're open 24 hours.

OAKBROOK LANE
10015 Dorchester Road   875-2776
Summerville

This popular bowling spot features 32 automated lanes, a pro shop, game room, snack bar and lounge. Several leagues call Oakbrook "home" and there's a children's playroom for league members. Fees are variable according to hours and league membership. Hours are 9:00 AM to 11:30 PM weekdays, and Friday and Saturday 9:00 AM to 2:00 AM.

ROYAL-Z-LANES
106 Central Avenue   875-2776
Goose Creek

Both summer and winter bowling leagues play here (along with the public) at this Goose Creek facility with 36 AMF lanes with automatic scorers, a game room, snack bar and lounge. A playroom for children of league bowlers is provided. Hours are 9:00 AM to midnight, Monday through Thursday; 9:00 AM to 2:00 AM Friday and Saturday; and Sunday, noon to 11:00 PM. Take I-26 to Goose Creek exit and follow Highway 52 to Central

Avenue (at Jim Walter Homes).

Camping

GIVHANS FERRY STATE PARK
Highway 61   873-0692
15 miles west of Summerville

Old-timers may remember this as Edisto State Park — opened in 1935 for family recreation along the Edisto River. When Edisto Beach State Park opened the following year, this park was renamed to avoid confusion. In so doing, the state chose to honor Captain Philip Givhans, an early patriot and Edisto River plantation owner who fed and gave fresh horses to the freedom fighters during the Revolution. The shallow, sandy-bottomed stretch of the Edisto on Givhans' land was once a safe place to ferry goods, livestock and people across the river.

Today, Givhans Ferry State Park offers trails and ball-playing fields, picnic areas, and swimming on the Edisto River (no lifeguards are on duty, however). Their facilities include 25 camp sites with water and electrical hookups, plus four fully-furnished vacation cabins that rent for less than $200 per week. Campsites are $9 per night. Advance reservations are strongly encouraged as bookings at these bargain rates are usually done well in advance. Drive west on Highway 61 from Summerville to the park entrance.

Day Camps

Many north area day-care centers and churches have summer day camp programs for children (see Child Care chapter). Also, county-run day camps can be found through Charleston County Parks and Recreation Department at 762-2172. North Charleston's day camp programs are organized through the city park system at 745-1028 (see North Charleston Parks). In Dorchester County, call the school system at 873-2901; in Berkeley County, call 761-8049.

Stock Car Racing

SUMMERVILLE SPEEDWAY
Central Avenue   873-3438

Fans of stock car racing will find this local track a hot spot on weekend nights. They regularly schedule NASCAR DASH Division racing along with their weekly races for Late-Model Stocks, Super Stocks, and Thunder & Lightning, plus their two other Four-Cylinder divisions. They run under the lights with grandstand seating; adult admission is $10; youngsters eight to 12, $3; and children under eight are free. Call ahead for race schedule times and additional information.

Parks

North Charleston Parks And Recreation Centers

FRANKIE'S FUN PARK
5000 Ashley Phosphate Road   767-1376
(across from Waccamau Pottery)
North Charleston

While not a public park in the traditional municipal sense,

Frankie's Fun Park more than qualifies as a recreation center — just ask any kid! This theme-park-like destination features a pavilion and 35 acres of fun for all ages. You'll find 36 holes of tropical miniature golf, both a road course and an oval racetrack for go-carts, 9-position batting cages, and a bumper boat lake (where children under seven can ride free with an adult). Inside the main pavilion is a state-of-the-art game room where more than 100 electronic games await the nimble of hand and mind. There's also a lighted, 90-position golf driving range with mat and turf tees plus target greens — great for night play.

Admission to the park is free, while tickets to most rides are $3.50 for a five-minute ride. Bulk tickets are 5 for $15. Miniature golf is $4 for 18 holes; $6 for 36 holes. Hours are 10:00 AM to midnight, Monday through Saturday; and Sunday, 11:00 AM to midnight. Driving range hours are 10:00 AM to 10:00 PM, Monday through Thursday; Friday, 10:00 AM to midnight; Saturday, 9:00 AM to midnight; and Sunday, 11:00 AM to 10:00 PM.

North Charleston Community Centers

The city of North Charleston has a series of community centers with varied recreational facilities for adults and children of all ages. During the summer months, these centers often have day camps and other planned activities for the out-of-school set. Check the following list for the community center nearest you and call for a run-down on their current adult activities, youth programs and sports facilities:

Collins Park & Pool
4155 Fellowship Road (at Monitor Street), North Charleston, 552-9446.

Danny Jones Gymnasium Complex
5000 Lackawanna Blvd., (office) 745-1032, (pool) 745-1034; (tennis center) 745-1033.

Felix Pinckney Community Center
Montague Ave. at Hassell Ave., North Charleston, 745-1036.

Live Oak Community Center
2012 Success Street, North Charleston, 745-1037.

Highland Terrace Community Center
2401 Richardson Dr., North Charleston, 745-1041.

North Park Village
3947-A Hilliyard Dr., North Charleston, 745-1040.

North Woods Community Center
8348 Greenridge Road, N. Charleston, 572-5401.

Pepper Hill Ball Park and Community Center
7695 Brandywine Rd., North Charleston, 767-0865.

Senior Citizens Building
1103 Marquis Rd., North Charleston, 745-1038.
Whipper Barony Park
3855 Chestnut St., North Charleston, 745-1039.

Summerville Parks And Recreation Centers

Summerville likes to be known as "America's Hometown," and that's a fair and accurate assessment. Good times in Summerville have acomfortable, homegrown flavor. Just off Main Street in the center of Summerville, for instance, is the quaint, Victorian city park named Azalea — for obvious reasons. Here, in the rolling leafy setting in the very heart of town are eight acres of azaleas (dozens of varieties), dogwood, wisteria and crepe myrtle with interlacing walking paths beside reflecting ponds. Open to the public year round, Azalea Park is at its peak bloom in the spring. It is always the central showpiece for Summerville's annual Flowertown Festival in late March and early April.

We've grouped the area's parks and playgrounds together as a single category for brevity. A wide range of youth and adult sports programs are offered by local volunteer and service organizations. Recreational facilities are available at the following Summerville area public parks:

Doty Field on North Hickory Street has football and baseball fields plus tennis courts. **Azalea Park** on South Main Street offers tennis courts and quiet walking paths. **Laurel Street Playground** on South Laurel Street has tennis courts and a childrens' playground. **Walnut Street Playground** on North Walnut Street has a good playground for small children. **Alston Playground** on Highway 78 West has baseball fields.

Old Fort Dorchester State Park
Dorchester Road   873-1740

This historic site has — in addition to the ruins of old Fort Dorchester — playing fields and a nice picnic area (see Dorchester County History).

North Area
Worship

As we described in our Charleston Worship chapter, the Lowcountry's long tradition of religious tolerance and diversification is truly remarkable. This is especially true of the early historic churches of the peninsula city and the quaint little Chapels of Ease described in Daytrips and Berkeley County Historic Sites. But this same wide-ranging tolerance and diversification is true of the north area —in churches from North Charleston through Summerville.

Again, we are attempting to recognize only those denominations that publicize their existence And because schedules for services change seasonally here in the Lowcountry, we make only general references to morning or evening worship. Call the church office for specific details, or check the *Post and Courier's* Saturday listing.

Adventist

SUMMERVILLE COMMUNITY
SEVENTH-DAY ADVENTIST
520 Gahagan Road   *821-4787 or*
Summerville   *821-4588*
This Summerville area church has about 140 members and meets on Saturday for a regular Bible study and morning worship service. There is a Wednesday evening service also. A mothers' room for young children is provided during services.

Baptist

CHARLESTON HEIGHTS BAPTIST
2005 Reynolds Avenue   *554-9459*
North Charleston
This church of about 250 active members, near the Navy base, offers Sunday School, two regular morning worship services and evening worship every Sunday. A prayer service on Wednesday evening is also well attended. A nursery is provided during services. From Charleston, take the Cosgrove exit off I-26 to Rivers; then turn right and stay left on Rivers to Reynolds Avenue.

COOPER RIVER BAPTIST CHURCH
1059 Crawford Street   *747-7389*
North Charleston
This is one of the larger Baptist churches in the north area with a regular Sunday morning attendance of about 300. Sunday School and regular morning worship is followed by Church Training and evening worship on Sunday evening. A Wednesday evening prayer service is also a part of this

church's tradition. Take the East Montague exit off I-26 all the way to Park Circle. Then take Montague Avenue several blocks to North Charleston High School and turn right on Jenkens Avenue to Crawford.

HILLCREST BAPTIST CHURCH
3595 Ashley Phosphate Road   552-1495
North Charleston

One of the largest congregations in the north area, this church holds two morning worship services plus Sunday School each week. Church Training and evening worship are on Sunday evening. There is a Wednesday evening prayer service and a nursery is provided for all services. Take I-26 to Ashley Phosphate Road and turn left at the light.

NORTHWOODS BAPTIST CHURCH
2200 Greenwich Road   553-3281
North Charleston

Sunday School and morning worship are followed by an evening Church Training and worship service. This church with nearly 280 members is located in the north area. Take I-26 past Ashley Phosphate to the Goose Creek/Moncks Corner exit. At Rivers Avenue at the light, take a left on Greenwich Road. All visitors are welcome.

RIVERBEND BAPTIST CHURCH
999 Michigan Avenue   552-4995
(near the AFB) North Charleston

This growing Baptist congregation is largely made up of local personnel from the AFB and retired Air Force and Navy folk living in the North Charleston area. They

have Bible study and worship service (each) twice on Sunday. Wednesday evening is prayer meeting. This church also has an on-site day care facility and kindergarten; call 552-2357. Take Dorchester Road to the main gate of Charleston Air Force Base. Just past the light, see the sign for the church across the street from the base commissary.

SUMMERVILLE BAPTIST CHURCH
417 Central Avenue, Summerville 873-2440

Two morning services, Sunday School and an evening service are held in this large Baptist church on Central at Carolina in downtown Summerville. The church is celebrating nearly a century at this location. They have ongoing programs for all ages. Visitors are warmly welcomed.

Catholic

ST. JOHN'S CHURCH
3921 St. John's Avenue, North Charleston

This church celebrates a Saturday evening Mass and three Sunday Masses. Confession is on Saturday afternoon and by appointment. Turn north from MacMillan Avenue at the main gates of the Naval Base. All are welcome.

ST. THOMAS THE APOSTLE
6650 Dorchester Road, North Charleston

Located between Charleston International Airport and the Air Force Base in North Charleston, this church holds one Saturday Mass with a Sacrament of Reconciliation and two Sunday Masses.

Christian

KING'S WAY CHRISTIAN CHURCH
Myers Road, Goose Creek   *821-1961*

Two Sunday morning worship services plus Sunday School and one evening service are regularly held in this Goose Creek Christian church near Hwy. 176. A nursery is provided for all services. Take Short-Cut Road near Summerville to Myers Road off Hwy. 176.

SUMMERVILLE CHRISTIAN CHURCH
Hwy. 78-E, Ladson   *871-2014*

Morning Sunday School is followed by regular worship plus one evening service each week. Youth and adult classes are on Sunday evenings and there's a Wednesday evening prayer meeting with Bible study for youth and adult classes. From Charleston, take the College Park exit off I-26 and turn right on Hwy. 78 to one mile past Exchange Park (toward Summerville).

Church Of Christ

NORTH CHARLESTON CHURCH OF CHRIST
6337 Rivers Avenue   *553-4963*
North Charleston

Sunday morning Bible study is followed by a worship service in this North Charleston church. Another service is held Sunday evening. Bible study is every Wednesday evening. An attended nursery is available for all services. Visitors are welcome.

Episcopal

ST. GEORGE'S EPISCOPAL CHURCH
9110 Dorchester Road,
Summerville   *873-0772*

Holy Eucharist services are held twice each Sunday along with a regular Sunday School. A nursery is provided during services. The church is located across from King's Grant on Dorchester Road.

ST. THOMAS EPISCOPAL CHURCH
1150 E. Montague Ave.   *747-0479*
North Charleston

Each Sunday morning, Holy Eucharist is celebrated twice with a sermon following the second service. A nursery is provided for the late service, only. Take I-26 to the Montague East exit.

Lutheran

GRACE LUTHERAN CHURCH
1600 Old Trolley Road   *871-5444*
Summerville

This (Missouri Synod) Lutheran church holds two morning services during the winter months plus a Sunday School. A nursery is provided for the late service only.

Nazarene

DORCHESTER ROAD CHURCH OF THE NAZARENE
5391 Dorchester Road   *552-7365*
Charleston Heights

Early Church School is immediately followed by a morning worship service here. Another service takes place later in the evening.

Every Wednesday evening is Family Night with organized activities for all ages. A nursery is provided for children during all services.

United Methodist

BETHANY UNITED METHODIST
118 West 3rd South Street   873-1230
Summerville

This large Summerville congregation holds Sunday morning Church School for all ages plus two morning worship services. Sunday evening, the Methodist Youth Fellowship meets. Wednesday evening is choir practice. A nursery is provided for all services. Visitors are welcome. The church is located between South Main and Central Avenue in downtown Summerville.

NORTH CHARLESTON UNITED METHODIST CHURCH
1125 East Montague Avenue   744-6669
North Charleston

This large United Methodist congregation holds services on Sunday morning along with early Church School and an evening youth program. The church also operates an on-site licensed day care center. Take the East Montague exit off I-26.

Nondenominational

UNITY CHURCH OF CHARLESTON
2535 Leeds Avenue   566-0600
North Charleston

This nondenominational group holds morning services weekly along with an early youth education/nursery. Wednesday afternoon there is a prayer service followed by World Religion Class. Visitors are welcome.

Summerville
History

*I*n Summerville, you're 25 miles inland from the Atlantic Ocean, on a ridge 75 feet above sea level. The longleaf pine forest all around you helps keep temperatures moderate while the air is scented with refreshing pine vapors borne on soft sea breezes.

These are the basic elements which first attracted a few planter families to build summer camps in this higher pineland spot — away from the mosquitoes and deadly swamp fevers which plagued the lower areas. The first few families to establish summer homes came between the end of the Revolution and 1790. By 1828, 23 houses were counted in the village. Two years later, a chapel of ease to St. Paul's Episcopal Church was built — indicating a growing trend on behalf of some families to maintain full-time residences there.

These "summer" homes were often built high on pilings with large, wraparound porches to catch the breezes. Today, you can still find many of them scattered randomly in the half-mile area around St. Paul's Episcopal Church in an area now called "Old Town."

By 1832, the South Carolina Railroad had come to Summerville and, the new areas of growth (un-like Old Town) had the benefit of a plan; regularly spaced streets running parallel to and at right angles to the tracks. A large, open space was reserved for a town square and today's Town Hall overlooks that site. Victorian commercial buildings soon sprang up around the square; many of them still standing. And with its railroad connection to Charleston at last in place, the once sleepy village started to grow rapidly. In 1847, Summerville was incorporated.

A series of fever epidemics struck Charleston during the late 1850s sending even more new residents to this relatively fever-free locale. As a Charleston newspaper lamented during those difficult years, "the eyes of Charleston sadly turned toward Summerville...." By 1860, the population had grown to 1,088 residents; 548 white, 540 black.

The Civil War brought an abrupt end to Summerville's growth and prosperity. Not until the end of the century would the town see another boom. When it did come, however, it would bring the pineland village international fame.

In 1889, a world congress of specialists in respiratory diseases met in Paris and named Summerville, South Carolina, one of the two best resort areas in the world for the cure of lung and throat disorders. This widely publicized "Tuberculosis Congress" introduced a whole new era in Summerville's history.

Special excursion trains came in from New York and St. Louis and numerous establishments were built to accommodate the flood of health-minded visitors. The grandest of these establishments was the Pine Forest Inn (no longer standing) where President Theodore Roosevelt (among other luminaries) stayed.

The fame of Summerville as a health resort waned with the coming of the Depression in the 1930s. But WWII and the postwar prosperity it brought to the Lowcountry gave the town new reason to succeed.

Summerville has traditionally been known as a center for azalea culture. The lush landscaped gardens and homes all seem to be an extension of the city's own Azalea Park (on Main Street). Indeed, come spring, Summerville is justifiably called "Flowertown in the Pines."

Summerville Attractions

Visitors to Summerville may first want to check in at the Chamber of Commerce, 106 E. Doty Avenue (873-2931) just a block off Main Street near Town Square. This quaint old Summerville house serves as a mini "welcome center"

with newcomer information, maps, brochures, and friendly advice.

FLOWERTOWN FESTIVAL

Every year, Summerville's biggest bash is the Flowertown Festival — when the town is ablaze in color. It is scheduled to coincide with the area's remarkable and quite spectacular azalea, camellia, and dogwood bloom. And by the calendar, that means two weeks before Easter or one week after — depending on where Easter falls. In 1994, the dates will be April 8, 9, and 10.

The whole town participates in the festival, which has been held since 1973, and includes parades, concerts, dancing, a food fair, a health fair, kiddie rides, historic house tours, and craft exhibits of all kinds.

In fact, the Flowertown Festival (originally sponsored as a fundraiser for the Summerville Family YMCA) is highly regarded in artistic circles up and down the Eastern seaboard. The quality of crafts displayed here is unusually good.

Every year, tens of thousands of visitors attend the three-day event and celebrate spring in the Lowcountry. The atmosphere is like an old-fashioned country fair. For more specific Flowertown Festival information, write The Greater Summerville Chamber of Commerce, P.O. Drawer 670, Summerville SC 29484, or call 873-2931.

SUMMERVILLE — DORCHESTER MUSEUM
100 E. Doty Avenue   875-9666
Officially opened in 1993 for

the Flowertown Festival, Summerville's newest museum gives visitors a fascinating look at the city's past. The inspiration for the museum was simple enough — it was intended to be a place where the area's children could learn about their own "home town" and visitors could see some of the city's rich and romantic past.

The building, formerly a police station, is in the same block as the Chamber of Commerce — less than a block from Town Square.

Here, you'll find local fossils, natural history, memorabilia from an earlier Summerville, and photographic displays showing the city and Dorchester County from the days following the Great Earthquake of 1886 to the present day. The emphasis is on the area's historic architecture and Summerville's many memorable characters.

For now, the museum is open on weekends only — staffed by volunteers. But we hope their hours will expand very soon.

Summerville's "Old Town"

(A DRIVING TOUR)

The section of your *Insiders' Guide* called Inside Dorchester County has a brief history of the town of Summerville. Your driving tour through Summerville's "Old Town" section will be more meaningful after reading it.

The shady, winding streets of this part of Summerville bring to mind the days when this was a summer retreat for wealthy planters. The charming homes and well-kept gardens seem little changed from those days — in the mid-1800s — or from those in the 1890s when Summerville was a world-famous health resort.

If you're coming from Charleston along Hwy. 61 (the old Ashley River Road), veer to the right on Bacons Bridge Road or Hwy. 165. This will lead you into Summerville at South Main Street or Hwy. 17-A. Turn onto W. Carolina Avenue and start your "Old Town" tour with St. Paul's Episcopal Church.

If you're coming via I-26 (from Charleston), take the 2nd Summerville exit onto Hwy. 17-A. Be sure to follow the signs (Summerville is to the left, Moncks Corner is on the right).

Follow Hwy. 17-A or Main Street all the way through town past Azalea Park and W. 5th Street. When you see W. Carolina Avenue, turn right and follow it to St. Paul's Episcopal Church.

You may want to briefly pause in the church parking lot, do your reading, and proceed from there.

St. Paul's Episcopal Church

The history of St. Paul's Episcopal Church dates back to 1828 when the Rev. Philip Gadsden, rector of another Lowcountry chapel of ease, followed the growing number of communicants moving to the thriving village of Summerville.

At first, services were held in the leaky old village hall or in some parishioner's residence. But in 1829 a decision was made to build a proper house of worship. The first church building, dedicated in 1832, stood just a few feet south of the present structure. But Summerville's rapid growth soon made this simple wooden structure far too small, so by 1857 a new church (the present building) was built at a cost of $5,000. In 1877 the church was extended by 20 feet; the present stained glass window and communion rail being added at that time.

The terrible earthquake that struck Charleston and Summerville on the night of August 31, 1886 badly damaged the building but repairs were soon made. (Note the earthquake rods running through the structure.)

Early in the 20th century, there was a movement to replace the 1857 building with a more modern structure. Fortunately, those plans were never realized. Today St. Paul's rector, vestry, and congregation work to preserve the old church where it continues to serve the community and be an architectural focal point for Old Town and Summerville itself.

Note the church parking lot exit signs which will lead you out to Gadsden Street where you turn left. This will bring you back onto W. Carolina Avenue where you turn right. *Immediately* turn left onto Sumter Avenue where in a few short blocks you can encounter at least 11 architecturally significant homes or "cottages" dating from the mid- to late 19th century.

On your right:

The Gelzer Brothers House (c. 1819)

413 Sumter Avenue

This home, like several others on this end of Sumter Avenue, was actually built facing a street no longer in existence. You're viewing what was originally the rear of this very early dwelling for Summerville's Old Town.

On your left:

The Brailsford-Browning House (c. 1830)

408 Sumter Avenue

Here is an example of early Summerville architecture where the house is lifted high off the ground to catch cooler ocean breezes. The lower area was once open, (the present enclosure was added after 1915). Early records show this house was occupied by a Dr. W.M. Brailsford in 1838 when it was listed among the 29 houses then counted in the growing village of Summerville. During the Civil War, the public records of Colleton County were destroyed. Summerville was then in Colleton County; so the exact date of this house and the name of the original builder have been lost.

On the right:

THE BUCKHEIT HOUSE (c. 1884)
317 Sumter Avenue

Existing documentation indicates that in 1862, a baker from Charleston named Philip Buckheit bought this land. Perhaps because of the war, he didn't actually build this house until about 1884.

Again, on the right:

THE DISHER HOUSE (c. 1862)
303 Sumter Avenue

Deeds for this property go back to 1862 when Robert W. Disher bought two acres of land from A.W. Taylor. Disher's house (and presence) on this site must have been noteworthy since the adjoining street now named Charleston Street, was formerly known as Disher.

On the left:

THE WILLIAM PRIOLEAU HOUSE (1896)
302 Sumter Avenue

Built by a Charleston druggist, Dr. William H. Prioleau, this is one of the many Victorian homes built during the big health resort boom around the turn of the century. The lacy architectural style is called "Queen Anne."

On the right:

THE KINLOCH HOUSE (c. 1861)
233 Sumter Avenue

This house was built in 1861 (shortly after the shelling of Ft. Sumter in Charleston Harbor) on land formerly owned by the Rev. Philip Gadsden, the first rector of St. Paul's Episcopal Church.

On the left:

THE BROWNFIELD HOUSE (c. 1875)
320 Sumter Avenue

This residence belonged to the Brownfield family who on this property built a now defunct boarding school for girls known as The Brownfield Academy. In 1893, it was advertised as "Particularly desirable for Northern young ladies with impaired health who would probably be successful in following their studies in this health-giving climate."

On the left:

THE PURCELL HOUSE (c. 1820)
224 Sumter Avenue

Records date this home between 1811 and 1828. The architecture is typical of the very early hunting lodges or summer homes built here by the nearby planters.

On the right:

PREFERENCE (c. 1885)
223 Sumter Avenue

Note the West Indian character of this home. The broad porches and high elevation would have offered friendly shade and cool breezes to its residents and guests. Although the exact date of construction is unknown, this handsome Victorian house is thought to have been built for a Mary Webb around 1885.

On the left:

THE CHARLES BOYLE HOUSE (C. 1888)
220 Sumter Avenue

This house was built by Summerville attorney Charles Boyle around 1888 on land that at one time straddled the Colleton County/Berkeley County line.

On the right:

THE SAMUEL PRIOLEAU HOUSE (1887)
217 Sumter Avenue

This was the home of Dr. Samuel Prioleau, in whose honor the first Summerville Infirmary was named. The land was given to Dr. Prioleau's wife by her mother, Mrs. Benjamin Rhett, who lived next door.

On the left:

THE SAMUEL LORD-ELIZABETH ARDEN HOUSE (1891)
208 Sumter Avenue

This handsome Victorian house was built for Samuel Lord in 1891 by the same contractor who built the town's celebrated Pine Forest Inn. With its three stories and impressive double piazzas, the ornate house was purchased in 1938 by Elizabeth Arden, the famous cosmetic firm magnate, who used it as her winter retreat. It remained in her possession until 1954.

And finally, on the right:

THE RHETT HOUSE (1882)
205 Sumter Avenue

Dr. Benjamin Rhett served as a surgeon for the Confederacy and later practiced medicine in Summerville. His Victorian house was built on land that was once owned by the South Carolina Canal and Railroad Company during Summerville's first boom days in the 1830s. For further information on Summerville, see Inside Dorchester County).

Now, stay to the right on Sumter Avenue until it intersects with W. 5th Street (at the First Baptist Church). Turn right and follow W. 5th Street back to Main. Then turn left and follow Hwy 17-A through town until you see signs for I-26 (south), the fastest route back to Charleston.

Summerville
Restaurants

*D*espite Summerville's small size, it offers a good selection of dining options. From Greek or Chinese to full course meals or only desserts — there's a place to satisfy any hunger. The $-symbol scale we give with each entry is meant to provide an idea of cost per entree so you can plan ahead:

Under $10	**$**
$10 - $15	**$$**
$16 - $20	**$$$**
$21 - and up	**$$$$**

Bon appetit!

THE CONTINENTAL CORNER
123 W. Richardson Avenue   871-1160
FAX 871-1165
$ - $$ *Most major credit cards*

Here's a friendly spot offering Greek foods and desserts with interesting lunch and dinner menus, plus specials of the day. Mixed drinks, beer, and wine are available, too. The Continental Corner offers complete carry-out and catering services and off-street parking, smoking and nonsmoking sections. It's open from 11:00 AM to 9:00 PM, Monday through Thursday; and from 11:00 AM until 9:30 PM on Friday and Saturday.

OSCAR'S PLACE
207 W. 5th North Street   871-3800
$$ *Most major credit cards*

Lunch and dinner menus here feature steaks, seafood, Mexican dishes, fresh fish, duck, veal, designer salads and sandwiches. Look for the evening blackboard specials Monday through Thursday until 10:00 PM; and Friday and Saturday until 11:00 PM. Otherwise, Oscar's is open Monday through Saturday. Lunch is served from 11:00 AM until 3:00 PM; the patio menu is offered from 3:00 until 5:00 PM; and dinner begins at 5:30 PM.

BoJo's
114 Central Ave.   875-3357
$ *Most major credit cards*

Here the place for seafood lovers with large appetites. The friendly, family atmosphere lends itself to Lowcountry favorites like Frogmore Stew and freshwater catfish. Bojo's is open for lunch Monday through Saturday, 11:00 AM to 2:30 PM. And every evening, dinner is served from 5:00 to 9:30 PM; except Sunday.

STEPHEN'S

100 Old Trolley Road	875-3413 or
	851-1511
$$	MC, V, D

Stephen's offers your favorite seafood, steaks, and salads along with cocktails. They're open from 5:00 to 9:00 PM, Tuesday through Friday, and 5:00 to 10:00 PM on Saturday. Most major credit cards are accepted.

THE TURTLE DELI

| 131 Central Avenue | 875-0380 |
| $ | MC, V |

This delightfully cozy spot is a popular lunchtime destination for those in search of generous deli sandwiches, daily soup and lunch specials, and homemade quiche and desserts. The Turtle Deli is featured in *Historic Restaurants of South Carolina* and is open from 11:00 AM to 2:45 PM, Monday through Saturday.

CHINESE EXPRESS

4665 Ladson Road	821-2128
(Corner of Dorchester and Ladson)	
$	MC, V

Chinese food lovers will find good, fast, family dining here with either dine-in or take-out service. The menu includes Szechuan and Hunan cuisine along with your Chinese favorites. They're open from 11:30 AM until 9:30 PM, Monday through Thursday; and 11:30 AM until 10:30 PM on Friday and Saturday.

GIANNI'S

| Ladson Square Shopping Center | 553-1272 |
| $ | No credit cards accepted |

Here's a place for Italian food lovers (and Greek food lovers, too). Gianni's is open from 10:00 AM to 10:00 PM, Monday through Thursday; and from 10:00 AM to 11:00 PM on Friday. They accept personal checks and cash only.

JUST CHEESECAKES, INC.

| 130 W. Richardson Avenue | 873-2776 |
| $ | MC, V |

Here's the topper for your Summerville visit: gourmet cheesecake and a cup of hot coffee — brought to you by the folks who make nothing else! Well, actually, you might find a giant muffin or a gourmet cake of some other ilk, but this is purely a dessert lover's heaven. The gates of this particular heaven swing open at 10:00 AM and close at 6:00 PM, Tuesday through Saturday.

Summerville
Shopping

The Central hub of Summerville was once Town Square — at Richardson Avenue and Main Street. This refreshing green space retains much of Summerville's Victorian charm. Actually, the park dates back to the original plans drawn up for the "New Town" of Summerville in 1832. It was designated as "a breathing place for la-dies and children." (Don't ask us where the men were supposed to breathe!) Later, it was officially named "Hutchinson Park" after the town's first mayor — elected in 1832 — and it soon became the town's business center.

At one end of the park, you'll see Summerville's Victorian train station with its sloping roof and

carved gingerbread. The other end is anchored by Summerville's third Town Hall, built in 1965.

Today, like in most other small towns across America, the majority of everyday shopping has moved out to suburban shopping malls. But Summerville's Town Square and the larger downtown area can rightfully claim a number of noteworthy shopping adventures.

Antiques

Summerville offers the antique buff a gold mine of shopping options. The merchandise, generally speaking, is more affordable than some of the fine, English imports found in Charleston's King Street shops. But the quality — in some cases — may be somewhat lower, too. Still, there's many a needle in the Summerville antique haystack. And the Insider with real curiosity, a sense of adventure, and a little patience is sure to have a great time shopping here.

ADELE'S ANTIQUES

109 S. Pine Street   *871-8249*

Adele's specializes in vintage clothing, jewelry, wedding gowns, European antiques, brass, clocks, and porcelain. Hours are noon to 5:00 PM, Tuesday through Saturday.

AFTERNOON ANTIQUES

405 W. 5th Street   *873-8897*
(Hwy. 78)

This shop features a fine collection of antiques, collectibles and gifts — plus a delightful tearoom for a shopper's respite. Hours are Tues-

day through Saturday, 10:00 AM to 5:00 PM.

ANTIQUES 'N STUFF

128 E. Richardson Avenue   *875-4155*

Here's a shop specializing in affordable antique furniture, glassware, jewelry, and other collectibles. Business hours are from 10:30 AM to 5:00 PM, Monday through Saturday.

B & N COLLECTIBLES

129 E. Richardson Ave.   *875-3735*

This spot specializes in Depression glass. Hours are 10:00 AM to 5:00 PM, Monday through Saturday.

CARRIAGE HOUSE COLLECTIBLES

1213 S. Main Street   *873-5704*

This shop's specialty is American and country antiques and accessories. The store hours are from 9:00 AM to 5:00 PM, Monday through Saturday.

THE CONSIGNMENT GALLERY, INC.

200 N. Main Street   *851-1674*

Here you'll find good deals on antiques, pre-owned furniture and collectibles. As the name implies, this is a consignment shop which both sells and receives merchandise; they will accept for sale your quality furniture and accessories.

COUNTRY STORE & ANTIQUES

1106 N. Main Street   *871-7548*

This shop carries American country, primitive antiques, gifts, and other collectibles. In particular, they carry Tom Clark and All God's Children figurines. Hours

The Frank Smith residence, Richardson and Pine Street.

are from 10:00 AM to 5:30 PM, Monday through Saturday.

EARLY TRADITIONS

87 Old Trolley Road   851-1627

This shop features a wide assortment of antiques, gifts and collectibles. Their regular hours are 10:00 AM to 5:00 PM, Tuesday through Friday. They're open on Sundays — by chance.

GRANNY'S ATTIC

71 Old Trolley Road   871-6838

This is an eclectic offering of antiques, collectibles, and gifts. Business hours are from 10:30 AM to 5:00 PM, except Wednesday and Sundays when the shop is closed.

LOWCOUNTRY ANTIQUES & COLLECTIBLES

89 Old Trolley Road   873-7101

This shop specializes in American period and primitive furniture, china, glassware, pottery, quilts and decorative items. Also, they carry the artwork of Summerville artist Colleen Strioff.

Hours are 10:00 AM to 5:00 PM, Tuesday through Saturday.

PEOPLE, PLACES & QUILTS

129 W. Richardson Avenue   871-8872

Here's a delightful little shop for unique American folk art, small antiques, and a large assortment of handmade quilts. Business hours are from 10:00 AM to 5:00 PM, Monday through Saturday.

REMEMBER WHEN

301 Old Trolley Road   821-1018

Here's a shop for those interested in primitive antiques, gifts and collectibles. Business hours are from 10:00 AM to 5:30 PM, Monday through Saturday; and 1:00 to 5:00 PM on Sunday.

SPECIAL BLESSINGS

129 W. Richardson Avenue   873-3994 or
875-5254

This shop carries furniture, glassware, dishes, toys, and accessories. Business hours are 10:00 AM to 5:00 PM, Monday through Saturday.

STALL HOUSE ANTIQUES
211 Stallsville Loop   875-0241

Stall House specializes in American period antique furniture and accessories. Business hours are from 10:30 AM to 5:00 PM, Tuesday through Saturday.

TOWN FAIR ANTIQUES, THE PROUD PUFFIN, PIECES OF OLD AND VILLAGE SHOPPE
131 E. Richardson Avenue   873-3462

This is an old Summerville house containing four antique dealers carrying a wide assortment of merchandise which includes furniture, rugs, glassware, books, clocks, original art, estate jewelry, and accessories. The shops are open from 10:30 AM to 5:00 PM, Monday through Saturday.

TIMELESS TREASURES ANTIQUES AND COLLECTIBLES
126 S. Main Street   875-9207 or
                                     744-1563

This shop has a little of everything — from fine antique furniture to ceramics and china to antique art. Hours are 10:00 AM to 5:00 PM, Monday through Saturday.

TROLLEY STATION ANTIQUES AND COLLECTIBLES
118 E. Richardson Avenue   821-7611

This spot is a cornucopia of merchandise with 300 square feet of Victorian fun. The selection includes furniture, glass, collectibles, vintage baseball cards, toys and primitives. They specialize in vintage lunch boxes — possibly the largest selection in the state. Business hours are 10:00 AM to 5:00 PM, Monday through Saturday (closed Tuesday), and 1:00 to 5:00 PM Sunday.

Crafts And Galleries

FRAME DESIGN
800 Main Street   871-6373

Just across the street from Rollings Elementary School, this art gallery and frame shop offers a mix of artwork that ranges from local artists to wildlife to florals to posters. Hours are 10:00 AM to 5:30 PM, Monday through Friday; and from 10:00 AM to 2:00 PM on Saturday.

GAILLARD STUDIO
129 West Richardson Avenue   851-6879

This small shop located in the renovated Cauthen's Hardware Store features the work of local artist, Ravenel Gaillard. Along with large scale recent original works, there are numerous smaller paintings and an assortment of attractive prints. Much of Gaillard's work recaptures his Lowcountry childhood in colorful, whimsical scenes of country life. Hours are 10:00 AM to 5:00 PM, Tuesday through Saturday; open Sunday and Monday by appointment.

THE FINISHING TOUCH
134 S. Main Street   873-2531

This charming specialty shop offers a variety of fine crafts, original artwork, and custom framing. Located in what was once Summerville's first department store, this shop features the work of Tom Timm, known as "The Custom Woodcrafter," whose artistry is legendary. The shop is open from 10:00

AM to 5:00 PM, Monday through Saturday.

GALLERY TWO
120 N. Main Street   *873-5396*

This art gallery and custom frame shop offers fine art prints, limited editions, and original watercolor and oil paintings. The gallery also features museum matting, special mounting, and handmade shadowboxes. Business hours are from 10:00 AM to 6:00 PM, Monday through Friday; and 10:00 AM to 2:00 PM on Saturday.

Books

ALL BOOKS & CO.
145 Central Avenue   *871-2772*

Here's Summerville's best selection of children's books, fiction and nonfiction, best-sellers, books on tape, and regional works. They carry bookmarks, greeting cards, gift certificates, and other gift items for readers. Hours are 10:00 AM to 6:00 PM, Monday through Friday, and 10:00 AM to 5:00 PM on Saturday.

Clothing — Children

CAROUSEL BOUTIQUE
125 Central Avenue   *821-8853*

This children's specialty shop offers traditional clothing with personality — tailored for newborns to size 14. They also carry quality consignments, handmade gifts, Charleston bonnets, and hand-painted apparel. The shop is open from 11:00 AM to 5:00 PM, Tuesday through Saturday. Special appointments can be made upon request.

Home And Garden

THE VILLAGE GREEN
132 W. Richardson Avenue   *871-1766*

This is a unique garden shop — in a town famous for its unique and beautiful gardens. Look here for interesting one-of-a-kind items from birdhouses to lawn furniture and other outdoor accessories. Hours are Tuesday through Saturday, 10:00 AM to 5:00 PM.

Photo: The Post and Courier

Picturesque Summerville Street.

Summerville
Accommodations

*T*hough the accommodations available in Summerville are more limited than in some of the surrounding areas, we recommend a couple of bed and breakfasts that are real gems. You might want to check ahead about their policies concerning children and pets. For those on a slightly tighter budget, there are several other alternatives. You choose.

The following scale will help you plan what your stay will cost per night, based on two adults.

$50 and under	$
$51 - $75	$$
$76 - $95	$$$
$96 - $110	$$$$
$110 and up	$$$$$

BED & BREAKFAST OF SUMMERVILLE

304 S. Hampton Street   *871-5275*
$$ - $$$ *No credit cards*

In the heart of Summerville's historic district you'll find the Guest Quarters of The Blake Washington House (c. 1865). This bed and breakfast is listed on the National Register of Historic Places. You can relax by the sparkling pool in the summer, or sit by a sleepy fire in the winter. But call well ahead of your arrival for reservations, only one room (with private bath) is offered.

COMFORT INN

1005 Jockey Court   *851-2333*
$$ - $$$ *Most major credit cards*

This chain motel is conveniently located at I-26 and Highway 17-A South. There's a pool and pool house with hot tub, exercise facilities, and a dry sauna. The ample rooms feature double queen or king beds — plus there are luxury suites (with whirlpool baths) available.

THE WOODLANDS

329 Old Postern Road   *875-2602*
$$$-$$$$ *MC, V, AX*

This grand and pillared (once) private home is now a grand bed and breakfast with twenty elegantly furnished guest rooms. The refurbished Woodlands (formerly Gadsden manor) will open in the fall of 1994 with a restaurant and intimate cocktail lounge. A complimentary breakfast is included with your room. Some of the public rooms are available for private parties or corporate events.

HOLIDAY INN OF SUMMERVILLE

120 Holiday Inn Drive   *875-3300*
$$ - $$$ *Most major credit cards*

Here's an old friend of family travelers with affordable single and double accommodations. You'll find a pool and a full-service restaurant plus a lounge with nightly entertainment.

Photo: The Post and Courier

The Edmundston Alston House.

Greater Charleston
Attractions

*H*owever varied the attractions of the Lowcountry and Greater Charleston may be, this is a place where people are drawn to, captured by, and never completely escape the clutches of...history. In fact, it's even fair to say we primarily offer history — a deeper, richer, more romantic history (and more of it) — than any other Colonial city in America. At least, that's the traditional and prevailing Charlestonian attitude.

Whether you're a newcomer to the Lowcountry (and a soon-to-be Insider, yourself), or you're merely a visitor to this gentle land, it's easy to become overwhelmed by the amount of history offered here — and the seriousness with which Charlestonians deal with it in their daily lives.

Charlestonians very much want to share their history with newcomers and guests. They share it proudly — just as long as you pay close attention, clearly make an effort to learn, and seek factual information from reliable sources. In other words, the true story about Charleston is a far better story than the tired Southern cliches some folks might expect to find. The good listener is richly rewarded for the investment of time and attention.

For obvious economic reasons and other reasons equally valid (like pride and passion), the subject of tourism in historic Charleston is seriously studied. There are many points of view, of course. But tourism has been — for many years — a rather sensitive and often volatile topic of discussion.

A good example of this can be found in a Chamber of Commerce brochure published for the tourist market in 1904. Charleston is described like a lady, one of unquestionable dignity, who has been forced onto the wicked stage of tourism by unseemly circumstances far beyond her control:

"The conservatism which has always characterized Charleston has hitherto prevented her merits from becoming so widely known as they should be. But conservatism in matters connected with the welfare of the community is no longer in accord with the spirit of our times....

"Charleston has always been justly famed for her hospitality, and still delights to honor all those who are deserving of (her) respect and admiration."

Then, with further Victorian modesty, the brochure goes on to laud the city's (apparently unlimited) historical attractions:

"The lover of history finds deep interest in her (Charleston's) connection with every important historical event from the planting of the early colonies down to the present day...and the sentimentally inclined can discover in the city and vicinity the scenes of many a legend and story."

Obviously, tourism and Charleston are very old friends.

Charleston and tourist *management*, on the other hand, are relatively recent acquaintances. In other words, the sheer volume of visitors (especially over the past decade) has finally begun to impact the fragile charm Charlestonians have stubbornly held onto for the past 300 years.

The quaint, genteel and quiet residential flavor of the 18th century peninsular city (even with its 19th- and 20th-century scars) is by definition incompatible with the economic, cultural and environmental consequences of five million tourists who visit the city annually. This collision of mores and economics has resulted in a very carefully planned and closely monitored tourism experience for today's Charleston visitor. We, as the city's guests — whether for a week or a lifetime — are very much the fortunate winners in this tug-of-war between *now* and *then*.

Because we truly care and because it helps to preserve our city's unique cultural identity, Charleston's historic attractions are (for the greatest part) well organized, highly accessible and intelligently interpreted. There are delightful Charleston experiences for

visitors of all ages and all areas of interest (academic American history, notwithstanding).

In this chapter, we will begin to orient you by steering you to visitor centers. Then, we'll take you on a written "tour" of this area's brightest and best attractions, beginning with the House Museums, then the Plantations and Gardens, followed by Forts and Other Museums. There is a lot to see and do here, and we hope this guide will help you plan well and miss nothing of interest to you.

Visitor Centers

CHARLESTON VISITOR RECEPTION & TRANSPORTATION CENTER

375 Meeting Street   853-8000

Because parking in the old, historic district is nearly always a problem, visitors are encouraged to make their first destination the Charleston Visitor and Transportation Center. Its location on "upper" (meaning the northern end of) Meeting Street offers visitors a welcome opportunity to leave their cars behind and see Charleston's large historic district (mostly the southern end of the peninsula) via any of several alternative transportation options.

The Visitor Center building, erected in 1856 by the South Carolina Railroad and originally used as a freight depot, makes a perfect place to get your bearings and plan your adventure in historic Charleston. Inside, you'll find an overview of the peninsular city in the form of a large diorama while a multi-screen video display introduces you to the

Drayton Hall

Circa 1738

A masterpiece of design and craftsmanship, the oldest and finest Georgian Palladian plantation home in the United States.

National Trust for Historic Preservation

Daily Tours on the Hour
Museum Shop

Hwy. 61 (Ashley River Rd.)

9 miles from Charleston in the Ashley River Historic District
(803) 766-0188

sights and sounds you're likely to encounter here. You'll find a comprehensive collection of free brochures, maps, fliers and other publications detailing the special tours, dining adventures and lodging options, as well as various recreation options and transportation venues.

Guided walking tours usually begin in the mornings and last about two hours. The cost is from $10 to $12. You may also choose a comfortable, air-conditioned minibus. These guided, motorized tours take about an hour and prices range from $10 to $20. Or, you might want to take one of Charleston's famous (guided) carriage tours and see the city at clip-clop pace. (See our chapter on Tour Guides for detailed information on these services.)

Incidentally, with all the horse-drawn carriage tours available, you may be pleased to learn that Charleston horses wear "diapers." Should a horse's diaper need changing and the street in any way becomes sullied (they say it happens even to the *best* horses), there's a very civilized Charleston solution. A special truck patrols the carriage routes during tour hours carrying a huge, blue tank of perfumed disinfectant. In the event of an "accident," carriage drivers are instructed to throw out flags to mark the spot. Then, the truck is dispatched to the scene for a welcome squirt, a quick wash and an apology.

Free shuttles leave the old depot at 15- or 20-minute intervals and carry passengers to the old City Market in the heart of downtown Charleston, so it's very possible to "do" Charleston and leave your car here in the lot.

Also, at the Visitor and Transportation Center, you'll find the 20-minute slide presentation called "Forever Charleston." This latest audiovisual introduction to the cornucopia of Charleston history and culture is a good one. The work includes some remarkable photography by three of Charleston's nationally known photographers; Tom Blagden Jr., Ron Anton Rocz and Bill Struhs.

In air-conditioned comfort, you'll see breathtaking vistas over and beyond the city, and you'll see (up close) some of the architectural detail that has been the signature of historic Charleston for at least 200 years. You'll hear tidbits from some of the city's local philosophers and you'll get to peek behind the (usually) closed gates into a few Charlestonian gardens and life-styles.

"Forever Charleston" is shown every 30 minutes from 9:00 AM to 5:00 PM daily. The admission charge is $2.50 for adults, $2.00 for seniors, $1.00 for youths (6 - 12), and it's free for children under 6.

The Visitor Reception and Transportation Center is open daily from 8:30 AM to 5:30 PM.

THE FRANCES R. EDMUNDS CENTER FOR HISTORIC PRESERVATION
108 Meeting Street   *724-8484*

Those who find themselves downtown and in the vicinity of 108 Meeting Street (across from the Mills House) have another option for starting their Historic Charleston odyssey. The Frances R.

Edmunds Center for Historic Preservation is its official name, but it's Historic Charleston Foundation's offering to visitor orientation. Here you'll find a well planned cultural and architectural overview, plus free and friendly tourist advice.

The Center's museum shop carries a fine array of merchandise, including many items from the Foundation's Reproduction Collections. And you'll find a comprehensive selection of books and reference materials relating to preservation, restoration, and Charleston's 18th- and 19th-century cultural life. Also, this is where you may buy tickets to the Foundation's signature house museum, the Nathaniel Russell House, and the (Middleton Place Foundation's) Edmundston-Alston House (see House Museums). The Frances R. Edmunds Center is open Monday through Saturday from 10:00 AM to 5:00 PM. Sunday hours are from 2:00 to 5:00 PM.

THE PRESERVATION SOCIETY BOOKSTORE

147 King Street   *723-4381*

Another friendly oasis for the footsore traveler (especially those touring the many antique shops scattered along King Street) is The Preservation Society of Charleston's bookstore.

The bookstore offers a fine collection of books and reference materials pertaining to Charleston and the Lowcountry, and the accommodating staff offers free tourist information, as well.

Every fall, from the end of September through October, The Preservation Society's evening candlelight tours are very popular and it's a lovely time of year to see the city. Tickets often sell out early, but you might check here at the last minute and be able to join one of the neighborhood tours of private homes.

This building is the headquarters and Resource Center for the organization (founded in 1920) originally known as "The Society for the Preservation of Old Dwelling Houses," one of America's premiere preservation organizations. (See the Architectural Preservation chapter.)

The Preservation Society Bookstore is open from 10:00 AM to 5:00 PM, Monday through Saturday.

House Museums

According to a recently completed study, peninsular Charleston still contains more than 2,800 historic buildings rated as "architecturally significant." Overwhelm-

Insiders Like:
Wading through a sea of fuchsia and white azalea blossoms during the annual spring bloom at Magnolia Gardens.

Insiders' Tip

ing as that may seem, it's even more amazing to realize that by far the vast majority of those buildings are private homes. And of these homes, literally hundreds could legitimately qualify as house museums — not only for their exterior architectural sophistication but for their sumptuous interiors, as well. In fact, preserving these homes and their remarkable collections of art, china, fine furniture and fabrics has become an integral part of today's Charleston life-style.

It's staggering to think that even after Charleston's many devastating earthquakes, wars, fires and hurricanes — not to mention the ever-changing tides of the city's economy — these houses still stand. Not a few of them still contain their original furnishings and treasured family heirlooms, some having been in place since before the American Revolution.

While most of these historic homes remain in private hands (only rarely opened to public tours), seven Charleston house museums offer visitors unique adventures "behind closed doors."

Most of the following house museums are open year round and operated by various nonprofit preservation organizations in the city (see our Architectural Preservation chapter for more information). Others are privately owned and operated as business entities. In either case, Charleston's house museums afford a fascinating glimpse of the style and sophistication of the city's interiors during a number of heydays in the development of decorative arts.

From 18th-century Georgian to late 19th-century Victorian, Charleston's house museums are presented, here, in the chronological order of their construction dates. As a quick reference for those who don't happen to keep the eight basic architectural styles of historic Charleston constantly top-of-mind, the following definitions (courtesy of Historic Charleston Foundation and the National Trust for Historic Preservation) are offered:

Colonial — refers to the period from 1690 to 1740. Look for a very low foundation, beaded clapboard siding, a high-pitched gable roof (sometimes with flared eaves), hipped dormers and raised panel shutters. A good Charleston example is the John Lining House, 106 Broad Street (at King Street).

Georgian — refers to the architectural style popular in England during the reign of Ann and the four Georges. Here in America, the style is generally assigned to the years 1700 to 1790. Look for a hipped roof, box chimneys, triangular pediments (often with oval lights), columns, a raised basement and a belt course between floors. An excellent Charleston example is the Miles Brewton House, 27 King Street.

Federal — refers to the American architectural style seen chiefly between the years 1790 and 1820. In England, the style is called ADAM, in reference to the English/Irish architect, Robert Adam. Look for geometric rooms, ironwork balconies, a low pitched roof, decorative bands around interior rooms and exterior trim, spiral stairs and

elliptical fan lights. A fine Charleston example is The Nathaniel Russell House, 51 Meeting Street.

Classic Revival — is the architectural return to the lines and the look of ancient Greece (and later, Rome). It was popular in America from about 1820 to 1875. Look for large, heavy columns and capitals, temple pediments, triglyph and guttae and all the other details in classic Greek architectural order. In Charleston, a great example is Beth Elohim Synagogue, 90 Hasell Street.

Gothic Revival — refers to the period between 1850 and 1885 when many American buildings referenced the up-reaching lines of Western European architecture between the 12th and 16th centuries. Look for pointed arches, buttresses, stone tracery and finials. One excellent Charleston example is the French Huguenot Church, 136 Church Street.

Italianate — refers to the popular building style seen here between 1830 and 1900. Look for paired brackets and round head arches, balustrades, a low pitched roof and the loggia (or veranda). A classic Charleston example is the Col. John Ashe House, 26 South Battery.

Victorian — refers, of course, to England's Queen Victoria who reigned from 1836 to 1901. In American architecture, however, it was a popular style between the years 1860 to 1915. Look for a multi-gabled roof, elaborate wood bracket work (sometimes called gingerbread), turrets and decorative roof decorations. A rare Charleston example is the Sottile House on Green Street (on the College of Charleston campus).

Art Deco — refers to the highly stylized look that many American buildings took during the years between the world wars, roughly 1920 to 1940. Look for decorative panels, narrow windows, flat roofs and multicolored bands. Charleston's outstanding example is the Riviera Theatre, 225-227 King Street.

THE THOMAS ELFE HOUSE (1760)
54 Queen Street

At this writing, The Thomas Elfe House is for sale. This delightfully miniature single house is one of Charleston's wonderful little treasures that for the past several years has been open to the public on a limited basis. That may well continue to be true in the future. You might call Information to find any new listing for tour information concerning this house.

Any serious student of fine Charleston-made 18th-century furniture or any antique buff with a nose for history will want to see this house. For that reason, its description is included here.

The Thomas Elfe House was built well before the American Revolution. It was just a craftsman's home, and a modest one at that — like many others throughout the city. The particular craftsman who owned this one, however, was most extraordinary. Thomas Elfe arrived in Charleston about 1747 from England. He brought with him a unique skill for woodworking. Here in Charleston, he became one of the most prolific and acclaimed cabinetmakers of the Colonial era. His work appears in many other house museums and private homes in Charleston as well as in other fine museums throughout the country.

During the period of 1768 to 1775, his own record books show that he created more than 1,500 pieces of cabinetwork. He worked primarily in mahogany and his distinctive fretwork, unique leg design and inner-drawer construction are the telltale signs of Thomas Elfe craftsmanship.

Restored in 1970, the house interiors show many finishing touches that are attributed to its first, now-famous owner. All four rooms display exquisitely proportioned fireplace walls of cypress paneling. There are china cabinets and deftly scaled closets artfully worked into each chimney alcove. And the slightly lowered dadoes give the effect of higher ceilings and greater space.

While this is still a private home, the fact that its first owner was a major contributor to the art and life-style of colonial Charleston makes it interesting today. It is hoped The Thomas Elfe House will continue to be available to the public in some capacity in the future.

THE HEYWARD-WASHINGTON HOUSE (1772)
87 Church Street   722-0354

This handsome, early Charleston "dwelling house" is now known by two names — because of two prominent Americans associated with it; one an owner, the other a distinguished guest.

It was built in 1772 by Daniel Heyward, a wealthy rice planter and the father of Thomas Heyward, Jr., a signer of the Declaration of Independence for South Carolina. It is documented that the latter Heyward lived in the house until 1794.

In 1791, President George Washington made a grand tour of the new nation and included Charleston on his itinerary. In anticipation of this distinguished visitor, the city rented Heyward's house for Washington's accommodations and Mr. Heyward was thus displaced to his country house for the duration.

In Washington's diary, he recorded his visit to the property saying, "The lodgings provided for me in this place were very good, being the furnished house of a gentleman at present residing in the country; but occupied by a person placed there on purpose to accommodate me."

Today, the house is furnished with a magnificent collection of period antiques, especially some fine Charleston-made furniture of the 18th century. Look for the famous Holmes bookcase that still bears the scars of an incoming British mortar from the days of the American Revolution.

This is the only 18th-century house museum in the city with original outbuildings (kitchen, carriage house and necessary) still a part of its courtyard. You'll also find a small formal garden in keeping with the period of the house.

The Heyward-Washington House was saved from destruction in the early 20th century by the Preservation Society of Charleston. It is now a National Historic Landmark owned and operated by The Charleston Museum. It's open daily, Monday through Saturday, from 10:00 AM to 5:00 PM; and Sunday from 1:00 to 5:00 PM. No entry is allowed after 4:30 PM. Admission is $5 for adults and $3 for children ages 3 to 12. (The Charleston Museum offers discounted combination ticket prices for all four of their museum sites, $15 for adults, $9 for children; or the two-site ticket package for $9.)

THE JOSEPH MANIGAULT HOUSE (1803)
350 Meeting Street   723-2926

At the beginning of the 19th century, Charleston architecture was still very much dominated by what was fashionable in Mother England. This house, designed and built in 1803 by Charleston's gentleman-architect, Gabriel Manigault (for his brother, Joseph) was certainly no exception. Today, it remains one of America's most beautiful examples of the graceful Adam style.

Both Manigault brothers were wealthy rice planters with sophisticated tastes. Gabriel had studied in Geneva and London where the Adam influence was at its height and he maintained an extensive architectural library of his own.

Local students of architecture — young and old — have learned that one of the best sources of hard-to-find architectural reference materials in the Lowcountry is Drayton Hall's Preservation Shop. They carry lots of fascinating crafts and fine merchandise related to preservation and/or plantation life. You'll also find that their book selection is a delightful surprise.

Insiders' Tip

The house is distinguished by one of the most graceful staircases in the city and displays an outstanding collection of Charleston, American, English and French furniture of the period.

Don't miss the charming Gate Temple in the rear garden. During the 1920s, when The Manigault House was very nearly torn down in the name of progress, Gabriel Manigault's classical Gate Temple was used as the rest room for an oil company's service station located then on the garden site. Later, during W.W.II, the house served as a USO canteen for servicemen passing through Charleston's busy Navy yard en route to battle stations overseas.

Today, it is a National Historic Landmark owned and operated by The Charleston Museum. Hours are from 10:00 AM to 5:00 PM, Monday through Saturday; and 1:00 to 5:00 PM on Sunday. Last tour is at 4:30 PM. Admission is $5 for adults and $3 for children ages 3 to 12.

THE NATHANIEL RUSSELL HOUSE (1808)

51 Meeting Street   723-1623

The prominent shipping merchant, Nathaniel Russell, decided to build his great mansion on Meeting Street — practically within sight of the busy wharves that brought him wealth. When his house was completed in 1808, Russell was 71 years old and he had reportedly spent $80,000 on the project — an enormous sum at that time.

Like the Manigault house, Russell's new home was inspired by the work of English architect, Robert Adam, whose delicate style was influenced by the airy classical designs only recently uncovered (literally) in the Italian excavations of Pompeii and Herculaneum.

Today's visitor is immediately dazzled by the dramatic free-flying elliptical stairway floating up through three floors without any visible means of support.

The finely proportioned geometric rooms are furnished with another outstanding collection of Charleston, English and French pieces — including rare china, silver and paintings.

Unlike most other Charleston house museums, the Russell House has never been through a sad period of decline and disrepair. First, as a fine town house, then as the home of a South Carolina governor, and later a school for girls, and even a convent — 51 Meeting Street has always been a respected and cared-for landmark. Today, it is owned and operated by Historic Charleston Foundation, an organization that has done much to preserve and enhance the city's architectural heritage. (See our Architectural Preservation chapter.)

The house is open for tours Monday through Saturday, from 10:00 AM to 5:00 PM; and Sunday, 2:00 to 5:00 PM; the last tour begins at 4:40 PM. They're closed on Christmas Day. Admission is $5; a combination admission ticket for this house and the Edmondston-Alston House is $8.

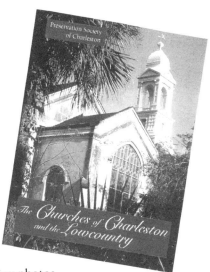

THE EDMUNDSTON-ALSTON HOUSE (1828-1838)

21 East Battery   *722-7171*

Charles Edmundston, another wealthy merchant and wharf owner, built this handsome dwelling in 1828 where he could enjoy an uninterrupted view over the expanse of Charleston Harbor. After a decade, the house was bought by Colonel William Alston, a rice planter. His son, Charles, redecorated the house in the 1830s favoring the fashionable Greek Revival style.

Incredibly, today's visitor can find many family documents, portraits, silver pieces and fine furnishings — and Charles Alston's almost intact library — all dating from the 1830s.

The house is notable for its unusual Regency woodwork, as well as its uncompromising views. The intimacy and authentic details of the house may leave guests feeling as if the Alston's have only recently left the property — perhaps on a visit to the country.

Today, the Edmundston-Alston House is owned by the Middleton Place Foundation. Tours are offered daily, Tuesday through Saturday, from 10:00 AM to 4:40 PM; and Sunday and Monday from 1:30 to 4:40 PM. Admission is $5; or $8 in combination with admission to The Nathaniel Russell House.

THE AIKEN-RHETT HOUSE (1817-1833-1857)

48 Elizabeth Street at Judith St.   *723-1159*

Unlike any other house museum in Charleston, the Aiken-Rhett house is a time capsule of Charleston history and taste. It was the home of Governor William Aiken from 1833-1887, and it owes most of its eerie charm to him.

The structure was built in 1817 by John Robinson as a typical Charleston single house — like so many others built in Charleston at the time. However, under the later ownership of South Carolina railroad magnate William Aiken (who was governor at the time of the Civil War), the house was drastically altered and enlarged. First, in 1833, it was remodeled to conform to the bold Greek Revival style popular at the time. Then, again in 1857, alterations were made in the Rococo Revival style gaining popularity in antebellum Charleston.

Again, an uncanny amount of furnishings and other objects belonging to Gov. and Mrs. Aiken can still be found here — including elaborate chandeliers the couple brought back from Paris in the 1830s, as well as portraits, statuary and library volumes. The difference here is that much of the house is unrestored. It is preserved, instead, largely as it was presented to The Charleston Museum in 1975 by descendants of the Aiken family.

As a result, the visitor can almost feel the presence of Jefferson Davis, President of the Confederacy, who was a guest in the house in 1863. You can easily picture Confederate General P.G.T. Beauregard using the house as his headquarters during Charleston's almost relentless 1864 bombardment by Federal troops. And the haunting, life-sized portrait of Mrs. Aiken dressed in finery belies her emotional and economic hardship after the war when

MIDDLETON PLACE

Middleton Place is a carefully preserved 18th-century plantation that encompasses America's oldest landscaped Gardens, the Middleton Place House, and the Plantation Stableyards. Located on the Ashley River Rd. (Hwy. 61), 14 miles northwest of Charleston. Open every day: 9 am – 5 pm. Middleton Place Restaurant serves Low Country recipes for lunch daily & dinner on Fri. & Sat. evenings.

(803) 556-6020 or toll-free: 1-800-782-3608

MIDDLETON INN
AT MIDDLETON PLACE

The Middleton Inn has fireplaces in every room, spectacular views of the Ashley River, a swimming pool, clay tennis courts and miles of nature trails...a 20th century compliment to the 18th and 19th century Middleton Place National Historic Landmark.

(803) 556-0500 or toll free: 1-800-543-4774
Ashley River Road, Charleston, South Carolina 29414

the governor was arrested and imprisoned for treason.

The fragile textures of time and the changing fortunes of war very much show in this house museum. Surely, this is its most romantic and enduring charm.

Although a more academic restoration of the property is ongoing (and is undoubtedly required for its long-term survival), the proud but tattered Aiken-Rhett House is a must-see. It is open for tours Monday through Saturday from 10:00 AM to 5:00 PM; and Sunday from 1:00 to 5:00 PM. The last tour is at 4:30 PM. Admission is $5 for adults and $3 for children (ages 3 - 12). Combination tickets for this, the Manigault House and the Heyward-Washington House are available here and at The Charleston Museum.

THE CALHOUN MANSION (1876)
16 Meeting Street   722-8205

Here is one of Charleston's few Victorian palaces. The reason Victoriana is possibly underrepresented in Charleston's decorative arts is largely an economic one; Charleston's economy was devastated by the Civil War. Clearly, during most of the Victorian era (1860-1915), no great amount of mansion-building was done here. But the 25-room, 24,000-sq.-ft., elaborately decorated house called The Calhoun Mansion is one spectacular exception.

It was built by George Walton Williams, a wealthy merchant and banker, who was (unlike most southern families) financially undaunted by the war. At the time of construction, the house was immodestly described in New York, Atlanta and Charleston newspapers as "the handsomest and most complete home in the South, if not the country."

The Calhoun Mansion has 14-ft. ceilings, ornate plaster mouldings and all the elaborate woodwork, lighting fixtures and window treatments you'd expect of the period. A grand staircase reaches up to a 75-ft. domed ceiling and there's a ballroom with a glass skylight reaching 45 feet high. A remarkable collection of fine furnishings of the Victorian era make a grandiose statement in this fascinating anomaly of Charleston's decorative arts.

The house is open for tours from 10:00 AM until 4:00 PM, Wednesday through Sunday. Admission is $10 for adults, $5 for children ages 6 to 15, and children under 6, free. Special tours may be arranged upon request.

Plantations and Gardens

Without a doubt, no visit to Charleston is complete without a journey to the plantations. And nowhere is Charleston's late, great plantation culture more in evidence than along the old route to Summerville — via the Ashley River Road (S.C. Hwy. 61).

This is the state's oldest highway and it once provided the back road access to some of the most beautiful Colonial plantations in the Lowcountry. Primary access to the early plantations was by river — a much faster, more convenient route.

Photo: The Post and Courier

A puma at Charles Towne Landing.

It might be helpful to remember that much of the wealth and sophistication of Charleston in the 18th and 19th centuries was derived from the plantation system. And the plantation system was, after all, an agricultural economy based on the practice of slavery. The opulence and wealth so evident (today) in the downtown Charleston house museums (built during that same period) may be viewed with newfound perspective when remembering this grim reality.

Here is where the Charleston visitor may be prey to a trite, old southern cliché. There was a time when the bucolic romanticism of the "Old South" largely swirled around the moonlit and magnolia-scented lives of southern aristocracy. While some of that romantic image may be partly true, it is by no means the *whole* story.

Today (much more than in the past) greater emphasis is being placed on showing visitors a more realistic picture of the society as a whole. That includes the lives of slaves, tradespeople, merchants, women and children. Look for that emerging "new" slant as you go about your adventures on the old plantations.

Also, it might be helpful to know that America's version of the plantation system didn't originate here at all. Like about everything else in the early colonies, it was imported. It came to Charleston from England via the West Indies. In fact, many of Charleston's early planter families emigrated from older plantations in The Barbados.

While a number of influences brought the concept of slavery to America, it flourished here in the Lowcountry. Today's visitor has a rare opportunity to see the plantation system in its various forms and eras. Today's more enlightened views include the chance to see where much of it began...and where it ended.

Here's a suggested route you may want to take:

Once across the Ashley River bridge at the foot of Spring Street (off I-26 and Hwy. 17 South), you'll drive through Charleston's post W.W.II urban sprawl. You may choose to start your plantation tour at the very beginning, at Charles Towne Landing 1670, South Carolina's unique state park now on the site of the colony's original settlement. There, you'll get to explore a reconstruction of an early settler's cabin and see the "experimental garden" where test crops of various kinds held the settler's best hope for survival in this brave, new world.

Next, you may want to take the same architectural quantum leap Charlestonians did — from that early, crude settler's cabin to the classical grandeur of (1738) Drayton Hall, which was built along the Ashley River's west bank only a generation later.

Then, at Middleton Place (developed c. 1740) and Magnolia Plantation (started in the 1680s and expanded c. 1840) you may want to explore the vast gardens so important to these early planter families. Magnolia's informal design (typical of 19th-century gardens) makes an interesting contrast to Middleton's strict geometric patterns (so popular in 18th-century France).

The geometrically designed formal gardens at Middleton Place show the incredible strength of Europe's artistic influence here in Charleston (40 years prior to the American Revolution).

At Middleton Place House (1755) you can trace the story of the distinguished Middleton family which included Arthur (1742-1787) signer of the Declaration of Independence. And at the Middleton Place stable yards, you can interact with the daily activities of a working plantation.

In the spring, you'll want to include Cypress Gardens, originally part of Dean Hall plantation on the Cooper River. Follow Hwy. 61 (from Middleton Place) to Hwy. 165 and join Hwy. 17-A through Summerville to Moncks Corner and follow the signs.

There, in a 163-acre black water cypress swamp is an incredible azalea garden begun in the 1920s and now owned and operated by the City of Charleston's Department of Parks. You'll find charming little bateaux (flat bottomed boats) to use and there are three miles of walking paths through the vibrant spring colors reflected in the mirrorlike waters.

Back through Charleston and six miles north along Hwy. 17 is Boone Hall, the picturesque, 738-acre plantation used extensively in the ABC-TV mini-series, "North and South," filmed in and around Charleston a few years ago. Boone Hall's best features include the famous three-quarter mile avenue of live oaks and the original "slave street" of nine brick slave cabins (c. 1743).

You won't be able to visit all these plantations in a single day. If you must select only a sampling of greater Charleston's plantation culture, perhaps the following in-depth and more detailed review of these sites will help you choose.

You won't regret the investment of time and travel it takes to digest these plantations and gardens. They're so much a part of the city — so vital to its development — that to see only one part and not the other might seriously handicap your understanding of the area as a whole.

CHARLES TOWNE LANDING 1670
1500 Old Towne Road, Hwy. 171   556-4450
between I-26 and Hwy. 17

Surely this is one of South Carolina's (if not America's) most unusual state parks. Charles Towne Landing 1670 was created in 1970 on the plantation belonging to Dr. and Mrs. Joseph I. Waring as part of the state's 300th anniversary celebration.

Today, the property isn't presented to the public as a "plantation" per se. Rather, the vast acreage is devoted to recreating and interpreting the first English settlement in the Carolinas that occurred on this plantation site in 1670.

Once inside the gate, visitors travel down a long alley bordered by ancient live oaks and swamp. Eventually you come to a parking lot and a large complex of modern buildings that serve as a starting point for your adventure.

Here are some highlights:

If at all possible, begin your visit with the wonderful 30-minute film, "Carolina," shown free in the nearby theater pavilion at regularly scheduled intervals. This film, directed by Carlos Romers in 1969 features wonderful music by the London Philharmonic Orchestra

and is still the best introduction to Charleston around. Filmed entirely without the on-screen presence of live actors, this motion picture sensitively traces the settlers' long, arduous voyage across the Atlantic and shows the strange, new world that awaited them. The camera celebrates their eventual success with a feast of the city's art, flowers and rich architectural detail. The film clearly gives newcomers a sense of the first settlers' struggle and what must have been their surprise and wonderment at this wild, new land that would hold their future.

The giant Exhibit Pavilion included an unusual underground museum that interpreted the first 100 years of the colony with artifacts, exhibits, recordings and art. This area was closed due to damages sustained in Hurricane Hugo and has not reopened as of this printing.

Along the river, you may board a full-scale replica of a typical 17th-century trading vessel called the *Adventure*. Picture it as a common work vehicle of the early plantation system — plying the waters with fur pelts, indigo shipments and rice to sell at the wharves in Charleston. These boats also carried supplies to the widely scattered plantations upriver.

The Animal Forest is a 20-acre natural habitat zoo with wolves, puma, bear, bison, snakes and alligators — all a part of the Lowcountry landscape when settlers arrived in the 1670s.

The Settlers' Life area with its replica Colonial buildings is a hands-on example of the early colonists'

The Ashley River Road

Before Hurricane Hugo struck the Lowcountry in September of 1989 - destroying an estimated 7 million board-feet of prime, standing lumber - the Ashley River Road was oak-lined, moss-laden, sun-dappled and almost unbearably beautiful. Certainly, that's how many Lowcountry old-timers remember it.

Most of the huge oak trees were hundreds of years old and stood so close to the road they became a hazard to speeding cars. So, for several years, every serious accident (and there were many) became a new excuse to remove more trees and more of the old road's ambiance. Then, the slow but relentless encroachment of commercial businesses and the addition of real estate developments took an even higher toll on the once scenic highway.

But even now, along the few miles between Drayton Hall and Middleton Place, you'll find stretches of the old Ashley River Road that are still intact. That is, the oaks reach up and over the road creating a sun-filtered canopy through which you'll feel you're driving into the past.

Remember, the Ashley River is always on your right - sometimes just through the trees. Bear in mind, too, that the old road (originally an Indian trail) was only a back road to the plantations; it was slow, rutted and practically impossible in wet weather. Most social and business traffic to and from these far flung plantations was by water. Thus, the great houses actually faced the river, the avenue to all agricultural wealth.

If you look carefully, you'll notice some unexplained, low ridges along the roadside. Chances are, these are old rice dikes indicating where the land was flooded and the fields cultivated for rice.

In other places through the forest (now drastically thinned by Hugo), you'll see larger, unnatural-looking mounds - especially noticeable in the wintertime. These are the outcroppings from old, abandoned phosphate mines.

After the Civil War, during the late 1870s, phosphate (an early fertilizer product) was discovered in the ground along the west bank of the Ashley. For a brief but reckless period, this entire landscape was crudely stripmined. As ecologically careless and harmful as these practices were, the phosphate era provided desperately needed income for a few of the old planter families who had somehow managed to hold onto their properties through the war and Reconstruction.

If the phosphate mining years were not the Ashley River's finest hour, at least they helped rescue what little was left of the plantations after the cataclysmic year of 1865.

In February of that year, as the war was winding down, Union troops advanced toward Charleston, via the Ashley River Road, looting and burning as they came. Of all the great houses once standing along the high, west bank of the river, only Drayton Hall survived.

Once, there were scores of plantations along the Ashley. They had wonderful, lyrical names: there was "MacBeth" and "Runnymede," "Millbrook" and "Schievelin".... Today, three of the old properties are open to the public; Drayton Hall, Magnolia and Middleton Place. Each is unique and remarkable in a different way. Each offers special insight into the Ashley River's fascinating plantation story.

Insiders' Tip

daily life. You'll see candle-making, open fire cooking, woodworking, even the colony's first printing press in action — depending on the season and the weather. Often, special exhibits and demonstrations can be found here on holidays.

Charles Towne Landing 1670 is open all year. The hours are 9:00 AM to 5:00 PM except during June through August when the park stays open until 6:00 PM. Picnic tables, a snack bar and a gift shop are all on site. The park is largely accessible to handicapped visitors.

Admission is $5 for adults, $2.50 for children (ages 6-14), $2.50 for seniors, and free for handicapped visitors and children under 6. Bicycle rentals are $2 per hour with a $2 deposit. Tram tours are $1 per person.

DRAYTON HALL

3380 Ashley River Road   766-0188

Not a tour of a reconstructed, working plantation or the collected decorative arts from a bygone era, Drayton Hall offers an adventure in architecture. Yes, architecture...and a great deal more.

It should be seen and experienced — if for no other reason — because it is the sole survivor of the ugly 1865 rampage by Union troops who looted and burned nearly every other plantation house along the Ashley River. But see Drayton Hall for even better reasons: because it is a survivor of so much more — so many other changes, influences, forces and times.

It was built between 1738 and 1742 as the country seat of John Drayton (1716-1779) whose family

had emigrated to Charles Towne from The Barbados and settled nearby at Magnolia Plantation a generation earlier.

The house is considered to be the oldest and finest example of Georgian-Palladian architecture in America. Its recessed, two-story portico may have been inspired by Italy's Villa Pisani, designed in 1552 by Andrea Palladio. The portico is one of the architectural signatures of Palladinism and Drayton Hall's portico may be one of the earliest built in America.

In any case, the story of how this very sophisticated English Palladian villa came to be built along the west bank of the Ashley, how it survived the ravages of time, war, earthquake and hurricane is a fascinating saga.

Maybe the greatest curiosity of all is how the old Drayton house survived the enormous forces of changing architectural taste. Oddly, the house was never modernized for 20th-century use. Drayton Hall has never seen plumbing nor central heat; it never had gas installed for lighting or heating purposes, its only link with modern electricity is the one meager line that brings life to its sadly necessary modern security system. Incredibly, some rooms in the house still bear original coats of paint.

Quite simply, Drayton Hall is an architectural time capsule. The structure remains almost untouched as an eloquent statement about 18th-century thinking, craftsmanship, technology and design. It's one of the few sites left in Colonial America so pure, unaltered and uncompromised by time.

Visitors will find the Drayton Hall story — how it all came to pass — "interpreted" by a small group of professional guides. These storytellers lead you through 250 years of time, family genealogy, architectural history, and a smattering of the economic and social realities of the plantation system.

A word or two about "interpretation" might be helpful here. Because each guide at Drayton Hall develops his or her own perspective of the house, every tour will be slightly different. That is, each guide bears the responsibility of interpreting and synthesizing the tremendous amount of research data collected about the property. You hear "their words," not a written script. Thus, return visits will only deepen your understanding of the house, its people and its times.

The bare fact that you're touring 15 unfurnished rooms is hardly noticeable since each room is chockfull of interesting information and rich, architectural detail.

Drayton Hall comes to life because imagination is a wonderful artist. Imagination can paint in the faded colors of Drayton Hall's early days when the settlement of Charles Towne was barely 70 years old. It can flesh out the heavy, antebellum days when the Ashley River plantation system was in its zenith. Now, through imagination, the visitor can even see Drayton Hall in the grim, dark days following the Civil War — when vagrants and vandals used it at will. Imagination can find the returning prosperity and almost hear the laughter of the Drayton parties

and other family occasions held there as recently as the 1960s. All it takes is an informed interpreter and your listening ear.

Research is an ongoing process at Drayton Hall. The future calls for recording oral histories of the Drayton family as well as the African-Americans so closely associated with the house and its survival.

Preserved but unrestored, Drayton Hall's faded hues and subtle shading, its frayed places and telling stains — are all pure Charleston. The house serves to illuminate the whole Ashley River plantation system in a rare and strangely haunting light.

An ongoing project at Drayton Hall is their education program for school youngsters (ages K through 12). Several curriculum-coordinated programs feature student tours, plantation games, archaeology studies and preservation workshops for both teachers and students.

The property is now jointly owned by the National Trust for Historic Preservation and the South Carolina Department of Parks, Recreation and Tourism. Tours are offered on the hour, November through February, from 10:00 AM to 3:00 PM; and March through October, 10:00 AM to 4:00 PM. A written tour in English, French or German can be purchased. Group rates, AAA and military discounts, handicapped access and (prearranged) student programs are available. Admission is $7 for adults, $4 for students (ages 5 to 18), and free to all members of the National Trust and Friends of Drayton Hall.

MAGNOLIA PLANTATION AND GARDENS

Highway 61   571-1266

This is where Thomas Drayton, Jr., father of Drayton Hall's John Drayton, settled when he came to Charles Towne in 1676 — a successful English planter from the island of Barbados. Early on, the home he built for himself and his family was destroyed by fire. The house built to replace it was subsequently burned by Union troops in 1865. The present structure is said to have been a Drayton family hunting lodge that was moved down the Ashley River in 1873 and placed atop the foundations of the old plantation house.

Magnolia Plantation is the original (and continuing) home of the Drayton family — now owned and managed by a ninth generation descendant.

Magnolia Plantation is famous for its expansive, informal (English style) gardens which are the legacy of the Rev. John Grimke-Drayton, who was the plantation's owner during the Civil War and whose parish was nearby at St. Andrews. In 1843, Rev. Grimke-Drayton imported numerous specimens of Camellia Japonica and in 1848, Azalea Indica. Then, due to a bout with tuberculosis in the late 1840s, he left his parish for a time and devoted himself entirely to his garden.

By 1870, despite the tragedy of the war and the burning of the main house, the gardens at Magnolia Plantation had grown both in size and reputation. That year, the property was first opened to the public. Paddle-wheeled steamboats from Charleston made regularly scheduled excursions to Magnolia where tourists relaxed, took picnics and strolled along the blossom-laden paths.

For all its lacy bridges arching gracefully over the mirrorlike cypress ponds, one little-known and smaller area is well worth finding. Look for the garden called "Flowerdale." This is where it all began. Here is Magnolia's earliest garden area (begun in the late 1680s), and it was possibly the inspiration for the Rev. Grimke-Drayton's larger, more ambitious plan a century and a half later.

Surely, he sat here in the 1850s pondering the moral issues facing his plantation world as the political storm clouds gathered over the South. Perhaps it was amidst the beauty of Flowerdale where he first thought of expanding the garden plan to create an oasis of beauty so lasting it might someday sustain his family home....

Today, the gardens boast 250 varieties of azaleas and 900 varieties of camellias. These, plus many other flowers added through the years, give Magnolia Gardens colorful bloom all year long. Its most spectacular season, however, is spring when the dazzling, vibrant azalea colors seem to vibrate on the landscape for as far as the eye can see.

Visitors can get an overview of the property in a 12- minute video on the plantation's history shown at regular intervals in the orientation theater.

Magnolia Plantation offers additional activities for nature lovers. Canoes can be rented to glide through the eerie beauty of its 125-acre waterfowl refuge. There are walking and bicycle trails plus a wildlife observation tower that's very popular with bird-watchers. There's an herb garden, a horticultural maze, an antebellum cabin, a typical Ashley River rice barge, and even a petting zoo for children (and adults, as well). You'll find picnic areas, a snack shop and a gift shop there, too.

The property is open daily from 8:00 AM to 5:00 PM. Group rates are available. Admission is $8 for adults ($3 more includes admission to the Audubon Swamp Garden) and the house tour is an additional $4. Prices may be slightly higher in the spring.

AUDUBON SWAMP GARDEN

At Magnolia Gardens   571-1266
Highway 6 I

Recently, Magnolia Plantation and Gardens has added a new element, the Audubon Swamp Garden. This separate attraction encompasses a 60-acre, black water cypress and tupelo swamp. The visitor has the opportunity to see an otherwise inaccessible natural area via boardwalks, dikes and bridges which provide an intimate view of the horticultural beauty and wildlife (including alligators).

The swamp garden gets its name from the great 19th-century American naturalist and wildlife artist, John James Audubon, who visited Magnolia in search of water bird specimens during his many lengthy stays in Charleston.

This attraction is operated separately from the rest of Magnolia Plantation and may be seen at half the admission price of Magnolia's general admission ($4 for adults).

MIDDLETON PLACE

Highway 6 I   556-6020

Middleton is one of the Lowcountry's most famous plantations and another National Historic Landmark along the rich and fascinating Ashley. This was the home of Henry Middleton, President of the First Continental Congress, and his son Arthur, signer of the Declaration of Independence.

The sheer size and scope of Middleton's gardens tell us a great deal about the man and his grand vision. When he began his garden plan in 1741 (the framework of which remains unchanged today) the French influence for a formal, geometric design was still very much in vogue. This was the Age of Reason — where philosophy held that the essence of true beauty lay in humankind's conquest over nature. Thus, all great gardens of the time imposed order and geometric form over the otherwise natural, unruly landscape.

Reportedly, it took 100 slaves almost a decade to complete the sweeping terraces, walks and artificial lakes — the vistas so pleasing to the eye today. But the gardens at Middleton Place are only part of the plantation story interpreted here. Unlike some of the plantations closer and more convenient to Charleston, Middleton Place was a world unto itself. The 12-acre greensward with its grazing sheep and strutting peacocks creates an unforgettable image for the first-time visitor. But this bucolic, pastoral scene belies the frenzy of activity and the vast labor force needed to maintain this busy world.

Recently opened on the Middleton Place grounds is Eliza's House, an actual freedman's dwelling now furnished as it might have been found in the 1870s — lived in by African-Americans who stayed on the plantation after Emancipation. The Middleton Place Foundation has ongoing research into the lives of slaves, freedmen and tradespeople who were so important to the Middleton Place scene.

The lively Plantation Stable yards will give you another glimpse into that busy world with its active displays of day-to-day life. Chances are, you'll find a blacksmith, a potter, weavers and carpenters, all busy at work and eager to explain and/or demonstrate their skills.

The main house, built sometime before 1741 was — like Magnolia's — burned in 1865 by Union Troops. It is said the soldiers drank wine and dined in splendor at Middleton Place house, then set fire to it as they left....

The south flanker building (added about 1755) was least damaged by the fire and it was essentially rebuilt in the early years of this century in its present form. Inside, you'll find Middleton family memorabilia displayed along with a remarkable collection of important family portraits, including works by Benjamin West and Thomas Sully.

Not to be missed is the view of the Ashley River from the high terraces of the gardens. The green grass ripples down the hillside and into the graceful Butterfly Lakes below. Off to one side, the old Rice Mill counterbalances the picture-perfect composition of the landscape.

In addition to the sensitive and skillful interpretation of Middleton's glorious past, there's an unexpected contemporary side to the plantation's present day life. Just past the old Rice Mill, a path leads into the forest and up a hill to the 55-room Middleton Inn, a unique riverside oasis for discerning travelers.

Middleton Inn was designed by Charleston architect W.G. Clark and it seems to have been born "of" the forest, rather than "in" it. With vine-covered stucco and unblinking glass walls, each suite looks out over a green, woodland setting and the quiet waters of the Ashley River. A visit to the Inn is well worth the short stroll from "yesterday" into "tomorrow" (see Charleston Accommodations).

The Inn has won numerous architectural awards plus a place in *Time* magazine's "10 Best of '86" list and a spread in *Architectural Digest Travels* (Fall, 1986).

Middleton Place is open daily. Hours are 9:00 AM to 5:00 PM for the gardens and stable yards. The House tours begin at 10:00 AM, except on Mondays when they begin at 1:30 PM. Rates are: $10 for adults and $5 for children (ages 6 to 12). House tour admission is an additional $5 per person. Group

The "Best Friend of Charleston" Comes Home

The first steam locomotive built to offer regular passenger and freight service in the United States took off from Charleston in 1830. A near-exact replica of that train, known as "The Best Friend", finally came back in the summer of 1993 to rest and be displayed in a building next to the Visitor Reception and Transportation Center. And you can see it there...free of charge.

The replica (built in 1928 and refurbished in 1969) was originally commissioned by Norfolk Southern Railroad Company to celebrate the 100th anniversary of its parent company, The South Carolina Canal and Railroad Company.

The now curious-looking train (consisting of an engine, a tender and two open passenger coaches) made its first run on Christmas Day of 1830. About 140 brave Charlestonians climbed aboard the contraption at Line Street and chugged a dazzling six miles out to Dorchester Road — as far as tracks had been laid.

Newspaper accounts of the time said, "We flew on the wings of the wind at the varied speed of 15 to 25 miles per hour." Eventually, tracks were extended 136 miles inland to Hamburg (S. C.) establishing forever a new transportation industry for the United States.

As for the original "Best Friend," sadly — it came to an early demise. Just six months into the operation (in June of 1831), a fireman grew annoyed at the constant hiss of escaping steam and decided to quiet the problem by sitting down on the safety valve. The engine exploded, killing him, scalding the engineer, and destroying the locomotive. Somewhere in this story there must be an important object lesson...something about never sitting down where you hear a hiss?

Insiders' Tip

rates are available and food service functions may be arranged on the property.

CYPRESS GARDENS
Off Hwy. 52   553-0515
Eight miles south of Moncks Corner

For those with time and the inclination to go even further afield, there's yet another treat in store. Discover the beauty and wonder of Cypress Gardens — a true southern cypress swamp, a water forest of uncommon natural beauty. This park, once part of Dean Hall Plantation, is now owned and operated by the City of Charleston. You'll find meandering foot paths for hikers, but the traditional way to see Cypress Gardens is by bateau — flat-bottomed boats poled or paddled by expert young boatmen who are always on hand to do the work for a small price. You have the option of rowing yourself, if you like, but the serenity of the black waters mirroring springtime azaleas, dogwoods, daffodils and wisteria deserves your undivided attention. Call ahead for seasonal hours and admission prices; usual hours are 9:00 AM to 5:00 PM. (See Berkeley County, Cypress Gardens)

Forts

Among the most visited attractions in the Lowcountry are the area's famous forts — standing today in mute testimony to the great strategic role Charleston Harbor played during the past 300 years.

Of course, the most famous of these fortresses is the legendary Fort Sumter...where the Civil War began. But Greater Charleston has a number of other forts and former military fortifications that offer fascinating stories for the serious historian...and for us regular Insiders, too. There's Fort Moultrie on Sullivans Island plus Fort Johnson on Johns Island (now site of the South Carolina Wildlife and Marine Resources Center); and there's Battery Wagner on Morris Island.

We'll sketch brief histories of these sites — just enough to send you off to see the real thing and get a taste of the very real drama and sacrifice associated with these places.

FORT SUMTER NATIONAL MONUMENT
Charleston Harbor

Almost every Charlestonian knows the story by heart: The year was 1861. South Carolina had seceded from the Union. And yet — just a few miles east, there at the mouth of Charleston Harbor — Union forces were still stationed at Fort Sumter.

The Confederacy officially demanded that Fort Sumter be vacated, but the North adamantly refused. At 4:30 AM on the morning of April 12, a mortar shell burst over the fort — fired from nearby Fort Johnson. The Civil War had begun.

At first — largely as a matter of honor — the Union forces defended the fort. But after 34 hours, they surrendered. It was practically a bloodless battle; no one was killed, and only a few men were wounded.

Amazingly, the Confederates held Fort Sumter for the next 27 months—against what was the heaviest bombardment the world had ever seen. Over the course of almost two years, no less than 46,000 shells (approximately 3,500 tons of metal) were fired at the island fort. In the end, the Confederate troops abandoned Fort Sumter; they never surrendered. It was February 17, 1865. By the following April, the war and the cause would be lost.

Today, Fort Sumter is a national monument administered by the National Park Service of the U.S. Department of the Interior. It is still accessible only by boat, and the only public tour of this tiny man-made island is offered through Fort Sumter Tours.

You can board the Fort Sumter Tour Boat at either of two locations; Charleston's City Marina on Lockwood Blvd., or at Patriots Point in Mount Pleasant (across the Cooper River). The trip out to Fort Sumter takes about an hour and fifteen minutes. It affords delightful views of Charleston's waterfront and the tip of the peninsula — from an ocean voyager's point of view. (There's a separate, two-hour nonstop tour that includes a cruise under the Cooper River bridges on up to the vast U.S. Naval Base in North Charleston.) The specially-built sight-seeing boats are clean, safe and have on-board rest room facilities.

In any case, you'll need to check in for your tour at least fifteen minutes early (for ticketing and boarding). Departure times vary according to season and the weather, so call ahead for departure information; 722-1691. During the busy, summer season, there are usually three tours a day from each location.

Rates are $9 for adults, $4.50 for children under 12, and children under 5 are free. You can buy your tickets at the dock. Handicapped access is available only at the City Marina departure location. Group rates are available, but advance reservations for groups are encouraged.

FORT MOULTRIE

(West) Middle Street   883-3123
Sullivans Island

From the earliest days of European settlement along the eastern seaboard, coastal fortifications were set up to guard the newly found and potentially vulnerable harbors. Here at Fort Moultrie, visitors can see two centuries of coastal defenses evolve in a unique restoration operated today by the National Parks Service.

In its 171-year history (from 1776 to 1947) Fort Moultrie has defended Charleston Harbor twice. The first time was during the Revolutionary War when 30 cannons from the original fort drove off a British fleet mounting 200 guns in a ferocious nine-hour battle. This time, Charleston was saved from British occupation and the fort was justifiably named in honor of its commander, William Moultrie.

The second time the fort defended the city was during the Civil War. For nearly two years, the Charleston forts (and the city itself) were bombarded from both land and sea. The (then) masonry walls of Forts Sumter and Moultrie crumbled under the relentless shelling, but the forts were able to hold back the Union attacks.

Today, the fort has been restored to portray the major periods of its history — five different sections of the fort and two outlying areas — each mounting typical weapons and representing a different historical period. Visitors move steadily backwards in time from the World War II Harbor Entrance Control Post to the original palmetto log fort of 1776.

Fort Moultrie is open from 9:00 AM to 6:00 PM in the summer and from 9:00 AM to 5:00 PM in the winter. It is closed on Christmas Day. Groups should make reservations for guided tours. Pets are not allowed.

From Charleston, take Hwy. 17 N. (Business) through Mt. Pleasant to Sullivans Island, and turn right on Middle Street. The fort is located about a mile and a half from the intersection.

FORT JOHNSON
Wildlife & Marine Resources Center   762-5000
James Island

Another Charleston area fortress steeped in history and adaptively reused for modern needs is Fort Johnson. Since the early 1970s, the waterfront James Island site has been the home of the South Carolina Wildlife and Marine Resources Department which researches and promotes the state's marine industries.

But savvy military buffs know Fort Johnson in another role. Like Fort Moultrie, this site has military significance dating back several hundred years.

No trace now exists of the original Fort Johnson that was constructed on the site in about 1708. It was named for Sir Nathaniel Johnson, Proprietary Governor of the Carolinas at the time. A second fort was constructed in 1759 and reportedly portions of that structure remain as "tabby" ruins there today. (Tabby is an early building material made from crushed lime and oyster shell.)

Records show the fort was occupied in 1775 by three companies of South Carolina militia under the leadership of Lt. Col. Motte. During the American Revolution the fort remained in Colonial hands until 1780 when the British forces advancing on Charleston reported finding it abandoned. A third fort was built in 1793, but a hurricane destroyed it in 1800. Some work on Fort Johnson was done during the War of 1812, but the following year another storm destroyed that progress. Shortly afterward, Fort Johnson was dropped from official reports of United States fortifications.

During early 1861, South Carolina state troops erected mortar batteries and an earthwork of three guns on the old fortress site. Unbeknownst to most Americans, the actual signal shot that opened the bombardment of Fort Sumter and marked the beginning of the Civil War was fired from the east mortar battery of Fort Johnson on April 12, 1861. Fort Sumter was fired upon; not vice versa.

During the Civil War, building activity increased until Fort

Johnson became an entrenched camp mounting 26 guns and mortars. However, apart from routine artillery firing from the site, the only major action at the fort occurred on July 3, 1864, when its Confederate defenders repulsed two Union regiments totaling about 1,000 men. The Union forces sustained 26 casualties and lost 140 men as captives. The Confederate loss was one killed and three wounded. On the night of February 17, 1865, Fort Johnson was evacuated during the general Confederate withdrawal from Charleston Harbor.

After the Civil War, Fort Johnson became a quarantine station operated by the state and the City of Charleston. It continued to be used in that capacity until the 1950s.

BATTERY WAGNER

Of all the forts and battlegrounds that dot the Lowcountry landscape and pay quiet tribute to the area's military history, perhaps the most muted one concerns Battery Wagner on Morris Island. The story is a brief one in the long struggle of the Civil War but it is a significant one...and one that is especially poignant today.

In 1989, the story of Battery Wagner was portrayed in the film "Glory," which starred Matthew Broderick, Denzel Washington and Morgan Freeman.

Time and tides have long since removed all traces of Battery Wagner. Today, Morris Island is vacant and uninhabited. It was recently annexed by the City of

Charleston and will someday be developed and become a vital part of the ever growing metropolitan area surrounding the city. But whatever its future may hold, the story of Morris Island will always include the story of Battery Wagner and the 54th Massachusetts Regiment.

Because Charleston was the "cradle of Secession" it was a primary target for the Union's high command. On June 16, 1862, the Union forces' first attempt to capture the city failed at the Battle of Secessionville on James Island. Union commanders decided to mount a two-pronged attack using both land and naval forces. There were two possible lines of approach to the city: through Sullivans Island, which was heavily defended, or through Morris Island, which was more lightly guarded. On Morris Island the main defense was Battery Wagner, a quickly built fortification with thick sand walls and more than a dozen cannons.

Choosing the Morris Island approach, Union forces landed on July 10, 1863, and opened fire the following day with little success. A week later, they tried again. Even after a 10-hour artillery bombardment Battery Wagner stood firm.

At dusk on July 18th, the Union infantry advanced up the beach toward heavily defended Battery Wagner. Spearheading the attack was the 54th Massachusetts Regiment under the leadership of Colonel Robert G. Shaw, the 25-year-old son of a wealthy Boston abolitionist. The regiment under Shaw's command was made up entirely of free blacks from the North

— one of the 167 black units that fought against the Confederacy in the Civil War.

The bloody hand-to-hand struggle at Battery Wagner saw 272 men from the 54th (more than 40 percent of the unit) fall dead and 1,500 Union forces lost — including Colonel Shaw.

The valor and courage displayed in the battle proved once and for all to northern and southern leaders that black soldiers could and would fight. The story of the 54th was widely publicized at the time and, as a result, the Union Army began to enlist blacks in growing numbers. By 1865, a total of 178,895 black soldiers had enlisted, which constituted 12 percent of the North's fighting forces.

The fight for Battery Wagner continued for ten more weeks until the Confederates finally abandoned the work on September 6. The 54th continued to serve along the southeast coast for the remainder of the war. It was mustered out of service in Mt. Pleasant on August 20, 1865.

Other Sites And Museums

THE BATTERY

For starters, Charleston's White Point Gardens (or The Battery, as most people know it) shouldn't officially be called "an attraction" like a museum or a fort. But on the other hand, it's a darn good bet that no first-time visitor to the city ever left here without making a point to walk there — or at least drive by.

In a city where almost every other building or street holds some historical significance, few sites have afforded a better view of Charleston's 300-year-long parade of history than The Battery.

That seaside corner of land at the end of East Bay Street where it turns and becomes Murray Boulevard is now a pleasant park with statues and monuments, long-silent cannons and spreading live oak trees. There's even a Victorian bandstand that looks like it could sport a uniformed Sousa band any Sunday afternoon. But the atmosphere here on The Battery hasn't been always so serene.

The battery has been a prominent feature in Charleston since the earliest days of the English settlement. Then, it was known as "Oyster Point" because it was little more than a marshy beach covered in oyster shells — bleached white in the Carolina sun.

At first, it was mostly a navigational aid for the sailing vessels going in and out of the harbor. The peninsula was still unsettled and the (first) colonial effort was farther upstream on the banks of the Ashley River at what is now called Charles Towne Landing.

Later, when the settlement was moved to the much more defensible peninsula site, the Point was a popular fishing area — too low and too easily flooded to be much of anything else. Charts used during the years 1708 to 1711 show only a "watch tower" on the site and just a few residences built nearby.

Remember, Charles Towne was still a walled city at that time; the southernmost wall being several "blocks" north, near what is now the Shrine Temple on East Bay Street. The Point was definitely a "suburban" location.

The area took a decidedly higher public profile — about a decade later — when the pirate Stede Bonnet (pronounced "Bonay") and some 40 or 50 scalawags just like him were hanged there from makeshift gallows. These executions were apparently quite effective in bringing an end to the pirate activity which had plagued the Carolina coast.

The first of several real forts built on the site came along as early as 1737. This and subsequent fortifications were crudely built, however, and none lasted long against the tyranny of the sea. By the time of the American Revolution, White Point was virtually at the city's door — no longer considered a strategic site for defense.

Hurricanes in 1800 and again in 1804 reduced whatever fortification remained there to rubble. Another fort, this version constructed for the War of 1812, apparently gave White Point a new popular name; The Battery. At least, the new name appears on maps beginning about 1833.

The Four Corners of Law

The intersection of Meeting and Broad Streets is known in Charleston as "The Four Corners of Law." The old line (mostly used by carriage drivers these days) is meant to imply that you can do literally everything legally important in life right here at this Charleston intersection. On the first corner you can get your mail (at the oldest operating Post Office building in South Carolina). On the second corner you can get married (at St. Michael's Episcopal Church — built in 1761 — where George Washington once worshiped). On the third corner you can pay your taxes (at Charleston's County Court House — now undergoing extensive restoration). And on the fourth corner you can get divorced (at Charleston's City Hall — built in 1801).

This attitude ranks right up there with the other one that graciously allows, "The Ashley and Cooper Rivers come together at Charleston...to form the Atlantic Ocean."

Insiders' Tip

The seawall constructed along East Battery (the "high" one) was built after a storm in 1885. Storms and repairs have traded blows at the seawall for many years — in 1893, 1911, 1959, and of course (Hugo) in 1989.

The area's use as a park dates back to 1837 when the city rearranged certain streets to establish White Point Gardens. It was here, from this vantage point, that Charlestonians watched the battle between Confederate fortifications across the river and the small band of Union troops holed up in Fort Sumter, April 12, 1861. What a beginning that was!

Once the war had started, this peaceful little garden was torn up and convulsed into two massive earthwork batteries — part of Charleston's inner line of defense. And while one of these battery sites housed a huge Blakely rifle (one of the two largest weapons in the Confederacy), neither battery ever fired a shot in anger. (Some incoming artillery rounds probably landed here during the extended bombardment of the city from late 1863 until Charleston fell in February 1865.)

The end of the Civil War was the end of The Battery's role in Charleston's military defense. Although, here, several subsequent wars have left poignant souvenirs behind for remembrance. Today, no less than 26 cannons and monuments now dot The Battery's landscape — each of which is described on a nearby plaque or description.

Over the years, The Battery has become something of a balm for the Charlestonian soul. In 1977,

Warren Ripley wrote a detailed booklet called *The Battery* which is still available through *The Post-Courier* office (577-7111). In it, he sums up the reasons why The Battery is so special....

"It has watched the elaborate drill of colonial militia...and the 'goose step' of Hitler's sailors on parade before W.W.II. It has suffered through 'reenactments' of historic events it witnessed in the first place...seen parades, air shows, and fireworks displays without number."

"It has observed three centuries of ocean traffic...watched the evolution from sailing ship to steam and nuclear propulsion as warships and cargo slipped in and out of port.

"It has echoed Sunday afternoon band concerts and heard the weekday cries of street vendors hawking wares to the neighborhood homes. It has harked to the whispers of countless lovers and warmed to the daylight shouts of happy, playing children."

For Charlestonians — clearly The Battery is more than a pleasant little park. Far more.

THE BELLS OF ST. MICHAEL'S

If your timing is lucky, a visit to the very heart of Charleston and its "Four Corners of Law" (the intersection of Broad and Meeting Streets) will be delightfully punctuated by the resonant chime of mighty church bells ringing overhead.

Indeed, the bells of St. Michael's Episcopal Church make more than just a pleasant sound; their ringing is very much a part of

Charleston — one of its oldest and most endearing attractions. In fact, their ringing is another of Charleston's object lessons in faithful perseverance, stubborn southern survival, and the fleet passage of time.

St. Michael's Episcopal Church, built in 1761, (see Charleston Worship) is the oldest church edifice on the peninsula, and the second oldest congregation in the city. Here is the church where George Washington worshiped on his famous 1791 official Presidential tour that included a stay in Charleston. (See The Heyward-Washington House)

The eight bronze bells hanging in St. Michael's spire were originally cast at the Whitechapel Foundry of London in 1764. Church records say the bells first sounded here in Charleston on September 21 of that same year — having safely made their first journey across the Atlantic Ocean. Amazingly, three times since then, the bells have made that long journey back to England.

Their first journey "home" was in 1782 during the War of Independence. The bells had rung in defiance of the Crown during Charleston's protest of the Stamp Act (1765) and British soldiers confiscated them as a punishing prize of war. Once back on English soil, however, the bells were purchased by a private speculator and promptly returned to Charleston and placed in St. Michael's spire.

Then, in 1862 during the War Between the States, seven of the bells were removed from the steeple and taken to Columbia for what was

hoped to be safekeeping. Charleston was such a likely target, many of the city's treasures were sent to Columbia at that time to escape the Union's wrath. Only the large tenor bell was left behind — to ring the alarm for Charlestonians still in the city. In 1865, the year Charleston fell, the bell rang dutifully until it cracked.

Meanwhile, General William T. Sherman's Union army selected upstate Columbia as an artillery target and South Carolina's entire capitol city burned in what was one of the most dramatic episodes of the war.

In 1866, St. Michael's vestry arranged to have the seven charred bells from Columbia and the one cracked bell remaining in the church returned to England — to be recast once more in their original molds at the (still in business) Whitechapel Foundry.

When they were returned in 1867, church records show that the melodies of "Home Again" and "Auld Lang Syne" rang from St. Michael's steeple.

The last journey of the bells — back to England and the (still going) Whitechapel Foundry was in 1993. Their recasting (once more in their original molds) was part of St. Michael's $3.8 million restoration and repair project undertaken as a result of damages suffered in Hurricane Hugo (1989).

The bells of St. Michael's rang anew on July 4, 1993, in a special day-long hand ringing ceremony — done in the English style. Nostalgic Charlestonians from all denominations made special trips past St.

Michael's all that day — just to hear the bells, celebrate Independence Day, and acknowledge another homecoming for the bells of St. Michael's for Charleston and its "Four Corners of Law."

THE POSTAL HISTORY MUSEUM
Meeting at Broad Streets

Unknown to most of the tourists who pass through the intersection of Meeting and Broad Streets (The Four Corners of Law), there's a *free* and fascinating little gem right there — deftly tucked into one of the corners.

The Postal History Museum is a special room *inside* the Charleston Post Office showing visitors some of the interesting tidbits of postal history associated with this coastal colonial town.

For instance, Charleston's first Postmaster (on the job before 1694!) was actually the Powder Receiver who not only collected a percentage of gun powder from every ship that arrived — he was also responsible for the mail. He was required to post incoming letters in a public room in his house for a period of 30 days. He collected his commission only when the letters were picked up by the recipient.

Imagine being in London in 1700... addressing a letter to "John Doe, Charles Towne, Carolina"...and it *getting there*!

This little museum is a *must* for philatelists or anyone else who ever wondered how 18th- and 19th-century mail was handled. And here's a great excuse to go in and see Charleston's elaborately detailed 1896 post office building — the oldest continuously operating Post Office in the Carolinas.

THE POWDER MAGAZINE
79 Cumberland Street

Only a couple of blocks from the bustling market area, is — quite simply — the oldest public building in the Carolinas. And yet, as Charleston attractions go, the Powder Magazine is relatively unknown to tourists (and to some locals, as well).

Perhaps the site is overlooked because it's dramatically upstaged by Charleston's sumptuous house museums and romantic streetscapes. And in truth, the utilitarian Powder Magazine actually predates Charleston's legendary esthetics. It was built for a time when the still-new English settlement was predominantly interested in self defense — basic survival.

In the early years of the 18th century, Charles Towne was still threatened by Spanish forces, hostile Indians, rowdy packs of buccaneers, and occasionally a French attack. It was still a walled city, fortified against surprise attack.

In August of 1702, a survey of the armament in Charles Towne reported "2,306 lbs. of gunpowder, 496 shot of all kind, 28 great guns, 47 Grenada guns, 360 cartridges and 500 lbs. of pewter shot."

In his formal request for additional cannons, the Royal Governor requested "a suitable store of shot and powder...(to) make Carolina impregnable." And so, in 1703, the crown approved and funded such a building which was completed (on what is now Cumberland Street) in 1713.

The Powder Magazine was the domain of the Powder Receiver, a newly appointed city official entitled to accept a gunpowder tax levied on all merchant ships entering Charleston Harbor during this period. The building served its originally intended purpose for many decades. But eventually — in an early colonial version of today's base closings — it was deemed unnecessary (or too small) and sold into private hands.

This multi-gabled, tile-roofed, architectural oddity was almost forgotten by historians until the early 1900s. In 1902, it was purchased by The National Society of Colonial Dames of America in the State of South Carolina.

It was maintained and operated as a small museum until 1991 when water damage, roof deterioration and time had finally taken too high a toll. What the Powder Magazine needed (to survive at all) was a major stabilization and restoration — beyond the resources of the owners.

In an agreement whereby Historic Charleston Foundation (see Architectural Preservation) will do the needed work under a 99-year lease, The Powder Magazine is presently undergoing a $400,000 preservation. This includes a temporary roof over the entire structure, allowing the massive walls to dry out before necessary repairs can be made. And much needed archaeological and archival research on the site is included.

Meanwhile, exhibits belonging to The Colonial Dames will be on display at The Old Exchange and Provost Dungeon, 122 East Bay Street (at Broad), 792-5020.

THE CHARLESTON MUSEUM
360 Meeting Street   722-2996

Located directly across Meeting Street from the Visitors Reception and Transportation Center is one of Charleston's finest gems: The Charleston Museum, founded in 1773. Because it is the first and oldest museum in America, the Museum's collection predates all modern thinking about what should be kept or discarded in preserving the artifacts of a culture.

Instead, the Charleston Museum is heir to the collected memorabilia of real American patriots, early Charlestonian families, early Colonial thinkers, explorers, scientists and planters. It is their opinion of what mattered to them...and what they thought should matter to us today. Although the collection is housed in modern buildings and it has the benefit of modern conservation methods and enlightened interpretation, the collection is uniquely eloquent. It speaks of a city that knew it was great...and sought to record itself for posterity. That difference, alone, makes The Charleston Museum a must see.

The museum's scope is the social and natural history of Charleston and the South Carolina coastal region. Objects from natural science, cultural history, historical archaeology, ornithology and ethnology are presented to illustrate the importance each had in the history of this area.

The Charleston Silver Exhibit contains internationally recognized work by local silversmiths in a beautifully mounted display. Pieces date from Colonial times through the late 19th century.

Visitors will see what the Museum's many archaeological excavations reveal about some of the city's best — and worst — times. Some artifacts date from the early Colonial period while others are from the Civil War years. Some exhibits focus on early Native Americans who lived in this region. Others trace changes in trade and commerce, the expansive rice and cotton plantation systems, and the important contributions made by blacks.

Children will be intrigued by the "Discover Me" room with amazing things to touch, see and do. They'll see toys from the past, games children played, the clothes they wore, furniture they used and more. The photographs, ceramics, pewter and tools reveal a very personal portrait of Charlestonians from the past.

Because the Charlestonian life-style is so much a part of the city and its history, the three house museums owned and operated by the museum are an important part of its offering. (See the Aiken-Rhett House at 48 Elizabeth Street; the Heyward-Washington House, 87 Church Street, and the Joseph Manigault House, and 350 Meeting Street — as described in the House Museums section of this chapter.) Here in appropriate settings, you'll see some of the museum's remarkable collection of antique furniture and decorative arts.

The Charleston Museum is open Monday through Saturday from 9:00 AM to 5:00 PM; and Sunday, 1:00 to 5:00 PM. Admission is $5 for adults, and $3 for children (ages 3 to 12).

THE OLD EXCHANGE AND PROVOST DUNGEON

122 East Bay Street   727-2165
(at Broad), Charleston

A public building has stood on this site since Charles Towne was moved from its original settlement (see the Charles Towne Landing entry earlier in this chapter) to its present location in 1680. The early settlers built their Court of Guard here. They imprisoned pirates and Indians in its lower level and held their town meetings upstairs in the hall.

The British built the present building on the site to create an impressive presence in the bustling Colonial port. With its striking Palladian architecture, the Exchange surely did just that. It was completed in 1771 and quickly became the social, political and economic hub of the growing city.

From its steps, the independent colony of South Carolina was publicly declared in March 1776. During the Revolution the building was converted to a British prison where signers of the Declaration of Independence were held. In 1788 the convention to ratify the U.S. Constitution met in the building. And President George Washington was lavishly entertained here several times during his southern tour.

From 1818 until 1896, the building served both the federal and confederate governments as Charleston's Post Office. In 1917,

Photo: The Post and Courier

The African-American exhibit at the Charleston Museum.

the U.S. Congress deeded the building to the Daughters of the American Revolution of South Carolina.

During an excavation of the dungeon in 1965, part of the original seawall of Charles Towne was discovered. Today, the Old Exchange & Provost Dungeon is leased to the State of South Carolina and is open to the public as a museum. The building has two halls that are available to rent for private events.

Hours are 9:00 AM to 5:00 PM, daily. Admission is $3 for adults, $1.50 for children ages 7 to 12, and children under 6 are admitted free. Senior discounts and group rates are available.

GIBBES MUSEUM OF ART
135 Meeting Street   *722-2706*

Established in 1905 by the Carolina Art Association, the Gibbes Museum of Art stands a block and a half north of the Four Corners of Law. As locations go, that's fairly close to what Charlestonians traditionally believe to be eternal truth. And, clearly, the Gibbes represents what is very close to an unbroken stream of uplifting experiences in art.

Members, residents of the city, and visitors all have access to a distinguished and growing collection along with year round exhibitions, educational programs and special events.

The building itself stands as a memorial to James Shoolbred Gibbes, a wealthy Charlestonian who bequeathed funds to the City of Charleston and the Carolina Art Association to create a permanent home for the Association's collection.

Today, that rich and fascinating collection includes American paintings, prints and drawings from the 18th century to the present. There are landscapes, genre scenes, views of Charleston and portraits of notable South Carolinians. Faces associated with history (and architectural landmarks all over the Low-country) seem to come to life there. You'll find Thomas Middleton painted by Benjamin West, and Charles Izard Manigault by Thomas Sully. There's John C. Calhoun painted by Rembrandt Peale plus an outstanding collection of more than 400 exquisite, hand-painted miniature portraits of 18th- and 19th-century Charlestonians.

The Elizabeth Wallace Miniature Rooms can be seen — 10 miniature interiors representing different traditions in American and French architecture, decorative arts and design. The Gibbes also has an outstanding collection of early Japanese woodblock prints in a special Oriental Gallery.

In addition to the regular schedule of exhibitions on loan from international, national and regional collections, the Gibbes presents major exhibitions in the visual arts during the Spoleto Festival U.S.A. every May through June.

Members and the public are invited to join museum tours, gallery talks, lectures, seminars, meet-the-artist events, films, videotapes and specialized videos for schools and community groups.

One of the most popular aspects of the Gibbes is the Museum Shop, which offers an excellent selection of art books, posters, note cards, jewelry and other gift items. Shop early for the best Christmas cards every year! Museum members receive a 10 percent discount on all purchases there. Admission to the shop is free and the shop is open during regular museum hours.

The Gibbes has a working stu-dio at 76 Queen Street which provides professional instruction in everything from painting and photography to textile silk-screening and jewelry-making. Classes and workshops are designed for all ages and levels of experience. Contact the Gibbes Museum Studio at 577-7275 for additional information.

Memberships to the Gibbes Museum of Art are renewable on an annual basis. Dues are tax deductible. You'll find applications for membership at the information desk or you can call the Gibbes at 722-2706. Guided tours are available by appointment. Call the education department to make arrangements.

Admission is $3 for adults, $2 for students and senior citizens, and $1 for children while members are admitted free. Museum hours are 10:00 AM to 5:00 PM Tuesday through Saturday, and 1:00 to 5:00 PM Sunday and Monday. The Gibbes is fully accessible to the handicapped.

PATRIOTS POINT NAVAL AND MARITIME MUSEUM

40 Patriots Point Road   884-2727
Mt. Pleasant

YORKTOWN (AIRCRAFT CARRIER)

No one comes or goes through Charleston via Hwy. 17 across the Cooper River bridges without noticing the giant aircraft carrier moored off Mt. Pleasant. It dominates (no, *commands*) a vast stretch of the Cooper's Mt. Pleasant shore at its very gates into Charleston Harbor.

She is none other than the

Photo: The Post and Courier

The Adventure and a nuclear submarine in Charleston Harbor.

Yorktown (CV-10), the famous "Fighting Lady" of World War II and the proud flagship of Patriots Point, the world's largest naval and maritime museum.

Of the five vessels permanently anchored there and open to the public, the *Yorktown* is the most impressive. She was commissioned on April 15, 1943, in the darkest days of the war. She fought valiantly in some of the worst engagements ever witnessed at sea. Her planes inflicted heavy losses against the Japanese at Truk and the Marninas, and she supported the American ground troops in the Philippines, at bloody Iwo Jima and Okinawa.

Shortly after she was commissioned and sent into battle, 20th Century Fox put a film crew on board to record — on still-rare Technicolor film — the continuing war story of a "typical" navy carrier in action. The spectacular footage shot at unnamed, secret locations during (then) unnamed battles became the Academy Award-winning documentary feature of 1944. The film was called "The Fighting Lady" and today it is shown daily at the *Yorktown's* on-board theater at regularly scheduled intervals. Don't miss it; nothing brings the World War II drama of the *Yorktown* to life like this amazing celluloid time-capsule. The terrible explosions and blistering fires, the fierce fighting, and all the brave young faces who served on her are there (hopefully) forever — to be seen and appreciated by generations then unborn.

But the *Yorktown's* story doesn't end there. Not at all. She patrolled the western Pacific during the Cold War and she even fought in Vietnam. In fact, the *Yorktown* received the crew of Apollo 8 in 1968, the first manned space flight around the moon.

The flight deck, hanger deck and many of the *Yorktown* crew's living and working quarters are open to visitors today. You'll find actual carrier aircraft and Vietnam War era anti-sub planes on display. And there are fascinating exhibits on everything from mines to shipbuilding.

One of the newest exhibits is the true-to-scale Vietnam Naval Support Base — showing the living conditions and operations (work) areas of a typical support base during the Vietnam War. Also recently added is the Medal of Honor Museum — featuring displays representing the eight different eras of our military history during which the Medal of Honor was awarded. You'll see actual Medals of Honor and some of the artifacts related to their original recipients.

Mercifully, you'll find a snack bar on board the *Yorktown* and another in the (riverside) gift shop, so excited youngsters and foot-weary veterans can stop for lunch and a rest.

Considering all there is to see, Patriots Point Naval and Maritime Museum is a real bargain. Admission is $8 for adults, $4 for children (ages 6 to 11), and free for children under 6. But plan on spending the better part of your day at Patriots Point; there's still much more to see.

SAVANNAH (NUCLEAR SHIP)

Insiders (roughly) our age may remember the *Savannah* from our trusty grade school newspaper, *The Weekly Reader*. She was christened "the world's first nuclear-powered merchant ship," and she was widely hailed as the great, new, coming thing in maritime technology. Her sleek, modern lines were big news and they seemed almost otherworldly to the 1950s school children trying to cope with the wonders and worries of the nuclear age.

The gleaming white ship still cuts a handsome profile against the cold, grey hardware of World War II and the warm green hues of the surrounding marsh. But the Cold War world wasn't ready for a nuclear powered merchant marine fleet. She only sailed the world's oceans for eight years — from 1959 to 1967 — but she proved the practicality of atomic power in working ships, if not working politics. During her entire career, she burned only 163 pounds of uranium, the equivalent of 28.8 million gallons of fossil fuel oil. Today, all nuclear fuels have been entirely removed and *Savannah's* upper decks and unique "white" engine room are open to visitors.

LAFFEY (DESTROYER)

The heroic destroyer *Laffey* (DD-724), which was commissioned on February 8, 1944, participated in the giant D-Day landings of Allied troops at Normandy four months later. Transferred to the Pacific, she was struck by five Japanese Kamikaze suicide planes and hit by three bombs during one hour on April 16, 1945, off Okinawa. Her gallant crew not only kept her afloat, but managed to shoot down eleven planes during the attack. After World War II, the Laffey served during the Korean War and then in the Atlantic Fleet until she was decommissioned in 1975.

A tour route on the *Laffey* lets you see her bridge, battle stations, living quarters and various displays of destroyer activities.

CLAMAGORE (SUBMARINE)

The World War II submarine *Clamagore* (SS-343) was commissioned on June 28, 1945. She operated in the Atlantic and Mediterranean throughout her entire career and patrolled tense Cuban waters during 1962. Twice modified, she survived as one of the U.S. Navy's last diesel-powered subs until she was decommissioned in 1975.

The *Clamagore's* tour route covers her control room, berth and mess areas, engine rooms, maneuvering room and displays of submarine warfare. Note: spaces are very cramped on board. Visitors with health problems — or claustrophobia — are cautioned.

INGHAM (COAST GUARD CUTTER)

The *Ingham* was the most decorated vessel in the U.S. service with a total of 18 ribbons earned during her career of more than 50 years. Commissioned in 1936, the *Ingham* took part in 31 World War II convoys, six Pacific patrols and three Vietnam tours. In 1942, she sank the German *U-boat 626* with one depth charge, which was called

"Ingham's Hole-in-One." In recent years, the cutter tracked illegal boat immigrants and drug runners. She was decommissioned in 1988 and is now open for tours.

MUSEUM ON THE COMMON
The Common   849-9000
217 Lucas Street, Mt. Pleasant

First opened in September of 1992 — on the third anniversary of Hurricane Hugo — this small but fascinating museum is dedicated to the people and events that shaped the history of the East Cooper area from Awendaw to the Old Village of Mt. Pleasant.

The major exhibit is "Hurricane Hugo Revisited," — first mounted in Columbia at The State Museum and reassembled here in its new permanent home. The Hugo Room is a multisensory exploration of the sights and sounds and feel of the 1989 storm. It focuses on the drastic changes Hugo brought to the natural environment as well as the changes it bought in human terms.

And while that event is slowly fading from the memory of most Americans, Hugo is still very vivid to those who were here to live it. So great was (and is) the Lowcountry's need and desire to put the storm behind us, this museum exhibit is one of the few areas in greater Charleston where the Hugo experience is displayed or "interpreted" for visitors.

Other exhibits include "Pirates of the Carolinas, Shipwrecks of East Cooper," and "Osceola — Seminole Indian Chief" (who is buried east of the Cooper River on Sullivans Island). Civil War buffs will like "Blockade Running, 1861 - 1865," and children can learn about "Sea Creatures of the Carolina Province."

This young but growing museum is a delightful discovery for those with limited time who don't want to drive over the (Cooper River) bridge and into peninsula traffic. Best of all, admission is *free.* Hours are Monday through Saturday from 10:00 AM to 6:00 PM.

THE CITADEL MUSEUM
171 Moultrie Street, Charleston   792-6846

This museum features the history of The Citadel, the Military College of South Carolina. It covers the entire history of the school, from 1842 to the present. Various displays represent the military, academic, social and athletic aspects of cadet life.

The museum is located on campus — on the third floor of the Daniel Library, which is the first building on the right inside The Citadel's main gates.

Hours are from 2:00 to 5:00 PM, Sunday through Friday, and noon to 5:00 PM on Saturday. The museum is closed for college, national and religious holidays. There is no charge for admission.

JOHN RIVERS
COMMUNICATIONS MUSEUM
College of Charleston   792-5810 or
58 George Street, Charleston   792-8016

The College of Charleston's John Rivers Communications Museum offers a unique opportunity to explore the world of broadcasting and communications. John M.

Rivers was a Charleston-born banker, businessman, and broadcasting executive who introduced television to the Lowcountry in 1957.

Visitors to the museum can hear early sound recordings, learn about the lives of famous inventors such as Marconi and Edison, and trace the advancements in science from the camera to television, from the phonograph to radio.

The museum is open Monday through Friday from noon to 4:00 PM, except during College of Charleston holidays. Summer hours may vary. Group tours are conducted by appointment only; call the museum to schedule one. Admission is free but donations are appreciated.

"Frankly my dear, *It's the best tour you'll ever have!"*

See It All With The Best Of Charleston
ADVENTURE SIGHTSEEING
A CHARLESTON FAMILY OWNED BUSINESS
1 & 2 Hour Historic City Tours

- See Ft. Sumter from the Battery ● Rainbow Row
- Catfish Row ● Old City Market ● Historic Mansions
- Churches ● The Citadel & Much More!

All tours include a stop at the Battery where you
will hear about the War Between The States
and see where it actually began.

**Tours leave the Visitor's Center DAILY.
for Reservations & free Downtown pick-up**
call 762-0088

Telephones Operating 8:00 am-10:00 pm Daily!

- Walking Tours ● Group Tours ● Convention
Planning ● Guide Service Also Available.

ADVENTURE SIGHTSEEING
762-0088 OR 1-800-722-5394

Ask about our Insider's Special

Greater Charleston
Tour Guides

*U*pon first impression, visitors to Charleston are usually primarily taken with the city's readily apparent architectural charm. Part of that fascination comes from the unspoken stories that leap to mind of Charleston's fairly obvious good times. People quickly want to know more about how a city of such architectural style and sophistication — *in fact* — evolved.

And so, the second impulse visitors usually feel is the need to seek out some kind of tour. Visitors want a visual and geographic overview, a point of reference, some sense of perspective. And most of all, they want to hear some of the stories recounting Charleston when everything (now) old was shiny and new, independence was still a dream, and Charleston was already famous as the brightest jewel in the British Colonial crown.

That's why the telling of Charleston's story has literally become an industry. It's important enough that to become an official, licensed tour guide here, one must take a city-sponsored course (and pass very tough written and oral exams) just to get the job. Charlestonians, you see, care *enormously* that their story be well-told. That's simply because the real truth is so interesting that amateurism, half-truths and downright lies (told by a tour guide) are considered wholly unnecessary, deceitful and *not at all* Charlestonian.

Tours of the city are available in several forms. Most of the walking or riding (be that in a carriage or car/van) tours depart from the Visitor's Center on Meeting Street or from The Market area. You may also choose to meet a private guide at your inn or hotel and depart from there. Cruising tours leave, for the most part, from the City Marina or Patriots Point in Mt. Pleasant. It might also be helpful to you to read over the Visitor Center section of our Attractions chapter since these places are excellent sources of information about the city's tour services. Here are some of the tours currently available that we consider especially good and interesting:

ADVENTURE SIGHTSEEING
762-0088 OR 1-800-722-5394

This company offers a variety of one- and two-hour tours of the historic district with special features like The Citadel Dress Parade (on Fridays only), a tour through The Old Exchange or one of Charleston's famous house museums, or a walking tour down

Charleston's narrow streets. They have free pick-up service from downtown hotels, the Visitor's Center, The City Market, and the City Marina. Reservations are required. Adult fares are $11; children $7 (for 1-hour tour). Adult fares are $17; children $9 (for 2-hour tours). All tours include one house museum and a complete history of the city.

ARCHITECTURAL WALKING TOURS
893-2327 or 722-2345
These are two-hour tours of Charleston's remarkable architectural heritage. The 18th-century tour begins at 10 AM; the 19th-century at 2 PM. Both tours depart daily from the lobby of the Planters Inn. The charge is $10 per person.

ASSOCIATED GUIDES OF HISTORIC CHARLESTON
724-6419
Tour the city, the gardens, plantations and house museums with a private guide in their autos. Phone for reservations from 8:30 AM to 5 PM daily.

CAROLINA LOWCOUNTRY TOURS
797-1045
Licensed guides conduct two-hour tours through Charleston's historic district in air-conditioned mini-buses. The fare is $19.50 for adults, $7 for children. (They schedule several tours a day.) Call ahead for shuttle service from your hotel.

CHARLESTON GUIDE SERVICE
722-8240 or 723-4402 or 724-5367
These are private auto tours of the city, the gardens and plantations, offered daily. Make advance reservations through the answering service.

CHARLESTON HOSPITALITY TOURS
722-6858
This company offers private car and walking tours of the historic city, the gardens and rice plantations. Call for rates and availability.

CHARLESTON HARBOR TOURS
722-1691
This is a 2-hour, narrated (with an emphasis on history), non-stop cruise touring the harbor, the U.S. Navy Base and the Port of Charleston facilities. The boat departs from Patriots Point in Mt. Pleasant. Adult fares are $8.50 for adults, $4.25 for children under 12.

CAPE ROMAIN NATIONAL WILDLIFE REFUGE
884-5523
Once-a-day boat trips to Cape Romain for birding, shelling, hiking, beach walking and surf fishing are available on Friday, Saturday and Sunday. Call Capt. Lyle Finnell in Mt. Pleasant for more information.

COASTAL EXPEDITIONS
884-7684
Scheduled and spontaneous kayak tours are an unusual way to see the coastal waterways. Don't be shy because you've never snuggled into one of these sleek boats before — half day tours include an instruction clinic. Rates vary, but two samples are: a half-day Shem Creek Tour, $35, and a full-day Adventure Tour, $55.

Photo: The Post and Courier

Visitors on a tour at Meeting and South Battery.

COLONIAL COACH AND TROLLEY COMPANY
795-3000

These tours are about 75 minutes long and feature over 100 points of interest in Charleston's historic district. The live, narrated tours are aboard reproductions of 19th-century trolleys and stop at the Battery for great views of Fort Sumter and Charleston Harbor. Trolleys depart from the City Market at "quarter 'til" and from the Visitor Center "on the hour." Adult fares are $11; children are $6 (for ages 4 through 12).

CHARLESTON TEA PARTY WALKING TOUR
577-5896

These private walking tours last about two hours and end with tea served in a private garden. They leave from the Meeting Street Inn, 173 Meeting Street, at 9 AM (a little later in the cooler months) and from St. Philips Church at 2 PM. The charge is $10 per person. Call for reservation.

CHARLESTON STROLLS
884-9505

This is a leisurely stroll through Charleston's oldest section — including the old walled city, St. Michael's Church and Catfish Row. See early 18th- and 19th-century architecture and hear about the history in between. Tours departs from the Omni Hotel lobby at 9:30 AM, and from the Mills House Courtyard at 10 AM. Call for reservations. The adult rate is $12; children are welcome free.

CHARLES TOWNE TOURS

This is a cassette walking and/or driving tour that includes a map. They are offered through the Mills House — ask at the Concierge Desk or in the Gift Shop. They rent for $8.50.

CIVIL WAR WALKING TOUR OF CHARLESTON
722-7033

This walking tour departs from the Mills House Courtyard, 115 Meeting Street, at 9 AM, Wednesday through Sunday, March through December. You'll hear the personal accounts and colorful anecdotes of the late Charlestonians who lived through it all. The tour includes photo comparisons of Charleston in the 1860s with today's views. Reservations are appreciated. Adult rate is $12, children under 12 are free.

COLONIAL CITY AND PLANTATION TOURS
871-2828

This company has a comprehensive schedule of downtown tours via air-conditioned van (both 1- and 2-hour versions), Friday Citadel Dress Parade tours, and plantation tours that are well-paced so you can enjoy each site. City tours depart from the Visitors Center at 8:45 and 11 AM, and at 1:45 and 4:30 PM. Adult fare is $10 for the 1-hour trip, $18 for the 2-hour one. Children's fare is half-price. The Citadel Dress Parade tour (on Fridays only) lasts three hours, with adult fare at $20 and kids half-price. They also offer a 2-day tour of four plantations for $30 per adult. All coupons (even competitors') are honored.

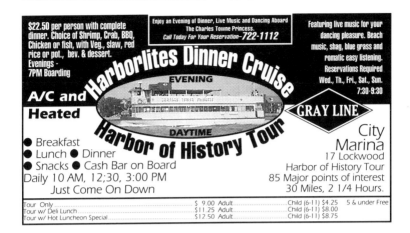
DINNER & HARBOR CRUISE
722-2628

Enjoy an evening cruise that includes a seated dinner and live entertainment plus dancing on board the yacht, *Spirit of Charleston.* Rates and schedules change seasonally. Call ahead for reservations and information before 1 PM on the day of the cruise. This tour departs from the City Marina on Lockwood Drive.

FORT SUMTER TOURS
722-1691

This tour visits the Fort Sumter National Monument where the Civil War began. Boats leave from the City Marina on Lockwood Drive and from Patriots Point in Mt. Pleasant. Adult fares are $8.50, children (6 to 11) are $4.25. Children under 5 are free.

GRAY LINE HARBOR OF HISTORY TOUR
722-1112 or 1-8—0344-4483

This 30-mile, non-stop tour covers more than 85 major points of interest in Charleston's famous harbor. The boat departs from the City Marina on Lockwood Drive at 10 AM, 12:30 and 3 PM daily. Adult fares are $9; children (6 to 11) are $5; children under 6 tour free.

GRAY LINE TROLLEYETTE (BUS) TOURS
722-4444

Gray Line offers two tours Charleston's historic district in an air-conditioned mini-van with large windows. There's an Express Tour (1 hour) and a Grand Tour (2 hours) available. The narrated tour highlights all the major landmarks and the Grand Tour includes an interior visit to the Old Exchange Building and Provost Dungeon. Tours leave from the Visitors Center at 9:30 and 11:30 AM, 1:30 and 3:30 PM. Adult fare is $10.50; children under 12, $6. The Grand Tour rate is $18 for adults, $11 for children under 12.

If you want to take a combined bus and boat tour, that rate is $22.50 for adults, $13.50 for children. You may want to ask your hotel clerk or concierge to book your reservations — they have plenty of experience here.

HISTORIC CHARLESTON WALKING TOURS (WITH DAVID FARROW)
722-6460

These walking tours leave daily from the downtown Days Inn at 9:30 AM (and from the corner of N. Market and Church at 10 AM), and return 12:30 and 6:30 PM. David is a native Charlestonian and a writer whose publications (and video) reflect his knowledge of the city. Adult rates are $10, children under 12 are free.

NATURE TOURS BY WATER
768-7294

See some of Mother Nature's wonders by boat (four to six passengers required). Watch dolphins, birds and the shoreline sights. Tours leave from Bohicket Marina, 1880 Andell Bluff Blvd., Seabrook Island. Reservations are required.

NATURE WALKS
723-6171

Special nature walks are scheduled by appointment through The Audubon Shop, 245 King Street. These tours are especially popular with birders and plant lovers visiting the Lowcountry. Some tours are in downtown Charleston, others go afield. Call for guide availability and specific information.

OLD SOUTH CARRIAGE COMPANY
723-9712

These are the carriage tours with guides wearing red sashes (Confederate uniforms, of sorts). The tours last 40 to 50 minutes narrated by licensed guides. They depart from 14 Anson Street (the corner of N. Market and Anson) every 20 minutes beginning at 9 AM daily. Adult fares are $13, children are $5 (ages 3 to 11).

OLDE TOWNE CARRIAGE COMPANY
722-1315

These carriage tours by licensed guides leave from the corner of N. Market and Church streets starting at 9 AM until dusk. Tours run from 45 minutes to an hour and the company offers free parking. Adult fares are $12, children are $5 (ages 3 to 11).

PALMETTO CARRIAGE TOURS
723-8145

Here's a one-hour carriage tour narrated by experienced guides as you meander through antebellum neighborhoods at a clip-clop pace. Tours begin and terminate at the Rainbow Market, 40 North market Street, daily from 9 AM to dusk.

They offer shuttle service from the Visitors Center and several downtown hotels. Adult fares are $14, children are $5 (for ages 4 to 11).

SHELLING SHUTTLES
768-1280

Here's another Seabrook Island offering that leaves from Bohicket Marina. The round-trip boat ride includes a visit to a barrier island for shelling, exploring and nature-watching. The rate is $40. Reservations are required.

THE COMPLETE WALKING TOUR OF HISTORIC CHARLESTON

This is a self-guided walking tour book — available at the Visitor Center and area bookstores. The price is $3.95.

SOUTHERN WINDJAMMER TOURS
Ripley Light Marina
Charleston Harbor   795-1180

Ah, here's a fantasy that's delightfully achievable. See Charleston from the water as countless settlers and 19th-century immigrants saw it — from the decks of a tall ship, the schooner *Pride.*

She's 84 ft. long and is U.S. Coast Guard certified to carry 49 day passengers or 20 overnight guests. Choose from a 2-hour cruise of Charleston Harbor for would-be sailors with limited time or take their five-day, four-night cruise to Savannah, Ga., for a longer sailing adventure.

Experienced sailors and quick learners may help with the ship, or you can simply sit back and enjoy the wind, the sea and the unexpected pleasure of almost soundless propulsion. Rediscover the noble and ancient art of sailing.

Daytrippers may bring their own food and drinks (alcohol is permitted in moderation), but the Savannah trip includes meals, cocktails and one night out at a chic restaurant in Savannah.

The 2-hour fare is $15 for adults; $10 for children (ages 1 to 10); babies under 12 months are free. The Savannah cruise fare is $395 per person. Call for departure dates and reservations.

Photo: The Post and Courier

An East Battery hitching post.

Greater Charleston
Architectural
Preservation

*I*f anything is more remarkable than Charleston's softly pastel streets, the graceful church spires, the elegant old homes with their exquisite interiors — it has to be the fact that any of it still exists at all.

No other Colonial city has suffered so many calamities so often as Charleston. Time after time, fire has left vast areas of the city in ashes. Twice the city has been bombarded during war — once by the British during the Revolution and once again by northern cannon in the War Between the States.

Then, Mother Nature has repeatedly hurled fierce hurricanes and tornadoes at the city and it has been cracked and shaken periodically by terrible earthquakes.

And yet, as you walk through the large and little streets south of Calhoun, you find them lined with fascinating architectural relics of the past. It's hard to imagine that much of what looks so timeless and permanent today could so easily have been swept away by any number of man-made calamities or some climatic happenstance.

Indeed, Charleston's ethic of architectural preservation (and restoration) is certainly no accident. Rather, it's the result of hard work and sacrifice by a few early visionaries and the regularly tested courage of today's preservation organizations.

Insiders — new or old — need to know about these organizations. You need to know what dues already have been paid to properly stand guard against the pitfalls and challenges that lie ahead. Historic preservation in Charleston remains an active and vital force. The organizations responsible for keeping Charleston beautiful continue to need public support and enlightened participation.

What follows is a brief description of Charleston's principle preservation organizations along with membership and other support information.

THE PRESERVATION SOCIETY OF CHARLESTON

147 King Street   722-4630 or 723-4381

In the early 1920s, Charleston was fortunate to have a remarkable group of people who sensed the value of their own town and its historic buildings. These people jealously guarded that heritage and saved a great portion of it from its two worst enemies: the many decades of past neglect and the future's natural gravitation toward urban "renewal."

The city's first preservation organization, The Society for the Preservation of Old Dwelling Houses, was founded in 1920 and incorporated in 1928. It evolved into what is now The Preservation Society of Charleston.

The organization is dedicated to preserving the heritage of Charleston. Its varied activities include advocacy on behalf of protective acquisition and restoration of historic properties, active participation in meetings of Charleston's Board of Architectural Review, and representation at a variety of city meetings and boards dealing with preservation issues.

The Society works to keep both its membership and the general public well informed about current preservation philosophies, techniques and issues. To do so, they publish a quarterly newsletter, *Preservation Progress*, and the Society has regular meetings with informative speakers.

In 1931, the Society played an important role in promoting the first Historic Zoning Ordinance in the United States. Other successes have included the initial "saving" of the Joseph Manigault House and the Heyward-Washington House (see our section called House Museums in the Attractions chapter) and the East Bay Street area now known as "Rainbow Row."

In its early years, the Society obtained financial support from the generosity of its founding members. Today, it continues to depend in large part on its members (grown to approximately 2,300 scattered all over the country) for monetary and moral support. To augment this base, the Society engages in limited publishing efforts and maintains a bookstore open to the public at its King Street headquarters. Additionally, the Society sponsors annual Fall House and Garden Tours which are highly popular with tourists. Funds earned from these activities are used to further preservation objectives.

Annual memberships extend from January through December. Dues are: Student, $15; Individual, $25; Family, $35; Contributing, $50; Sustaining, $100; Patron, $150; Benefactor, $500; and Life Membership, $1,000.

The Preservation Society qualifies as a nonprofit, tax-exempt institution. Membership dues and contributions may be deducted for income and estate tax purposes. Memorial gifts are invited. Write The Preservation Society of Charleston, Box 521, Charleston, South Carolina, 29402.

HISTORIC CHARLESTON FOUNDATION

11 Fulton Street   723-1623

Historic Charleston Foundation is a nonprofit educational organization dedicated to the preservation and physical conservation of our nation's architectural and cultural heritage as represented in Charleston and the Carolina Lowcountry.

Organized and incorporated in 1947, the Foundation has undertaken programs that concentrate on property conservation, plus neighborhood and commercial/business zone revitalization. The

Foundation seeks the stabilization of Charleston's architecturally significant urban environment — which traces its origin back to the 1670s.

The Foundation's primary efforts have centered in Charleston's Old and Historic District — the oldest in the United States — which encompasses more than 3,600 rated structures and represents approximately 25 percent of the city's land mass.

Additional preservation efforts and survey work extend into the outlying tri-county area, which constitutes the original settlement area of the Carolinas.

Foundation programs serve as realistic, economically feasible alternatives to urban decay; provide protection for vulnerable buildings, housing and neighborhoods; and promote heritage education and citizen participation in urban planning. The Foundation's efforts in these areas serve as models for many other communities throughout the nation.

The work of the Foundation is divided into five basic areas: Preservation Programs; House Museum and Curatorial; Heritage Tours and Education; Historic Charleston Foundation Reproductions; Public Relations and Development.

Staff offices for the Foundation are presently located at 11 Fulton Street, with additional offices at the Nathaniel Russell House, 51 Meeting Street; the Frances R. Edmunds Preservation Center, 108 Meeting Street; and the Historic Charleston Foundation Reproduction Shop at 105 Broad Street.

Historic Charleston Foundation has no membership, but its work is augmented by the active support of approximately 700 volunteers who annually donate in excess of 8,000 hours to Foundation programs and events. The largest concentration of volunteer support is provided by the Board of Trustees, home owners and docents for the enormously popular Festival of Houses and Gardens each spring. Volunteer opportunities also include duties as house museum docents and service on standing and special interest committees.

Financial support for Foundation programs derives from a variety of sources which include earned and endowment income, public and private grant monies, and tax-deductible gifts of cash securities or objects.

The Foundation needs and welcomes gifts from those who wish to participate in the study, conservation and protection of

Insiders Like:
Springtime Tea Rooms — complete with okra soup and even shrimp paste sandwiches. The annual "Courtyard Tea Room" at the Confederate Home on Broad Street is sponsored by the Charleston Family Y in March and April (call 723-6473), coinciding roughly with the Old St. Andrews Parish Episcopal Church Tea Room (call 766-1541).

Insiders' Tip

Charleston's heritage. All contributions and bequests to the Foundation's programs are tax-deductible, as provided by law.

THE SOUTH CAROLINA HISTORICAL SOCIETY

100 Meeting Street   *723-3225*

In 1855, as the last of America's revolutionary generation was dying off, their recorded thoughts, accomplishments and aspirations were dying, too. The founders of The South Carolina Historical Society recognized this fact and saw the need to preserve existing records of that era for the future of South Carolina and for the generations yet to come.

That year, they invited "contributions of every sort ... (to) illustrate ... social, political or ecclesiastical (life), our industry, (and) our resources...." This 19th-century call for the vanishing evidence of South Carolina's past became the foundation for the Society's collection.

Simply restated for today, the Society's mandate is "to collect information respecting every portion of our state, to preserve it, and when deemed advisable, to publish it."

The Society's holdings now constitute South Carolina's most important private repository of history. Here, members and researchers find and study the papers of governors, congressmen, generals, architects, poets, artists, soldiers and planters ... along with young girls' diaries and love letters, and the records of churches, banks, grocery stores, plantations and shipping companies. They all record the rhythms of South Carolina daily life.

In addition, there are files on nearly 4,000 South Carolina families, more than 40,000 maps, photographs and architectural drawings, and 30,000 books, pamphlets and serials which trace the lives of South Carolinians, then and now.

Over the past decade, researchers have flocked to the Society in record numbers; historians, genealogists, authors, lawyers, scholars and filmmakers.

The South Carolina Historical Society seeks membership among all who share an interest in the state's past — students and adults, natives and newcomers. Members enjoy a rich variety of programs and benefits, including the quarterly *South Carolina Historical Magazine*, their newsletter, *Carologue*, and invitations to Society-sponsored lectures, tours and social functions.

The Society maintains offices and their collection in The Fireproof Building, on Charleston's Meeting Street, built in 1826 and designed by South Carolina's premiere antebellum architect, Robert Mills.

Membership dues are relatively modest to encourage easy participation by all those interested in South Carolina history. They are: Student, $25; Regular (individual or family), $40; Libraries, $50; Contributor, $60; Sustainer, $100-$499; Sponsor, $500 - $999. Higher level memberships are also available.

For a membership application or more information, write S.C. Historical Society, 100 Meeting Street, Charleston, S.C. 29401-2299.

Greater Charleston
Antiques

*F*or the Insider who wants to buy, sell, study or just window shop (for) antiques — Charleston represents the *Motherlode*. Because it was first an English city, Charleston's sense of taste in antiques is decidedly British. And fittingly, Charleston's many antique shops and galleries — many of which are located along King Street — reflect that English bias.

Bear in mind, the Lowcountry was first claimed and settled by English aristocrats who brought along their aristocratic taste in furnishings. And if they couldn't import their hearts' desires for finery and furniture, they imported tradesmen who could recreate it for them here on this side of the Atlantic.

The affluent, British-educated 18th-century Charlestonians proudly decorated their homes with the latest in English good taste — as an obvious symbol of their cultural status and social position. Long after Britain ceased being a factor in the colonies, politically speaking, colonists looked to Mother England for direction in taste. In fact, this artistic/cultural co-dependency has lingered in Charleston for well over two hundred years.

Of course, during the late-18th and mid-19th centuries dramatic events greatly altered the city's economic health. There were earthquakes, wars, fires and storms — all of which took their toll on Charleston's grandeur (including the city's remarkable collection of antiques). The collapse of the indigo and rice trades, the hardships of Reconstruction, and the opening of America's vast western frontier left poor Charleston few viable resources with which to rebuild its economy.

Many of the elegant old homes fell into neglect as Southern families struggled to cope with all the social and economic changes swirling around them. In many cases, their only recourse was to sell some of the old family furniture, silver, crystal and china remaining from the former days of glory. Charleston did what she had to do in order to survive.

By the early 1900s, a few savvy antique dealers from New York had discovered Charleston's cache of truly fine English furnishings. They soon learned that the quality of the furniture was outmatched only by the city's economic distress. By the 1920s, what amounted to an antique industry was going strong in Charleston.

Happily, Charleston no

longer relies on furnishings from her native homes and the misfortunes of her old families to fill today's antique shops and galleries. Now, ships carrying huge 40-ft. containers filled with English antiques regularly arrive in Charleston harbor. Much of the merchandise therein gets sold in local shops, while some of it goes on to discerning dealers all over America. Still, Charleston enjoys the lion's share of the top quality merchandise — largely because of the demand. (Many of Charleston's old homes were built to showcase such furnishings, and each new owner has the opportunity to refurbish.)

From St. Michael's Alley and King Street to the shops in Mt. Pleasant and along Savannah Highway, dozens of opportunities exist to shop for some of the best antiques sold in America.

We've listed, here, some of the shops you may want to explore.

A'RIGA IV
208 King Street   *577-3075*

This shop carries a wide assortment of interesting early ceramics, decorative arts and period accessories. You'll find some fascinating antique medical and scientific instruments, too. A'riga IV is open from 10:00 AM to 5:00 PM, Monday through Saturday.

ACHITRAVE
202 King Street   *577-2860*

Architrave carries fine American 18th- and early 19th-century

furniture along with chandeliers, other lighting fixtures and decorative accessories. The shop is open from 10:00 AM to 5:00 PM, Monday through Saturday.

ACQUISITIONS
273 East Bay Street 577-8004 and 722-0238
This shop offers interior design services and specializes in English pine (originals and reproductions), English mahogany and antique painted furniture. It's open from 10:00 AM to 5:00 PM, Monday through Saturday.

AMELIA LOUISE
192 King Street   723-3175
This shop is an ever-changing kaleidoscope of 18th- and 19th-century antiques. Their slant is toward the decorative and the unusual with many accessories and objets d'art. Amelia Louise is open from 10:00 AM to 5:00 PM, Monday through Saturday.

AMERICAN STERLING GALLERIES
195 King Street   723-7197
Here's a shop offering a comprehensive sterling pattern matching service (both active and obsolete patterns) along with assorted hollowware and in-house appraisal services. They do some buying, too. The shop is open from 10:00 AM to 5:00 PM, Monday through Saturday.

ELIZABETH AUSTIN ANTIQUES
165 King Street   722-8227
Elizabeth Austin Antiques is another fine shop specializing in antique silver, jewelry, furniture and authentic accessories. The owner offers appraisal services, too, for insurance and estate purposes. The shop is open from 10:00 AM to 5:00 PM, Monday through Saturday.

GEORGE C. BIRLANT & COMPANY
191 King Street   722-3842
This is one of Charleston's oldest antique emporiums, having been around since 1929. They are direct importers of English 18th- and 19th-century furniture, silver, china, crystal and brass. Birlant is open from 9:00 AM to 5:30 PM, Monday through Saturday.

BRASS AND SILVER WORKSHOP
758 St. Andrews Blvd.   571-4342
This is a store dedicated only to select furnishing and accessories, silver plating, repairs and full restorations of all metals and fine art. Hours are from 10:00 AM to 4:00 PM, Monday through Friday.

CROGAN'S JEWEL BOX
308 King Street   723-6589
Crogan's is a shop dealing in elegant antique jewelry and affordable estate silver, hollowware and estate jewels. They're open from 9:30 AM to 5:30 PM, Monday through Saturday (see Shopping section).

CAROLINA PRINTS
188 King Street   723-2266
This shop deals in pre-1945 American art, antique prints, sporting art, Southern genre and museum-quality framing. The hours are from 10:00 AM to 5:00 PM, Mon-

day through Saturday.

CENTURY HOUSE ANTIQUES
85 Church Street   *722-6248*

Century House is a shop dealing in English and Chinese export porcelain of the 18th and 19th centuries. Business hours are from 10:00 AM to 5:00 PM, Monday through Saturday (but closed on Wednesday).

CHARLESTON INTERIORS & GARDENS
91 Broad Street   *577-9003*

Here's where you can expect the unexpected in antiques, gifts, accessories, art and garden ornaments. Business hours are from 10:00 AM to 5:30 PM, Monday through Saturday or call for an appointment.

COLEMAN FINE ART
7 Broad Street   *853-7000*

Coleman's specializes in art restoration and framing. The shop features portrait and figure painting by Mary Whyte, plus other artists. Hours are from 10:00 AM to 5:00 PM, Monday through Saturday.

D. BIGDA ANTIQUES
178 King Street   *722-0148*

This is another King Street dealer with a handsome collection of antique furniture from various periods, hard-to-find old sterling, interesting prints, paintings and collectibles — plus a nice assortment of estate jewelry. Hours are 10:00 AM to 5:00 PM , Monday through Saturday.

DEM GEMS OF CHARLESTON
18-A Anson Street   *723-0678*
or 1-800-538-6286

Only a block north of Market Street (toward Calhoun), catty corner from Hoppin' John's, is this fun collection of antiques and decorator items. There's an array of gift items and mementos of yesteryear all displayed in a small, classic Charleston Single House. Business hours are Monday, Thursday, Friday and Saturday from 10:30 AM to 6:00 PM ; Sunday from noon to 5:00 PM ; and closed Tuesday and Wednesday.

DI RESTA ANTIQUES
200 King Street   *853-8502*

This shop features Continental, English and American antiques with a special emphasis on equestrian art. They do some buying, too. They're open from 10:00 AM to 5:00 PM , Monday through Saturday.

EAST BAY ANTIQUE MARKET
28 Hasel Street   *577-3621*

You'll find a vast collection of goodies from more than 20 independent dealers who display their wares jointly in this convenient location, across from Harris Teeter. This market has everything, from old photographs to fine 19th-century dining furniture. This is a great shop for people who love hunting for those old collectibles that stir memories of yore. Hours are Monday through Saturday, 10:00 AM to 5:00 PM ; Sunday, 1 PM to 6:00 PM .

ESTATE ANTIQUES
155 King Street   723-2362

This is where you'll find a wide assortment of fine American 18th- and 19th-century furniture plus Oriental rugs and decorative accessories. The shop is open from 10:00 AM to 5:30 PM, Monday through Saturday.

THE GOAT CART
18 East Elliot Street   722-1128

This charming little nook is the original consignment shop with an assortment of antiques, trifles, Oriental furniture, porcelains, decorative items, rugs and 18th- and 19th-century American and English furniture. Hours are from 10:00 AM to 4:00 PM , Monday through Friday; 10:00 AM to 1:00 PM on Saturday.

GOLDEN AND ASSOCIATES ANTIQUES
206 King Street   723-8886

Golden and Associates carries English and American 18th- and 19th-century furniture, mirrors, and chandeliers. Shipping arrangements can be made to retail and the trades. Business hours are from 10:00 AM to 5:00 PM , Monday through Saturday.

THE GREY GOOSE ANTIQUES MALL AND AUCTION GALLERY
1011 St. Andrews Blvd.   763-9131

This is Charleston's upscale antique mall and auction gallery with over 1,500 square feet of changing merchandise. Business hours are 10:00 AM to 6:00 PM , Monday through Saturday.

GRANNY'S GOODIES
332 East Bay Street   577-6200

Here's a fun and funky shop specializing in vintage clothing for ladies and men, along with a wide variety of collectibles, furniture and jewelry from the near and distant past. Granny's is open from 10:30 AM to 6:00 PM , Monday through Saturday; 1:00 PM to 5:00 PM on Sunday.

INDIGO
189 East Bay Street   853-9206

This is a relatively new shop as King Street antiques go, but they carry a delightful collection of English 19th-century furniture, some Victorian pine, select folk art, wrought iron, plus decorative accessories and international crafts. Business hours are 9:00 AM to 5:30 PM, Monday through Saturday.

JAMES ISLAND ANTIQUES
2028 Maybank Highway   762-1415

Here, special shoppers will find 17th-, 18th-, and 19th-century furniture and accessories, including blue and white Staffordshire, pearlware, decorated stoneware, pewter, iron, tinware and woodenware. This shop is open by chance or by appointment.

JOHN GIBSON ANTIQUES
183 King Street   *722-0909*

This firm has been dealing in antiques on King street for nearly 20 years. Their crowded and fascinating shop features 19th-century furniture along with some fine old reproductions. Estate appraisal services are offered. Hours are from 9:00 AM to 5:30 PM , Monday through Saturday.

JOINT VENTURE JEWELRY, LTD.
185 King Street   *722-6730*

This is the area's largest estate and pre-owned fine jewelry consignment shop. It's open from 10:00 AM to 5:30 PM, Monday through Saturday.

LIVINGSTON & SONS ANTIQUES, INC.
163 King Street (also 2137 Savannah Hwy.)
723-9697, 556-6162, or 556-3502.

Livingston's is a direct importer of fine English and European antiques whose displays can be seen in their King Street shop or in their 30,000-sq.-ft. warehouse on Savannah Hwy. (US 17 South). Hours are 8:30 AM to 6:00 PM , Monday through Friday; 10:00 AM to 4:00 PM on Saturday.

PEACOCK ALLEY
9 Princess Street   *722-6056*

Here's a charming assortment of fine antiques, reproductions and decorative accessories located in a restored warehouse just off King Street. Their merchandise includes some interesting consignments from Charleston homes. Hours are 10:00 AM to 5:00 PM , Monday through Friday.

PERIOD ANTIQUES
194 King Street   *723-2724*

Period Antiques has an interesting, unusual and changing selection of choice American and European antiques, including furniture, paintings, mirrors and decorative accessories. It's open from 10:00 AM to 5:00 PM , Monday through Saturday.

PETTERSON ANTIQUES
201 King Street   *723-5714*

They bill themselves as "the last curiosity shop in America." In addition to furniture, their merchandise includes classical eclectic curios, objets d'art, books, porcelain, Depression glass, old art and decorative accessories. Appraisals are offered and they have full auction service as well. Hours are 9:30 AM to 5:30 PM, Monday through Saturday; 1:00 to 4:00 PM on Sunday.

PIAZZA
5 Fulton Street   *577-5094*

Here's a place specializing in antique needlepoint pillows and footstools, decorative antique furniture and accessories, plus unusual small gifts. Business hours are from 10:00 AM to 5:00 PM , Monday through Saturday.

MICHAEL B. POLIRER
123 King Street   *722-7488*

The shop offers a variety of furniture and accessories, silverware and jewelry — both purchased and

sold. Business hours are 9:30 AM to 5:00 PM , Monday through Saturday.

ROUMILLAT'S ANTIQUES
2241 Savannah Hwy.
Charleston (West Ashley)   766-8899
and 225 Meeting Street   722-0302

This is something of a departure from the veddy, veddy serious antique tradition of King Street in Charleston — but it's an awful lot of fun. Roumillat's has a vast array of used furniture and antiques that can turn out to surprise you. Some people find real gems in the rough. They say their selection is American and English antiques, Victorian, Edwardian and plain old-fashioned stuff. Call ahead for directions and the twice-monthly auction dates. Then go and enjoy. Hours are 10:00 AM to 6:00 PM , Monday through Saturday; and they're open Sunday afternoons 1:00 PM to 5:00 PM .

SAMUEL E. MCINTOSH, LIMITED
223-225 Meeting Street   577-6138

This is a fine source for 18th- and 19th-century English furniture and accessories, European porcelains, American prints and maps and fine reproductions. Hours are from 10:00 AM to 5:00 PM , Wednesday through Saturday.

SHALIMAR ANTIQUES

2418 Savannah Hwy.   *766-1529*

This shop, located five miles south of the Ashley River Bridge on Hwy. 17, has a large stock of quality antiques, clocks and furniture. They offer expert clock restoration and carry the area's largest stock of American primitives.

TERRACE OAKS ANTIQUES MALL

2037 Maybank Hwy.   *795-9689*

Here in a convenient mall atmosphere with 11,000 sq. ft. of space and free parking, you'll find American, English, primitive, country and collectable antiques. The mall hours are 10:00 AM to 6:00 PM , Monday through Saturday; and 1:00 PM to 6:00 PM on Sunday.

UPSTAIRS-DOWNSTAIRS

5 Fulton Street   *577-7042*

This shop carries architectural antiques, mantels, iron work, garden ornaments, imported tiles, lighting fixtures, furniture and accessories. Hours are 10:00 AM to 5:00 PM , Monday through Saturday.

VENDUE HOUSE ANTIQUES

9 Queen Street   *577-5462*

This beautiful shop, located in a 19th-century building in Charleston's fascinating "French Quarter," offers period English antiques, distinctive art objects and unusual gifts. Hours are 10:00 AM to 5:00 PM , Monday through Saturday.

VERDI ANTIQUES & ACCESSORIES

196 King Street   *723-3953*

This shop offers an interesting combination of Continental, French and American Empire, plus painted furnishings and other accessories. Business hours are 10:00 AM to 5:00 PM , Monday through Saturday.

VIRGINIA'S ANTIQUES

1011 St. Andrews Blvd.   *763-9131*

This shop, within the Grey Goose Antiques Mall, specializes in antique jewelry, sterling silver, porcelain, glass and objet d'art.

152 A.D.

152 King Street   *577-7042*

This is a shop decorators will love. And why not? The "A" stands for antiques and the "D" is for decor. They display a delightful assortment of unusual ideas for the eclectic home or office, including lamps, accessories, architectural items (mantels, moldings, etc.) plus some garden ornaments. Hours are Monday through Saturday, 10:00 AM to 5:00 PM and by appointment.

179 1/2 KING STREET

179 King Street   *577-0591*

The shop carries unique antique furnishings and decorative objects. Business hours are 10:00 AM to 5:00 PM , or by appointment.

Greater Charleston
Arts

Some people would tell you the verdict on Charleston and The Arts is still out — that after an early, spectacular (i.e. historic) start, the city fell artistically asleep and has been asleep since...well, the Civil War. Others would have you believe this is a virtual mecca for experi-mental and traditional art forms of all kinds — if only during Spoleto. And the truth probably lies some-where in between. There have been times, like the 1920s and early '30s, when Charleston seemed to feel artistic stirrings that resulted in truly exciting art.

Photo: The Post and Courier

The Artist Guild sponsors a Sidewalk Show on several weekends preceeding Spoleto.

In literature, there was Charleston's DuBose Heyward (1885 - 1940) whose legendary 1925 novel, *Porgy*, inspired a "renaissance" of artistic effort in and about the city and its people. The story — for those who may not know it — is factually based on the life of a poor, black, crippled street vendor and his tragic love for an abused, drug-addicted woman. The novelist's playwright wife, Dorothy, coauthored the stage play, which opened on Broadway in 1927.

Meanwhile, in 1926, none other than George Gershwin — already famous for his "Rhapsody in Blue" and headed for immortality as a composer of American musical standards — was fascinated by the story of Porgy. He felt it was just the vehicle he was looking for in order to compose a uniquely "American" opera. With the help of his lyricist-brother, Ira, and the Heywards, the project eventually made the magical transformation from the written page to the legitimate New York stage.

One of Charleston's favorite legends is about the summer George Gershwin spent here in Charleston (actually, in a beach house on Folly Beach) working on the opera. Yes, he did come here. And no, the house no longer stands — it washed out to sea years ago in a storm long since forgotten (although you might hear otherwise).

Although it took several years, the now world-famous and hauntingly beautiful opera known as *"Porgy and Bess"* was finally produced by New York's Theatre Guild in 1935. While it was never a staggering financial success (not much was in 1935), the work was universally and artistically acclaimed.

Since then, the opera has played all over the world, including in Milan's prestigious La Scala. But no audience could love it more than a Charleston audience does — where it was performed most recently in 1990 in a marvelous production at Gaillard Municipal Auditorium.

Neither Dubose Heyward nor George Gershwin would live to see *"Porgy and Bess"* reach the full zenith of its fame. Gershwin died of a brain tumor in 1937, and Heyward succumbed to a heart attack in 1940. The Heywards, along with their daughter, are buried in the graveyard of St. Philip's Church, not far from the "real" Catfish Row on Church Street — just below Broad.

Another highlight of Charleston's artistic "renaissance" would be the work of Alice Ravenel Huger Smith (1887 - 1858), watercolorist and "preservationist" of the Lowcountry's rice plantation landscapes.

In the late 1930s, when she began to realize that the old plantation life-style — especially the great rice plantation life-style of the 1850s — was dying out and might soon be forgotten, she recorded it in a series of paintings that are now integral to the permanent collection of the Gibbes Museum of Art (see Attractions, Other Museums).

Another important artist of the "renaissance" years would have to be Elizabeth O'Neill Verner (1883-1979). Her fascination with the architecture and streetscapes of Charleston can be traced back as early as 1903. One passion was etching, and her works (many illustrations of Charleston) are highly acclaimed. The work of Elizabeth O'Neill Verner, from about 1923 until the late 1960s, has almost come to "define" Charleston's renaissance "school" of art (see Galleries, Tradd Street Press).

But what about today? And what is all this "Spoleto" hoopla all about?

Festivals

SPOLETO FESTIVAL USA

Not every newcomer to the Lowcountry is familiar with the city's spectacular showcase for the arts called "Spoleto Festival USA." By the same token, no one stays in Charleston very long before hearing "Spoleto this...and Spoleto that...."

For openers, know that Spoleto (pronounced "Spo-LAY-toe," like tomato) is the New World counterpart to the summertime arts extravaganza in Spoleto, Italy, called the "Festival of Two Worlds." The latter was founded back in 1958 by Pulitzer Prize-winning composer-librettist-director Gian Carlo Menotti.

Menotti saw the little medieval town of Spoleto's rich architectural heritage, suitable performing facilities and central European location (about 60 miles north of Rome) as the perfect backdrop for an interdisciplinary celebration and exchange for international artists — young and old, rich and poor.

By 1977, Menotti was looking for an American home for his festival and for many of the same kinds of reasons, Charleston neatly filled the bill. With encouragement from Charleston's mayor, other impor-

Few Charlestonians, now, remember the fact that when Dubose and Dorothy Heyward were preparing for the 1927 stage production of *Porgy and Bess*, set designers arrived from New York to get the feel and flavor of the rotting but picturesque "tenements" where the characters of the play lived and loved. Much of what is now prime real estate "below Broad Street," would have been ideal (at the time) as typical Charleston slum dwellings. And the actual drawings that eventually were translated into the original production's sets were based on the rear of 99-101 East Bay Street — now in the heart of "Rainbow Row." Anyone who has been graciously entertained in that home (and many, many have) will recognize the arched kitchen-house steps and the other architectural similarities woven so artfully into the sets for this unforgettable production.

Insiders' Tip

tant members of the local community and the National Endowment for the Arts, Spoleto Festival USA premiered as a two-week long explosion of opera, jazz, theater and dance (including classical ballet) exploring famous and obscure traditional works as well as the new and the avant garde. The rest, as they say, has been history.

Charleston takes on a special glow during the festival. Almost anyone would agree with that. Maybe it's the international critics who review the performances in every day's special section of the *Post and Courier*, or the crowded restaurants and traffic-clogged streets. Perhaps it's the joyful noises that seem to be floating on the air all over town, the street performers, the sudden profusion of art galleries, and the excitement of a population swollen with young, talented people. But for whatever reasons, Spoleto is a time of great fun — and good art.

Don't miss it.

But alas, when the festival is over and they pack up the sets and costumes and truck them off to other more-distant parts...take heart. The Arts — and we mean quality billings — don't die out completely here, they just (thankfully, perhaps) slow down a bit after those weeks of saturation. You do have to work a little harder, however, to pursue them. Remember that the spirit of Spoleto fosters the development of greater and more appreciative audiences for arts activities in and around Charleston — *all* through the year.

Piccolo Spoleto

Piccolo Spoleto (translated "Little Spoleto") is the City of Charleston saying, "Encore! Encore!" It is Charleston's official companion festival (a series of festivals, really) running concurrently with the internationally acclaimed Spoleto Festival USA.

Piccolo's focus, however, is on local and regional talent of every artistic discipline. There are literally hundreds of events offered every year through Piccolo — most of which are relatively low-cost or free of charge.

Expect to see performances ranging from chamber music to provocative theater, to experimental dance, to visual arts.

One of Piccolo Spoleto's most popular events is the annual appearance of June Bonner's Coconut Club — a festive performance site and chic late-night watering hole that recreates the feel and fun of big-city nightclubs of the '40s and '50s. There are usually afternoon and evening shows, so everyone gets a chance to come in and play.

The city's Office of Cultural Affairs handles the project and sees to it, through its Artreach Program, that the festival's high spirits and fine performances get exported to artistically neglected sections of the community — where the arts can be experienced by everyone, regardless of economic status or educational background.

MOJA Arts Festival

The MOJA Arts Festival in the fall is the City of Charleston's celebration of the Lowcountry's rich and wonderful heritage from the African and Caribbean cultures. This 16-day performance schedule offers exciting theater, visual arts, dance, music, films and lectures.

"MOJA" is a Swahili word meaning "one" and "unity," therefore — "the source" and/or "the beginning." So the city's celebration of black arts is indeed appropriately named, since Charleston was the port of entry for thousands of slaves during the 18th and early 19th centuries and their contribution to America's culture is enormous. The festival is sponsored by the city's Office of Cultural Affairs and is funded in part by the South Carolina Arts Commission.

Theater

In the 18th century when Charles Towne was the capital of the Colonial province and thriving port of entry, there were reports in England that it was "the gayest, politest and richest place in America." So, naturally, it became one of the first American towns to patronize the arts and sciences — including the world of drama.

According to Eola Willis and her copious 1933 study of the city's early theatrical life, *The Charleston Stage in the 18th Century*, drama was alive and well here — as early as the

1730s. The city's first newspaper, *The Charleston Gazette* describes at some length the first theatrical season of 1734. That year on January 18, the *Gazette* carried the following notice:

"On Friday the 24th instant, in the Court-Room will be attempted a Tragedy called 'The Orphan, or the Unhappy Marriage.' Tickets will be delivered out on Tuesday next at Mr. Shepheard's at 40s each."

Apparently, the season's opening performance was a hit because on February 8th, the *Gazette* published its first "review" in which the prologue to "The Orphan" was reprinted in its entirety.

Then, quickly following on February 18th, "The Opera of Flora or Hob in the Well" opened with the dance of the two Pierrots and the pantomime of "Harlequin and Scaramouch." This was another first for Charleston theater, the first time a musical play had been performed on American shores. Apparently, the theatrical life of Charleston, South Carolina, was off and running by 1734 — and shines just as brilliantly today.

DOCK STREET THEATRE

Much ado is made about Charleston's many "firsts" and not the least of those stories is the one about the Dock Street Theatre being the first and oldest theater in America.

Well, let's split hairs here — just for accuracy's sake. It has been academically decided that the first theater in America was erected in Williamsburg, Virginia, in the second decade of the 18th century. The second was built in New York in 1732. The third was in Charles Towne in 1736, while Philadelphia didn't have a playhouse until 1749.

In the early 18th century, certain buildings were called "theatres" through they were no more than Long Rooms — rooms big enough to hold a crowd. These places were lacking a traditional stage and other theatrical facilities. The 1734 production of "The Orphan" was actually performed in a court room — just such a place.

Charleston's first theater was on the site of the old Planter's Hotel on Church Street. Church Street was then the only principal street running the entire length of the city. It ended at White Point, which is now known as The Battery (see Attractions, The Battery). Thus Church Street was the thoroughfare for all the traffic to and from the bustling and noisy docks. It made good sense to build a theater near this main traffic route, so in 1736 the first building was constructed on the south side of Queen (then called "Dock") Street, just a little west of heavily traveled Church Street.

Records show it was less than 100 yards from the Huguenot Church and St. Philip's. It was said to have had a stage, pit boxes and a gallery Perhaps some ill fate soon befell this building, because no mention of it is found after 1737.

Eventually, a second theater was constructed nearby, and an early hotel was built on the rear portion of the old theater lot. The year was 1800. It was called The Planters Hotel because it was a popular lodging for Lowcountry planters and their families who would leave their plantations at certain times of the year. It was customary to be in town for the winter social season and for Race Week. In 1835, the Planters Hotel was remodeled and expanded.

The old Planters Hotel is the structure that was still standing (but in ruins) when in the 1930s the WPA — giving work to unemployed architects and craftsmen during the Depression — rebuilt it as the theater we know today.

Technically, it is the oldest building still standing that was part of a Colonial theatrical enterprise. But the charming stage proscenium and the handsome paneled boxes we picture today as the Dock Street Theatre were not around to hear the prologue to "The Orphan" — not in 1734, anyway. It would be nearly two hundred years later that Charleston's own Dubose Heyward, already famous for his novel, *Porgy*, would write a special dedication for the occasion. It was November 26, 1937 and the reconstructed theater was to be called the "Dock Street" in honor of those early Charleston productions on the site.

None of the above takes anything away from the Dock Street Theatre's enormous popularity and charm — or the tremendously important role it plays in the theatrical life of the city today.

The reconstruction of the Dock Street auditorium recaptures the spirit of early Georgian theaters. It seats 463 people, has a pit, and a parquet of 13 boxes. The walls are paneled with natural local black cypress, rubbed soft and mellow. The wood was treated with an old formula of iron filings dissolved in vinegar, and then waxed — which brings out the grain. The lighting fixtures carry out the feeling of candle brackets and the cove ceiling has exceptional acoustic properties — as theaters of the time often did. Over the stage hangs a carved wood bas-relief of the Royal Arms of England (obligatory in all Georgian theaters), duplicated from an original that still hangs above the altar in Goose Creek's Chapel of Ease — built in 1711 (see Berkeley County, Historic Sites).

The Dock Street 's stage has a proscenium opening of 34 feet (somewhat larger than the original would have had) and features an apron forestage with "proscenium doors" on either side. This is quite typical of Georgian theaters. Today's Dock Street stage floor is flat where the original most likely was raked. The Reconstructed Dock Street was never intended to be a museum piece, but rather it was recreated to serve as a modern theater — capable of handling a wide variety of productions and become, once again, an integral part of Charleston's rich cultural life.

NORTH CHARLESTON COLISEUM
5001 Coliseum Drive   529-5050
North Charleston

Opened in 1993, the much-anticipated North Charleston Coliseum is the largest and most diverse indoor entertainment facility in South Carolina. Various seating configurations are possible, but generally speaking, the Coliseum's capacity is 14,000 seats. Because of this, the Greater Charleston area is now a viable audience for some of the biggest traveling shows and sports attractions in America. In its first year of operation the Coliseum has attracted Neil Diamond, Ringling Brothers Barnum and Bailey Circus, Reba McEntire, Metallica, World Cup Figure Skating, NHL Hockey and NCAA Basketball.

The Coliseum is also the permanent home of the South Carolina Stingrays Hockey Club which began play in the East Coast Hockey League in the fall of 1993.

Tickets for all Coliseum events can be purchased by phone at (803) 577-4500, the Coliseum Box Office or any SCAT Outlet.

Insiders Like:
Listening to the promising sounds of students doing their vocal exercises — floating down from June Bonner's vocal studio upstairs at the Dock Street Theatre.

Insiders' Tip

To get there, take the Montague Avenue exit off I-26 and follow the signs, or take the Montague Avenue exit off I-526 (Mark Clark Expressway).

SCAT locations are as follows:

Visitor Reception Center
375 Meeting Street, Charleston, 720-5618

Harbour Music
Orange Grove Plaza, (West Ashley) Charleston, 763-0303

Harbour Music
Aviation Square, 6185 N. Rivers Avenue, North Charleston, 572-6716

Harbour Music
Wando Crossing, 1501-6 Hwy. 17, North Mt. Pleasant, 884-5206

Leon's Menswear
975 Bacons Bridge Road, Suite 108, Summerville, 871-5029

Oakbrook Auto Center
1920 Old Trolley Road, Summerville, 871-6782

Monkey Music
320 King Street, Charleston, 723-7200

MWR Office
Naval Station, Bldg. 644, Code 15, North Charleston, 743-5233

MWR Office
Naval Weapons Station, Bldg. 708 Jefferson Street, Goose Creek, 764-7601

CHARLESTON AREA ARTS COUNCIL
207 East Bay Street, Suite 208   577-7137

The Charleston Area Arts Council is a great clearing house for information on the Lowcountry arts scene. If you're looking for a place to get an overview of arts activity in this area, this is the place to start. Actually, the CAAC is an umbrella agency that supports the arts — like the Trident Chamber of Commerce supports the Lowcountry business community. It's private, nonprofit, and supported by city and state grants; private foundations; corporate, group and individual members — about 450 members in all.

In spirit, the CAAC is based on the idea that — even in the arts — there's strength in numbers. And smaller arts organizations can accomplish more and be more financially successful when working together sharing creative ideas, facilities, promotional tools and management expertise.

The CAAC publishes a comprehensive calendar of events in conjunction with the Trident Chamber of Commerce to be included in every newcomer's packet. And their arts information hotline is now part of the News4 *Telesource* system (Dial 720-9248, Category ARTS, 2787). For a membership application or to receive more information on the Charleston Area Arts Council, call 577-7137 or write P.O. Box 21295, 207 East Bay Street, Suite 208, Charleston, SC 29413-2195.

OFFICE OF CULTURAL AFFAIRS
City of Charleston, Dock Street Theatre
Charleston   724-7305

This is the City of Charleston's office which advocates, services and helps fund the various arts organizations that help promote the city. It produces the MOJA Arts Festival each fall and Piccolo Spoleto in the spring. Call Diane Abbey, Director, for more details; or write The City of Charleston's Office of Cultural Affairs, 133 Church Street, Charleston, SC 29401.

Theatre

According to the League of Charleston Theaters, which is a support organization of Lowcountry performing arts groups and theater companies, their combined output is formidable. Their figures show they contributed $24,000 to the city's 1993 Piccolo Spoleto earnings. Member groups presented a total of 71 performances during the festival which were attended by more than 9,500 people.

Thumbnail sketches of some of Greater Charleston's theater groups follow:

AFRICAN AMERICAN REPERTORY COMPANY
28-B Blake Street, Charleston   577-2347

This group tours area schools and neighboring communities with plays about and by African Americans. For more information contact Derek Stuart.

AMAZING STAGE COMPANY
133 Church Street,
Suite 7, Charleston   577-5967

This group presents a full season of family-oriented plays and children's theater during an October through April season in the Dock Street Theatre. They offer various educational programs which explore stage management, scene study, projection and creative dramatics for beginners and advanced students, as well. Volunteers are encouraged to contact the theater to become involved; call Julian Wiles.

CENTER STAGE/DEPARTMENT OF THEATER, COLLEGE OF CHARLESTON, SIMONS CENTER FOR THE ARTS
Charleston   953-5600

Center Stage is the student organization at the College of Charleston which (together with the

SCAT Ticket Outlets are scattered throughout the Greater Charleston area to make ticket-buying for major events easier, quicker and more accessible to people living on the outskirts of the Lowcountry. Incidently, SCAT is the acronym for South Carolina Automated Ticketing — and they handle tickets for almost every major event, attraction and performance in the Lowcountry — at every major venue from the Dock Street Theater to Gaillard Auditorium to the Coliseum. The system is computerized so that a buyer in Summerville, for instance, has just as good a chance for a choice seat as does the fella who stands in line at the theater box office. It's truly an equal-opportunity, first-come, first-served system.

Insiders' Tip

Department of Theater) produces a varied season from October through April in the Emmett Robinson Theater. Student productions are staged in the Simons Center's flexible and highly creative Theater 220. For more information, contact Allen Lyndrup or Mary Holloway.

PREMIERE THEATER AT THE COLLEGE OF CHARLESTON DEPARTMENT OF THEATER COLLEGE OF CHARLESTON

Simons Center for the Arts   953-5805

Contemporary plays featuring the work of local professionals as well as faculty and graduate students from the College of Charleston Theater Department are staged by this group. For additional information contact Allen Lyndrup.

CHARLESTON ACTORS THEATER SOCIETY (C.A.T.S)

20-B Blake Street, Charleston   767-8731

This is an African-American company that works with new scripts in staged readings. They have occasional productions in Charleston and they also tour with the Artreach program. They have performed musicals during recent Piccolo Spoleto festivals. For more information, contact B. Spencer Prior.

CHARLESTON REPERTORY THEATER

931 Ashley Avenue, Charleston   577-7952

This group has traditionally produced classic one-act plays and new scripts as a part of "Off the Fringe" at Piccolo Spoleto. The company is currently expanding with regular offerings of longer contemporary plays. Their intention is to provide theater artists with a frame-

work organization under which new productions can take place. Call David Frederick for more information.

CHARLESTON THEATREWORKS

701 East Bay Street,
Charleston   853-5648

Currently, Theatreworks offers an extensive education program for children. Work is underway to finish a space for the theater school that would also be used for performances. They hope to produce a regular season of adult and children's plays this year. They are interested in recruiting volunteers. Call Mary Cimino for more information.

FLOWERTOWN PLAYERS

Box 1322, Summerville   875-9251

This is a community theater located in Summerville whose educational and literary objectives are to stimulate interest in the arts, music, literature and drama in people of all ages. They have a regular season of productions and their own home facility in downtown Summerville. Volunteers are welcome. Call Betty Sue Collins or Jerry Musselman for more information.

FOOTLIGHT PLAYERS

107 East Bay Street, Charleston   722-7521

This group recently celebrated their 60th season producing quality community theater in Charleston. They enjoy strong support from the traditional Charleston community for their long-standing record of exposing local audiences to interesting, instructive and cultural plays. Volunteers are welcome. Call Kit Lyons for additional information.

ROBERT IVEY BALLET/PRODUCTIONS
1910 Savannah Highway, Charleston   566-1343

Although Robert Ivey Ballet is primarily a dance company with a full-time studio, this production operation offers popular musicals on a fairly regular basis. Last summer, the RIB produced Hamlet at the Dock Street Theatre. For their theater productions, open auditions are held. Call Sharon Hodge or Robert Ivey for more information.

SHERI GRACE PRODUCTIONS
299 East Bay Street, Charleston   723-9291

Sheri Grace Productions has produced dinner theater at various venues throughout the Charleston area   They occasionally perform through a special arrangement with Events by Stephen Duvall.

TIGHTROPE PRODUCTIONS
29 Anita Drive
Charleston   766-6158

Although it has no set season of performances, Tightrope Productions is one of the most active theatrical organizations in the area — networking local actors, singers, dancers, and support personnel with Charleston's corporate/convention industry. They do everything from full-length plays and musicals to street theater, characterizations, and audience-participation drama. Lou White is their producer/director.

WORKSHOP SUMMER THEATRE
P.O. Box 32192
Charleston   722-4487

This all-volunteer organization has a unique focus on community theater at the grass-roots level. They are dedicated to providing talented newcomers and first-time directors with a forum for the dramatic arts. Now in their 17th season, the Workshop Summer Theatre usually (but not always) performs in the Footlight Players Workshop, and usually (but not always) during the summer months. For more information, contact the current director through their P.O. box, or the switchboard at Footlight Players.

Dance

BALLET ACADEMY OF CHARLESTON
1662 Savannah Hwy.   769-6932 or
Charleston   795-7779

The Ballet Academy of Charleston is under the direction Mara Meir, former ballerina with Ballet de Paris, and prima ballerina of the Israeli Opera. This is a fee-based school offering scheduled semesters of classical ballet training for children aged 4 through 17, with separate adult classes.

Children's trial classes are offered. No recital performances are held; parents view their children's progress through regularly scheduled open classes and conferences with the director.

ANONYMITY DANCE COMPANY
26 27th Avenue
Isle of Palms   886-6104

This professional modern dance company has been Charleston-based since 1985. They perform throughout the state with a wide repertoire of styles and works. The company is available for master classes in technique, improvisation, choreography, and classroom creativity for children. Contact Jennifer D. Strelkauskas, Artistic Director, for more information.

CHARLESTON BALLET THEATRE
280 Meeting Street, Charleston   723-7334

This energetic group presents professional dance concerts in Charleston and throughout the Southeast. They perform in their own facility during the city's Piccolo Spoleto, too. Their wide range of performances include such classics as *The Nutcracker, Sleeping Beauty* and *Swan Lake*. Call Don Cantwell for more information.

ROBERT IVY BALLET
1910 Savannah Highway,
Charleston   556-1343

The Robert Ivy Ballet promotes all aspects of dance education through local performances outreach to the larger community. The Robert Ivy Ballet's International Touring Company has represented the United States in the USSR and in South America. Call Robert Ivey for more information.

Music

CHARLESTON BOYS CHOIR
571-7207

This is a performing arts organization composed of fourth through eighth grade boys who love to sing. Chosen by audition, the boys rehearse twice weekly during the school year and perform sacred and secular music throughout the Lowcountry. Call Director Tim Shepard for more information.

CHARLESTON COMMUNITY BAND
556-3463

Now in its 18th year, this all-volunteer concert band performs 20 free concerts a year in various locations throughout the area. The group provides a wonderful opportunity for talented local adults to continue their musical pursuits.

CHARLESTON CONCERT ASSOCIATION
722-7667

This organization continues a 250-year-old tradition of presenting concerts in Charleston and brings various national and international companies to perform classical works at the Gaillard Municipal Auditorium. Season tickets are available. Contact Jason Nichols for more information.

CHARLESTON SYMPHONY ORCHESTRA
(Offices) 14 George Street   723-7528

Charleston has a long, rich and varied musical history; records indicate several different orchestras were organized in the city in the years from 1819 to 1919. Today, the organization known as the Charleston Symphony Orchestra has been in existence for more than 50 years.

In December of 1936, Miss Maud Winthrup Gibbon and Mrs. Martha Laurens Patterson founded what is known today as the Charleston Symphony Orchestra and they presented a concert in Hibernian Hall on Meeting Street.

The orchestra provided music for the official grand opening of the newly restored Dock Street Theatre in 1936. And the Dock Street became their official "home" for the first three years.

Through the 1940s and '50s, Memminger Auditorium was home for the group as they brought in such famous artists as Robert Merrill, Jan Pierce, Blanche Theirbom and Eleanor Steber. The orchestra played under the batons of conductors J. Albert Frecht, Tony Hadgi, Don Mills, and from 1962 to 1982 Maestro Lucien DeGroote.

In the late 1970s, the orchestra emerged as a fully professional organization with the employment of a core of full-time, conservatory-trained, first chair players. It achieved "Metropolitan" status in the American Symphony Orchestra League and adopted Gaillard Auditorium as their official home.

In 1984, David Stahl became the Music Director and Conductor. Under his leadership, the CSO became one of the leading arts organizations in the southeast. The orchestra's budget increased from $250,000 in 1984 to more than $1.5 million. Maestro Stahl and his assistant conductor, Lon Shull, plus a resident orchestra of 33 professional full-time musicians, perform a demanding concert schedule on stage and throughout the community — including special events and school programs throughout the state.

The orchestra has four major concert series — Masterworks, Chamber Orchestra, Light & Lively and Pops. In addition, the CSO performs other special concerts that cover a broad range of musical tastes.

During the 1992-93 season, the CSO set a goal of reaching 70,000 students via in-school concerts throughout the Greater Charleston (tri-county) area. CSO receives funds from the City of Charleston, the South Carolina Arts Commission and The National Endowment for the Arts.

Individual ticket sales are handled through SCAT locations; all season tickets are sold through the CSO offices at 14 George Street. Call 723-9693.

Look for the whimsical "frogs" by Lowcountry metal sculptor Charles Smith at Charleston Crafts, Inc. They're unforgettable.

Insiders' Tip

CHARLESTON SYMPHONY
ORCHESTRA LEAGUE

14 George Street, Charleston   766-2161

The 300-member Charleston Symphony Orchestra League serves the orchestra in many ways — although they're mostly known in the community as sponsors of the annual Symphony Gala and the Symphony Designer Showhouse.

Through fund-raising events, the League provides major financial support to the orchestra. They annually award scholarships to orchestra musicians for advanced study and to school-age musicians who are members of the Charleston County Youth Orchestra. Members volunteer many hours of service in the CSO office, promoting the orchestra, aiding in the sale of season tickets, and serving as concert ushers. The League welcomes any who wish to join and help in the support of the CSO.

CHARLESTON SYMPHONY SINGERS
GUILD

c/o 98 Wentworth Street   795-0506

The Singers Guild was organized in 1978 as the choral complement of the Charleston Symphony Orchestra. They are conducted by the group's founder, Emily Remington, who also serves as organist/choirmaster of Grace Episcopal Church. The group performs with the Charleston Symphony Orchestra in major works several times a year. In addition to the large concert group, there are two smaller performance groups which appear throughout the season. The Chamber Singers, under the direction of (CSO) Assistant Conductor Lon

Shull, perform twentieth century music. The second group, Songs of the South, is under the direction of Dr. Hank Martin and performs Civil War era music for conventions and local organizations.

Participation in Singers Guild groups is by audition. Auditions are held at regular intervals. Call Val Hirsch for more information.

EAST COOPER CONCERT SERIES

1516 Pine Island View
Mt. Pleasant   881-5027

This annual four-concert series, held on Saturday night at 8:00 PM at Christ Our King Church, 1122 Russell Drive in Mt. Pleasant, benefits East Cooper Community Outreach. Admission price to all concert events is a monetary donation or a food/paper product. Performers include various ensembles from the Charleston Symphony Orchestra, visiting concert choirs, and individual artists. Contact Lorna Tedesco for scheduling and more details.

Galleries

With so much history and architecture to share, Charleston may not be known primarily as an artists' colony. But, the city has produced a number of fine artists over the years. The charming illustrations of Elizabeth O'Neill Verner in the 1920s, '30s and '40s were certainly not the first artistic views of the city to catch the public's eye — but they were, and still are, among the most popular. There were others like Charles Fraser and Samuel Morse (the inventor of the telegraph) who were portraitists of great talent who worked here. Some of those artists and their works are on display at the Gibbes Museum of Art (see Attractions, Other Museums).

Today, downtown Charleston hosts an amazing array of fine art galleries that expand the view and the viewpoint far beyond the city Mrs. Verner loved to draw. Generally, when you're browsing in any of the downtown galleries, you're within easy walking distance from another...and another...and another.

The serious shopper with an appetite to see more than just a few galleries may want to park the car and ride Charleston's DASH shuttle system between stops. Take the Meeting-King Street route.

THE AFRICAN AMERICAN GALLERY
43 John Street   722-8224

There is always a colorful and changing collection here at this showcase for African and African-American art. Located just across from the Visitors Center, their exhibition room features original works from local, national and international artists. New exhibits are mounted every two months. Their prints and custom framing department has over 1,500 limited edition prints and posters. Their wearable art and gifts section includes one-of-a-kind garments imported from Africa. Jewelry from local craftsfolk, imported baskets, carvings and pottery are excellent gift ideas, too.

The African American Gallery offers a number of educational programs to schools, local commu-

nity groups and out-of-town visitors. These include gallery tours, lectures, poetry readings, meet-the-artist events, classes, workshops, multimedia presentations and more. African American Heritage tours to areas of historic importance in and around Charleston are offered in conjunction with licensed tour guides. Excursions and educational trips to Africa can be arranged through the gallery as well. Hours are 10:00 AM to 6:00 PM, Monday through Saturday.

AMERICAN ORIGINALS
153 East Bay Street   853-5034

Located between Broad and Queen Streets, this gallery carries decorative fine crafts and wearable art. Look for their silks and batik, tile art, metal sculpture, pottery, jewelry and 32mobiles. Hours are 10:00 AM to 5:30 PM, Monday through Saturday; Sunday hours are 1:00 to 5:00 PM.

THE AUDUBON SHOP AND GALLERY
245 King Street   723-6171

This is a favorite gallery of nature lovers and wildlife fans. You'll find old and new limited edition nature prints, traditional Audubon prints, 19th-century city views, engravings and antique plates. They carry original wildlife art and a wide assortment of merchandise related to birding, star gazing and nature study. Look for their good selection of children's nature-related educational materials, too. Hours are 9:30 AM to 5:30 PM, Monday through Saturday; and noon to 5:30 on Sunday.

BIRDS I VIEW GALLERY
119-A Church Street 723-1276 or 795-9661

Anne Worsham Richardson is a South Carolina artist and naturalist who is recognized all across America for her wildlife paintings — especially her birds. She maintains a private wildlife sanctuary outside her studio where she often takes in sick or injured birds. They frequently recover under her care and are reissued into the wild; but while they are healing, many birds have been "models" for her paintings. She has received many honors over the last few years; her latest being her induction into the South Carolina Hall of Fame at Myrtle Beach. Her gallery hours are 10:00 AM to 5:00 PM, Monday through Saturday.

BLUE KNIGHT GALLERY
816 St. Andrews Blvd
Charleston   556-9373

Across the Ashley River about a mile down St. Andrews Blvd., the Blue Knight Gallery is making a name for itself as a source for affordable artwork. Pre-matted and framed prints and posters as well as imported original oils are featured here. Especially nice is their work with painting restoration and conservation. And, they have a custom framing department that's well stocked and creative. Hours are 10:00 AM to 5:00 PM, Monday through Saturday.

CAROLINA PRINTS AND FRAMES
188 King Street   723-2266

This gallery specializes in American art pre-1945 and what they call "Sporting Art." It has been around for over 25 years — putting artists and collectors together. You'll find a wonderful selection of antique prints, original paintings and botanicals by Besler, Schwert and others. They carry Audubon prints and architectural drawings, too. Their staff is qualified to act as framing consultants as well. Hours are 9:00 AM to 5:00 PM, Tuesday through Saturday.

CHARLESTON CRAFTS, INC.
38 Queen Street   723-2938

This gallery, located just around the corner from the Dock Street Theatre, is the only permanent showcase for craft artists in South Carolina. Their exhibits include clay, fiber, wood, jewelry, metals, glass, photography, paper, traditional crafts, basketry, leather, toys and even soap making. Their juried membership offers a wide variety of gifts — from traditional to contemporary, from utilitarian to decorative, from affordable to exclusive. Demonstrations and featured crafts artists change every week. Hours are from 10:00 AM to 5:00 PM, Monday through Saturday; and Sunday from 1:00 to 5:00 PM.

COLEMAN FINE ART
7 Broad St.   853-7000

This is the needle in the haystack for anyone looking for an art restoration specialist. Services here include cleaning and revarnishing damaged or dirty oil paintings plus museum and custom framing for art of all kinds. They carry original works and some limited edition prints, as well. Commissions are accepted for portraits by Mary

Whyte. Hours are Monday through Saturday, 10:00 AM to 5:00 PM, or by appointment.

COURTENAY GALLERY
45 Courtenay Drive   792-6611

Located within MUSC's new Student Life and Wellness Center — between MUSC and the Veteran's Hospital — the Courtenay Gallery focuses on art for the mind and the spirit. Their exhibitions of twentieth century works by area artists change on a three month schedule and admission is free and open to the public. Special tours may be arranged for schools, senior citizens and community organizations through Susan Ravenel. Hours are 6:30 AM to 9:00 PM, Monday through Friday; 9:00 AM to 5:00 PM on Saturday; and 1:00 to 7:00 PM on Sunday.

COURTYARD ART GALLERY
195 1/2 King Street   723-9172

This gallery features ten Lowcountry artists and mounts special shows each month. Look for works by Jim Reed, Joann Davis, E. Charlisle Vorwerk, Coleen Cooper Stoioff, Bill Zobel, Jean Sinclair Beck, Lila Gray Cauthen, Amelia Rose Smith, Joanne Evans and Amelia Whaley. Hours are Monday through Saturday, 10:00 AM to 5:00 PM.

EAST BAY ART CO-OP
153 East Bay Street   853-5034

This gallery features contemporary paintings and sculpture by distinguished local artists. Included are mixed media paintings by Julie Rivers; photos and sculpture by Bob Brown. Look for works by nine other artists and sculptors in this unique and refreshing space. Admission is free. Hours are 10:00 AM to 5:30 PM, Monday through Saturday; Sunday hours are from 1:00 to 5:00 PM.

ERIC-CHRISTOPHER'S STUDIO OF HAND ENGRAVING
57 Broad Street   723-3604

Eric-Christopher (one name, two words) studied at the Corcoran School of Art in Washington, DC; with Barbara Norman in London; and Norman Dobbins in Germany. His craft is hand-engraved glass and he works with local cabinetmakers and framers in the execution of his custom designs. His work can be seen at his Broad Street studio or call for an appointment. Estimates are provided free.

EAST BAY GALLERY
264 King Street   723-5567

This gallery offers "the unusual and beautiful" in contemporary American crafts. Their companion gallery in Mt. Pleasant is located in Moultrie Plaza, 636 Coleman Blvd. (849-9602). Hours are from 10:00 AM until 6:00 PM, daily.

FRASER STUDIO & GALLERY
292 King Street   577-6039

West Fraser is an accomplished artist whose subjects range from cityscapes to portraits. His realistic paintings show a distinctive understanding of light and color — with an uncanny attention to detail. He has won numerous awards, and international publications have recognized his work. His studio includes the work of Mary Edna Fraser, a batik artist specializing in large-scale silk paintings and sculptures. Look for this fine combination of oils, batiks, limited edition reproductions and posters. Commissions are accepted. Gallery hours are 1:00 to 5:00 PM, Monday through Friday, or by appointment.

GALLERY EAST

15 Mid Atlantic Wharf 722-2858

Located in a renovated cotton warehouse only a block from Waterfront Park, this gallery features a large selection of local artwork, jewelry and sculpture. They carry limited and open edition prints and posters, too. Their custom framing department offers French matting and unusually creative matting ideas. Shipping and gift wrapping are available. Hours are 10:00 AM to 5:00 PM, Tuesday through Saturday, or by appointment. From May through August, hours are 10:00 AM to 5:00 PM, and noon to 4 PM on Sunday.

GALLERY TWELVE

290 King Street 723-0311

This storefront gallery features the work of award-winning Charleston artists and is the city's oldest artists' co-op. Look here for works by Otis Conklin, Jim Reed, Victoria Platt Ellis, Carolyn M. Epperly, Caroll W. Rivers, Margaret Hall Hoybach, Coleen Cooper Stoiff, Margaret Petterson, Nicki Williams, Connie Poulnot, Joan Davis, Daryl Knox, Diane Ratner, Karen Weihs and Patsy Tidwell-Slavens. Hours are Monday through Saturday, 10:00 AM to 5:00 PM, and by appointment.

GALLERIES WEST INDIES

73 Broad Street 720-8876

This gallery features African sculptures and new works by local artists Henri Vial and Alexander Luke Wallace. Hours are 10:00 AM to 5:00 PM, Monday through Sunday. Admission is free.

HALSEY-McCALLUM STUDIOS

20 Fulton Street 723-5966

Longtime favorites William Halsey and his wife, Corrie McCallum, show their remarkable contemporary works in their Fulton Street studio (second right turn off King St. past the Omni). This is the William Halsey for whom the College of Charleston named their student gallery in the Simons Center for the Arts on St. Philips Street. Call for an appointment.

THE GOIN GALLERY

309 King Street 722-4895

This is Charleston's largest gallery of contemporary art. All the work is original — by local and regional artists. They frequently mount special one-person or group exhibitions. They also carry fine, hand-pulled prints, Spoleto and Wildlife Festival posters, plus a fine selection of Charleston scenes. Their framing department is particularly good and appraisal services are available. Hours are 10:00 AM to 5:30 PM, Monday through Saturday.

JOHN DOYLE STUDIO

354.5 King Street   *723-3269*

Visitors to the Market Area who stop in at A.W. Shucks for lunch or for oysters and beer are totally surrounded by the unique work of Charleston artist John Doyle. His bold colors and striking figures are filled with life and a special warmth. Doyle's studio is on King Street, and special showings of his work or private commissions can be arranged. Call 723-3269 for specifics.

LOWCOUNTRY ARTISTS, LTD.

87 Hasell Street, next to
Omni parking garage   *577-9295*

Nine local artists operate this gallery in what was an old book-bindery shop. The quaint gallery has a fine selection of original watercolors, woodcuts, pottery, oils and prints. Their specialty is Charleston and Lowcountry scenes. You'll also find collages, hand painted tiles, colored pencil drawings, linocuts, monoprints, etchings and other graphics, too. Portrait, fine art and commercial art commissions are welcomed. Every month, one of the participating artists has a show of "new works." Hours are 10:00 AM to 5:00 PM, Monday through Saturday, or by appointment.

NINA LIU AND FRIENDS

24 State Street   *722-2724*

Nina calls this "a gallery of contemporary art objects." We call it fun. This quaint gallery makes a bold statement with a distinctive collection of glass, porcelain, jewelry, decorative ceramics and fiber art. Solo shows by nationally known artists are featured periodically, and you'll find paintings and sculpture there, too. The gallery is located in the downstairs rooms of a 19th-century town house in what is called "The French Quarter." Hours are 10:00 AM to 5:00 PM, Monday through Saturday, or by appointment.

SOUTH CAROLINA CENTER FOR PHOTOGRAPHY

132 East Bay Street   *723-6457*

This is a refreshing and well-mounted gallery exclusively for the display and sale of fine art photography — showing works by members of the prestigious South Carolina Photographers Guild. Hours are Monday through Friday, 10:00 AM to 3:00 PM. Call about Saturday hours. Admission is free.

Insiders Like:
Reading *Master Skylark* and *The Doctor to the Dead, Anthology of Black Legends and Ghost Stories*, by native son John Bennett. Bennett, who was born in 1865 and died in 1956, achieved much recognition as a writer, artist and illustrator before founding the Poetry Society of the South with Dubose Heyward.

Insiders' Tip

STEVEN JORDAN GALLERY

463 W. Coleman Blvd.,
Mt. Pleasant 881-1644

While not exactly on downtown Charleston's beaten gallery path, Steve Jordan's enormously popular work is well worth the trip over to Mt. Pleasant. He works primarily in transparent watercolor and occasionally in acrylics and pastel. His subjects range from Lowcountry scenes to international subjects. For ten years, Jordan was on the faculty at the Gibbes Museum of Art and is a member of AWS (American Watercolor Society). Over 30 of his works are available in print. His gallery includes hand-crafted jewelry, pottery and some sculpture. Hours are 10:00 AM to 6:00 PM, Monday through Thursday; 10:00 AM to 7:00 PM, Friday and Saturday; and 1:00 to 6:00 PM on Sunday.

TIDWELL-SLAVENS GALLERY

323 King Street 723-3167

This gallery features prints and oils from local, state and nationally known artists. Look for color graphics and original watercolors, too. Hours are 9:00 AM to 6:00 PM, weekdays and Saturdays. Sunday hours are from 1:00 to 4:00 PM, or by appointment.

UTOPIA

27 Broad Street 853-9510

This small, avant-garde gallery on Charleston's very traditional Broad Street seems like a non-sequitur, but it's a welcome and refreshing break. They display "alternative" fashions and art. Hours are Monday through Saturday, 11:00 AM to 6:00 PM.

VIRGINIA FOUCHE' BOLTON STUDIO & GALLERY

127 Meeting Street 577-9351

Another well-known and very popular Charleston artist and teacher is Virginia Fouche' (pronounced "fu-shay") Bolton. Her sensitive and colorful Charleston cityscapes and charming Lowcountry scenes are usually done in watercolor — as originals. However, her gallery offers lithographs and miniatures of her work, as well. Over the years, Ms. Bolton has received many awards and honors; the latest being a Grumbacher Silver Medallion. Her works hang in public and private collections across the country. Her Charleston gallery is managed by her daughter, Lucy Berryman. Hours are 10:00 AM to 5:00 PM, Monday through Saturday.

Greater Charleston
African-American
Heritage

**AVERY RESEARCH CENTER
FOR AFRICAN-AMERICAN
HISTORY AND CULTURE**

125 Bull Street
Charleston   *727-2009*

The rich culture of South Carolina African Americans has been recognized for many years for its unique national significance. However, the materials that document this culture have been widely scattered over the years and much of it has already been lost. The Avery Research Center for African American History and Culture of the College of Charleston was established to document, preserve and make public the unique historical and cultural heritage of this significant group — for this and future generations.

In October of 1990, The Center was officially established at 125 Bull Street in Charleston's historic district. Here, at long last, a growing archival collection and on-site museum could share the purpose of gathering together these valuable materials and encouraging scholarship on the subject.

The Research Center is located on the site of the former Avery Normal Institute — the local normal and college preparatory school which served Charleston's black community for nearly 100 years.

Avery Normal Institute was organized in October of 1865 by black minister F.L. Cardozo of the American Missionary Association for (in his words) "the education of colored children." In 1868, the school moved into the Bull Street building just five blocks west of the College of Charleston. There — for nearly a century — the school produced teachers for the community and gifted leaders for South Carolina and the nation.

The Center is actively soliciting manuscript collections — the personal and professional papers of individuals and organizations, oral and video histories, photographic records and other related documents. Donors may be assured their gifts will receive the care needed to store and preserve them.

The archival collections are regularly used to present exhibits and educational programs for the public. These activities are planned in conjunction with local and national African American celebrations and holidays.

The Reading Room of the Avery Research Center is open to the public Monday through Friday from, 1:30 PM to 4:30 PM. Morning hours are available by appointment.

Tours of the building and the museum galleries are conducted between 2:00 PM and 4:00 PM. Group tours are available by appointment.

Written inquiries about the Center or its archives should be addressed to: Avery Research Center for African American History and Culture, 125 Bull Street, College of Charleston, SC 29424. For more information, call Dr. Myrtle Glascoe, College of Charleston, (803) 727-2009.

SLAVE AUCTION BUILDING
6 Chalmers Street, Charleston

During slavery, Charleston passed an ordinance which said all slave sales had to be held in licensed market buildings. One of these buildings still exists on the downtown cobblestone street called Chalmers (between Church and State). For many years, it was a museum for black folk art and open to the public. The building has been vacant for several years.

The Basket Ladies

One particular art form practiced here in the Lowcountry has been recognized and celebrated virtually all over the world. It's found in the art museums of New York and Rome; it's among the Smithsonian collections; and it's evident along the sidewalks of Charleston's "Four Corners of Law" at Meeting and Broad. You'll find it downtown in the old Market, too, as well as here and there along Lowcountry highways — especially Hwy. 17 N.

We're talking about the weaving of sweetgrass baskets, a traditional African-American art form practiced here in the Lowcountry since the early 18th century.

These baskets are handmade of long bunches of sweetgrass, pine needles and bulrush, which are bound together with fiber strips from native Palmetto trees. They are coiled and formed to create a wide variety of baskets — all shapes and sizes, each one unique — which are both functional and beautiful in their own right.

Creating these baskets requires skilled craftsmanship and long hours of hard work. A simple, average basket may take twelve hours or more...while larger, more complicated versions may take up to two or three months to create.

Insiders' Tip

BOONE HALL PLANTATION

U.S. 17 North
Mt. Pleasant   **884-4371**

Once one of the largest cotton plantations in the south, Boone Hall dates back all the way back to the 1680s. At one time, it housed more than 1,000 slaves. Nine of the original slave houses still stand on "Slave Street." These structures, now frequently used by filmmakers for their stark authenticity, are open to the public on this still-working farm.

Boone Hall is open Monday through Saturday from 8:30 AM to 6:30 PM; and Sundays from 1:00 to 5:00 PM. (See Daytrips, Boone Hall.)

CABBAGE ROW

89-91 Church Street, Charleston

This downtown area was claimed as the inspirational setting for DuBose Heyward's 1925 book, *Porgy,* and George and Ira Gershwin's beloved folk opera *Porgy and Bess* (which premiered in 1935). "Cab-

The craft of weaving sweetgrass baskets has been a part of the Lowcountry since the early days of slavery. The skills are largely passed on from generation to generation. Traditionally, the men harvest the fiber and other plant materials from the local marshes and swamps; then the women weave the baskets.

While the bulrush, pine needles and palmetto strips are indigenous to and available here in the Lowcountry, coastal land development has begun to threaten their supply. Today, some basket weavers must go to Florida and along the Savannah River in Georgia in search of their sweetgrass. Because of this threat to one of the Lowcountry's most endearing traditions, Historic Charleston Foundation has recently sponsored a test project on James Island to cultivate sweetgrass as a crop. At this writing, the first crop of sweetgrass (several acres) is flourishing and it looks like the sweetgrass basket tradition — in terms of raw material, at least — may be more secure than it's been in years.

The result of all this labor and talent is truly unique. Each sweetgrass basket is utilitarian and beautiful, rich in the natural tones of the varied grasses, and elegant in its ethnic simplicity. Be sure to discover the wonderful sweetgrass baskets of the South Carolina Lowcountry.

Insiders' Tip

bage Row," the scene of the story, got its name from the vegetables regularly sold by area black residents from their carts and window sills here. Today, this section houses quaint little shops, but anyone familiar with the opera and its stage settings will see that this place (and the alleys around and behind it) could easily have been the original scene.

Was there ever a *real* Porgy? Was the story based on truth?

Many Charlestonians recall a poor, crippled man who lived here (in the early 1920s) and who used a small goat cart to get around. The other details of the story are hard to pin down on any one individual. But Charleston certainly had enclaves of black families who struggled against very difficult times. And their saga of survival and social interdependence was (and is) inspiring. Charleston clearly has hurricanes — and in those days storms struck with little warning. And surely then, as now, the ugly specter of drugs and violence influenced these people's lives and loves dramatically.

ELIZA'S HOUSE AT MIDDLETON PLACE

Rt. 4, Ashley River Road
Charleston, SC 29414   556-6020

After the Civil War, a number of freed slaves wanted to remain living and working on the huge rice plantation that was Middleton Place. They built "Eliza's House" for themselves in the 1870s. The building has recently been restored and is shown along with the other outbuildings which house demonstrations of weaving, spinning, blacksmithing, candle making, carpentry and pottery making — all tasks of the plantation slaves.

Eliza's House is open daily, from 9:00 AM to 5:00 PM. House tours are Tuesday through Sunday, from 10:00 AM to 4:30 PM. Contact Mrs. Alada Shinault-Smalls, Interpretive Coordinator for African-American History at Middleton Place for more information. (See Attractions, Middleton Place.)

DRAYTON HALL

3380 Ashley River Road
Charleston 29414   766-0188

This colonial era plantation house is shown to the public today as an architectural museum. It is considered to be the finest and earliest example of Palladian architecture in America. Built between 1738 and 1742, the structure is a monument to the 18th century European and African American artisans who displayed remarkably early and sophisticated skills. Now a property of the National Trust for Historic Preservation, Drayton Hall's Research and Education Departments are in the vanguard of the nation's effort to document and acknowledge the contribution of African Americans to the colonial south. Special events and educational programs at Drayton Hall offer insight into this culture and its modern legacy. For more information, contact Dr. George W. McDaniel, Director; or Megett Lavin, Education Director. Drayton Hall is open daily, except Christmas and Thanksgiving. (See Attractions, Drayton Hall.)

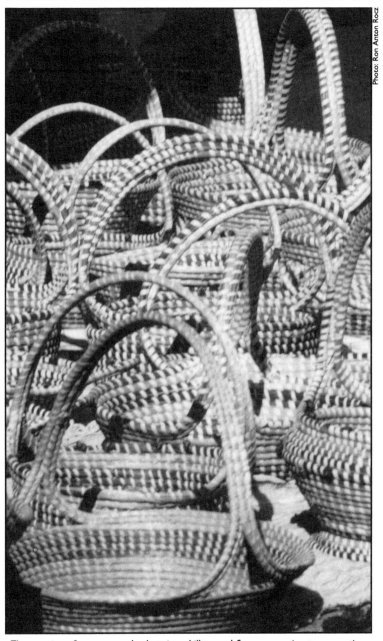

The weaving of sweet grass baskets is a skill passed from generation to generation.

CHARLESTON MUSEUM

360 Meeting Street
Charleston, SC 29403   722-2996

America's first museum, founded in 1773, has exhibits and art featuring African-American life in the South Carolina Lowcountry. Additional photographs and treasured information on African-American history and culture are housed in the museum's archives. Archival research is welcome; call the museum for an appointment. The Charleston Museum is open Monday through Saturday, from 9:00 AM to 5:00 PM. (See Attractions, Charleston Museum.)

BATTERY WAGNER

Morris Island

The first Union regiment of free black soldiers, the now-famous 54th Massachusetts Volunteer Infantry Regiment, fought on Morris Island during the Civil War. The bloody battle was an undeniable confirmation of the bravery, courage, and valor of the black soldiers and their willingness to fight for the North. Although the site is not (yet) memorialized formally, the island can be viewed during the Fort Sumter harbor tours which leave from Patriots Point in Mt. Pleasant or from Charleston's City Marina on Lockwood Blvd. Call 884-2727 for departure times. (See Attractions, Battery Wagner.)

Greater Charleston
Annual Events

Tradition is important to Low-country residents, and successful events often fall into that category. The Chamber of Commerce (853-5000) and the Office of Cultural Affairs (724-7305) are good clearing houses for many activities, but tickets or detailed information is available for specific events by contacting the numbers listed below.

January

"Hot" Festival
Hampton Park, City of Charleston Recreation Department, 724-7327

February

The Charleston Blues Festival
Lowcountry Blues Society, P.O. Box 291, Mt. Pleasant, S.C., 29464, or King Street Palace, 723-1075 or 722-3263
Lowcountry Oyster Festival
185 East Bay Street, Suite 206, Charleston, 29401, 577-4030
Royal Hanneford Circus
Gaillard Auditorium, 577-4500
Southeastern Wildlife Exposition
Dept. R.P.O. Box 20159, Charleston, 29413-0159
Valentine's Event
Citadel Mall, City of Charleston Recreation Department, 724-7327

March

Clyde Beatty-Cole Brothers Circus
Exchange Park, Ladson, 572-3161
Drayton Hall Annual Candlelight Concert
Drayton Hall, 3380 Ashley River Road
Festival of Houses
P.O. Box 1120, Charleston, 29402, 723-1623
Flowertown Festival
Summerville Family YMCA, 900 Crosscreek Dr., 29485, 871-9622
Kite Flying Day
Isle of Palms Park, Isle of Palms Recreation Department, 886-8294
Mini Walk (2 mile)
Downtown Charleston, City of Charleston Recreation Department, 724-7327
Ride, Charleston, Ride (10K)
Hampton Park, City of Charleston Recreation Department, 724-7327
Sunday Art in the Park Series
Hampton Park, City of Charleston Cultural Affairs, 724-7305
Tour Au Charleston (Biking Event)
Downtown Charleston, City of Charleston Recreation Department, 724-7327
"Wheel Good Time"

Hampton Park, City of Charleston Recreation Department, 724-7327

The Women's Show
Woman to Woman Magazine and Fox 24 TV, 884-0156

Cajun Festival
861 Riverland Drive, Charleston, 29412, 762-2172

April

Dinosaur Egg Hunt
Playground Road Complex, St. Andrews Parks & Playground Commission, 763-3850

Easter Bunny
Citadel Mall, Mall Merchants, 766-8511

Easter Bunny
Northwoods Mall, Mall Merchants, 797-3060

Easter Egg Hunt
Isle of Palms Park, Isle of Palms Recreational Department, 886-8294

Easter Event
Hampton Park, City of Charleston Recreational Department, 724-7327

Flowertown Festival
Summerville YWCA, 871-9622

Cooper River Bridge Run & Walk
MUSC Wellness Center, 45 Courtnay Drive, Charleston, 29401, 792-1586

Kid's Fair
Gaillard Auditorium, Jewish Community Center, 571-6565

Seafood Festival
P.O. Box 745, Mt. Pleasant, 884-2528

Charleston Jazz Festival
SCAT, 577-4500

Blessing of the Fleet
PO Box 745, Mt. Pleasant, 29464, 884-2528

May

Ashley Whippet Invitational
Isle of Palms Park, Isle of Palms Recreation Department, 886-8294

Festival Piccolo Spoleto
City of Charleston Cultural Affairs Office, 724-7305

Spoleto Festival U.S.A.
P.O. Box 157, Charleston, 29402, 722-2764

June

Piccolo Spoleto Finale
Hampton Park, City of Charleston Recreation Department, 724-7327

Sand Sculpting Contest
10th Street Beach, Isle of Palms, Isle of Palms Recreation Department, 886-8294

Arthur Smith/Johnson Outboards King Mackerel Tournament
P.O. Box 834, Charleston, 29402 (704) 366-4387

July

Celebration of Summer
Hampton Park, City of Charleston Recreation Department, 724-7327

Festival of the Fourth (Fireworks)
Brittlebank Park, Local radio stations, 577-6947

August

Kids Cane Pole Tournament
James Island County Park, Charleston County Parks and Recreation Commission, 762-2172

Summer Shine
Isle of Palms Park, Isle of Palms

Recreation Department, 886-8294
Folly River Float Frenzy and Fish Fry, 588-9258

September

Annual House and Garden Candle-light Tours
The Preservation Society, P.O. Box 521, Charleston, 29402, 722-4630
Buddy Bream Fishing Tournament
Charles Towne Landing, 556-4450
Caboose Wazgoose
Sullivans Island, East Cooper Arts Council, 881-0153
Children's Fishing Festival
Colonial Lake, City of Charleston Recreation Department, 884-0832
Children's Festival
Mt. Pleasant Recreation Department, 884-2528
Scottish Games and
Highland Gathering
The Scottish Society of Charleston, P.O. Box 254, Mt. Pleasant, 29465, 884-4371
A Taste of Charleston
Greater Charleston Restaurant Association, 185 East Bay Street, 577-4030
Charleston Maritime Festival
P.O. Box 20159, Charleston, 29402, 722-4630 or 1-800-221-5273

October

Children's Art Exhibit and MOJA Festival
Different locations, City of Charleston Cultural Affairs Office, 724-7305
Children's Festival
Mt. Pleasant, Mt. Pleasant Recreation Department, 884-2528
Coastal Carolina Fair
Exchange Club of Charleston, 572-3161
Halloween Carnival
Isle of Palms, Isle of Palms Recreation Department Exchange Club, 886-8294
Halloween Event
Hampton Park, City of Charleston Recreation Department, 724-7327
Halloween Festival/Trick or Treat Village
Playground Road Complex, St. Andrews Park & Playground Commission, 763-3850
MOJA Arts Festival
The Office of Cultural Affairs, 133 Church Street, 724-7305
Poe Festival
Sullivans Island, East Cooper Arts Council, 881-0153

November

Arts and Crafts Festival
Drayton Hall, 766-0188

Insiders Like:
The traditional graduation exercises held every spring at Ashley Hall — where the girls wear white dresses and carry arm loads of crimson roses.

Insiders' Tip

Battle of Sessionville Re-Enactment
795-3049 or 747-6656
Festival of Lights
James Island County Park, 795-7275
Plantation Days
Middleton Place, Ashley River Road,
Charleston, 29414, 556-6020
Thanksgiving Art Contest
Isle of Palms Recreation Center,
Isle of Palms Recreation Depart-
ment, 886-8294
Charleston Cup
South Carolina Jockey Club and
Stono Ferry, 766-6208

December

African-American Spirituals
Drayton Hall, Ashley River Road,
Charleston, 29414, 766-0188
Ashley Hall Christmas Play
Location varies, Ashley Hall School,
722-4088
**Breakfast With Santa and
Gift Making Workshop**
Playground Road Gymnasium, St.
Andrews Parks Playground Com-
mission, 763-3850

Boat Parade
Charleston Harbor, Parade of Boats
Committee, 884-7227
Candy Cane Lane
King Street, City of Charleston, 724-
3796
Family Yuletide in the Stableyard
Middleton Place, Middleton Place
Foundation, 556-6020
Kid's Christmas Crafts Show
Marion Square, City of Charleston
Recreation Department, 724-7327
Santa's Arrival on King Street
King Street, City of Charleston, 724-
3796
Visits With Santa Claus
Citadel Mall, Mall Merchants, 766-8511
Visits With Santa Claus
Northwoods Mall Merchants, 797-3060
Santa's Train Ride
Charles Towne Square Mall, Mall
Merchants, 554-7945
Winter Wonderland
Omni Hotel, Camp Happy Days,
571-4336

A Lowcountry
Daytrip

*H*ere is an adventure into the very heart of the Lowcountry. It's a day-long journey into a land of rivers and a fascinating look at some of South Carolina's early agricultural history.

In the 18th and early 19th centuries, this land and its waters spawned a rich, romantic, but fragile culture — largely based on a single cash crop: rice. Any real understanding of the Lowcountry and its ethic includes an appreciation for rice and the major role it played in the development of the area.

Toward that end, we'll visit the sleepy fishing village of McClellanville, once a cooler summer place for old plantation families...more recently the brave survivor of 1989s devastating Hurricane Hugo.

We'll pay a call on two important 18th-century plantations presented to the public in totally different (but valid) ways. And we'll explore old Georgetown, formerly the "rice capital of South Carolina." On the way, we'll encounter charming little chapels of ease that served the faithful plantation dwellers so far flung and isolated in South Carolina's earlier days.

And finally, we'll wander the quiet paths of Brookgreen Gardens, a unique and unexpected museum of 19th- and 20th-century American sculpture built on lands once granted to Lowcountry colonists by King George II of England.

Start at the foot of Charleston's Cooper River Bridge, on S.C. Hwy. 17 North. Follow the signs on the bridge marked, "Georgetown. Hwy. 17-701." DO NOT take the right turn at the far end of the bridge leading to the village of Mt. Pleasant.

THE COOPER RIVER BRIDGES

Once described as "a new traffic epoch" by its Jazz Age builders, the old "Cooper River Bridge" on your left is now the overcrowded, often cursed, foil for rush hour commuters to and from peninsular Charleston. Officially named the John P. Grace Memorial Bridge in honor of a former Charleston mayor, the span was the 5th longest suspension bridge in the world when it was opened in 1929. It took 14 months to complete at a cost of more than $5.7 million and 14 lives. Its narrow, roller-coaster, 2.7 mile-long ride provides a spectacular view of the Cooper River for some travelers; sweaty palms and a pounding heart for many others.

In 1946, the freighter *Nicara-*

gua Victory, adrift in gale force winds, crashed into the eastern approach of the bridge tearing away a 100-yard section of the roadway — sending one car with its family of five into a watery grave below. So vital was this Charleston to Mt. Pleasant traffic link that an old iron bridge was barged in to serve as a temporary patch. Huge cranes hoisted it up to the span so cars could gingerly cross while permanent repairs were planned.

By 1966, increasing traffic and a more impatient public demanded better access to and from the peninsula, so a second and wider span was added. The new bridge was named the Silas N. Pearman Bridge in honor of a South Carolina Commissioner of Public Works.

Continue along the U.S. 17 Bypass for about 8 miles through commercial development. Then, look to your right for a small, tin-roofed chapel with an octagonal cupola. Pull into the churchyard through the open gate.

CHRIST EPISCOPAL CHURCH

Here's your first chance to encounter one of the Lowcountry's most charming "undiscovered" treasures, one of the little-known but much-loved chapels of ease. Millions of tourists visit the area and never even know these little "testimonies" to the Lowcountry's bygone plantation era still exist. But they do exist — in various forms and in varied states of repair and use.

First, however, a little background information is required:

The colony of Carolina was founded with the Anglican church named as its established religious force. Early on, Anglican congregations received financial assistance from the British government to construct appropriate houses of worship. These first Anglican churches also tended to benefit from the generosity of wealthy planters in their congregations. As a result, these churches were built with greater architectural sophistication than those of other religious organizations. And it's mostly these better-built, early Anglican structures that survive today as mute witness to the strength of religion in the early colonies and the isolation of plantation life.

Christ Church Parish was one of ten parishes established by the Church Act of 1706. The following year, a wooden building was in place on this site serving a slowly growing number of communicants. When fire destroyed the wooden building in 1725, a new brick structure was completed in 1726.

In 1782, British soldiers burned the church to the walls during the Revolution and it wasn't rebuilt until about 1800. In 1865, during the Civil War, fire all but destroyed the church again; and although it was once more rebuilt, regular services were discontinued by 1874. Finally, in 1925, both the structure and the congregation were restored by descendants of early Christ Church Parish families.

Despite its long, hard struggle for survival, Christ Church is a viable, active congregation today. Sunday services are: Holy Eucharist, 8:00, 9:00, and 11:15 AM.

Chances are, your initial excursions into the Lowcountry's plantation past led you along the Ashley River, not the Cooper. If so, you missed the opportunity to visit some of the vast plantations that once flourished along the Cooper. Not the least of them is Boone Hall Plantation...and here's your chance.

To find Boone Hall, cross the double highway opposite Christ Church to Longpoint Road and look for the sign. Less than a mile up Longpoint Road on your right is Boone Hall's entrance.

BOONE HALL PLANTATION
Highway 17 North   *884-4371*

Boone Hall Plantation is a 738-acre estate dating back to the 1680s when the Lords Proprietor made this sizable land grant to an early English settler, Major John Boone.

During the 18th and 19th centuries, Boone Hall was a thriving cotton plantation covering more than 17,000 acres. Brick was also a plantation product: they were used in the construction of the original mansion, cotton gin house, slave cabins and circular smokehouse. Later, Boone Hall was famous for its large groves of pecan trees, many of which are still productive today.

Boone Hall is a favorite of photographers and filmmakers because of its magnificent avenue of live oaks and the nine original, unrestored slave cabins (c. 1743) which once housed the plantation's skilled craftspeople and the house servants. The original Boone Hall mansion was lost in a tragic fire and the present structure dates from the mid-1930s.

It's interesting to note that this is where extensive location filming was done for the Warner Brothers/ABC-TV mini-series, "North and South."

Admission is: Adults, $4.25, children 6-12, $1.00. The property is open all year except Thanksgiving and Christmas Day, Monday through Saturday, 9 AM to 5 PM., Sundays 1 to 4 PM. From April 1 through Labor Day, the hours are 8:30 AM to 6:30 PM, Sundays 1 to 5 PM.

Now, return to S.C. Hwy. 17 and turn left. (Note the double lane road and cross over the two oncoming lanes before turning left.) Keep following S.C. Hwy. 17 straight ahead and note the signs designating the Francis Marion National Forest on both sides of the highway.

THE FRANCIS MARION NATIONAL FOREST

This quarter-million acre tract includes sections of both Charles-

---

Insiders Like:
Crabbing off an old dock along some Lowcountry creek with nothing more than a scoop net and a raw chicken neck tied to a string.

Insiders' Tip

ton and Berkeley Counties. Once the battleground where the legendary General Francis Marion (the "swamp fox") engaged Col. Banastre Tarleton's British troops during the American Revolution, this vast park is now a wildlife reserve and a microcosm of Lowcountry habitat as it miraculously inches back to life after the ravages of Hurricane Hugo in 1989.

Continue on S.C. Hwy. 17. At about mile 33, look for the sign on the right marking the intersection of S.C. Hwy. 45. Turn right to discover McClellanville.

McClellanville

This sleepy old fishing village nestled amongst the live oaks along Jeremy Creek was once the summer haven for planters living on the Santee River. More recently, however, McClellanville is best known as one of the small towns that bravely and miraculously survived Hurricane Hugo.

Eons before the town was known as McClellanville, it was one of the small villages occupied by the Sewee Indians. Archeology shows it's one of the few sites in South Carolina that has been continuously occupied by humans for thousands of years.

The beginnings of the existing village date back to the mid-1800s when rice planters on the Santee River built retreats there — away from the disease-ridden, backwater plantations. A devastating hurricane in 1822 had completely wiped out a village of planter homes on nearby Cedar Island and the new site was thought to be safer from storms. Then, after the Civil War, some of the area planters were forced to completely abandon their plantations and move into the little summer village on a permanent basis.

McClellanville wasn't actually "McClellanville" for many years until it became necessary to christen it something for post office and other "municipal" purposes. Several names were discussed, including "Jeremy" or "Jerryville" — after the creek of the same name. And even "Romain" was considered — after Cape Romain. But the village was finally named "McClellanville" for one of its early citizens, A. J. McClellan.

In the 1920s, it became one of the first places in the state where shrimpers from the west coast of Florida would come to trawl the rich coastal waters for shrimp. Eventually, the town developed into one of the major shrimp ports in the state.

The old buildings in McClellanville reflect the architectural development of the town from a summer retreat for plantation families to a thriving, incorporated town. You'll find residential, commercial, religious and educational properties dating from the 1860s to the 1930s.

Of the hundreds of thousands of stories spawned by the forces of Hurricane Hugo on September 21, 1989, the story of McClellanville is among the most memorable.

A small plaque has been placed on a wall near the cafeteria door in McClellanville's Lincoln

Photo: The Post and Courier

Motorboating on the creek.

High School. It's a little more than six feet above the floor and it shows how high the water rose that night. But no 8" x 10" plaque can measure the level of fear experienced by the 400 or so people who had gathered there for shelter against the storm.

In the pitch black night — as the storm center pushed violently over peninsular Charleston some 35 miles to the south — the accompanying tidal surge rushed in on McClellanville with horrendous force and speed.

What was essentially the entire black population of the town had just settled in for what they hoped would be only a moderately uncomfortable night. There was excitement, to be sure. And dread. And worry. But the primary concern was getting the children and older people settled in as comfortably as possible. Toward that end, people were scattered throughout the building in various hallways and classrooms.

Suddenly, they heard a strange, rushing noise above the already fierce storm. Cold, black water rushed in from everywhere pinning the exit doors shut and turning the school into a nightmarish death trap.

Some people scrambled onto the bleachers in the gymnasium as the waters quickly climbed after them. Others crowded up onto the school's stage and literally held their children over their heads as the water surged in — up to their chests.

They sang and prayed and cried and comforted each other throughout the seemingly endless night. Then, finally, the water began to recede. What the stunned survivors found outside by dawn's earliest light was literally unrecognizable....

Amazingly, no one drowned in the McClellanville calamity at Lincoln High School. One life was lost — later. But it could so easily have been a disaster with hundreds of lives lost.

Today, McClellanville is remarkably recovered. If you drive into the village via Pinckney Street, note the New Wappetaw Presbyterian Church (c. 1830) on the right. Sunday services there start at 11 AM; Sunday School begins at 10.

Turn right on Oak Street and drive about two blocks to St. James Santee Episcopal Church (whose congregation dates back to c. 1706) This charmingly pure, shingle-Gothic structure was built in 1890.

Don't leave town before you drive up to the docks for a view of McClellanville shrimp fleet harbored there along the Intracoastal Waterway.

Return to Highway 17 North via Pinckney Street and turn right. About 100 yards up the road, a sign marks the intersection of South Santee Road (marked S.C. 857). Turn left and follow it to the entrance of Hampton Plantation.

HAMPTON PLANTATION (c. 1750)

The origins of Hampton Plantation can be traced back to the earliest European settlement of the Santee delta. The Horry family, who built and developed the property, were descendants of French Huguenots who had emigrated to Carolina in search of religious freedom and economic advancement.

The Horrys are thought to have acquired the land on which Hampton now stands during the period between 1700 and 1730. The actual date of construction for Hampton's main house is not clearly known, but according to early records, "(it) was built about the year 1750 by Col. Daniel Horry...."

The Horry land holdings on Wambaw Creek comprised some 5,000 acres and they were worked in the traditional manner — like most of the other Lowcountry plantations at the time. Rice was grown on the swamp lands along the water and these rice fields were carefully connected by a complicated system of canals and ditches. The fields were flooded and drained as the demands of the rice growing season required.

Indigo (used in the dying of wool) was another Hampton cash crop. For a time, there was a profitable demand for indigo because England used it in vast quantities for the dying of British naval uniforms.

In fact, the Daniel Horry who supposedly built Hampton Plantation married the daughter of a famous South Carolinian credited with growing the first successful indigo crop in the Lowcountry. Her name was Eliza Lucas Pinckney. As a young widow, the legendary Mrs. Pinckney more or less attached herself to her daughter's household and, for over twenty years, played a major role in the daily life at Hampton.

During the American Revolution, while most of the prominent men were "off" engaging the British enemy at various places, a colony of wives and children sought refuge at Hampton — relatively isolated from the military action. The dozen or so ladies sheltered there represented something of a Who's Who of South Carolina Colonial history. Women with names such as Drayton, Middleton, Rutledge, Izard and Huger were in attendance at various times.

Hampton's famous portico plays another interesting role in the plantation's long story. It may have been built specifically to impress one of Hampton's early distinguished visitors.

In 1791, President George Washington made a grand tour through the still very young United States of America. On May 5th, according to Washington's own diary, he "breakfasted and dined at Mrs. Horry's about 16 miles from Georgetown." The traditional story is that as the President was brought up the steps of the glorious new portico at Hampton, Mrs. Horry and her mother, along with the youngest Horry daughter, greeted Washington wearing "sashes and bandeaux" hand-painted with likenesses of the President.

Another story is that Washington was asked whether or not a young oak tree growing directly in front of the house should be removed to improve the view. The President is supposed to have suggested the tree be spared — and so it was. At any rate, what remains of a giant old live oak can still be seen today located directly in front of the house.

Circumstances found the actual welfare of Hampton Plantation left largely up to the Horry women during the busy years between the Revolution and the beginning of the Civil War. As ownership passed from daughter to daughter (and the married name became Rutledge), Hampton faded as a viable agricultural operation.

In 1865, at the age of 22, the young master of Hampton — Henry Middleton Rutledge — joined the Twenty-Fifth Regiment of North Carolina. Eventually, he was elected to lead his unit through the war. Before the war was over, his regiment had suffered 200 killed in action, 280 dead from disease, and 470 wounded — with 140 of those wounded more than once.

Of course, life at Hampton was drastically altered following the war. The family struggled to cope with the financial requirements of maintaining the house, but the drastically altered economic climate made life very difficult. Rice was no longer profitable, and Hampton was too far from the struggling markets to try and raise cotton, corn or tobacco in any volume.

Hampton, during those years, must have presented quite a strange juxtaposition; the proud, classical portico surrounded by a lawn planted in string beans and crowded with chickens....

By 1923, both Col. Henry Rutledge and his wife, Margaret

Hamilton Seabrook, were dead. Hampton sat empty and neglected for a number of years until 1937 when the Colonel's youngest son, Archibald Rutledge, retired to his family's ancestral home.

Archibald Rutledge was a man of letters; he'd published his first book of poetry in 1907. His prowess with poetry and prose always reflected his love and nostalgia for life on the Santee. By 1934, in recognition of his burgeoning literary reputation, Archibald Rutledge was named poet laureate of South Carolina.

In 1941, he published his most popular work, *Home by the River*, in which he described his efforts to restore Hampton Plantation to its former glory. Over the course of more than 30 years, hundreds of visitors were eventually received at Hampton — drawn to the plantation and its owner by the popular works of Archibald Rutledge.

By 1971, in failing health, Rutledge sold the house and seventy-five acres to the State of South Carolina. He died in 1973 and was buried in the family cemetery on Hampton's grounds.

When Hampton Plantation became a state park, the house had been unoccupied for several years. Initial inspections quickly indicated that an extensive renovation would be absolutely necessary. While documentary research about the house and its owners went on, another story began to unfold: the evolution of the house itself.

The exposed fabric of the house revealed that most of the interior walls had been covered with modern materials over the course of the previous century. And as the newer surfaces were removed, the ancient framework of Hampton was exposed. This afforded researchers an excellent opportunity to display sections of the original house as well as the different patterns of modernization and change that evolved in a Lowcountry plantation house on the Santee delta.

Like Drayton Hall on the Ashley River, Hampton Plantation offers visitors an architectural look at the sophisticated lifestyles pursued by some of the Lowcountry's earliest families.

Hampton Plantation (the state park) with its picnic grounds and screened cabanas is open Thursday through Monday from 9 AM to 6 PM. The house is open from 1 to 4 PM. Admission is $2 for adults, $1 for youths aged 6 to 16, and it's free for children under 6. Call 803-546-9361 for more information.

As you leave Hampton and return to S.C. 857, turn right. This will bring you to a sandy road leading off to the left. This remote and almost abandoned stretch of wilderness eventually brings you to another early "chapel of ease" — this one built for the spiritual needs of the planters along the Santee delta.

Bear in mind, you're well off the beaten track, here. Real Insiders shouldn't be daunted by a lonely, sandy road leading apparently into the pages of history and the beguiling mists of time.... But we'd better say, here, that if the road is wet and muddy — proceed at your own risk. If you see recent tire tracks, you can be safely encouraged to try it. When you get there, you won't be disappointed....

St. James Santee
Church (c. 1768)

Finding this incredibly sophisticated, early architectural treasure sitting here in the (apparent) wilderness is your first surprise. Your second jolt may be learning it was built (in about 1768) not as the first, but the fourth church to serve St. James Santee Parish. But let this simple fact dramatically say just how important religion was to these early Carolina settlers.

St. James Parish was a thriving neighborhood of planters who petitioned the church for a "new" chapel that would be more conveniently located near Wambaw Creek. The building eventually provided for them was completed shortly after the completion of St. Michael's in Charleston at Meeting and Broad streets. In fact, the impressive design of St. Michaels may have actually influenced this structure, in that both designs employ the use of two bold, classical porticos. Here the porticos are supported by four, gently fluted brick columns complete with brick bases and brick (Doric) capitals.

If you're lucky, the church may be open and you can see the high-backed, boxed pews separated by a cross axis of clay tile flooring. If the church isn't open, discreet window peeking is definitely called for.

Amazingly, these beautiful, hand-hewn box pews have never been painted — ever — although sometime in the 18th century they were rearranged so the chancel might face the east wall. What is (now) the rear portico has been enclosed as a vestry room, and the simple pulpit on the north wall is a modern replacement. But the general ambiance of this little chapel in the wilderness is overwhelmingly authentic.

Sitting here so proudly in this quiet, woodland setting, St. James Santee Church seems to generate its own will to survive. So haunting was this relic of the Lowcountry's plantation past that, although the church's communion silver was stolen during the Civil War, it was quietly returned at a later date....

In the churchyard, barely legible tombstones (best translated from paper rubbings) relate stories of fierce Revolutionary battles and

If you managed to do everything on this daytrip in a single day, you are to be congratulated — and summarily sent home for a long, quiet rest! Chances are, you learned miles and miles ago that the Lowcountry is a fascinating and almost endless adventure in history. The pace you set is strictly your call. Whether you spend a day... or two... or stay for a lifetime, the journey is unforgettable. Our hope is that this Insiders' daytrip guide has helped you along the way.

Insiders' Tip

the closely held relationships between the strong, early families of the Santee delta.

Turn around and go back to Hwy. 17 and (turn right) heading northeast toward Georgetown. At what should be about mile 56, there's a sweeping curve in the road which preludes the delta of the South Santee River and its plantation system.

Your vista both to the right and to the left is not natural marsh but what remains of vast rice fields, once worked by 19th-century slaves when Georgetown was the "rice capital of the Carolinas."

Just across the high bridge over the North Santee — another branch of the Santee's widespread water shed to the Atlantic — you'll encounter the white-painted gates of Hopsewee Plantation on your left.

HOPSEWEE PLANTATION

Hwy. 17, twelve miles
south of Georgetown   *546-7891*

Hopsewee Plantation was built in 1740 and was the birthplace of Thomas Lynch, Jr., a signer of the Declaration of Independence. This is the only rice plantation in Georgetown County that is presently open to the public.

Amazingly, only four families have ever owned Hopsewee. Today, it is owned by Mr. and Mrs. James T. Maynard who graciously open their house and grounds to the public. Theirs is a remarkably refreshing attitude toward historic preservation in that the Maynards live in Hopsewee — but with a respect for and obligation to its place in history.

Although the main house at Hopsewee has been modernized for today's living, it is handsomely furnished with antiques and period furniture, which make it very easy to picture life here as it was in Thomas Lynch's day.

Be sure to visit the cook house/slave cabin — so few of them survive today. This one is furnished with tools, crockery and cooking utensils appropriate to its original purpose. It's important to realize that the work in these "dependency" structures — like the backbreaking work done in the rice fields — made the more formal life of the main house possible.

Hopsewee is located on the North Santee River overlooking the former rice fields of the river's delta. Imagine the beautiful views Lynch was able to see every day...as he pondered the dangers and daring consequences of national independence.

Hopsewee is open Tuesday through Saturday, 10 AM to 5 PM. It's closed on holidays, but special tours can be arranged in advance by appointment. Admission is $5 for adults, $2 for children (ages 6 to 18), and for cars entering the grounds but not touring the house, the fee is $2.

Continuing north on Hwy. 17 (for about 12 more miles past Hopsewee Plantation) you'll cross a high bridge over the Sampit River and pass a large industrial complex on your right. Then, once in Georgetown proper, turn right off Hwy. 17 and you'll quickly find yourself downtown.

GEORGETOWN

More than any other South Carolina community of its size, age and historical importance, Georgetown is respectful of its past. What the visitor sees here today — streets and streets of charming 18th- and 19th-century homes — reflects this consciousness quite beautifully.

Several preservation organizations in the community can share the credit for this effort. They include the Georgetown County Historical Society, the Georgetown County Historical Commission, and the Historic Georgetown County Foundation. These groups were instrumental in collecting data pertaining to the community, marking and preserving historic homes and sites, and educating new generations about the former "Rice Capitol of the South."

Downtown Georgetown was recently revitalized and now has interesting shops and restaurants backed up against the once bustling riverfront docks.

At the intersection of Front and Scriven streets, you'll see an interesting old brick building with a clock tower. This is Georgetown's famous Rice Museum — and it's a great first stop toward understanding the giant rice industry that once made Georgetown the thriving agricultural focus of the Lowcountry.

THE RICE MUSEUM

Front and Scriven streets   *546-73423*

The real story of the rice culture of Georgetown County is one of the most exciting and colorful chapters in the history of South Carolina — maybe even the whole history of American agriculture. It's all been captured here in The Rice Museum through fascinating maps, pictures, artifacts, exhibits and intricate dioramas that portray a rice crop from planting through processing and eventual shipment to markets all over the world.

The Rice museum is located in the Old Market Building which locals call "the town clock." This clock tower has become the architectural symbol of Georgetown and this is an appropriate place to browse through booklets and tourist information pertaining Georgetown County.

Sometime in 1993, The Rice Museum will inaugurate an exciting new exhibit called "The Brown's Ferry Vessel." This is what remains of an early commercial river vessel that once plied the waters of the Carolina coast during the first half of the 18th century. (Heretofore, very little has been known about South Carolina river vessels of this early period.)

This one, which was carrying a load of bricks when it sank near Brown's Ferry in about 1740, has been excavated from its long-time resting place and laboriously preserved for eventual display. The remaining section of its hull and keel will shed invaluable light on a dimly lit facet of the Lowcountry's transportation history.

Museum hours are 9:30 AM to 4:30 PM, Monday through Saturday. Admission is $2 for adults; but for students, children and members of the museum, admission is free. Included in this small fee is admission to the next door gallery which features changing exhibits of paintings, crafts, and sculpture relating to Georgetown. The Gallery is open 10 AM to 4 PM.

Eighteen miles north of Georgetown — still on Hwy. 17 — is the entrance to another adventure; Brookgreen Gardens. And it's an adventure well worth the long drive.

BROOKGREEN GARDENS
Hwy. 17, eighteen miles
north of Georgetown　　　*800-849-1931*

Brookgreen Gardens plugs nicely into the plantation theme of this daytrip in that the property encompasses four 18th- and 19th-century plantations; The Oaks, Springfield, Laurel Hill, and (old) Brookgreen. But since the late 1920s, agriculture has hardly been the primary harvest here. Instead, Brookgreen now has 350 acres of beautifully landscaped gardens specifically designed to display over 500 pieces of outdoor sculpture — all created by leading American artists of the 19th and 20th centuries.

The idea for Brookgreen Gardens was the brainchild of noted American sculptor Anna Hyatt Huntington, who with her late husband (philanthropist Archer M. Huntington), planned and endowed the museum back in the 1930s.

Today, the property is man-aged by a private organization, Brookgreen Gardens, a Society for the Southeastern Flora and Fauna. You may choose to get an initial orientation at the Visitors' Pavilion and have some overview of the property. Or, you may want to wander the seemingly endless paths and encounter the breathtaking sculpture by "surprise." There's also a Nature Area where wild animals native to these plantations are housed in natural settings — yet accessible to view.

Brookgreen's hours are from 9:30 AM to 4:45 PM, every day except Christmas. Admission is $5 for adults, $2 for children (ages 6 to 12), and free for children 6 and under.

Greater Charleston
Spectator Sports

When most people in this area think of "sports," tennis, golf, swimming and other participatory activities come to mind. But, neither visitors nor locals should overlook the excellent professional and collegiate sports that are available here for our enjoyment. There's nothing like taking off for a day at the stadium to watch the great American sport of baseball, and the Charleston Riverdogs provide action-packed play. It's also exciting to see the big-name professionals who regularly show up at the area resorts for golf and tennis matches. And, who among us doesn't enjoy an autumn afternoon spent cheering on the college football team...even if our own college days are but a dim memory! So, take some time off from your own sports regimen to sit for a while and watch the pros at action. You'll probably find yourself screaming "hey batter, batter, batter!" right along with the best of 'em!

Professional Sports

GOLF AND TENNIS
World class professional and amateur tournaments are held regularly at the major resorts in the area. For instance, the 1990 PGA Cup Matches were held at Kiawah's Turtle Point, while the 1991 Ryder Cup Matches were played on Kiawah's Ocean Course. For more information, contact: Kiawah (768-2121); Wild Dunes (886-2164); or Seabrook Island (768-1000).

BASEBALL
Charleston Riverdogs, a minor league team, is a Class A farm team of the Texas Rangers. The Rainbow's season runs April through September, with 72 home games at College Park. Locals turn out regularly and appreciate the special reduced admission games throughout spring and summer. For ticket information, call 723-7241.

Insiders Like:
Tailgating before football games in the parking lot at Johnson Hagood Stadium, home of The Citadel's Bulldogs.

Insiders' Tip

Collegiate Sports

With several higher education institutions in the area, opportunities for spectating at college sporting events are abundant. The most popular are, of course, football, baseball and basketball, but you can also catch soccer, track and field and other events if you are interested. For ticket information, contact: Charleston Southern at 863-7679; The Citadel at 792-5121; and the College of Charleston at 792-5556.

Sailboat Racing

Regattas are popular events, particularly in the warmer months. A schedule is set in January and is posted in the area yacht clubs. Spectators often enjoy watching these races from the Battery.

Stock Car Racing

SUMMERVILLE SPEEDWAY

Fans of stock car racing will find this local track, on Central Avenue in Summerville — complete with lighted track and grandstand seating — a hot spot on weekend nights. Regularly scheduled events include NASCAR DASH Division racing as well as weekly races for Late-Model Stocks, Super Stocks, Thunder & Lighting, and two other four-cylinder divisions. Call 873-3438 for race schedules and additional information.

Greater Charleston
Golf

Greater Charleston can take justifiable pride in the variety of golf challenges available to the area's visitors and residents.

If you're a serious tournament player with world-class experience or if you're just one of those relatively harmless twice-a-year duffers, Charleston has you well covered when it comes to golf. After all, this is the site of America's very first golf course...among the city's other claims to fame.

From the world-ranked resort courses to the ever-popular public tracts, from the private courses to the semi-private offerings, it's literally possible to golf every day for nearly a month and play a different 18-hole course.

As you might expect, nearly every golf course in the Lowcountry has had some kind of renovation since the devastation caused by Hurricane Hugo in 1989. As a result — and as a general rule — all the area courses are in excellent shape today.

DESIGNER GOLF COURSES

Every course is different in some way. Each has it's own charm and individual characteristics — not to mention frustrations. And that may, in part, be due to the fact that most of the world's best golf architects have designed courses here in the Lowcountry. You'll find the work of Pete Dye, Tom Fazio, Arthur Hills, Jack Nicklaus, Gary Player, Robert Trent Jones and Rees Jones among them.

Pete Dye's name is one of the biggest in the industry. His most famous courses include Harbour Town on Hilton Head Island, and the Stadium Course at PGA West in La Quinta, California. Dye's most recent offering is The Ocean Course at Kiawah Island — which hosted the 1991 Ryder Cup matches. The Ocean Course rivals Tom Fazio's Lowcountry masterpiece, The Links Course at Wild Dunes Resort, which is ranked among the world's best.

Fazio's golf courses are possibly the most popular here in the Lowcountry because he designed both courses on Wild Dunes (The Links and Harbor Course) and he also did Kiawah's popular Osprey Point.

Where Pete Dye frequently uses railroad ties (almost a signature of his work), Arthur Hills on the other hand prefers to use more of the site's natural elements in his designs. Hills did the new course at Dunes West which opened in 1991 and showcased the 1992 Amoco

A LEGEND IN THE MAKING.

Charleston National Country Club has already established its golfing credentials. The developers are now ready to claim the high ground as East Cooper's premiere residential community. Unlike many other golf-oriented communities where golf is often secondary to sprawling development, Charleston National is authentically designed around a world class Rees Jones championship course.

Our neighborhoods are small and intimate, so the clubhouse, pool and tennis facilities will never be too crowded for residents and members to enjoy. And with only a limited number of golfing memberships available, Charleston National will always remain the exclusive enclave of those who wish to preserve the very best of the country club tradition.

Come out today and see for yourself why Charleston National is the Lowcountry's finest authentic country club community. Rees Jones himself called it one of golf's most elite venues. You can call it home.

A LEGEND IN THE MAKING INDEED.

Charleston National

HIGHWAY 17 NORTH • MT. PLEASANT
JUST 6 MILES NORTH OF I-526
884-7705
HOMESITES MARKETED EXCLUSIVELY by JOE GRIFFITH REALTY INC.
STEPHEN A. GRIFFITH, BROKER

9C966251

Centel Championship. Hills' other famous golf course designs include Eagle Trace, a TPC course in Coral Springs, Florida — cited in *Golf Digest's* "100 Best Courses in America."

Another name to note among the Charleston area's most popular golf designers is Tom Jackson, who gave us Patriot's Point in Mt. Pleasant back in 1981. He's also responsible for the course on Edisto Island at Fairfield Ocean Ridge (1978), as well as the one at Crowfield Plantation (1980) in Goose Greek.

SIGNATURE HOLES

Patriot's Point has the famous No. 17 hole, a par-3, 112-yard (white tees) island green which catches the uninitiated off guard. This hole requires the player to take into careful consideration the ever-changing winds off Charleston Harbor.

The No. 6 hole at Fairfield Ocean Ridge is another island hole that can be a spoiler. It's a tough 380-yard, par-4 challenge.

Crowfield Plantation, which opened in 1990, offers their par-5, 500-yard, No. 7 hole which features treacherous mounds that make the players feel like they've found a bit of old Scotland.

Rees Jones' Charleston National design, which opened in 1990, features the demanding No. 15 hole, a par-3, 183-yarder from the white tees. It plays 210 yards from the blue tees and has a innocent-looking little pond on the right that attracts errant balls like a magnet.

SCENERY

Pete Dye's Ocean Course and Tom Fazio's Links Course both make spectacular use of the Atlantic Ocean in their designs. Dye's Wild Dunes design, Harbor Course, uses the Intracoastal Waterway as a backdrop. The Links at Stono Ferry, designed by Ron Garl in 1989, is another opportunity to play along the colorful and busy Intracoastal.

But most of the Lowcountry's golf courses take full advantage of the beautiful salt marshes — signature of the Lowcountry itself — in their layout designs. Gary Player's Marsh Point, at Kiawah, is probably the best example. It has been known to happen that a curious alligator has occasionally wandered onto the course. The unofficial rule is: let the 'gator keep the ball, no penalty stroke incurred.

In fact, the whole area's multiple charms make the Lowcountry a favorite destination for those "golf widows and widowers" and the assorted family members who often get swept up in a spouse's or parent's pursuit of the sport.

The rationalization usually goes something like this:

While golfers are challenged to play the many private, semi-private, and public courses located throughout the area, the unenlightened can always explore the beautiful Lowcountry plantations, the splendid museums, the beaches and interesting shops and thus stay content and amused....

Another benefit of Charleston golf is that because there's so much else to do here, the area courses are relatively uncrowded.

That means excellent starting times and an unhurried atmosphere.

We're providing, here, brief profiles of the area courses. So tee up when it suits you, and tee off on eighteen relaxing and scenic Lowcountry holes. You'll find descriptions of who designed the courses and when, plus who can play them...and where to call for more details.

Charleston Area Golf Courses

CHARLESTON MUNICIPAL GOLF COURSE

2110 Maybank Hwy., Charleston 795-6517

This public course, located only five minutes from downtown Charleston, has been around since 1929. Although it lost some 350 mature trees in Hugo's wrath, the course has been beautifully replanted and is now in very good shape. The par-72 course is 6,400 yards long with small greens and well-tended fairways. There's an on-site pro shop with a snack bar. PGA- and LPGA-trained instructors are on hand for lessons, and this is the only public course in South Carolina with a Henry Griffitts club-fitting system available to beginners and experts alike. Club and cart rentals are available. Call about a week in advance for tee times.

CHARLESTON NATIONAL COUNTRY CLUB

1360 National Dr.,
Mt. Pleasant   884-7799

The idea for Charleston National Country Club was conceived more than 20 years ago, but the once-private golf community was just coming into focus when Hugo struck in 1989. Redesigned and refurbished with input from original designer Rees Jones, the par-72, 18-hole course (now semi-private) is 6,900 yards long from the back tees. Charleston National has an beautiful 8,000-sq.-ft. clubhouse with luxury amenities including a pool and tennis center. This is the home course for the College of Charleston and The Citadel golf teams. Call ahead for fees and reservations.

CROWFIELD GOLF AND COUNTRY CLUB

300 Hamlet Circle (U.S.-176),
Goose Creek   764-4618

Crowfield Golf & Country Club offers championship golfing on a semi-private course designed in 1990 by Tom Jackson and Bob Spence. Their 18-hole layout is slightly "Scottish" in that it has rolling tundra accompanied by acres of fairway and greenside bunkers. Shooting ability is of prime importance, here. Undulating greens and imaginative pin placements test the nerves of the most skilled players.

Crowfield's pro shop is well stocked and there's a restaurant and cocktail lounge on site. Tee times are accepted up to one week in advance. Call ahead.

DUNES WEST
3003 Dunes West Blvd.,
Mt. Pleasant   **856-9378**
Located 10 miles northeast of Charleston in the fast-growing East Cooper section of the city, Dunes West is part of a new 4,700-acre residential community currently in development. Their highly rated course — set on a high, marshy peninsula bounded by three tidal creeks — was designed by Arthur Hills. Like its sister course on Isle of Palms, Dunes West takes full advantage of its natural setting. The opening holes, cut from tall pines, have fairway corridors leading to elevated and bunkered greens. The back nine has a typical Lowcountry flavor with moss-draped oaks lining the fairways and expansive views of the marsh from several of the tees and greens. There's a handsome new clubhouse built on the foundations of an old plantation house with every modern luxury amenity. The Hills course at Dunes West was the site of the 1992 Amoco Centel Championship. Dunes West is semi-private; call ahead for fees and reservations.

THE LINKS AT STONO FERRY
5365 Forest Oaks Drive,
Hollywood   **763-1817**
This 18-hole, par-72 championship course (owned and managed by Jim Colbert Golf, Inc.) is located on S.C. Hwy. 162, off Hwy. 17 South near the little town of Hollywood. The Links opened in 1980 and was designed by Tom Fazio to accompany the exclusive Stono Ferry Plantation development. It is open to the public seven days a week. You'll find a complete pro shop and a driving range, and a full-service restaurant. PGA-trained teaching pros are on hand and rental clubs are available. Advanced registration is required.

PATRIOTS POINT GOLF LINKS
100 Clubhouse Road (Off Hwy. 17 Business)
Mt. Pleasant   **881-0042**
Operated by Kemper Sports Management, this 18-hole public course is located just across the Cooper River bridges in Mt. Pleasant, just off Hwy. 17 North near the towering U.S.S. *Yorktown* anchored in Charleston Harbor. The par-72 layout affords spectacular views of the harbor with ocean-going cargo ships and Navy vessels frequently passing by. The course is 6,838 yards in length from the back tees (5,562 yards from the front) with well-contoured fairways and well-bunkered greens. Amenities include a complete pro shop, a driving range, rental clubs and electric carts. A grill and snack bar is available, too. Call ahead for reservations and fees.

PINE FOREST COUNTRY CLUB
1001 Congressional Blvd.
Summerville   **851-1193**
The 18-holes at Pine Forest Country Club wind through the tall Summerville pines with some live oaks, dogwoods, and a lake system thrown in for good measure. Designed by golf architect Bob Spence,

and managed by Kemper, this is one of the newest and most talked-about USGA courses in the Lowcountry. With an equal representation of straightaways, doglegs, and elevation changes, this course is nicely balanced — with fun in store for golfers of all capacities. Rental clubs and electric carts are available; call ahead for reservations and fees.

SHADOWMOSS PLANTATION GOLF CLUB
20 Dunvegan Drive (off Hwy. 61),
Charleston   556-8251 or 1-800-338-4971

Public play is welcome at this scenic course designed by Russell Breeden and opened in 1970 along Hwy. 61, the old Ashley River Road. In 1986, the 18-hole, par-72 course was extensively renovated and several water hazards were added to increase the challenge. Other modifications were made after Hurricane Hugo. The course cuts through pines, oaks and hickory, through a mosaic of ponds and streams in an area once dotted with early 18th- and 19th-century plantations. You'll find a well-stocked pro shop, a snack bar, grill/lounge, and locker rooms. There's also a putting green, a chipping green and a driving range. Tee times can be arranged though a number of local hotels and inns or by calling the Shadowmoss toll-free number.

EAGLE LANDING
1500 Eagle Landing Blvd.,
Hanahan   797-1667

This semi-private, executive-length (regulation ball) golf course has recently been renovated and is under new management. Their up-dated clubhouse features a fully-stocked pro shop and a snack bar. Pro instruction and rental carts are available. You'll find a driving range, putting greens and a well-maintained setting for this golf opportunity next to the Eagle Landing community. Memberships are available.

GOLF AT WILD DUNES
Isle of Palms 886-6000 or 1-800-845-8880

Only 15 miles from Charleston is Wild Dunes, which was named one of the top 12 golf resorts in America by *Golf Magazine.* It features two Tom Fazio-designed golf courses. The Links opened in 1980, with a 6,722-yard, par-72 layout, whose two finishing holes are right on the Atlantic ocean. *Golf Magazine* currently includes The Links among the top 40 courses in the country and places it 63rd on their "100 Greatest Courses in the World" list.

The Harbor Course, which opened in 1986, has four holes set directly along the Intracoastal Waterway. With a par-70, the 6,402-yard layout challenges players with two holes that play from one island to another across the Yacht Harbor.

For information on both Wild Dunes golf courses, call the main switchboard and ask for each course by name.

GOLF ON KIAWAH ISLAND
Kiawah Island   768-2121

Internationally famous Kiawah Island offers no less than four separate and distinct golf layouts for the adventurous Lowcountry golfer. Their challenge is so widespread that there's great opportunity for the tour elite, low handicappers, and the average players. Choose from Marsh Point, Turtle Point, Osprey Point and the newest offering—The Ocean Course, made famous by the internationally televised 1991 Ryder Cup Matches.

Each of the Kiawah golf courses is semi-private — available to homeowners, guests visiting the island and Lowcountry vacationers who specifically call for reservations to play (24-hrs. in advance). Call 768-2121, Kiawah's main switchboard, and check with each course individually for tee times and greens fees.

Marsh Point, the island's first golf course, is par-71 with water on 13 holes. Designed by Gary Player and opened in 1976, it is 6,333 yards long.

Turtle Point, designed by Jack Nicklaus, is a par-72 course, 6,889 yards long with three dramatic holes right on the ocean. It opened in 1981.

Osprey Point was designed by Tom Fazio in 1988. This 6,840-yard long course has three natural lakes and a par of 72.

The Ocean Course was designed by Pete Dye and completed just in time for the International Ryder Cup Matches in 1991. *Golf Digest* named The Ocean Course the "best new resort course of the year," and voted it among the top 100 in the world. And the cliff-hanger finish of the 21-hour 1991 Ryder Cup put the course on the "must play" list of pros and amateurs everywhere. Our only caution is...beware the distraction caused by the three-mile stretch of spectacular undeveloped Atlantic beachfront; it's a real spoiler

to that eye-on-the-ball concentration. For reservations or more golfing information, call Kiawah's main switchboard and ask for each course by name.

GOLF ON SEABROOK ISLAND
Seabrook Island   768-1000
or 1-800-824-2475

Golf on Seabrook Island is limited to island residents, friends of club members, and visiting resort guests. There are two distinctively different golf challenges on the island; Crooked Oaks — designed by Robert Trent Jones, and Ocean Winds — designed by Willard Byrd.

Crooked Oaks is a par-72, 6910-yard course that meanders through the lush maritime forest and around several black water lagoons. Ocean Winds, slightly newer, is a par-72 course, 6,549 yards long, that plays a bit closer the to the ocean.

Seabrook golfers enjoy the benefits of a full-scale clubhouse facility, a large scale pro shop, plus clinics and private instruction offered by an excellent teaching staff. Call the Seabrook main exchange and ask for either course regarding tee times and fees.

FAIRFIELD OCEAN RIDGE
One King Cotton Rd.
Edisto Beach   723-0325
or 803-869-2561 Ext. 5162

Called the Country Club at Edisto, the Fairfield Ocean Ridge golf course is a semi-private 18-hole championship layout designed by Tom Jackson in 1976 and considerably updated since then. The 6,400-yard course features water holes, dense subtropical vegetation and (for early risers) frequent visits by native wildlife. Fairfield has its share of old bull 'gators, but local wisdom says they prefer to sun and run — rather than fight.

The course has dune ridges throughout; where the second and third tees are now situated was once a Confederate Army stronghold! But the overall feel of the course is "natural," as it was primarily carved from tidal marsh and jungle-thick Lowcountry vegetation. The No. 1 green provides a spectacular view of the Atlantic.

Fairfield's other amenities add to the mix, and you'll find a fully-stocked pro shop with club and cart rentals available. Clinics and private instruction are offered by PGA-trained pros. Tee time reservations are required. Call their Charleston number or dial Edisto Beach direct for more information.

NAVY/AIR FORCE GOLF COURSES

There are two Navy-operated golf courses in the Greater Charleston area. Until further notice is given (re: base closure dates), both courses are open seven days a week and may be used by active duty and retired military, their family members, Reservists and Department of Defense civilian employees. Pro shops at both courses offer a complete line of golfing accessories as well as club and cart rentals.

One course is known as Indigo Plantation, an 18-hole layout located on the north end of the Naval base near the Cooper River Recreation Center. Call 743-5222 for tee times and fee information.

The other 18-hole course known as Redbank is located on the Naval Weapons station — situated along the banks of the Cooper River. Call Redbank Golf Club at 764-7802 for tee times and fees. Redbank also offers a driving range.

Greater Charleston
Boating

*B*oating in the Trident area is an integral part of the Lowcountry life-style. From moonlight sails, family picnics on barrier islands or morning hunts in the back creeks, to deep sea trips fishing for "the Big One," the boat is the best way to go. While it is possible to bring your own, buy or rent one while you are here, make certain that you acquire — in navigational terms — "local knowledge" before you leave shore. A home-study, Boater Education Course, which includes information about navigation rules, aids to navigation, legal requirements, safety equipment, trailering and coping with emergencies, is available at no charge by contacting: Boating Safety, at 762-5041. Also, the South Carolina Wildlife and Marine Resources Department (P.O. Box 167, Columbia, South Carolina 29202) publishes valuable, detailed information about our waterways.

If you are in the market for a new boat, shop the retail stores in the Trident Area for reliable sales and service. From the city out to Moncks Corner, some of the older, outstanding establishments include:

CHARLESTON YACHT SALES
3 Lockwood Boulevard   *577-5050*

These yacht brokers handle both sail and power boats, and also offer service, repairs, instruction, appraisals, deliveries, charters and surveys. Located next to the Charleston Municipal Marina, Charleston Yacht Sales has long been a fixture on the peninsula.

DUNCAN'S BOAT HARBOUR
1997 Bridge View Drive   *744-2628*

Duncan's, situated on the Ashley River in North Charleston, sells Bayliner boats ranging in size from runabouts to yachts. Open seven days a week, Duncan's is both a wet and dry storage marina.

HAMMOND MARINE INC.
105 North Highway 52   *761-8422*

Hammond Marine, in Moncks Corner, has been in business for more than 20 years and carries Johnson motors and parts, Crest pontoon boats and Duracraft john boats.

MARINE AND RV CENTER
2445 Highway 17 South   *556-8660*

Founded in 1957 — one of the first, if not the very first, boat shops on the peninsula — the Marine and RV Center has changed its location but not its dedication to quality products and service. Lines like Key West, Maxum, and Robalo, as well as motors by Johnson, Force, Yamaha and Mercury are displayed in Marine Center's large boat yard. Boat parts, accessories and services are also available. The Marine Center also carries the impressive Shasta and Wilderness campers as well as Coachmen and Shasta recreational vehicles.

RENKEN BOAT CENTER
5840 Dorchester Road　　　*767-0515*

Renken is located in North Charleston, and sells its own product: Renken Boats — built here since 1958. Motors by lines like MerCruiser and OMC as well as parts, service and accessories are available.

SEA RAY OF CHARLESTON
2225 Leeds Avenue　　　*747-1889*

This boat store is the area's exclusive Sea Ray dealer, selling sports boats, cruisers and even yachts up to 50 feet. Service and accessories are also offered.

SEELS OUTBOARD
1937 Savannah Hwy.　　　*556-2742*

Seels carries Evinrude engines, Grady White boats as well as Sea Swirls and Hydra Sports. Located on Savannah Highway, Seels is an established boat dealership which has been in operation since the 1960s.

Boat Docking

If you are interested in docking your boat at a Lowcountry marina, consider the following options:

ASHLEY MARINA
33 Lockwood Boulevard
Charleston, 29401　　　*722-1996*

Located at Intracoastal Marker 470 on the Ashley River, this marina is on the peninsula and convenient to all areas of the city. Diesel and gasoline are available at the fuel dock, and there is room for 860 feet of parking there. In addition to a captain's lounge, ship's store, showers and a laundromat, there is a fax machine and notary public on the premises. Transients are welcome here.

BOHICKET MARINA
1880 Andell Bluff Road Charleston, 29455
768-1280 or 800-845-2233

Next to Kiawah and Seabrook resorts, Bohicket is 20 miles south of Charleston but just seven miles from the Intracoastal Waterway. Within minutes, boaters are in the open sea. Bohicket's 190 wet slips and floating docks are on deep water, and dry storage is available. Secured shower and bathroom facilities and a laundromat, as well as 20 shops and three restaurants, make this marina a first class vacation destination. Boat charters and water tours are offered, and bicycles, rollerblades and videos can be rented. There is a ship's store, and bait and fuel can be purchased. Transients as well as long-term rentals are welcome.

BUZZARD'S ROOST MARINA
P.O. Box 12359
Charleston, 29412　　　*559-5516*

Near Intracoastal Marker 11, Buzzard's Roost is a deep water marina, just minutes from the city's

The Challenge America.

municipal golf course. There are 190 wet slips along with dockage for transients. A laundry, shower and fuel are available. A restaurant and small ship's store are located at the marina.

DOLPHIN COVE MARINA

2079 Austin Avenue   744-2562

Dolphin Cove is located on very deep waters of the Ashley River, a few miles past the City Marina. Gas is available here, as is complete on-site engine, hull and accessory service. Short-term dockage is available, and the facility is equipped with showers, a laundry, a lounge and restaurant.

GEORGE M. LOCKWOOD MUNICIPAL MARINA

17 Lockwood Drive
Charleston, 29401   724-7357

This marina is owned and operated by the City of Charleston, and is close to the peninsula's activity.

MARINA'S CAY MARINA

P.O. Box 12090
Charleston, 29412   588-2091

Marina's Cay is on the Folly River — part of Marina's Cay Resort — two miles from the ocean, and nine miles from the Intracoastal Waterway. Charleston's closest facility to the ocean, Marina's Cay has fuel, ice, supplies, snacks and 24-hour security.

RIPLEY LIGHT MARINA

766-2100

Located West of the Ashley, in the shadow of California Dreaming restaurant, Ripley Light has

showers, a laundry facility, a courtesy vehicle, floating concrete docks and boating supplies. Fuel, bait and even dry storage are available.

SHEM CREEK MARINA

526 Mill Street   884-3211

Shem Creek offers dry stacks (boat storage) and is an authorized Johnson, Evinrude and MerCruiser repair shop. Conveniently located for East Cooper residents, Shem Creek is often filled to capacity.

STONO MARINA

2409 Maybank Highway
John's Island, 29455   559-2307

Just four miles from the Charleston peninsula, Stono Marina is next to Buzzard's Roost Marina. The ship's store carries boat supplies, and ice is available. There are bathrooms and showers, but no laundry facility or fuel available.

TOLER'S COVE MARINA

Highway 703 at Intracoastal Waterway
Mount Pleasant, 29464   881-1888

East of the Cooper, Toler's Cove is across the harbor from Charleston and across the Intracoastal Waterway from Sullivans Island and Isle of Palms. The marina has tennis courts, visible from the causeway. There are also showers and a laundry, as well as gas, bait, ice and other necessities.

WILD DUNES YACHT HARBOR

P.O. Box 527
Isle of Palms, 29451   886-5100

Wild Dunes, on the Intracoastal Waterway at Wild Dunes Beach and Racquet Club, is

Trident Area Public Boat Landings

Berkeley County

Ramp #	Ramp Name	Body of Water
01	Henderson G. Guerry	Lake Moultrie
02	Thornley Forest II	Lake Moultrie
03	Hatchery Landing	Lake Moultrie
04	William Dennis	Tail Race Canal
05	Durham Creek	Durham Creek
06	Fred L. Day	Lake Moultrie
07	E. Jarvis Morris	Lake Moultrie
08	Mac Flood	Lake Moultrie
09	Spiers	Lake Marion
10	Rembert C. Dennis	Wadboo Creek
11	Highway 41	Santee River
12	John R. Bettis Boat Landing	Goose Creek Reservoir
13	Bushy Park	Cooper River and Back River Reservoir
14	Huger Park	Cooper River
15	Tailrace Rediversion Project	Santee

Charleston County

Ramp #	Ramp Name	Body of Water
01	Pier Point	Ashley River
02	Remley's Point	Wando River
03	Paradise	Wando River
04	Steamboat	North Edisto River
05	Flynn Street Wando Woods	Ashley River
06	Wappoo Cut	Wappoo Creek
07	Virginia Avenue Park	Cooper River
08	Robert E. Ashley	Jeremy Creek
09	Buck Hall	ICWW
10	Battery Island	Stono River
11	Folly River	Folly River Landing
12	Riverland Terrace	Elliot Cut
13	John P. Limehouse	Stono River
14	Cherry Point	Bohicket Creek
15	Bulow	Rantowles Creek
16	Moore's	ICWW
17	Still's	Wambaw Creek
18	Martin's	Edisto River
19	Penny Creek Landing	Penny Creek
20	Wiltown Bluff	Edisto River
21	Dawhoo Landing	Dawhoo River
22	Shem Creek Landing	Shem Creek
23	Live Oak	Big Bay Creek
24	Gadsonville	Copahee Sound
25	County Farm	Ashley River
26	Toogoodoo Landing	Toogoodoo Creek
27	City Marina	Ashley River

Dorchester County

Ramp #	Ramp Name	Body of Water
01	T.W. Messservy	Edisto River
02	T. Coke Weeks	Edisto River
03	Herbert H. Jessen Landing	Ashley River

a full-service marina with access to the resort's amenities — golf, tennis, swimming and a beach. There are floating docks, a restaurant, bathrooms, showers, a laundry and a ship's store with supplies for boating.

Boat Launching Areas

Those who wish to launch boats in this area will find a number of landings for public use. On weekends they are generally crowded, and early risers find it easier to park the car and trailer. For more information about any landing, contact the South Carolina Wildlife Department at 795-6350.

General Sailing And Boating Information

Sailors or aspiring sailors find plenty of company in the Lowcountry. If you are interested in learning more about the sport or about the regatta schedule, talk to the enthusiasts at one of the following entities:

SAILING ASSOCIATION — COLLEGE OF CHARLESTON
Municipal Yacht Basin   792-5547

ADULT SAILING CLASSES
The College of Charleston offers adult sailing classes which meet at the Municipal Yacht Basin. Equipment is furnished, and no advanced skills are required.

SAILSPORTS SAILBOARDS
1419 Ben Sawyer Boulevard   884-1508
Located in Mt. Pleasant, Sailsports offers lessons in windsurfing by certified instructors.

TIMEOUT
3 Lockwood Boulevard   577-5979
Downtown, next to the Charleston Municipal Marina, Timeout sells sailboats and windsurfing equipment as well as accessories. Lessons in windsurfing are also available.

COASTAL EXPEDITIONS
P.O. Box 556   884-7684
Sullivans Island, S.C. 29482
Coastal Expeditions rents kayaks (also sells used equipment) and offers kayak tours of the Lowcountry from the Santee to the ACE Basin, from the Congaree to the Coast. A quality operation, Coastal Expeditions welcomes beginners and experienced kayakers with invitations such as: "View the Oyster"; "Cape Romaine on Capers Island"; and "Historic Rice Fields and Freshwater Marsh."

Greater Charleston
Hunting and Fishing

*H*unting and fishing are major recreational traditions in the Trident area. When the Honorable William Elliott published *Carolina Sports by Land and Water,* in 1846, it was called a "description and defense" of these sports in the Lowcountry. Today, the best "defense" of the sports is that many who participate in them are also conservation-minded people who help implement and adhere to laws protecting wildlife. Limits and seasons as well as a licensing program are part of an overall system that fosters responsible sportsmanship and helps maintain diversity and numbers.

Hunting

Residents and visitors both can be licensed to hunt in the Trident area. And, from raccoons to deer, turkeys to ducks, there is still variety and quantity in Lowcountry habitats.

The South Carolina Wildlife and Marine Resources Department designates private land in the Trident area as Game Zone 6. The agency publishes a brochure in March that details areas, regulations, limits and check stations. For your copy, write to the department at P.O. Box 167, Columbia, S.C. 29202.

In addition to hunting by personal invitation on private property, there is land — marked as Waterfowl Management Areas (WMA) or U.S. Forest Service lands — on which public hunting is allowed. The Wildlife Department can furnish details about these areas and restrictions as well.

For information about the Wildlife Department's 12-hour Hunter Education Course contact: Hunter Education, SCWMRD, P.O. Box 167, Columbia, S.C. 29202, or call 734-4003. The course includes classroom instruction (covering hunting ethics, hunter/landowner relations and basic conservation and wildlife management principles) and hands-on experience in hunter safety and hunting techniques. This course is accepted by other states requiring certification.

Fees are subject to change, but the following list may be used as a guide:

RESIDENT FEES FOR HUNTING

State Hunting License	$12
Big Game Permit	$6
(Required statewide for deer, turkey and bear.)	
Turkey Tags	FREE
(All hunters, regardless of other license	

requirements, must have a set of Wild Turkey Tags in their possession while hunting.)

Junior Outdoorsman's License **$16**
(For residents age 16-17 only, includes WMA, big game, hunting and fishing privileges.)

State Migratory Waterfowl Stamp **$5.50**

NON-RESIDENT FEES FOR HUNTING LICENSES

Annual Hunting License	$75
Big Game Permit (For deer, turkey and bear)	$80
10-Day Hunting License	$50
3-Day Hunting License	$25
Shooting Preserve Permit	$8.50
WMA Permit	$76
State Migratory Waterfowl Stamp	$5.50

Fishing

The Trident area offers some of the best fishing on the East Coast. Berkeley County's lakes Marion and Moultrie include 170,000 acres with striped bass, largemouth bass, sunfish, white bass, crappie and catfish. Charleston County, blessed with at least 60 miles of protected coastline, is a fishing enthusiast's paradise. The fresh waters of the Ashley and Cooper rivers, with adjacent rice field breaks, as well as salt creeks, bays and the ocean are open to the public. Fish for largemouth bass, bream, trout, flounder or spot tail bass in these rivers, and bluefish in the harbor; or head out to the deep water for catch like dolphin, wahoo, marlin, sailfish or tuna. Dorchester County includes part of the Edisto River, home to striped bass and American shad — the roe of which, often served with grits, is a Lowcountry delicacy. Largemouth bass, redbreast and bluegill bream, as well as catfish, also swim the Edisto.

In an effort to protect the fish population, South Carolina has established regulations concerning limits and sizes of catches of fish, the use of seines and gill nets, and guidelines concerning crabbing, shrimping and other "fishing" activities. For specific information about seasons, rules, and licenses, contact the South Carolina Wildlife and Marine Resources Department (795-6350).

Deep sea fishing is a popular sport, and charter boats allow visitors and locals alike to enjoy the experience. Trips are on luxury boats, air-conditioned and large enough to ride out the ocean swells, yet small enough to put you on a first-name basis with the captain. Sometimes captains will allow special combinations (for instance, two in one party and two in another to make up a trip), or a half- or three-quarter-day charters. For an all day trip, plan on a long, physically challenging day, and bring plenty of sunscreen along with your hat. Boats generally leave hours before dawn and return when the sun is heading down. If you would prefer a half-day trip on a boat that accommodates dozens of people at a fraction of the cost, consider one of the large fishing boats that offer half- and full-day rates without the frills. These, too, are usually air-conditioned, so don't let the relentless sun scare you away. The following is a sampling:

Fishing boats open for charter in the Trident

Blockade Runner   722-1691

This custom-built 45' sport fisherman boat can be rented for private parties of up to six. The captain and his mate fish for tuna, dolphin, mackerel and other species off Charleston. According to season, rates vary from $650 to $1100.

Bohicket Charters   768-72994

Bohicket offers inshore and offshore fishing trips on a 46' yacht, and is located near Kiawah and Seabrook Islands. Boat rentals (13' Whalers to 21' skiffs) and tackle are also available, as are shelling trips, sunset cruises and even customized trips.

Carolina Clipper   884-2992

This large, comfortable boat is air-conditioned and takes off each day from Mt. Pleasant's Shem Creek. Full-day trips are $50 per person during the week, and $60 per person on Saturday, Sunday and holidays.

Captain Ivan's Island Charters   588-6060

Departing from the Charleston Marina, Captain Ivan's 30', wide beam boat (Coast Guard certified) has custom rods, reels and tackle.

Half day trips cost $300 for up to four people, and $65 for each additional person. Full day trips cost $550 for up to four people, and $100 per additional passenger. Charter fishing trips as well as specialty trips for tournaments are offered.

Dolphin Cove Marina Charters   744-2562

This charter company offers trips on the *Prime Time* as well as other boat rentals. The captain is licensed and experienced. Call for rates.

Happyniss Sportfishing Charters   881-1575

Docked at Toler's Cove, in Mt. Pleasant, this professional captain offers deep-sea sportfishing as well as harbor cruises on board an air-conditioned, twin-engine 42' Bertram. Rates are: four hours (half day), $575; six hours, $700; eight hours, $825; 12 hours, $1100. Two-hour cruises are also available for $190. A ten percent discount is in effect during the week.

J.J. Deep Sea Fishing   873-2065

This boat has been fishing out of Charleston for three decades, and goes out for a full day of fishing. The cost is $40 per person, which includes bait and equipment. It leaves from the Charleston City Marina.

Insiders Like:
Telling your northern friends and family that you went swimming in the still-warm Atlantic Ocean on Thanksgiving.

Insiders' Tip

Wild Dunes Yacht Harbor   *886-5100*

Wild Dunes offers inshore and offshore fishing trips with three-quarter-day and full-day options. Also, crabbing trips, shelling, beachcombing, motor and sailboat rentals, as well as sunset and moonlight cruises are available. Prices range from $6 to $1,000.

Fishing Licenses

Contact the South Carolina Wildlife and Marine Resources Department, P.O. Box 167, Columbia, S.C. 29202 for detailed information about licenses. For general guidelines, refer to the list below (which is subject to change):

RESIDENT FEES FOR FISHING LICENSES

State Fishing License	$10
Combination Fishing and Hunting License	$17
(Includes big game permit)	
Lakes and Reservoirs Permit	$3
14-Day Fishing License	$5
Sportsman's License	$44
(Includes WMA, big game, hunting and fishing privileges)	
Junior Outdoorsman's License	$16
(For residents age 16-17 only, includes WMA, big game, hunting and fishing privileges)	
Shrimp Baiting Permit	$25

NON-RESIDENT FEES FOR FISHING LICENSES

Annual Fishing License	$35
7-Day Fishing License	$11
Shrimp Baiting Permit	$500

Greater Charleston
Public and Private Schools

*R*ecords from the first general public school system in the Lowcountry date back to 1856. Today, separate public school systems are in place in Charleston, Berkeley and Dorchester Counties. More than 80,000 students in grades Kindergarten through 12 are enrolled at more than 115 schools in the four school districts: Berkeley County, Charleston County, Dorchester II and Dorchester IV. There are seven schools serving children with special education needs, four magnet schools for academically motivated students, as well as a SAIL (Students Actively Interested in Learning) program within regular public schools for children with high test scores and strong academic potential.

Charleston County Schools

Charleston County School District is the 75th largest in the country, with 44,000 students enrolled in 72 schools. It employs approximately 2,600 teachers and maintains an average pupil/teacher ratio of 19 to one.

Two vocational centers provide extensive occupational training in subjects running the gamut from carpentry to child care services, while advanced students ben-

efit from summer programs like the Summer Sail Program, which offers opportunities to 350 students exhibiting talent in the visual and performing arts.

The summer OASIS Program (Opportunity for Advanced Student Involvement in Systems) serves approximately 600 talented students at four separate locations throughout Charleston County. Special education programs directed at students with emotional, mental or physical handicaps are available through the Charleston County School District as well.

The district has been a trailblazer for the magnet school concept, with four locations: Buist Academy, Ashley River Creative Arts Elementary, Jennie Moore Elementary and the Academic Magnet High School. Magnet schools' educational programs provide an alternative curriculum that integrates resources from the community, higher education, the arts, business and technology.

The following is a breakdown of how many public schools are in Charleston County: elementary schools, 44; middle schools, 15; high schools, 11; and vocational schools, two.

For more information, contact the Charleston County School District at 15 Hutson Street, Charleston, 29403; phone 724-7733.

Because relying on the phone book for numbers to reach specific district offices (rather than the overall county office listed above) can be confusing, we have compiled a list of important contacts for easy reference:

Districts 1 and 2, 849-2873

Mt. Pleasant falls into these districts.

District 3, 762-2780

James Island is included in this district.

District 4, 745-7150

North Charleston is in District 4.

District 9, 762-2780

John's Island is in District 9.

District 10, 763-1500

West Ashley is located in District 10.

District 20, 724-7760

District 20 is peninsular Charleston.

District 23, 889-2291

St. Pauls, Edisto and Ravenel are included in District 23.

MAGNET SCHOOLS

Elementary   724-7760, 763-1500
High School   724-7760

These special schools serve a student population that is academically and/or artistically motivated. Located on the peninsula and West of the Ashley, they draw students from surrounding neighborhoods as well as areas spread throughout the district.

SAIL PROGRAMS

720-3010

This acronym stands for "Students Actively Interested in Learning," and the program is in place within the public school system. Offerings are innovative and challenging, and designed to stimulate the bright students who are accepted into the program.

HOME SCHOOLING

720-3024

Parents who wish to teach their children at home should contact the school system for specific guidelines and assistance.

Berkeley County Schools

Berkeley County School District is the third largest in the state with a student population of 27,825 enrolled in 35 different schools. The northern end of Berkeley County is rural and sparsely populated, while the area from Moncks Corner to Hanahan is suburbanized.

Nearly 500 new students are enrolled into the district each year because of the area's rapid growth. In the last 13 years, the district built nine new schools and 23 major additions to existing structures. By 1995, enrollment is expected to reach 30,000. The district has begun construction of two new elementary schools in the southern part of the county, designed to accommodate 800 students each. They are expected to be completed by the beginning of the 1992-1993 school year.

The district's curriculum is designed to meet the educational needs of all students, regardless of their academic achievement level. Accelerated students benefit from classes tailored to their advanced abilities. Average students receive a steady diet of core courses designed to prepare them for the challenges posed by college and postgraduate jobs. Remedial education is available for students requiring special attention in order to attain academic credit. Special education programs are targeted to children with handicaps ranging from the visually impaired to the educable mentally retarded. Berkeley County schools use the self-contained resource and itinerant teacher models for implementing instruction. All Berkeley County schools offer support personnel and services to students, including guidance counselors, psychologists and speech therapists.

This is a breakdown of the Berkeley County schools by number: elementary, 15; intermediate, two; middle schools, eight; high schools, eight; and vocational centers, two.

Contact the Berkeley County School District at P.O. Box 608, 229 Main Street, Moncks Corner, S.C., 29461; or, call 761-8600 or 723-4627.

Dorchester County Schools

Dorchester County has two school districts — Two and Four. District Two has been designated the second-fastest growing district in the state. A study conducted for the school district by The Citadel indicated that 95 percent of the residential growth projected for

Dorchester County before the year 2000 will occur in District Two. In addition, 98 percent of this growth is projected for the Oakbrook section of Summerville. School enrollment there jumped from 10,106 in 1979-1980 to 13,440 in 1990-1991.

District Two operates 13 schools, specializing in extracurricular activities for students in grades K through 12. Students graduating from Summerville High School, currently the district's only high school, have consistently outscored the state norms on SAT scores. Summerville seniors receive $500,000 in college scholarships each year.

Project Opportunity, an alternative program for young people in high school, is a special counseling and basic skills program aimed at lowering the dropout rate. This program is conducted at a school site during the afternoon and early evening.

District Two has four schools — Flowertown, Knightsville, Rollings Elementary and Summerville High — earning designations for deregulating school curriculum, allowing greater innovation in teaching methods and meeting the increasingly complex needs of young people.

District Two's school breakdown is as follows: elementary schools, nine; middle schools, three; and high schools, one. Contact Dorchester School District Two at 102 Greenwave Blvd., Summerville, S.C., 29483; or call 873-2901.

District Four is located on the outer region of Dorchester county and it's one of the smallest in the state with only 2,500 students. The district has one of the best pupil/teacher ratios in South Carolina, with one instructor per 18 students. The district sets high standards for its faculty, with nearly 39 percent of about 140 teachers earning master's degrees.

This district provides incentives for the professional growth and advancement of its faculty through in-service training programs and membership in the Salkehatchie Consortium, which provides graduate courses at no cost to teachers.

District Four curriculum is designed for students looking to enter the work force after high school, as well as students heading for college. Here's a breakdown of the district school by number: elementary schools, three; middle schools, one; and high schools, two.

Contact Dorchester School District Four at 500 Ridge Street, St. George, S.C., 29477, or call 563-4535.

Private Schools

There is an excellent selection of at least 25 independent schools in the area, ranging from parochial to all-girl. Some offer financial aid, and most sponsor open houses on campus for visitors. One source for more detailed information is the Tri-County Admissions Council, which publishes a brochure — complete with locator map, phone numbers and important facts about member schools. A copy of this publication is available from local Realtors as well as the Charleston Trident Chamber of Commerce. For contacts at nonmember schools, check the telephone directory. The following list of private schools is a sampling of what is available in the Greater Charleston area:

ADDLESTONE HEBREW ACADEMY
1639 Raoul Wallenberg Blvd.
Charleston, 29407   571-1105
Addlestone accepts children from 18 months through the 8th grade and provides secular as well as religious training. Conversational Hebrew classes are offered along with a full curriculum in elementary grades.

THE ARCHIBALD RUTLEDGE ACADEMY
10111 Old Cemetery Road, P.O. Box 520
McClellanville, S.C. 29458   887-3323
The Archibald Rutledge Academy, named for South Carolina's Poet Laureate, offers full college preparatory and general curricula for students in grades K through 12. The school's small

classes and updated facilities as well as an emphasis on surrounding ecological and cultural resources are important features.

ASHLEY HALL
172 Rutledge Avenue
Charleston, SC 29043   722-4088
Founded in 1909, Ashley Hall is a college preparatory day school dedicated to educating young women from early childhood through grade 12. One hundred percent of the school's graduates are accepted by colleges and universities across the nation.

BISHOP ENGLAND HIGH
203 Calhoun Street
Charleston, 29403-6193   724-8383
Bishop England High School is a Roman Catholic coeducational secondary school operated under the auspices of the Diocese of Charleston. Academic ability grouping is a unique feature of the school.

CHARLESTON DAY SCHOOL
15 Archdale Street
Charleston, 29401-1918   *722-7791*
Charleston Day School is a coeducational day school enrolling about 170 students in grades 1 - 8. Graduates go on to local day schools and to a variety of preparatory schools around the country.

CHARLES TOWNE MONTESSORI SCHOOL
56 Leinbach Drive
Charleston 29407
Located on a five-acre wooded campus West of the Ashley, Charles Towne Montessori accepts children ages 12 months to 12 years old and offers a learning environment in keeping with Montessori principles. There is a Studio Program (for the arts) as well as a Sports Program after school.

FIRST BAPTIST CHURCH SCHOOL
48 Meeting Street   *722-6645 or*
Charleston, 29401   *722-6646*
First Baptist Church School offers a college preparatory educa-tion in a Christian setting for grades K4 through 12. The academic cur-riculum is enriched by Bible study and extracurricular activities.

LORD BERKELEY ACADEMY
204 West Main Street
Moncks Corner, 29461   *761-8539*
Lord Berkeley is a coeduca-tional, college preparatory day school for students in grades K4 through 12. In addition to academic and extracurricular activities, Lord Berkeley offers such activities as ath-letics and service clubs.

LOW COUNTRY ACADEMY
2120 Wood Avenue
Charleston, 29414   *571-7740*
Low Country Academy has small classes, emphasizing the ba-sics in both general and college preparatory courses for students in grades 7 through 12. A summer program offers remediation and advancement opportunities.

Ashley Hall

Judith Webber Ross Early Childhood Center
Coeducational, Ages 2-4

Kindergarten through Grade 12, All Girls

Fully accredited by NAIS, SACS.

"Outstanding academic program in a caring atmosphere"

For more information, contact Admissions Representative.

172 Rutledge Ave., Charleston, SC 29403
(803) 722-4088, FAX (803) 723-3982.

Ashley Hall admits students of any race, color, religion, national or ethnic origin.

CHARLESTON DAY SCHOOL
FOUNDED 1937

15 Archdale Street
Charleston, South Carolina 29401-1918
803-722-7791

A top-quality program of academics, sports and activities in a small, warm, and caring environment. For boys and girls in grades 1 through 8. Nondiscriminatory admissions.

MASON PREPARATORY SCHOOL
56 Halsey Boulevard
Charleston, 29401   723-0664

The mission of Mason Preparatory School is to provide a solid academic foundation to students in grades 1 through 8. In addition to a well-rounded curriculum, a wide variety of after-school activities is offered.

PINEWOOD PREPARATORY SCHOOL
808 West Old Orangeburg Road
Summerville, 29483   873-1643

This coeducational, college preparatory day school enrolls students in K3 through 12. It offers a full developmental preschool and kindergarten program and a challenging academic program for its students.

PORTER GAUD SCHOOL
Albermarle Point
Charleston, 29407-7593   556-3620

Episcopal-related Porter-Gaud is a private, coeducational, college preparatory school with students in grades 1 through 12. All of its graduates go on to four-year colleges.

ST. PAUL'S COUNTRY DAY SCHOOL
5139 Gibson Road
Hollywood, 29445   889-2702

St. Paul's Country Day School provides an academic education in a nondenominational Christian atmosphere. Grades K through 12 attend classes on a 10-acre, consolidated campus.

SEA ISLAND ACADEMY
2024 Academy Drive
John's Island, SC 29455   559-5506

Sea Island Academy offers a college-preparatory curriculum stressing the fundamentals in all academic disciplines. The school accepts qualified students in grades K4 through 12.

TRI-COUNTY CATHOLIC ELEMENTARY SCHOOLS
A full academic course of all basic disciplines is offered at all

The Citadel
CO-EDUCATIONAL

EVENING COLLEGE
(FULL OR PART TIME)

OFFERING

BACHELOR DEGREES IN:
CIVIL AND ELECTRICAL ENGINEERING
BUSINESS ADMINISTRATION

GRADUATE DEGREES IN:
EDUCATION - BIOLOGY - MATHEMATICS
ENGLISH - HISTORY - PSYCHOLOGY -
BUSINESS ADMINISTRATION -PHYSICAL
EDUCATION - COMMUNITY & SCHOOL COUNSELING
- EDUCATIONAL ADMINISTRATION - LEADERSHIP
READING, CURRICULUM &
INSTRUCTION - SPECIAL EDUCATION

"AN EXCELLENT OPPORTUNITY TO FURTHER
YOUR EDUCATION AT YOUR OWN PACE"

FOR ADDITIONAL INFORMATION
(803)-953-5089
THE CITADEL EVENING COLLEGE

Catholic schools, in addition to the study of religion and Christian values. For more information, contact Diocesan Office of Education, 119 Broad Street, Charleston, 29401, at 724-8370.

TRIDENT ACADEMY
1455 Wakendaw Road
Mt. Pleasant, 29464   884-7046

Trident Academy serves children in grades 1-12 who have diagnosed learning disabilities. The basic philosophy at Trident is to teach students to compensate for their differences in learning, allowing them to mainstream as quickly as possible.

Colleges And Universities

Higher education has been a priority in the Lowcountry since the founding of the College of Charleston in 1770. Today, there are many academic institutions of advanced learning with expansive, formal campuses. In addition, there are small junior colleges, business colleges, branches of out-of-state colleges and universities, and even a culinary institute in the Trident area. Major institutions, with strong ties to greater Charleston, are described below:

CHARLESTON SOUTHERN UNIVERSITY
Interstate 26 and Highway 78   863-7075

When it was founded in 1964, Charleston Southern was Baptist College — the only church-affiliated college in this area. Now elevated to university status and ranked as the second largest in the state, it offers 28 undergraduate degrees as well as masters degrees in business administration, education and the art of teaching.

THE CITADEL
171 Moultrie St.   792-5000

Recently ranked by the *U.S. News and World Report* as one of "America's Best Colleges," The Citadel is an all-male, non-federal military college — the largest of its kind

in the United States. With a formal campus and regimented activities, The Citadel combines academic requirements with military training in the areas of discipline, responsiveness and leadership. Women show up on the grounds for social events and also at night for coeducational courses. Some undergraduate and a wide selection of graduate courses — including those leading to the MBA — are offered through the Citadel Evening College.

COLLEGE OF CHARLESTON/ UNIVERSITY OF CHARLESTON
66 George St.   *792-5507*

Recognized as the first municipal college in the United States and the oldest institution of higher learning in South Carolina, the College of Charleston offers 28 undergraduate degrees. Now called the University of Charleston, the masters program offers degrees in education, marine biology and public administration. The campus showcases incredibly beautiful landscaping, with botanical displays for every season.

JOHNSON & WALES CULINARY UNIVERSITY
701 East Bay Street   *723-4638*

Enrolling a dedicated group of students who enter the food services industry, Johnson & Wales is a nationally recognized culinary school. It also offers fascinating short courses in the culinary arts which are open to the community at large.

MEDICAL UNIVERSITY OF SOUTH CAROLINA
171 Ashley Avenue   *792-2300*

The oldest medical school in the south, MUSC was founded in 1824 and now is at the functional center of the largest medical complex in the state. The university includes six colleges: medicine, nursing, health related professions, pharmacy, dental medicine and graduate studies.

TRIDENT TECHNICAL COLLEGE
700 Rivers Ave.   *572-6111*

Trident Technical College is part of the state system, and offers two-year programs for a variety of technical degrees. There are three campuses — a main campus in North Charleston, a second on the peninsula, and a third in Berkeley County — together serving more students than any of the other colleges or universities in the area.

Greater Charleston
Child Care and Early Childhood Centers

*B*ecause many families are now two-career, there is a very real need here for full-time child care facilities — places that take care of children from early morning until after regular work hours. That's what this chapter is all about. Note that we have not included schools with abbreviated programs for toddlers because they are not geared to working parents (but, see the Schools chapter). Neither have we included private, business-affiliated operations run strictly for the children of employees, because they are closed to the public. On the other hand, we do list early childhood centers that are school-like but have full-day, year round schedules.

What follows is a sample listing of what is publicized. There seem to be more centers located West of the Ashley and in other parts of Greater Charleston than on the peninsula, and we hear parents complaining about that all the time. Often there are wait lists at popular establishments, and it would be a good idea to get your name on a few. We recommend that you schedule visits to any establishments you are considering during their working hours, so that you get a feel for the children, the care-givers and the facilities.

Remember that the State of South Carolina licenses day care centers only if they maintain standards such as cleanliness, acceptable student-teacher ratios and adequate space-per-child allotments. (Call the Department of Social Services at 792-7346 to request more detailed information about this process.) Before you make a decision about where to take your child, make sure the operation has an up-to-date license, and that the program itself fits your preference in terms of structure or freedom. Nose around the playground and check out the general atmosphere, but remember that this is real life: "kids will be kids," and you could stumble upon a "bad day" for everyone at a "good" day care or early childhood center.

Sometimes, a less costly alternative is to arrange child care in an individual's home. Such opportunities are advertised in the classified ad section of the local papers. Or, you can run an advertisement for a caregiver who will come into your home. There is a local placement service (Child Care Options, at 766-9590) which charges clients $25 to find three child care openings within two working days. It is affiliated with Neely's day care centers.

If you are able to provide

lodging and would enjoy a cultural exchange experience to augment the child care, you might consider contacting an au pair placement service such as AuPairCare (1-800-288-7786) for a live-in nanny. This service arranges for English-speaking, European au pairs between the ages of 18 and 25 to come to the United States for a year. Host families supply lodging, meals and a salary in return for 45 hours of child care per week. Unlike employees, au pairs function much like family members, sharing meals and social occasions, and a local community counselor is on hand to help the year go smoothly for both the au pair and the family. Those who have been involved with the program say it is a fun way to broaden their children's vision of world boundaries.

In the following pages, we will give you a rundown on some of the child care centers with good reputations in the area. We've broken the information up into the various cities in the Trident area so it will be more convenient for you to find a center nearest your work or home.

Charleston and West Ashley Area Child Care

BABYLAND
1534 Orange Grove Road   556-7222
Babyland accepts infants and children, and is open Monday through Friday, 6:30 AM - 6:15 PM. There are different rates by hour, day or week. Located near Ashley Plaza Mall, they have a nursery class for 2- and 3-year-olds, and kindergarten for 4- and 5-year-olds. It is state licensed and offers dancing, swimming, music, skating and field trips. Call for information about the ABC Program.

BUILDING BLOCKS
St. Andrews Shopping Center   769-6082
Operated by creative and certified teachers, Building Blocks offers drop-in (call ahead, though) babysitting and much more. Our children love the Rockin' Aerobics, Jumpnastics, and arts and crafts classes. Science programs, individual or group tutoring, math/reading enrichment classes and karate classes are also part of the program. Friday and Saturday night babysitting is available, and the facility (complete with soft gymnastic equipment) can be rented out for parties. Call for rates and information about all programs.

CHILD DEVELOPMENT CENTER
Ashley River Baptist Church   556-2681
This is a popular West Ashley program for children ages six weeks to five years old. Lunch is served, and the hours are from 7:00 AM to 6:00 PM. Children go on field trips and are exposed to Christian music.

GREATER ST. LUKE AFRICAN METHODIST EPISCOPAL DAY CARE CENTER
78 Gordon Street   577-7747
One of the few centers on the peninsula, this program accepts children ages six weeks to five years. Hours are 6:00 AM to 6:30 PM, and there is a distinctly religious atmosphere.

Quality
live-in child care...

with a special European *flair*.

- carefully screened European au pairs
- about $170/week for any size family
- AuPairCare counselors in your area

800-288-7786

AuPairCare

A U.S. Government-designated program.

HOPE'S TREASURE CHEST
24 Sycamore Road   766-8893

This West Ashley center is open Monday through Friday, 7 AM until 5:30 PM for children in preschool and kindergarten. Breakfast, lunch and snacks are served, and the center has dance, readiness and developmental programs.

JANICE'S CHRISTIAN DAY SCHOOL
2417 Savannah Hwy.   766-2944

Accepting infants through 12-year-olds, the school serves hot meals and has a Christian Education Program. Computer training and after school tutoring are offered.

JUDITH WEBBER ROSS EARLY CHILDHOOD CENTER
Ashley Hall, 172 Rutledge Avenue 722-4088

This early childhood center is a coeducational program for ages two through four, located on an established girls school's campus in Radcliffeborough. A new facility, qualified teachers and a unique setting make this a top choice on the peninsula.

KINDER-CARE LEARNING CENTER
17 Farmfield Road   571-6365

This chain is known for its clean, safe centers with a trained staff. This one is located at the head of Farmfield subdivision, West Ashley, just off Savannah Highway. Children ages six weeks to 12 years are accepted, and parents are always welcome. Also try the other West Ashley location:

KINDER-CARE LEARNING CENTER
1401 Ashley River Road   766-4535

This is a second location for Kinder-Care West of the Ashley.

LA PETITE ACADEMY
2523 Ashley River Road   556-5873

One of a chain, this academy accepts children ages six weeks to 12 years old. Before and after school care with transportation are available. It is state licensed and operates from 6:30 AM until 6:15 PM, year round.

LOVE 'N CARE
1613 Evergreen Street   766-4360

Love'n Care accepts children three months to six years, and serves lunch. Located west of the Ashley, it is licensed by the state, and offers extra programs such as swimming. Operating hours are Monday through Friday from 5:30 AM to 12:00 midnight. On Saturday, it is open from 6:30 AM until midnight.

LOVING AND LEARNING EDUCATIONAL CENTER
876 S. Colony Drive   571-0080

Children six weeks to 12 years are accepted at this well-liked West Ashley day care center. It is licensed by the state, and provides hot lunch and snacks. The hours are 6:30 AM until 6:00 PM. Ballet, tap, jumpnastics and field trips are pluses. After school care and transportation are available.

LUTHERAN CHURCH OF THE REDEEMER DAY CARE
714 Riverdale Drive   763-3368 or
*   571-6655*

This center, located behind the West Ashley Krispy Kreme, of-

Woodland Hall
Preschool & Kindergarten

Marsha Pringle, Owner
Kim Martin, Director

946 Whipple Road, Mount Pleasant
Call 884-8582

fers programs for two- through five-year-olds from 7:00 AM until 6:00 PM. There is after school care from 3:00 PM until 6:00 PM, and dancing, ceramics, swimming, jumpnastics and gymnastics are also offered.

MONTESSORI LEARNING CENTER
51 Pitt Street   720-8918
This is another good choice on the peninsula. Children are accepted from ages two-and-one-half to six years, and the hours run from 7:00 AM to 6:00 PM year round. Classes are small with lots of individual attention, and programs follow a Montessori philosophy.

NEELY'S EARLY CHILDHOOD EDUCATION CENTER INC.
1521 Wappoo Road   766-9590
Neely's includes three centers at three separate locations in West Ashley, tailored to the needs of children six weeks to four years old. Lunch is served, and the hours are from 7:00 AM to 6:00 PM. This

center has been in existence for more than 30 years and has many loyal alumni.

THE PLAYHOUSE
1534 Orange Grove Road   556-7222
Located West of the Ashley, this center and kindergarten accepts infants to 12-year-olds, is licensed by the state and offers a program with Orange Grove Elementary School. Hours are Monday through Friday, 6:30 AM until 6:15 PM. There is a physical fitness program, and after-school care and pickup for older children. Extra activities include swimming, music, dancing, educational field trips and skating, as well as soccer and tee ball teams for boys and girls. Call for information about the ABC Program.

THE PRESCHOOL ACADEMY, INC.
1002 Wappoo Road   763-3488
This center offers programs before and after school for children ages six weeks to 12 years.

There is transportation to and from elementary schools. Dance classes are an option, and hot meals are served daily. It is located on a West Ashley street that runs between Highways 17 South and 61.

Mount Pleasant Area Child Care

Mount Pleasant residents have convenient access to good child care facilities. We have listed some of the options, and suggest that parents also listen for word-of-mouth tips and read the want ads for additional possibilities.

CHARLOTTE'S LITTLE SCHOOLHOUSE
749 Bowman Road   884-2282

This center is open from 6:30 AM until 6:00 PM, and enrolls children ages six weeks to 12 years old. It offers a developmental program for toddlers up to two years, as well as a kindergarten program for three- to five-year-olds. Morning snack, hot lunch and an afternoon snack are provided, and after school care and school transportation as well as summer programs are available.

JUNGLE GYM INCORPORATED
280 W. Coleman Boulevard   884-0652

Located near Wonderworks and Baskin-Robbins in the Northcutt Plaza, this is part-time child care that operates Monday, Wednesday and Thursday for Mother's Morning Out from 9:00 AM until 12:45 PM. Babysitting is available by reservation from 1:00 PM until 5:00 PM, Monday through Wednesday, and Friday and Saturday night as well. There is also a playgroup on Saturday from 9:00 AM until 12 noon. Children love this place, and it is a perfect setup for birthday parties.

KINDER-CARE LEARNING CENTER
874 Lansing Drive   884-7839

This center is part of the Kinder-Care chain, which has seven locations in the Trident area. Appealing are the facts that it stays open from 6:00 AM until 6:30 PM, and that it has a trained staff who welcome parents anytime.

LITTLE LEARNER'S LODGE
116 Church Street   884-0511
(6 weeks to three years)
208 Church Street   884-4471
(3 years to 10 years)

This child development center is an affiliated Montessori school with two programs and separate facilities: one for six weeks to three years old, and one for three years to ten years old. It is open from 6:30 AM until 6:30 PM. Most teachers have degrees and are certified. There is after school pickup, as well as gymnastics, dance and summer camp options.

MONTESSORI OF MOUNT PLEASANT
414 Whilden St.   884-1117

This school is in the Old Village, and accepts children ages 18 months up to six years old. It is open from 7:00 AM until 6:00 PM. Teachers have college degrees and are Montessori certified. There are after school and summer programs such as cooking and drama, sports, tennis, swimming, gymnastics and Yamaha keyboard.

MOUNT PLEASANT

GRACE CENTER-INFANT
822 Johnnie Dodds Boulevard   884-9721

This is a strictly infant, Christian-oriented program, for children six weeks to 24 months. Hours are Monday through Friday from 6:30 AM until 6:00 PM.

THE O'QUINN SCHOOLS
955 Houston Northcutt Blvd.   881-8506

Linda O'Quinn's is one of the finest preschools and kindergartens in the area. There are two locations (see James Island, too) and they both offer a structured program for ages two through five. Included here are extra activities such as ballet, gym, and educational instruction in French, science and geography. Lunch and two snacks are served between 7:00 AM and 6:00 PM, Monday through Friday.

ROCKING HORSE CHILD CARE CENTER
973 Houston Northcutt Blvd.   881-0130

Rocking Horse is open from 6:30 AM until 6:00 PM, and accepts children from six weeks through 12 years old. A hot breakfast is available, and hot lunch as well as two snacks are served.

TATTLE TALES CHILD CARE DEVELOPMENT CENTER
1326 Ben Sawyer   881-6111

This center is not structured, and offers a homelike environment for children ages six weeks to five years. It is open 6:30 AM until 6:00 PM, and lunch is provided.

WOODLAND HALL PRESCHOOL KINDERGARTEN
946 Whipple Road   884-8582

Woodland Hall is a year round preschool for children ages two to five. While classes run in the morning from 8:30 until 12 PM, extended care is available from 7 AM until 6 PM. Woodland is well respected for the "extras" provided to students such as computer classes, ballet, gymnastics, jumpnastics and creative drama. Many parents also like the school's emphasis on manners and social interaction. Breakfast is available and hot lunch is served.

East Islands Area Child Care

There is talk of day care centers opening on the islands, but as we go to press only one is operational:

SULLIVANS ISLAND CHILD CARE
1856 Middle Street   883-9162

Sullivans Island Child Care is a full-day operation, offering care for children six weeks to nine years old. The program is not overly structured, but children do take naps. Cereal breakfast, hot lunch and two snacks are served during the day.

West Islands Area Child Care

CHILD AND INFANT DEVELOPMENT
1630 Harbor View Road   795-0659

This program accommodates children from infants six weeks old to school age. There are preschool activities as well as summer programs. Breakfast and lunch are served during the day. Hours are from 6:30 AM until 6:00 PM, Monday through Friday. Children take field trips, and dance, karate, computer and music are offered.

EPWORTH METHODIST CHURCH DAY CARE
1540 Camp Road   795-9551
Epworth Methodist takes children from six weeks to twelve years old. Hours are from 6:30 AM until 6:30 PM, Monday through Friday. A hot meal and snacks are served.

FIRST BAPTIST OF JOHNS ISLAND
3483 Maybank Highway   559-0368
First Baptist of Johns Island accepts infants six weeks old through kindergarten-age. There is a small student-teacher ratio, and a structured program. Students come from all over the area, and lunch is included in the cost of tuition.

FIRST KLASS EARLY CHILDHOOD LEARNING CENTER
933 Dupont Road   556-5555
First Klass offers an amazingly bright, clean and cheerful atmosphere with experienced, caring teachers for children ages six weeks through age 5. Hours are Monday through Friday, 6:00 AM until 6:00 PM, with hot lunch served. An excellent music program and classes in dance and gymnastics are offered. There is also an after school program (with van pickup at most West Ashley schools) and a summer program for 5-12 year olds (which includes field trips, arts/

crafts, swimming, skating and reading enrichment).

HARBOR VIEW PRESBYTERIAN CHURCH
900 Harbor View Road   795-8224
Harbor View accepts children age 18 months through the fifth grade (or eleven years old). Hours are 6:30 AM through 6:00 PM, five days a week. Hot lunch and snacks are served in a structured setting. There is plenty of time for fun, with music, crafts and outdoor play built into the program.

HOPE'S TREASURE CHEST
1528 Folly Road   795-9422
This James Island center takes children ages newborn to five years old. The structured program runs from 6:30 AM until 6:00 PM, Monday through Friday. Breakfast, lunch and snacks are provided throughout the day.

LA PETITE ACADEMY
902 Nabors Drive   795-0384
This James Island center accepts children six weeks to twelve years old. Hours are from 6:30 AM until 6:30 PM, Monday through Friday, and breakfast, lunch and snacks are served. Dance, gymnastics, computer and a summer camp are offered.

THE O'QUINN SCHOOLS
1567 Harbor View Road   795-6708
One of the best programs in the area, Linda O'Quinn's has an excellent, structured program for ages two through five. Extended hours are available from 7:00 AM until 6:00 PM, and lunch as well as

two snacks are served throughout the full day. The campus is set back off Harbor View on a deep, wooded lot with a fenced-in play area for the children. (See Mt. Pleasant section.)

LOVING AND LEARNING
958 Folly Road   *795-9183*

This James Island center accepts infants age six weeks through 12 years old. The program is structured, and hot lunch as well as snacks are served. Field trips, ballet and tap, gymnastics and even jumpnastics are offered as part of the fun at Loving and Learning. There is an after-school program and a pickup service for the school age kids.

Summerville/North Charleston Area Child Care

CHILD CARE CENTER OF SUMMERVILLE, INC.
414 S. Main Street   *873-8920*

This center, located in Azalea Park, offers a program for infants through elementary school (age 12). There's a play school for ages two through five, and transportation is provided to and from area schools. Their summer program includes a day camp for school-age children with swimming, field trips, arts and crafts and more. The hours are Monday through Friday from 6 AM to 6:30 PM. Drop-ins are welcome.

COLLEGE PARK CHRISTIAN DAY CARE CENTER
1011 College Park Road   *875-5921*

Accepting infants from six weeks to elementary age, this Christian program offers both day care and a preschool ABEKA curriculum. Activities include gymnastics, arts and crafts, games and daytrips. Their summer program includes swimming instruction. They're open year round, Monday through Friday, 6 AM to 6 PM.

FLOWERTOWN BAPTIST CHURCH DAY CARE
1305 Boone Hill Road   *875-6371*

This year round, full-day program is available to children six weeks to eight years old. Transportation from preschool and kindergarten is provided (the Flowertown and Newington bus stops just outside the school door). A hot lunch is provided plus morning and afternoon snacks. Hours are from 6 AM to 6:30 PM, Monday through Saturday.

THE GAZEBO SCHOOL
1264 Bacons Bridge Road   *873-3896*

This program is for children 18 months through fifth grade. Transportation is provided to and from area schools. Preschool is offered for three- and four-year-olds, and a private kindergarten for five-year-olds. They use ALPHA TIME for four- and five-year-olds. Summer camp activities include bowling, movies, swimming, and arts and crafts. Lunch is included. Hours are from 6:45 AM to 6:30 PM, Monday through Friday.

GOOD SHEPHERD SCHOOL OF DORCHESTER PRESBYTERIAN CHURCH

10290 Dorchester Road   875-8722

Affiliated with Dorchester Presbyterian Church, this program offers a preschool program in the morning and day care in the afternoon. Their hands-on, learning (Christian) atmosphere includes a hot lunch (breakfast optional), and the school is open from 6:30 AM to 6:30 PM, Monday through Friday.

HELPING HANDS DAY SCHOOL

Hwy. 17A-North (in Sangaree)   875-4621

This day care program is offered to children six weeks to 12 years. School bus pickup and delivery comes to the door. Activities include dance exercises, skating, movies, visits to parks and arts and crafts. Breakfast, lunch and snacks are provided. Hours are from 6:30 AM to 6 PM, Monday through Friday.

KOALA KARE CHILD CENTER

905 N. Cedar Street   871-3069

This program is for children six weeks to 12 years of age, and it includes a pre-kindergarten learning program for ages two through four. Breakfast, a hot lunch, and snacks are provided — as is transportation to and from area schools for older children. Their summer program includes swimming, horseback riding, field trips, movies and comprehensive arts and crafts. Hours are from 6 AM to 6:30 PM, Monday through Friday.

KIDS KORNER DAY CARE

Hwy. 78   873-5437

This day care facility is open to children six weeks old to 12 years old. Their Christian environment includes such activities as story time, show and tell, nature walks, visits to the library and movies. Breakfast, a hot lunch and snacks are served. Transportation is provided to and from area schools. Hours of operation are from 6 AM to 6 PM, Monday through Friday.

KINDER-CARE LEARNING CENTER

201 Miles-Jamison Road   871-7912

One of eight such centers in the greater Charleston area, this Kinder-Care offers a program for children ages six weeks to 12 years. Various programs for two-, three- and four-year-olds work with science, nature and children's literature to stimulate development. The center is open from 6 AM to 6 PM, Monday through Friday.

LA PETITE ACADEMY

1665 N Main Street   875-1190

One of a chain, the academy accepts children ages six weeks to 12 years old. Before and after school care with transportation is available. It is state licensed and operates from 6:30 AM to 6:30 PM, Monday through Friday, all year.

LA PETITE ACADEMY

1664 Old Trolley Road   875-1230

This is La Petite's second location in the Summerville area.

OAKBROOK CHILD DEVELOPMENT CENTER

901 Travelers Boulevard   871-3053

Oakbrook's large and impressive program accepts infants and toddlers through elementary school. Located near Oakbrook Office Park, the center offers a modified Montessori curriculum with music, art, dance, physical education, computers, literature, math, daytrips and more. There's also an excellent summer program. Hours are 6:30 AM to 6 PM, Monday though Friday.

RX (PRESCRIPTION) DAY CARE

801 Travelers Boulevard   821-2635

While this listing offers neither a regular full-day schedule nor a year round curriculum, they do provide a valuable service — day care for sick children in a facility staffed by a physician and a nurse. RX Day Care is owned and operated by the Ashley River Clinic. The facility has hourly rates and offers service to parents who cannot miss work due to a sick child.

TABERNACLE CHRISTIAN DAY SCHOOL

3670 Ladson Road   873-9190

This program, for children ages six weeks to 12 years, offers preschool Christian education. Their kindergarten program is for two-, three-, four- and five-year olds with ABEKA curriculum. Breakfast, lunch and snacks are included. Their summer program offers daytrips, arts and crafts and athletic challenges.

TINY TOTS TECH

328 Sangaree Parkway   871-3209

This program, offered for ages 6 weeks to 12 years, has K-2, K-3, K-4 and a private kindergarten for 5 year olds. They also offer after school activities and a full summer day camp. Activities include computer classes, dancing, gymnastics and piano lessons. They're open from 6 AM to 6 PM, Monday through Friday.

WE LUV DAY CARE CENTER

1262 Bacons Bridge Road
(at Farm Road)   821-8217

We Luv accepts children from six weeks old to age 12. Preschool education is for ages two to five, with after school activities, summer programs and transportation to and from area schools. Hours of operation are from 6 AM to 6:30 PM, Monday through Friday.

Greater Charleston
Medical Care

*L*ike about everyone else these days, we're concerned about medical care. But here in the Lowcountry, we're more fortunate than some. In the Greater Charleston area, there are nine major hospitals that provide patients with comprehensive services ranging from state-of-the-art neonatal care to heart and liver transplants. Altogether, these nine institutions offer some 2,500 hospital beds while more than 11,000 Charleston-area people are employed in the Lowcountry's health care industry.

While many rare and specific health care problems receive special attention through the Medical University of South Carolina, the Greater Charleston area is known for its excellent psychiatric and drug treatment facilities — including Charter Hospital of Charleston and Fenwick Hall. In addition, there are a host of nursing homes and rehabilitation facilities. The community is served by Meducare, a helicopter transport service that extends across a 150-mile radius, delivering patients to the region's hospitals within 35 minutes. Plus, the area is supported by highly rated Emergency Medical Services (EMS) vehicle units.

Walk-In Medical Centers

Visitors to the Greater Charleston area — and sometimes even locals — will want a handy reference to the neighborhood medical clinics for those minor (but otherwise vacation-spoiling) emergencies that sometimes befall the busy traveler.

The following list contains some of the prominent area clinics and private practices that will see patients on short-term notice. Most clinics are open every day for extended hours and no appointment is necessary. Also, note the "physicians referral" phone numbers and satellite clinics listed under the information for the area's major hospitals following these clinics.

EAST COOPER AREA
East Cooper Family Practice
913 Bowman Road, Mt. Pleasant, 884-5101
Mount Pleasant Pediatrics
1041 Johnnie Dodds Blvd., Mt. Pleasant, 881-0007

WEST ASHLEY AREA
Doctors Care
1851 Sam Rittenberg Blvd., Charleston, 556-5585
Emergicare
2049 Savannah Hwy., Charleston,

577-4101; Pharmacy, 571-4915
Franklin C. Fetter Family Health Center
3627 Maybank Hwy., Johns Island, 559-3676
James Island Medical Center
430 Folly Road, Charleston, 762-1440

NORTH CHARLESTON AREA
Atlantic Medical Center
8780 Rivers Ave., Suite 306, 572-8800
Doctor's Care
8091 Rivers Ave. (Northwoods Shopping Center), North Charleston, 572-7000
Lyman Medical Center
206 Goose Creek Blvd. (Hwy. 52), Goose Creek, 572-0433
Navcare (Navy Clinic)
2070 Northbrook Blvd., North Charleston, 764-4670
North Area Doctors Practice
2002 Reynolds Ave., North Charleston, 747-1855

SUMMERVILLE AREA
Doctors Care
1185 E. Dorchester Road, 871-7900

Hospitals

MEDICAL UNIVERSITY OF SOUTH CAROLINA (MUSC) MEDICAL CENTER
171 Ashley Avenue, Charleston, SC 29425
Hospital Operator: 792-2300

The MUSC Medical Center, a 585-bed teaching hospital, is the heartbeat of the Medical University of South Carolina. The Center, along with MUSC's Outpatient Clinic, serves patients not only from the Greater Charleston area, but those attracted to it from all over the state and the southeast.

In addition to more than 50 certificate baccalaureate, masters and doctoral programs in virtually all areas of the health sciences, MUSC offers continuing education programs that serve to help South Carolina's other health professionals stay current with the latest medical treatments and procedures.

Under the umbrella of MUSC are several specialty facilities including: the Albert Florens Storm Eye Institute, Children's Hospital, Family Medicine Center, the Heart Center, Hollings Oncology Center, the Institute of Psychiatry, and the University Diagnostic Center. For complete departmental listings, consult your phone directory.

You may call MUSC's physician referral service at 792-2844. The "information" number for patients' room location is 792-4535. Billing inquiries may be directed through the hospital's main operator at 792-2300. General visiting hours are from 11:00 AM to 8:30 PM daily.

ROPER HOSPITAL
316 Calhoun Street, Charleston, SC 29401
Hospital Operator: 724-2000

Roper Hospital is one of the Lowcountry's oldest and largest health care facilities. Today, with 421 beds and more than 1,500 employees, Roper can rightfully claim the phrase that accompanies their logo: "For generations...the hands of Experience."

Included in their special services is Roper Heart Care, a complete cardiac care facility that addresses prevention, diagnosis, treatment and rehabilitation. Roper Cancer Care offers compassionate care, state-of-the-art diagnostic and treatment services, plus special resources for cancer patients and their families. Roper's Neuroscience Center specializes is neurological disorders including epilepsy monitoring and surgery with advanced microscopy, ultrasound and laser technology.

The Women's and Children's Services includes a resource center, family-centered maternity care, lifestyle services, diagnostic breast and osteoporosis services, plastic and reconstructive surgery, maternity fitness and the Bright Beginnings Program.

Roper has eight diagnostic centers located throughout the Tri-County area. They are all open from 7:00 AM to 5:30 PM, Monday through Friday at the following locations:

Downtown at 71 Gadsden Street, phone 577-4747.

East Cooper at 1051 Johnnie Dodds Blvd, Suite A, phone 881-9678.

James Island at 333 Folly Road, phone 762-2320.

North Charleston at 3210 Landmark Drive, phone 767-4507.

West Ashley at 16 Farmfield Road, Bldg. 4, phone 571-4202.

West Ashley Surgery Center (outpatient ambulatory surgery services) at 18 Farmfield Road, phone 763-3763.

Downtown Campus Medical Office Building at 125 Doughty Street (on the first floor, above ground floor), phone 724-2086.

Summerville, at 700 N. Pine Street, phone 851-2170.

Roper Berkeley Center is Berkeley County's only 24-hour emergency outpatient diagnostic center. That address is 730 Stony Landing Road, Moncks Corner; phone 899-7700.

Roper's downtown emergency room is open 24 hours a day. The physician referral service, general health and medical information number is 720-1200. The Patient Information Desk is 724-2111 and provides room numbers or you may dial direct 724-2 + the room number. For patient billing inquiries, call 724-2950. General visiting hours are from 9:00 AM to 9:00 PM. Obstetrics visiting hours are from 11:00 AM to 9:00 PM.

TRIDENT REGIONAL MEDICAL CENTER

9330 Medical Plaza Drive (I-26 & Hwy. 78)
North Charleston, SC 29418
General information: 797-7000

This is the largest facility in Trident Regional's Health System with its four separate locations scattered throughout the Lowcountry. The Medical Center is a 300-bed acute care hospital employing more than 1,200 health care workers. They provide 24-hour emergency services. For patient information, call 797-5200, then dial 4 plus the room number. Trident's physician referral number is 797-3463.

(TRIDENT'S) SUMMERVILLE MEDICAL CENTER

295 Midland Parkway, Summerville
General information: 875-3993

Presently, the Summerville Center is expanding to a 100-bed facility with 24-hour emergency services. They sponsor numerous wellness programs for the community in addition to providing laboratory, (ACR accredited) mammography and physical rehabilitation services. The emergency room phone is 821-3838.

(TRIDENT'S) MONCKS CORNER MEDICAL CENTER
206 Rembert Dennis Blvd., Moncks Corner
General information: 761-8721

This facility, serving the residents of Berkeley County, sponsors a number of community wellness programs in addition to providing laboratory and (ACR accredited) mammography services.

(TRIDENT'S) ST. GEORGE DIAGNOSTIC CENTER
217 Parler Avenue, St. George
General information: 563-8452

This facility, serving Dorchester County residents, features a lab drawing station, (ACR accredited) mammography services, plus various community wellness programs.

BAKER HOSPITAL
2750 Speissegger Drive, North Charleston
General information: 744-2110

This 104-bed, private, not-for-profit, community hospital features a 24-hour emergency room, comprehensive outpatient services, plus an inpatient and outpatient chemical dependency unit. Call the main switchboard for their physician referral service. Visiting hours are from 10:00 AM to 9:00 PM.

Baker has a Medical Center at Goose Creek; the phone is 553-1915. Their Health Services Corporation Family Practice Clinic at Charleston Air Force Base is 556-4079.

Their (Baker's) Foot, Ankle & Leg Center of South Carolina is 747-4444.

The number for Emergency Dental Services at Baker is 745-2787.

BON SECOURS-ST. FRANCIS XAVIER HOSPITAL
135 Rutledge Avenue, Charleston
General information: 577-1000

Bon Secours-St. Francis Xavier Hospital is an acute care facility located on peninsular Charleston near the MUSC complex and Roper Hospital. Licensed for 362 beds, the hospital has been part of Charleston since 1882, organized by the Sisters of Charity of Our Lady of Mercy. In 1990, the hospital was transferred to the Sisters of Bon Secours. Now Bon Secours-St. Francis is part of the Bon Secours Health System made up of seven hospitals and 14 nursing home facilities throughout the United States.

The hospital offers a full range of services including emergency room, diagnostic procedures and medical-surgical treatment. This hospital is especially known for the 12-room birth suite, for their advanced level of endosurgical (minimal access surgery) techniques using lasers, and for housing the only hospital-based autologous blood center (which is a way of giving self-blood donations before surgical procedures) which now offers the option of frozen blood.

Their physician referral number is 577-11MD. Patient information and location is 577-1118. Home

Health Care services are at 556-4044. Call the main switchboard for specialty department numbers. Visiting hours are from 9:00 AM to 8:30 PM.

CHARLESTON MEMORIAL HOSPITAL
326 Calhoun Street, Charleston
General information: 577-0600.
Charleston Memorial is dedicated to serving the needs of patients in Charleston County. This was the first area hospital to open a fully operational emergency room. Today, Charleston Memorial's emergency treatment facility treats over 20,000 patients annually. Their inpatient facility has 172 beds and 36 bassinets. It contains general medical and surgical units, an intensive care unit, a psychiatric unit and a new obstetrical unit (opened in March of 1992). The hospital provides 24-hour emergency service as well as limited outpatient services. The hospital — owned by Charleston County and managed by MUSC — is presently building a new outpatient ambulatory care center (just next door) which will contain 86 examination rooms and provide laboratory, radiology and diagnostic services on site. It will also house prenatal clinics with ultrasound and amniocentesis available. Visiting house are from 11:00 AM to 8:00 PM daily.

EAST COOPER
COMMUNITY HOSPITAL
1200 Johnnie Dodds Blvd., Mt. Pleasant
General information: 881-0100
This hospital, serving the communities east of the Cooper River, has 100 beds and about 350 employ-ees. Formerly known as "AMI East Cooper," the facility opened in 1986 to provide acute care and 24-hour emergency room services. Call the main switchboard for patient information and room assignments. East Cooper's physician referral number is 881-4311. Visiting hours are from 9:00 AM to 9:00 PM daily.

R. H. JOHNSON VA
MEDICAL CENTER
109 Bee Street, Charleston
General information: 577-5011
This U.S. Veterans Affairs authorized 280-bed (with 930 employees) medical center provides acute, medical, surgical and psychiatric inpatient care plus primary and specialized outpatient care to veterans in a 13-county (South Carolina) primary service area. The satellite Savannah Outpatient Clinic shares some facilities and serves an additional 10-county area in Georgia plus three additional counties in South Carolina.

The VA Medical Center is affiliated with 45 different educational institutions, primarily MUSC, which is the main source of the center's paid resident staff. The hospital's 44 separate clinics treat a variety of health problems ranging from audiology care to vascular surgery. Call the main switchboard for additional information. Visiting hours are from 11:00 AM to 8:30 PM daily.

U.S. NAVAL HOSPITAL CHARLESTON
Rivers Ave. at McMillan Ave., North Charleston
General information: 743-5130
The Naval Hospital Charleston, located just outside the Naval Base main gate, provides a wide

range of inpatient and outpatient services for the area's large Naval community. In addition to the primary facility with its 250 beds (and 930 employees), the hospital operates branch clinics at the Naval Station, in the Navy Shipyard, and on the Naval Weapons Station.

Ambulance service is available for emergencies while on base and for residents of MenRiv Park housing at 743-5444. Ambulance service for Hunley Park residents is provided by the Charleston Air Force Base, but is also available at 743-5444.

The hospital's emergency room treats critically ill or injured patients 24 hours a day. It is located on the McMillan Ave. end of the hospital.

The Ambulatory Care Clinic provides treatment to acutely ill patients on an appointment and walk-in basis. Acutely ill children are treated in the Pediatric Clinic on an appointment basis. Specialty clinics are offered in many different areas, however, most require a referral from the Ambulatory Care Clinic.

The hospital provides a Family Practice Program that offers a wide range of services to enrolled members.

Call the Navy's Navcare Clinic near Northwoods Mall (2070 Northbrook Blvd.) at 764-4670 for prerecorded information; 764-4606 for mammography information; and 764-4354 for all other assistance.

The Naval Station Branch Medical Clinic phone number is 743-3390.

The Naval Shipyard Branch Medical Clinic phone number is 743-6812.

The Health Benefits Office at 743-5260 or 743-2996 assists patients in Champus and Medicare claims processing.

Naval Hospital visiting hours are from 1:00 to 8:00 PM daily.

Charleston holds many architectural surprises, such as this ornate ironwork.

Greater Charleston
Real Estate

When it comes to real estate, one thing is crystal clear; Greater Charleston has it all. You'll find everything from antebellum mansions, resort homes, luxury townhouses, beachfront condominiums, suburban dwellings, planned communities with starter homes, affordable apartments and every once in awhile...a fine old plantation.

Visitors and newcomers are sometimes stunned by the diversity of Lowcountry neighborhoods. This wide spectrum of real estate offerings is illuminated to some degree by the average selling prices for homes in the Greater Charleston area.

According to the Charleston Trident Multiple Listing Service, the average selling price for a home in the Tri-County area in 1992 was $100,562. And the breakdowns by specific areas were as follows:

The average price of a home in the West Ashley area was $98,820; West Islands, $115,543; North Charleston, $63,029; East Cooper, $131, 015; Peninsular Charleston $212,224; Dorchester County, $87,495; and Berkeley County, $80,942. (Remember these figures are only averages and you'll find a wide range of selling prices within each of the areas mentioned above.)

One of the best resources for specific real estate information in Greater Charleston is the Charleston Trident Association of Realtors. With nearly 2,000 members throughout Charleston, Dorchester and Berkeley counties (the Trident area), you can easily find a professional who can help you find the home that's right for you.

The companies selected to highlight in this guide are among the best. Of course, there are many others who are excellent, but space limitations forbid our providing a complete listing here. You may want to check your Yellow Pages for a real estate firm specializing in an area that's of particular interest to you. Or, contact the Charleston Trident Association of Realtors, 5675 Woodbine Avenue, Charleston, S.C. 29406. You'll find their office located just off the Remount Road exit ramp on the right off I-26; the phone is 747-0600.

Real Estate Companies

Of course, choosing a real estate company is a very personal matter. But because it is such an important decision, be sure you find an agent who truly understands you and your priorities. Sometimes that's easier said than done.

An agent who specializes in investment properties may not understand why you want to see only pre-Revolutionary houses or why an otherwise acceptable house won't do because grandmother's dining room furniture won't fit....

By the same token, an agent with a reputation for handling plantations and historic properties may not understand the needs of a first-time buyer, or the advantages of one school system over another....

But, in general the agents in the Greater Charleston area are well versed in the needs of a broad spectrum market. And, with the multi-listing services, almost any agent can show you any house or property you might be interested in the area. As with any business relationship, some frank discussions early on about what you're looking for (and in what price range) can help you avoid wasting time and patience — both yours and theirs. Just remember open communication with your real estate agent (or company) is your first key to finding the right home.

DOWNTOWN CHARLESTON PROPERTIES

Residential real estate in downtown Charleston can be a very specialized market. You're looking at properties with historic and aesthetic values that often override the considerations of ordinary shelter. And there is that awesome specter of restoration to consider — whether it's something already accomplished at great expense or it's something

you feel you want to tackle. Then, there are special tax strategies and things like "facade easements" to learn about — which can make owning a home in the historic district more affordable.

Sound complicated? It is. So it's best to get some help from people who deal with this on a daily basis. Here are some of the companies with plenty of experience in selling residential real estate in downtown Charleston.

ANN GREEN REAL ESTATE, INC.
41 Broad Street, Charleston   723-3900
This firm (currently with nine agents) has a highly successful Broad Street office specializing in downtown Charleston residential real estate. They also have a property management division which can be accessed by calling 720-5881.

ARTHUR RAVENEL REAL ESTATE COMPANY
635 East Bay Street   723-7847
This small family company has been in business since 1945. Their experienced agents can help you with purchases ranging from historic properties downtown, to waterfront properties, to commercial real estate.

JOSEPH P. RILEY REALTY
13 Broad Street, Charleston   723-3700
This downtown real estate firm has been around since 1937 — founded by the late father of long-time Charleston Mayor Joseph P. Riley, Jr. Agents associated with this firm have a knowledgeable perspective on the changing values of Charleston's residential real estate.

They have listings for local island properties and North Carolina mountain retreats as well.

DANIEL RAVENEL REAL ESTATE COMPANY

21 Broad Street, Charleston   723-7150

This company, begun in 1983, has 12 agents currently representing commercial, waterfront and downtown Charleston residential real estate. They specialize in historic properties and are corporate members of the National Trust for Historic Preservation. Most of their agents are native Charlestonians with special insights into the local real estate scene. The company also has offices on Sullivans Island and Isle of Palms. Their property management division number is 723-2763.

DISHER, HAMRICK & MYERS, INC.

480 East Bay Street, Charleston   577-4115

This 12-year-old company has seven full-time agents whose primary focus is on historic properties in downtown Charleston. All but one live in the historic district in old homes and relate to the area personally as well as professionally. Most have been through the restoration process and work well with clients facing that challenge...a perspective that clients find to be invaluable.

ANN CHAPMAN REAL ESTATE COMPANY

55 Broad Street, Charleston   723-7867

With almost 10 years experience in the field, this company's owner is a native Charlestonian who has made quite a name for herself in this sophisticated and specialized real estate market. The company prides itself on its ability to provide personal service and attention to detail.

READ & READ REALTORS

*37 Broad Street, Charleston   577-5400 or
1-800-421-3089*

Here's an old and well-established real estate firm handling sales, rentals and leasing in downtown Charleston and throughout the tri-county area. They have 10 agents with additional offices in West Ashley, North Charleston and East Cooper areas.

Tri-County Real Estate Companies

In addition to the independent real estate companies who specialize in historic properties or beach homes, there are the giant franchise networks available here — eager to meet your real estate needs. These companies offer newcomers complete, one-stop comprehensive real estate service—whether you're moving across the country or just across town. Look for names like Gallery of Homes, Better Homes & Gardens, Coldwell Banker, RE/MAX and ERA.

In fact, we're seeing a definite trend among some of the older, larger real estate companies toward joining these nationwide franchise networks. The idea here is that there's strength in numbers; that teamwork and standardization lead to better efficiency and greater success.

RE/MAX REALTORS (FORMERLY THE MAX HILL COMPANY)

This company, with more than 25 years experience in the local real estate market, recently joined the RE/MAX network. RE/MAX was No. 1 in Canada last year (No. 2 in the USA) for "number of actual transactions." Presently, about 20 fully trained and qualified

agents work out of three Lowcountry offices — in Mt. Pleasant, James Island and downtown Charleston. These locations are:

824 Johnnie Dodds Blvd., Mt. Pleasant	881-9925
33 Broad Street, downtown Charleston	577-3030
44 West Ashley Road, James Island	571-5220

COLDWELL BANKER O'SHAUGHNESSY REAL ESTATE SERVICE CENTER

Here's another company that was formerly a closely held family real estate empire — now networking nationally (and internationally) through Coldwell Banker. There are now nine Lowcountry offices ready to serve the newcomer who first calls their Relocation Office at 803-763-4610 or writes 1953 Sam Rittenberg Blvd., Charleston, SC 29407. Their offices are:

8252 Rivers Avenue, North Charleston	797-7799
118 Spring Hall Drive, Goose Creek	572-1213
1825 Trolley Road, Summerville	871-9000
900 Johnny Dodds Blvd. (East Cooper) Mt. Pleasant	884-1800
452 Folly Road, James Island	795-7810
1315 Ashely River Road, (West Ashley) Charleston	571-7400
343 East Bay Street, (Downtown) Charleston	577-2839
2359 Bohicket Road, Johns Island	559-5511
1024 Palm Blvd., Isle of Palms	886-8110

PRUDENTIAL CAROLINAS REALTY

This company operates a full-time, salaried staff in their Relocation Offices at 342 East Bay Street.

Newcomers may call toll-free 1-800-334-0171. Discuss your real estate needs with a trained staff able to help you with school applications, tax forms, tuition fees, handicapped accessibility...even career assistance. Then, you're referred to a hand-picked agent in one of these regional offices:

Archdale Office
7951 Dorchester Road,
Charleston Heights   552-2905
Goose Creek Office,
220 St. James Ave.,
Goose Creek   797-6121
Downtown Office, 342
East Bay Street, Charleston 722-4116
Mt. Pleasant Office, 786-A
Johnnie Dodds Blvd.   884-1622
Summerville Office, 132 N.
Main St., Summerville   873-0722
West Ashley Office,
1731 Savannah Hwy., Charleston 556-5800
Property Management Division
(for help with rentals)   722-4116

ERA REAL ESTATE

With more than 34,000 agents across the country, this company (which pioneered the concept of nationwide multiple listing) now gives the concept of networking new meaning. There are 12 offices between Myrtle Beach and Savannah. This scale of operation offers the seller a higher degree of security; i.e. if they don't sell your home, they'll buy it from you — so you can go ahead with your move. They offer the buyer a one-year warranty on your new home, too. They've recently added a feature, "electronic information service," which allows you to preview any ERA listed home in America on your own home computer. Local ERA companies include:

ERA American, 225 Hwy. 52,
Goose Creek   899-5777
ERA Locations, 625 Old Trolley Rd.,
Summerville   851-1600
ERA Harper,
9505 Hwy. 78, Ladson   797-0858
ERA Fox Everidge, 8735, North Park Blvd.,
North Charleston   797-3009
ERA Royce King, 745 Johnnie Dodds Blvd.
Mt. Pleasant,   881-0913

Beach-Resort Properties

Beach properties especially on the resort barrier islands like Kiawah, Seabrook and Isle of Palms (Wild Dunes) are considered to be a real estate specialty here in the Lowcountry. Several companies deal exclusively in resort properties while others have "resort divisions" or satellite offices that handle resort sales and rentals.

Because many of these beachfront homes are, in fact, second homes or would-be retirement homes for the owners, it's common to find the same real estate company who sold the property representing the owners in short-term leasing arrangements to carefully screened area visitors. Vacation rental packages offered under this kind of agreement usually are called "property management" services.

Some of the best of these companies are:

ISLE RESORT PROPERTIES
3714-G Bohicket Road   800-345-0085
                          or 768-3533

Whether you're looking for a vacation rental or permanent home, Isle Resort Properties can find the perfect villa, cottage, condo or home. Located in The Island Center, they serve Seabrook and Kiawah Islands, and Bohicket Marina. For a free brochure, call their toll-free number.

PAM HARRINGTON EXCLUSIVES

3690 Bohicket Road,   *768-0273 or*
Suite 2-C, Johns Island   *800-845-6966*

This company, headquartered near Kiawah in The Island Center, has a lion's share of business on Kiawah Island. They've been helping visitors secure luxury accommodations and premium real estate on Kiawah, Seabrook and Johns Island since 1978. Sales are handled through 768-3635.

CARROLL REALTY

103 Palm Blvd., Isle of Palms   *886-9600*

This firm, begun in 1981, specializes in the sale and rental of resort homes on Isle of Palms and Sullivan's Island. Their offices are located between the islands on Palm Boulevard.

OCEAN ONE REALTY, INC.

Island Center, Isle of Palms   *(800) 365-6114*
or 886-8333

An innovative, progressive company, Ocean One handles home sales, beach rentals and investment properties. They specialize in the islands but serve the greater Charleston area with equal concern and service. Their combination of sales office, property management and rental operation works together successfully to offer complete personalized service.

BEACHSIDE REAL ESTATE

Island Center,   *800-888-4056*
Isle of Palms   *or 886-4056*

Offering full, professional ser-

vice, Beachside Real Estate specializes in Island properties. The three principals are Island residents themselves, and have extensive combined experience, having been involved in the initial development of Wild Dunes. With their expertise, they can find you the perfect villa, townhouse or home for your vacation or year round living.

ISLAND REALTY

1304 Palm Blvd., Isle of Palms   *886-8144*

Since 1977, this firm has been a major player on the Isle of Palms (Wild Dunes) and Sullivan's Island property sales and resort rental scene. They have 19 sales agents and 10 full-time employees in their resort rental division. They also have a beachfront meeting and convention center with resort amenities available independently—complete with golf packages on Wild Dunes.

MARRONE REALTY

3232 Maybank Highway,
Johns Island   *559-0092*

This company has specialized in island real estate since 1985 and has an excellent reputation for service. They deal in resort homes, waterfront property and country acreage on Seabrook, Kiawah, Johns Island and Wadmalaw Island.

Apartment Rentals

DOWNTOWN CHARLESTON AREA

411 MEETING STREET

411 Meeting Street, Charleston   *723-2057*

These rents range from $395

to $650 per month for efficiencies, 1-bedroom/1-bath; 2-bedroom/1-bath; and 2 bedroom/1.5-bath units. These fully equipped apartments have almost every amenity possible — including a pool, Jacuzzi, club room and fenced parking with card access — all in the heart of downtown Charleston. Leases are 6 and 12 months (short-term leases are available on the efficiencies). Security deposit is $200 to $300. Pets are conditional. Management is by Lexington Group Properties.

FRED WICHMAN REALTORS
768 St. Andrews Blvd.,
Charleston   556-2100
Although this company's vast real estate holdings are mostly off-peninsula on James Island, West Ashley and Mt. Pleasant, they do handle a number of apartment rentals in the downtown area. Offerings range from efficiencies to 3-bedroom luxury apartments with every amenity and feature. Rentals here can range from $325 to $2,000. Call for details.

SERGEANT JASPER APARTMENTS
310 Broad Street   723-7544
This newly renovated high rise apartment building is at the very foot of trendy Broad Street — with spectacular views of the Ashley River and/or Colonial Lake. They offer a 1-room efficiency; 1-bedroom/1-bath; 2-bedroom/1-bath, and 2-bedrooms/2-baths units. Utilities and off-street parking are included. Rentals range from $440 to $850. A security deposit of one month's rent is required. Leases are 6 and 9 months. No pets are al-

lowed. Management (on-site) is by The Beach Company.

WEST ASHLEY AREA

ASHLEY CROSSING
2235 Ashley Crossing Drive,
West Ashley   571-5711
Rents range from $480 to $620 for these 1-bedroom/1-bath, 2-bedroom/2-bath apartments. Plush carpeting and window treatments are included. Patio doors lead off the master bedroom and living room to large balconies. Units have storage, fireplaces, cathedral ceilings and more. Amenities include a pool, Jacuzzi, tennis and volleyball courts and a fishing pier on a well-stocked lake. Leases are flexible; security deposit is $200. Pets are conditional. Management is by Chrisken Real Estate.

ASHLEY HALL GARDENS
2040 Ashley River Road,
West Ashley   766-2555
Rentals for these 2-bedroom/1.5-bath, 3-bedroom/2-bath garden apartments start at $425. Ceiling fans and carpeting are included. There's a pool and laundry on site, too. Lease agreements are monthly and six or 12 months. Security deposit is $150. Pets are welcome with a $150 fee. Some furnished units are available. Management is by Blake Shewmaker & Associates.

ASHLEY OAKS APARTMENTS
78 Ashley Hall Plantation Road,
Charleston   766-6369
The price range here for 1-bedroom/1-bath, 2-bedroom/2-bath, 3-bedroom townhouse/2-

bath, and 3-bedroom townhouse/ 2.5-bath is $380 to $580 a month. Water, sewer, sanitation and pest control are included. Amenities include two pools, two tennis courts, two basketball courts, volleyball and playground areas. Lease agreements are six and 12 months. Security deposit is $150. Pets are welcome (limited to 2) with a $100 fee assessed each pet. Management is by Duddlesten.

BRIERGREEN APARTMENTS
3 Sawgrass Road,
James Island 795-9232

Rentals here start at $450 for 1-bedroom/1-bath, 2-bedroom/1-bath, 3-bedroom/1.5-bath apartments close to James Island Park and Folly Beach. Water is furnished. Amenities include a tennis court, clubhouse, pool and children's playground. Lease agreements are six and 12 months with a military transfer clause. Security deposit is $225. Pets are welcome with a $150 deposit and a $75 fee. Management is by Darby Development.

CASTLEWOOD
885 Castlewood Blvd.,
Charleston 556-2030

These 2-bedroom/1.5-bath apartments near Citadel Mall and other shopping centers rent from $415 to $460 per month. Water and sewer are included. Washers and driers are available at a small cost. Amenities are two pools plus a kiddie pool, a Jacuzzi, clubhouse, exercise room, fishing lake, volleyball court, picnic areas and free basic cable TV. Lease agreements are 12 months and, at extra cost, six months. Security deposit is $200. No pets are allowed.

CHARLESTON ARMS
1551 Sam Rittenberg Blvd.,
Charleston 556-3303

These family-oriented rentals range from $395 to $480 for 1- and 2-bedroom units available in three different floor plans. Some have patios, others have balconies. Water is furnished. Amenities include two pools, a tennis court, an elevator, outside storage and laundry facilities. Leases are 6, 9 and 12 months; security deposits are negotiable. Pets are accepted (under 25 lbs.) with a fee of $75 and a deposit of $125.

DRAYTON QUARTER
2285 Ashley River Road
Charleston 763-2763

These 1-bedroom/1-bath; 2-bedroom/2-bath units range from $459 to $649 and feature a large screened-in patio or balcony. You'll find vaulted ceilings, fireplaces, and fine sports facilities — including a pool, lighted tennis court, volleyball, and Jacuzzi with a party gazebo and picnic area, too. Police, corporate, senior citizen and MUSC discounts are available. Pets are welcome (under 20 lbs.) and a security deposit is required. Management is by Balcor.

GEORGETOWN APARTMENTS
1476 Orange Grove Road,
Charleston 766-8783

These 1-, 2-, and 3-bedroom apartments rent from $395 to $555 and all have extremely spacious floor plans. Particularly noteworthy are the large bedrooms and ample storage space. Some have patios, others have balconies. There's a swimming pool, cabana and children's playground. Lease agreements are six, nine and 12 months (less than six-month leases are $50 more). Security deposits are conditional. Pets are accepted (under 25 lbs.) with a $125 deposit and a $75 fee. Management is by Griffin.

INDIGO CREEK
1735 Ashley Hall Road,
Charleston   *556-1233*
These apartments range from $375 to $460 for 1-bedroom/1-bath flat, 2-bedroom/2-bath flat, and 2-bedroom/1.5-bath townhouse units. Window treatments and ceiling fans are included. Amenities include a pool, volleyball and shuffleboard courts, clubhouse and more. Leases are six and 12 months. Security deposits range from $225 to $350 with a (conditional) pet. Management is by J.J. Kerr.

PLANTATION APARTMENTS
1840 Carriage Lane,
Charleston   *556-1188*
Close to Charles Towne Landing and shopping malls, these 1-, 2-, and 3-bedroom apartments have great variety. Both furnished and unfurnished units are available from $385 to $540 per month. Corporate units are available, too. Amenities include two pools, a clubhouse and a fenced-in playground. Leasing is six and 12 months. Security deposit is $100. Pets under 25 lbs. are accepted with a $75 fee and a $125 deposit. Management is by Griffin.

PLANTATION OAKS
2225 Ashley River Road
Charleston   *766-6122*
These 1-bedroom/1-bath and 2-bedroom/2-bath units range from $480 to $615. Leases are six months, with a security deposit of $200. These apartments have fireplaces, screened porches and furnished window treatments. There's a pool, two tennis courts, volleyball, a clubhouse and car wash. Some handicap units are available. Pets (25 lbs.) require a $150 deposit and $100 fee.

THE OAKS
1850 Ashley Crossing Lane
Charleston   *763-4661*
Rents here range from $460 to $590 with six- and 12-month lease options. They offer 1-bedroom/1-bath and 2-bedroom/2-bath units with fireplaces and built-in shelves. There's a pool (for swimming and water volleyball), Jacuzzi, two lighted tennis courts and planned social activities. Some furnished apartments are available. Pets are conditional with a $150 fee; and the security deposit is $150. Management is by Insignia.

PLANTERS TRACE
2222 Ashley River Road
Charleston   *571-0842*
Managed by InterSouth, these 1- and 2-bedroom/1-bath; 2-bedroom/2-bath; 3-bedroom/2-bath units range from $370 to $495. Lease options are six, nine and 12 months. There's either a fenced-in patio or a balcony with each unit plus a pool, tennis court, outside storage, and a clubhouse. Senior citizen discounts

are offered. Pets (20 lbs.) are conditional. Security deposit is $100.

WESTCHASE APARTMENTS
1742 Sam Rittenberg Blvd.,
West Ashley   *571-0471*

Rents here range from $400 to $565 for 1-bedroom/1-bath, 1-bedroom with den/1-bath, 2-bedroom/1-bath, 2-bedroom townhouse/1.5-bath, and 2-bedroom with den/1-bath units. All have dead-bolt locks, peep holes, and smoke detectors. Amenities include fireplaces, bay windows and window seats, clubhouse, pool and Jacuzzi, plus a lighted tennis court, boat parking and more. Lease agreements are seven through 12 months; security deposit is $125 per occupant. Small pets are allowed with a fee (limit of 2). Management is by the Paragon Group.

WINDJAMMER APARTMENTS
1742 Sam Rittenberg Blvd.,
West Ashley   *571-0471*

These 1-bedroom/1-bath, 1-bedroom with den/1-bath, 2-bedroom/1-bath, 2-bedroom townhouse/1.5-bath, and 2-bedroom with den/1-bath apartments range from $350 to $525. Some units have fireplaces, all have access to swimming pool, clubhouse and volleyball court. Water is included. Leases are six and 12 months; security deposit is $250. There is a mili-

tary transfer clause. Children and pets are welcome. The pet fee is $150. Management is by Love Properties.

MT. PLEASANT AREA

ANCHORAGE APARTMENTS
1700 Whipple Road,
Mt. Pleasant   *884-6906*

These units rent from $435 to $520 for 1-bedroom/1-bath, 2-bedroom/1.5-bath, and 3-bedroom/2-bath apartments. All kitchen appliances are included, plus window treatments. There's an on-site pool, two tennis courts and laundry facilities. Some furnished apartments are available. There is a military transfer clause. Pets are conditional with a fee of $100. Security deposit is $225. Management is by J.J. Kerr.

BAY CLUB
1481 Center Street Ext.
Mt. Pleasant   *881-9651*

These 1-bedroom/1-bath; 2-bedroom/2-bath units range from $460 to $605 with a 12-month lease and a transfer clause. Look for fireplaces, skylights, cathedral ceilings, patios or balconies and sports facilities (tennis, pool, Jacuzzi). Pet deposit is $100 (limit of one, under 25 lbs.), with a fee of $100. Security deposit is $150; management is by Tenmer.

Insiders' Tip

Insiders Like:
The holiday atmosphere of King Street and "Candy Cane Lane" during the whole Christmas season.

BEAUMONT TOWNHOUSES
2100 Emerald Terrace,
Mt. Pleasant   *881-9484*

These townhouse apartments range from $675 to $810 for 2-bedroom/2.5-bath and 3-bedroom/2.5-bath units. Kitchen appliances include microwave and self-cleaning oven. Water, sewer and monthly pest control are included. There's a pool, exercise room and a laundry on site. Leases are flexible. Security deposit is $200 per person with a military transfer clause. Pets are conditional with a nonrefundable $250 fee. Management is by Elk.

CRICKENTREE
1061 Hwy. 17 Bypass
Mt. Pleasant   *884-4334*

These rents start at $460 for the 1-bedroom/1-bath and 2-bedroom/2-bath units. Amenities here include a fireplace, patio or balcony, pool, lighted tennis courts and more. Water and pest control services are provided. Leases are six and 12 months with a military transfer clause. Security deposit is $225. Pets are conditional. Management is by Darby Development.

EAST RIDGE
269 Alexandria Road
Mt. Pleasant   *881-0013*

From Tenmer (management), these 1-bedroom/1-bath; 2-bedroom/2-bath, 3-bedroom/2-bath apartments range from $460 to $690. Lease options are nine and 12 months with transfer clause. Amenities include fireplaces, patios or balconies, outside storage, free basic cable, a pool, Jacuzzi, tennis courts and a car wash. Pet deposit is $100 with a $150 fee (un-

der 25 lbs., one per unit). Security deposit is $150.

HARBOR POINTE
331 Harbor Pointe Drive
Mt. Pleasant   *884-2345*

Here you'll find 1-bedroom/1-bath, 2-bedroom/1-bath, 2-bedroom/2-bath and 3-bedroom/2-bath units ranging from $470 to $735. Lease options are six and 12 months with a transfer clause. These units feature glass sun-rooms with lakefront views, vaulted ceilings, fireplaces, patios or balconies, a pool and two lighted tennis courts. Pets are conditional with a fee of $150; the security deposit is $200.

HIBBEN FERRY
1054 Anna Knapp Blvd.,
Mt. Pleasant   *884-6779*

Rentals range from $490 to $620 for these 1-bedroom/1-bath and 2-bedroom/2-bath units which include patios or balconies, fireplaces, window treatments, plus access to a pool and two tennis courts. You'll find outside storage, a clubhouse and designated sports areas for volleyball and basketball, plus fishing off their two piers on Shem Creek. Rent includes reverse osmosis water. Lease agreements are six and 12 months with a transfer clause; security deposits are $200. Pets are conditional. Management is by Insignia.

THE MEADOWS
Off Old Georgetown Road,   *881-2208*
Mt. Pleasant   *884-8970*

Rentals range upward from $505 for these 2-bedroom/1-bath and 3-bedroom/2-bath apartments. Amenities include a pool, attic storage and free basic cable TV. Leases are six and 12 months; security deposit is a month's rent. Pets are conditional (limited to one) with deposit of $100 and a fee of $100. Management is by Howell.

PACES WATCH
997 Johnny Dodds Blvd.,
Mt. Pleasant **884-6467**

Rates range between $445 and $750 for efficiency, 1-bedroom/1-bath, 2-bedroom/1-bath, 2-bedroom/2-bath apartments. Rent includes carpeting and window treatments, balconies or screened porches and fireplaces. Amenities include a fitness center with aerobic classes, a whirlpool spa, two lighted tennis courts and a car wash area. Reverse osmosis water, sewer, garbage collection and pest control are provided. Leases are six, nine and 12 months. The security deposit is $200. Pets are conditional with fees of $200. Management is by Trammell Crow.

PARISH PLACE
1175 Mathis Ferry Road,
Mt. Pleasant **884-9028**

Rents begin at $425 for 1-bedroom/1-bath, 2-bedroom/1-bath, and 3-bedroom/1.5-bath units only a mile from the Mark Clark Expressway. Carpeting and blinds are included. Residents have a pool plus tennis and basketball courts. Leases are six and 12 months with a military transfer clause. Security deposit is $225 minimum, pets are conditional with a fee of $75 and a deposit of $150. Management is by Darby.

PALMETTO PLANTATION
2011 Hwy. 17 N.
Mt. Pleasant **881-6800**

Just opened — these 1-bedroom/1-bath; 2-bedroom/1-bath; 2-bedroom/2-bath; and 3-bedroom/2-bath apartments range from $465 to $795. Lease options are six, nine and 12 months with a transfer clause. Look for vaulted ceilings, fireplaces, garden rooms with lake views, balconies or screened verandas, a great fitness center, optional covered parking, a pool, lighted tennis court, a playground, and concierge services. Pets are limited to one (20 lbs., 20") with a fee of $200 and a deposit of $100. The security deposit is $200. Management is by Aronov.

REMINGTON FOREST
Rifle Range Road,
Mt. Pleasant **884-9028 or 884-8970**

Duplex apartments here rent from $575 to $675 for 2-bedroom/2-bath, 3-bedroom/2-bath units. All have fireplaces, ceiling fans and attic storage. Amenities include a pool and free basic cable TV. Leases are six and 12 months, security deposit is $250 minimum. Pets are conditional (limited to one) with a fee of $100 and a deposit of $100. Management is by Howell & Associates.

RIVERWOOD APARTMENTS
1053 Rifle Range Road,
Mt. Pleasant **884-0731**

Rents here start at $430 for 1-bedroom/1-bath, 2-bedroom/1.5-bath, and 3-bedroom/2-bath apartments. All units have window treatments and there's a tennis court, pool and clubhouse on site. Lease options are six, nine and 12 months with a military transfer clause. Security deposit is $225. Pets are conditional. Management is by Darby Development.

RUNAWAY BAY
800 Runaway Bay,
Mt. Pleasant   881-8444

Units here rent from $490 to $690 per month for 1-bedroom/1-bath, 1-bedroom with den/1-bath, 2-bedroom/1-bath, 2-bedroom/2-bath, 2-bedroom deluxe/2-bath, and 2-bedroom with den/2-bath. Amenities include screened porches, fireplaces, vaulted ceilings, a weight room, a jogging trail/fitness course, pool with lap-lanes and more. Lease options are six and 12 months. Security deposits range from $200 to $300. Pets are conditional with a deposit of $100 and a fee of $150. Management is by America First.

SNEE FARM LAKES
1141-J Shadow Lake Drive,
Mt. Pleasant   884-1658

Rentals here range from $595 to $760, although you'll occasionally see special offers. Senior citizen rates are lower. Units are 2-bedroom/2-bath, 2-bedroom/2.5-bath, and 3-bedroom/3-bath apartments. All have large pantries and abundant closet space. Amenities include private patios, separate pools for adults and children, a private lake, car wash facilities and more. Some furnished townhouses are available. Leases are offered with a security deposit of $250. Pets are conditional with a fee of $100. Management is by Brownyard Investments.

THICKETT APARTMENTS
1900 Hwy. 17 By-Pass,
Mt. Pleasant   884-2876

These apartments start at $460 for 1-bedroom/1-bath and 2-bedroom/2-bath units. All have fireplaces and patios or balconies. Amenities include a pool, a lighted tennis court, a pond, a clubhouse and more. Lease agreements are nine and 12 months with a military transfer clause. Security deposit is $225. Pets are conditional. Management is by Darby.

NORTH CHARLESTON (EAST) AREA

AUDUBON PARK
Eagle Landing Blvd. (off Rivers)
Hanahan   569-0055

Near Northwoods Mall, these 1-bedroom/1-bath; 2-bedroom/2-bath; 3-bedroom/2-bath apartments range from $460 to $685. Lease options are six, nine and 12 months with a military transfer clause. Amenities include fireplaces, screened patios or balconies, a pool, a sports court, weight room, playground, picnic area with gas grills, plus access to Eagle Landing golf. Some handicap units are available. Pets are conditional with a $150 fee and a $150 deposit. Security deposit is $250; management is by Estates.

CENTURY OAKS
1501 E. Enterprise,
North Charleston   767-4525

These are single family homes and duplexes ranging from $270 to $385 per month. Rates include water, sewer, trash pickup and extermination services. They are located close to vocational and elementary schools. Leases are six and 12 months with a security deposit of $100 to $175. Pets are welcome with a $100 fee. Section 8 applications are accepted. Management is by Kerr Properties.

FARRINGTON PLACE
7927 St. Ives Road
North Charleston   *569-3509*
Offering 1-bedroom/1-bath; 2-bedroom/2-bath; and 3-bedroom/2-bath units, these rents range from $460 to $705. The lease agreements are the standard six-, nine- and 12-month options with a military transfer clause. You'll find cathedral ceilings, fireplaces, patios or balconies, a pool and tennis court, recreation room, clubhouse, exercise room with sauna/Jacuzzi, and additional storage. Security surveillance is available. Pets are conditional (under 25 lbs.) with a $100 deposit and $100 fee. Security deposit is $200; management is by H.V. McCoy.

NORTH COVE
7950 Crossroad Drive,
North Charleston   *572-8300*
Here are rents in the $435 to $635 range for 1-bedroom/1-bath, 2-bedroom/2-bath and 3-bedroom/2-bath apartments. Water is included. Amenities are fireplaces, patios or balconies, vaulted ceilings, skylights (in some), a pool, tennis court and playground. Leases are six, nine and 12 months with a transfer clause. Security deposit is $200. Pets are conditional with a fee of $100 and a $100 deposit. Management is by H.V. McCoy Properties.

PLANTERS CROSSING
7910 Crossroads Drive,
North Charleston   *572-0660*
Located close to Northwoods Mall and I-26, apartments here range from $390 to $485 for 1-bedroom/1-bath and 2-bedroom/2-bath units. All units include large pantries, carpeting and window treatments and some have fireplaces. Amenities include a pool, lighted tennis courts, a clubhouse, baseball and picnic areas and more. Leases are three, nine and 12 months. Security deposit is $100. Pets are conditional (under 20 lbs.). Management is by InterSouth.

RIVER PLACE
1920 McMillan Ave.,
North Charleston   *744-2743*
This assortment of 1-, 2-, and 3-bedroom flats and townhouses rents in the $325 to $435 range. Some are furnished, others not. Water, garbage pickup and monthly pest control are included. They have 24-hour security gates at the entrance plus two pools, volleyball and basketball courts, two playgrounds and more. Leases are six and 12 months with a military transfer clause. Security deposit is $100 to $200. No pets are allowed. Management is by LeLo.

NORTH AREA (WEST)

BRACKENBROOK APARTMENTS
Apartment Blvd.,
North Charleston   *552-1901*
These 1-bedroom/1-bath, 2-bedroom/1-bath and 3-bedroom/1.5-bath apartments start at $375 a month. Water and window treat-

ments are included. Amenities include a tennis court, pool and playground. Leases are six and 12 months with a military transfer clause. The security deposit is $200 ($150 for military). Pets are conditional with a $75 fee and a $150 deposit. Management is by Darby Development.

OAKRIDGE TOWNHOUSES
4230 Bonaparte Drive,
North Charleston   *767-2978*
Rental fees for these 2-bedroom/1.5-bath townhouses start at $390 a month. Water, sewer, garbage pickup and basic cable and HBO are included. Safety features are firewalls, dead-bolt locks and smoke detectors. Leases are six and 12 months; security deposit is $150. No pets are allowed.

PALMETTO TOWNHOUSES
7501 Peppercorn Lane,
North Charleston   *552-5606*
These 2-bedroom/1.5-bath townhouses just off Ashley Phosphate Road range from $365 to $395 per month. Water and pest control services are provided and window treatments are included. Lease agreements are six, nine and 12 months with a security deposit of $100. Pets are conditional (under 20 lbs.). Management is by InterSouth.

WAVERLY PLACE APARTMENTS
1900 Waverly Place Lane,
North Charleston   *767-4525*
Rental fees range from $435 to $615 for these 1-bedroom executive, 1-bedroom deluxe, 1-bedroom with den, 2-bedroom/2-bath units. Various models feature vaulted ceil-

ings, fireplaces and bay windows. Shared amenities include volleyball and racquetball courts, a pool, a lighted tennis court, clubhouse, Jacuzzi and an exercise room. There are on-site gazebos with grills for outdoor picnics. Lease agreements are six through 12 months. Security deposit is $200. Pets are conditional with a $200 deposit and a $15 fee per month. Management is by Summit Properties.

HANAHAN AREA

BROADMOOR APARTMENTS
5820 Murray Ave.
Hanahan   *747-0417*
Minutes from the military bases, hospitals, colleges and the airport (with public transportation close by), here are 1-bedroom/1-bath; 2-bedroom/1.5-bath; and 3-bedroom/2-bath apartments with lease options of six to 15 months (military transfer clause included). Rents range from $325 to $500 with a security deposit of $200. Pet fee is $100 with a $100 deposit.

COLONY SQUARE APARTMENTS
1100 River Road
Hanahan   *797-0211*
Rents here range from $335 to $425 for efficiency; 1-bedroom, 1-bath; and 2-bedroom, 1-bath units. There's a pool, clubhouse with party room, children's playground, a volleyball court and weight room on site. Leases are six and 12 months with a military transfer clause. Pets require a $250 fee, and the security deposit is $150.

RIVIERA APARTMENTS
6240 Old Point Road
Hanahan   553-0124

These 1- and 2-bedroom apartments rent from $385 to $435 with six- and 12-month lease agreements (military transfer clause included). A pool, outside storage, a view overlooking a tidal creek, and a private boat ramp are featured. Security deposit is $100, pets are $75 each with a $125 deposit. Management is by Griffin.

LADSON AREA

GRADUATES POINTE
1398 South University Drive
Ladson   572-2608

These are 2-bedroom/2-bath; 3-bedroom/2-bath, and 2.5-bath townhouses rent for $494 to $528 with six- and 12-month leases. Amenities include fireplaces, patios, garages, a pool, tennis court, playground, and a clubhouse. Security deposit is $250; with a pet fee of $150 (one pet only). Management is by Southeastern Properties.

OAKMONT VILLAGE
100 Oakmont Avenue
Ladson   871-3427

Here are 1- and 2-bedroom garden apartments or 2-bedroom townhouses ranging in price from $335 to $425 a month. Lease agreements are monthly, or six and 12 months. Units have carports, access to tennis facilities, a pool, and clubhouse. Security deposit is $150; with a pet fee of $150. Management is by Blake Shewmaker & Associates.

SUMMERVILLE AREA

AUTUMN WAY
101 Hutson Drive,
Summerville   873-5966

These 1-bedroom/1-bath and 2-bedroom/2-bath apartments range from $315 to $340 per month. Amenities include separate pools for adults and children, tennis courts and a children's playground. Monthly pest control is furnished, too. Both six- and 12-month leases are offered with military transfer clauses. The security deposit is $150. Pets are conditional with a fee of $100. Management is by Lane Properties.

DORCHESTER CROSSING
1660 Old Trolley Road,
Summerville   871-7410

Rents here range from $395 to $545 for 1-bedroom/1-bath, 2-bedroom/1.5-bath, 3-bedroom/2-bath apartments. Ask about occasional specials. Smoke detectors, water and outside storage are included. There's a jogging trail, pool, separate kiddie pool, two tennis courts, a clubhouse, playground, car wash area and more. Leases are three, six and 12 months with a military transfer clause. Security deposit is $150. Small pets are allowed with a $150 fee.

PLANTERS VILLAGE
112-B Luden Drive,
Summerville   821-8639 or 884-8970

These 1,200-sq.-ft., 2-bedroom/2.5-bath apartment rentals start at $475 per month. Two different floor plans are available. Both have fireplaces, separate dining rooms and patios. There's a pool on site, as well. Water and sewage are included. Lease agreements are six and 12 months with a military transfer clause. Security deposit is $150 or one month's rent. Pets are allowed (under 25 lbs.) with a $150 fee and a $150 deposit. Management is by Howell & Associates.

SAWBRANCH APARTMENTS
1815 Bacons Bridge Road,
Summerville   *871-6880*

Rents here begin at $380 a month for these family-oriented apartments with 1-bedroom/1-bath, 2-bedroom/2-bath, and 3-bedroom/1.5-bath units. Water and window treatments are provided. Amenities include a tennis court, play area and picnic grounds. Lease options are six and 12 months with a military transfer clause. There's a $225 security deposit. Pets are conditional. Management is by Darby Development.

SOMERSET
1225 Boone Hill Road,
Summerville   *873-6555*

Rates range from $389 to $499 for these apartments which vary in size from 1-bedroom/1-bath, 2-bedroom/1-bath, 2-bedroom/1.5-bath, 3-bedroom/1.5-bath to 3-bedroom/2-bath units. Some have patios, others balconies. All have dead-bolt locks and smoke detectors. Amenities include a pool, clubhouse and a guest apartment. Standard leases are six and 12 months, but shorter periods can be arranged (with a military transfer clause). Pets are allowed with a $150 fee. No security deposit is required. Management is

by Allstate.

TREEHAVEN
400 Pinewood Drive,
Summerville   *873-3356*

The rental range for these 1-bedroom/1-bath, 2-bedroom/1.5-bath, 3-bedroom/2-bath apartments is $320 to $430 a month. They are just off Central Avenue in a quiet, family setting. Amenities include a pool and a children's playground. Leases are six and 12 months with a military transfer clause. Security deposit is $200. Pets are conditional with a deposit of $100 and a $100 fee. Management is by J.J. Kerr.

WESTBURY MEWS
1425 Old Trolley Road
Summerville   *875-2005*

This attractive complex includes 1-bedroom/1-bath; 1-bedroom (Deluxe)/1-bath; 1-bedroom with den/1-bath; 2-bedroom/1-bath; 2-bedroom/2-bath; and 3-bedroom/2-bath units. Rents range from $380 to $640. Look for vaulted ceilings, (optional) fireplaces, screened porches, outdoor storage, pool, spa, clubhouse, exercise room, and a sanded volleyball court and playground. Leases are six and 12 months with a military transfer clause. Pets are conditional with a $150 fee and a $150 deposit.

Building Materials

BEN PETERS BRICK, INC.
1123 Ashley River Rd.   *556-1922*
8232 Rivers Avenue   *553-5555*

BERLIN G. MYERS LUMBER
350 N. Main, Summerville   *873-2010*

BUCK LUMBER & BUILDING SUPPLY, INC.

1911 Maybank Highway	795-0150

CAROLINA BUILDING MATERIALS & SALVAGE

2440 Meeting Street Road	744-2575

G.S. CARTER & SONS, INC.

2143 Heriot Street	577-6644

CONCRETE PRODUCTS CO.

39 Folly Road	556-2266

84 LUMBER

Rt. 176 & Rt. 52	797-6684
704 Johnnie Dodds Blvd.	884-8431

HOME QUARTERS WAREHOUSE

7665 Northwoods Blvd.	572-5885

HUGHES LUMBER AND BUILDING SUPPLY CO., INC.

82 Mary Street	577-6671

LOWE'S

4790 Marriott Drive	744-6286
8155 Rivers Ave.	572-5770
Hwy. 17 North	881-3400

PELICAN BUILDING CENTER

4450 Arco Lane	554-8280
3155 Maybank Hwy.	559-4190
111 Lumber Lane	553-5252

RED TOP BUILDING SUPPLY

3881 Savannah Hwy.	571-6262

SOUTHERN LUMBER AND MILLWORK CORP.

2031 King Street	744-6281

Greater Charleston
Retirement

With its mild climate and natural beauty, the Trident area is an attractive retirement destination. There are numerous residential communities geared to different stages of independence and a growing array of services in the business sector that are tailored to the needs of those enjoying their "golden years."

Special activities for seniors include the Lowcountry Senior Sports Classic, an event that includes golf, a fun walk, tennis, swimming, Frisbee golf, a cycling event, spin casting, darts, billiards bridge and more. For more information, call Laurie Clarke at 849-2061.

The Charleston County Community Education Program sponsors classes that are offered at various Charleston schools and are open (for a fee) to the public. Students may chose classes ranging from ceramics, piano and typing to smocking, flower arrangement and ballroom dancing. All ages are eligible to attend, and fees vary according to class. Seniors 60 years or older may take courses for $25 a semester at The College of Charleston, and for a $15 application fee at The Citadel.

Senior citizens' service organizations include a Senior Services Department at Bon Secours St. Francis Xavier Hospital (call 577-1212) and The Shepherd's Center of Charleston (call 722-2789).

A Resource Guide and Directory of Area Organizations and Community Resources is available for reference or purchase ($8.00) at the Charleston County Library, 404 King Street (call 723-1645).

Some stores discount merchandise for shoppers who are 60 years or older. Revco drugstore gives a 10 percent discount every day for Revco products, and on Wednesdays for all store items, while Eckerd offers discount coupons. Condons Department Store gives a 10 percent discount every Wednesday on all items, and Kerrisons Department Store gives a 10 percent discount every Monday between 10:00 AM and 1:00 PM, as well as all day on Sunday if open (the store closes some Sundays during the summer).

The following living arrangements for seniors in the Trident area are a sampling of what is available:

Resorts

Three well-known resorts in the Trident region, attracting retired executives (as full-time and vacation property owners) from across the nation, are Kiawah, Seabrook and Wild Dunes. Houses, villas and condominiums are available for those interested in upscale, planned community living. The island settings are beautiful, and there is easy access to tennis, golf, swimming, boating and social activities. There are no provisions for assisted living in these developments, but active seniors find the life-style ideal.

(See our Neighborhood sections in the East Islands and West Island sections for more information on these resorts.)

Retirement Apartment Buildings

CANTERBURY HOUSE
175 Market Street   *723-5553*

Those interested in relocating into an apartment building for seniors will find the Canterbury House an appealing option.

The Canterbury House is located on the peninsula, in easy walking distance of shopping on King and Market streets. A city location makes it convenient for volunteers to participate in special programs for residents. There is usually a lengthy waiting list of those interested in apartments here, so get your name on the list early if this is the place for you.

Retirement and Life Care Communities and Homes

BISHOP GADSDEN
EPISCOPAL COMMUNITY
1873 Camp Road   *762-3300*

Affiliated with the Episcopal Church, Bishop Gadsden is located on James Island. Members enjoy the benefits of group living (with such amenities as dining room privileges) in a lovely setting, and are often entertained — with lectures or presentations — by volunteers from Episcopal churches in the community. An assisted living option will be available in the near future.

COOPER HALL RETIREMENT COMMUNITY

937 Bowman Road   *884-6949*

Several options are available at Cooper Hall, including assisted living quarters and apartments. Assisted living quarters are studio, one- or two-bedroom apartments with kitchens and private bath. Services include laundry service, medical surveillance, three meals a day and activities.

Those in retirement living may chose from a one- or two-bedroom or one- or two-bedroom deluxe apartment with amenities such as an indoor swimming pool, pharmacy, beauty salon, laundry facilities and bridge rooms. There is a nurse on call at all hours, and the dining room has a menu from which guests may order as well.

THE ELMS OF CHARLESTON

9100 Elms Plantation   *572-5154 or 800-237-3460*

The Elms is a beautifully land-scaped, controlled access community of single-family homes for "prime time" living in style. Located next to Charleston Southern University and the Trident Regional Medical complex, the amenities of this retiree community are extensive and include an over 8,000-square-foot club with a fitness center, swimming pool, exercise area, spa, library and beauty/barber parlor. Shopping, dining, golf and other cultural opportunities are

Insiders Like:
The enticing aromas of the various coffee beans for sale at Fulford-Egan Coffees & Teas on Meeting Street near the Omni.

Insiders' Tip

within minutes away.

Management maintains the yard and home exteriors.

FRANKE-HOME

261 Calhoun Street   *577-4041*

This residential care facility, operated by Lutheran Homes of South Carolina, is located on the peninsula and offers private and semiprivate rooms with some assistance available. There is a full time staff of licensed practical nurses, certified nursing assistance, a chaplain, beauty care, bus trips, laundry, a library, exercise classes, entertainment, family support groups, a structured volunteer program, chapel services and special dietary assistance.

PRESBYTERIAN HOME
OF SOUTH CAROLINA

201 West Ninth North Street,
Summerville   *873-2550*

The independent living options at the Presbyterian Home include 59 outside cottages, 20 efficiency apartments and 17 two-bedroom apartments. Also, there are 120 residential rooms with private baths, and residents are served three meals a day. On site is a beauty shop, barber services and entertainment such as field trips to Spoleto, Monday night movies, ceramics, painting and exercise classes. Bible classes and chapel are conducted, and transportation to the doctor or shopping is furnished. A 90-bed infirmary is run by licensed nurses. Opened in 1958, this community gives priority to South Carolina Presbyterians.

SANDPIPER VILLAGE

1224 Village Crest Avenue,
Mt. Pleasant   *884-5735*

Sandpiper is located in Mt. Pleasant and offers large private and semiprivate rooms. Trained nurses are on duty around the clock, and the services of physical and speech therapists are available. A "Preferred Plan" includes extras ranging from medical exams to cable television. Daily activities and social events, bingo, bridge, arts and crafts, church services, a beauty and barber shop and even a lending library are available in the Sandpiper Village.

Greater Charleston
Media

Daily Newspapers

THE POST AND COURIER
*(Daily paid circulation: 112,286;
Sunday, 128,868)*
*134 Columbus Street,
Charleston, SC 29403-4800   577-7111*

As "the oldest daily newspaper in the South," this famous South Carolina publication appears Monday through Sunday and is published by the Evening Post Publishing Company. *The News and Courier* was founded in 1803; *The Evening Post* in 1894. The merger of these two daily papers as *The Post and Courier* on October 1, 1991 marked the beginning of a new era in Charleston newspaper publishing.

In 1990, the latest of several plant expansions took place when another 10-unit press was installed, doubling the press capacity. Additionally, computerization has advanced production to state-of-the-art, full-page pagination, making it one of the most modern newspaper publishing plants in America.

In keeping with a long tradition of service to the greater Charleston area, *The Post and Courier* now offers more than a daily newspaper to its customers. A weekly zoned section call *This Week* is published every Thursday and serves local news to the six communities comprising the Tri-County area. *The Post and Courier Extra* is a colorful, entertainment-oriented publication that is hand-delivered to 70,000 non-subscribers each week. And, the HomeX custom advertising delivery service can target geographically or demographically, and hand-deliver an advertising message or product sample to any area from a single street to entire zip codes.

Over the years, the staff has won numerous Associated Press awards and has been recognized by The Society for Professional Journalists.

Weekly Newspapers

AIRLIFT DISPATCH (USAF)
(Free distribution; published by the Charleston Air Force Base)
*c/o CCP South, 1365 Ashley River Road
Charleston, SC 29407   763-1800
FAX   763-0089*

With 7,500 copies per issue, this exclusive Charleston AFB newsletter is published 50 weeks per year (excluding the two Fridays after Christmas). It goes to 1,025 on-base private residences with the remainder issued to 60 pick-up points throughout the base. Copy deadline is Tuesday, noon. Space deadline for advertising is Monday, noon.

GOOSE CREEK GAZETTE

(Paid circulation, 4,500)
P.O. Box 304,
Goose Creek, SC 29445　　　　572-0511

This community weekly is published on Wednesday. Principal staff positions include: John Vernelson, Publisher and Bud Burnett, Advertising Manager. The deadline for news and photos is 5 PM on Friday.

HANAHAN NEWS

(Paid circulation, 1,500; total market coverage, 20,500)
P.O. Box 60580,
North Charleston, SC 29419-0580744-0246

Newsroom　　　　747-5773

This is a community-oriented weekly published on Wednesday. Principal staff positions include: Carl Meynardie, Publisher and Paul Meynardie, Advertising Manager. The deadline for news and photos is 5:30 PM on Thursday.

THE BERKELEY INDEPENDENT

(Paid circulation, 11,500; total market coverage, 22,000)
P.O. Box 427,
Moncks Corner, SC 29461　　761-6397
FAX　　　　　　　　　　　899-6996

As a community-based weekly appearing on Wednesday, the major staff positions are Allen Morris, Editor/Publisher and Deidirde Lynch, Advertising Director. The deadline for news and photos is 3:00 PM on Thursday.

THE CATALYST (MUSC)

(Free distribution; published by the Medical University of South Carolina)
c/o CCP South, 1365 Ashley River Road
Charleston, SC 29407　　　　763-1800
FAX　　　　　　　　　　　763-0089

Published weekly with 7,500 copies distributed every other Thursday evening, this tabloid is the MUSC faculty/staff newspaper. Text and editorial is produced by MUSC public relations. This publication reaches the highest concentration of degree-holding professionals in South Carolina. Copy deadline is Tuesday, noon. Space deadline for advertising is Monday, noon.

CHARLESTON CHRONICLE

(Paid circulation, 2,203; total market coverage, 6,000)
P.O. Box 20548,
Charleston, SC 29413　　　　723-2785
FAX　　　　　　　　　　　577-6099

This black-oriented weekly, published on Wednesday, has James J. French, Sr. as Editor and Gladys Hazel as Advertising Manager. The deadline for news and photos is Monday, noon.

COASTAL TIMES

(Paid circulation, 1,250; total market coverage, 5,000)
701 East Bay Street
PCC Box 1407,
Charleston, SC 29403　　　　723-5318

This community weekly with an African American slant is published on Wednesday with James Clyburn as Publisher and Mignon Clyburn as Assistant Publisher/Advertising Director. Deadline for news and photos is 10 AM on Monday.

MOULTRIE NEWS

(Total market coverage, 15,500)
P.O. Box 12110,
Charleston, SC 29422   849-1778
FAX   849-0214

This is a free weekly carrying community news for Mt. Pleasant, Sullivan's Island and Isle of Palms published on Wednesday. Charlie Diggle is Publisher and Advertising Manager. Deadline for news and photos is 5 PM on Friday.

THE JOURNAL

(Paid circulation and rack sales, 6,000)
P.O. Box 12110,
Charleston, SC 29422   849-1778
FAX   849-0214

This weekly carries community news for Charleston's West Ashley area, James Island and Folly Beach. Day of publication is Thursday. Charlie Diggle is Publisher and Advertising Manager. Deadline for news and photos is 5 PM on Friday.

NORTH CHARLESTON NEWS

(Total circulation, 10,500)
P.O. Box 60580,
North Charleston, SC 29419   744-8000

This community-based paper with local news is distributed free throughout the north area. It's published on Wednesday in conjunction with the *Hanahan News*. Paul Meynardie is Editor/Publisher and the deadline for news and photos is 5:30 PM on Thursday.

SUMMERVILLE JOURNAL-SCENE

(Paid circulation, 9,000; total market circulation, 23,000)
104 East Doty Avenue,
Summerville, SC 29483   873-9424
FAX   873-9432

This bi-weekly community paper is published on Wednesday and Friday with comprehensive coverage of the Summerville area and all of Dorchester County. Total market coverage day is the first Wednesday of every month. Major staff positions include William C. Collins, Editor/Publisher, and Dwane Stephens, Advertising Manager. Deadlines for news and photos are two days in advance of intended publication.

Tabloids

The tabloid press in Greater Charleston is on the upswing with several new special-interest newspapers holding sway against the long-time survivors in this highly competitive advertising market.

ARMED FORCES ALUMNI NEWS

(Distributed free with Airlift Dispatch; published by Charleston AFB)
c/o CCP South, 1365 Ashley River Road
Charleston, SC 29407   763-1800
FAX   763-0089

This quarterly tabloid is an insert for *Airlift Dispatch*, the weekly newspaper for Charleston Air Force Base. The editorial content, written under the aegis of the Retiree Activities Program, is geared for the 13,000 local retired military personnel living the greater Charleston area. Call for issue dates, deadlines and rate information.

CHARLESTON ARTS

(Published by Shoestring Publishing Company, Inc.)
Office: 132 East Bay Street, Charleston
P.O. Box 427
Bonneau, SC 29431   *723-6457*

This is a free publication distributed throughout the city of Charleston, acting as a voice of the local arts scene. The writers take on difficult and controversial subjects (like arts funding) and do extensive background research. Reviews of local arts offerings and gallery profiles are standard fare, plus you'll find a comprehensive calendar of area exhibitions, shows and special events. Recently, the publication has spawned a new subsidiary, *Berkeley County Arts (and more)*.

OMNIBUS

(Published by Dixie Media, Inc.)
Office: 1-A Pinckney Street, Charleston
P.O. Box 69
Charleston, SC 29401   *722-6771*

What can you say about a free tabloid that proudly claims to be "a picture paper for people who read"? Good writing, real humor, and a refreshingly irreverent view of the traditional Charleston scene all play important roles in this tabloid's success. This is, in fact, a long-time survivor in the sometimes deadly world of the avant garde tabloid press. Look for discussions of art, politics, food, books, music, theater and wry, entertaining observations of life in general. Charles L. (Pete) Wyrick, Jr. is Publisher/Editor; call for ad rates and publication deadlines.

UPWITH HERALD

(Published by Upwith Media)
334 East Bay Street, Suite G-164
Charleston, SC 29401   *577-5304*

This year-old weekly entertainment and review tabloid is a voice of Charleston's "too cool" crowd. It's just getting off to a good start in the teen and college market. Look for reviews of the local club scene and commentary on the area arts in general. MonGo Nicholl is Publisher/Editor. Input and information flows to and from the publication via voice mailbox (803/863-6363) which stays "open" 24-hours a day.

Television Stations

WCBD CHANNEL 2

P.O. Box 879,   *884-4141*
Charleston, SC 29402   *FAX 881-3410*

This is Charleston's ABC affiliate. William Evans, Jr. is General Manager, Steve Gleason is Program Director. PSAs may be sent in writing or on 1" videotape; material should be received two weeks in advance.

WCIV CHANNEL 4

888 Allbritton Blvd.,   *884-8513*
Mt. Pleasant, SC 29464   *FAX 849-2507*

Here's Charleston's NBC affiliate. Stephen Brock is General Manager, Celia Shaw is Program Director. Send PSAs in writing or on 1" or 3/4" videotape; material should be received one to two weeks in advance.

WCSC CHANNEL 5

P.O. Box 186,   723-8371
Charleston, SC 29402   FAX 723-0074

This is the local CBS affiliate. Jim Smith is General Manager, Charlie Thompson Program Director. PSAs may be sent in writing or on 1" videotape to Beverly Pigg; material should be received two weeks in advance.

WITV CHANNEL 7

P.O. Box 11000   737-3240
Columbia, SC 29211   FAX 737-3417
Newsroom   737-3370

This is Greater Charleston's PBS (Public Broadcasting) station, on the air from 6 AM until midnight. Henry Cauthen is General Manager, Jesse Bowers is Program Director. Contact Tom Fowler (in Columbia) for information regarding locally produced public affairs shows. No PSA's are accepted for direct broadcast.

WTAT CHANNEL 24

4301 Arco Lane,   744-2424
Charleston, SC 29418   FAX 554-9649

This is Charleston's Fox Broadcasting affiliate. They broadcast 24-hours a day. P. J. Ryal is General Manager, William Littleton is Program Director.

WCTP CHANNEL 36

1558 Ben Sawyer Blvd.,
Mt. Pleasant, SC 29464   884-3185

This is Charleston's only locally-owned and operated independent station. They feature popular syndicated programming and two locally produced shows; "Back Talk" with Bob Waters and "Video Jamz" with Anthony Baxter. President and General Manager is Arnold (Mr. B) Baynard, Vice President and Station Manager is Michael Baynard.

Radio Stations

Like the TV stations serving Greater Charleston, the radio stations here tend to serve the entire area, not just the local urban areas. Our listings briefly identify the area's most popular radio station's call letters, their AM or FM frequency, the dial numbers (where to find them), their current mailing address, phone and FAX numbers, and a brief description of the station's programming format.

WAVF FM "96-WAVE" (96.1)

1417 Remount Road,   554-4401,
North Charleston, SC 29406   FAX 566-0814

This 24-hour FM station offers "album-oriented rock" and appeals to the mainstream rock & roll fan. Their mix is about 70% classic rock, with 30% current hits. PSAs may be sent in writing; material should be received two to three weeks prior to airtime. Program Director is Dave Rossi.

WSUY FM, "SUNNY 100 FM" (100.5)

One Orange Grove Rd.,   556-5660
Charleston, SC 29407   FAX 763-0304

This 24-hour FM station has a "soft adult contemporary" format, offering music that's always soft and bright with half-hour long uninterrupted sets each hour. They never talk over the music, and they "say what they play." PSAs may be sent in writing or on cassette or reel-to-reel; material should be received seven days prior to airtime. Program Director is Dave Sousa.

WDXZ FM, "NEW MIX 104.5" (104.5)

One Orange Grove Road,   556-5660
Charleston, SC 29407   FAX 763-0304

This is Charleston's newest FM radio station playing "hot adult contemporary," the best of the '70s, '80s, and '90s. They like to say they're "maximum music, minimum talk." PSAs may be sent in writing or on cassette or reel-to-reel; material should be received seven days prior to airtime. Program Director is John King.

WEZL FM (103.5)

P.O. Box 747,   884-2534
Mt. Pleasant, SC 29465   FAX 884-1218

This is a popular 24-hour FM station with country music fans. They like the term "contemporary country" as it includes the many cross-over hits that country music has these days. They include a locally-produced public affairs show, "Community Forum," on Sunday mornings. PSAs may be sent in writing; material should be received two to three weeks prior to airtime. Their Program Director is T.J. Phillips.

WOKE AM (1340)

P.O. Box 30547,
Charleston, SC 29417   763-1340

Broadcasting from 5 AM to 12:30 AM, this family-oriented AM station features popular music, local information, year round sports programming (including high school basketball), and a strong sense of community spirit. Since 1946, the station has been on the air under the auspices of the Harry C. Weaver Broadcasting Corp. PSAs may be sent in writing or on reel-to-reel. Program Director is Buck Clayton.

WPAL AM (730)

P.O. Box 30999,   763-6330
Charleston, SC 29407   FAX: 769-4857

This 24-hour AM station features a progressive rhythm & blues format, coupled with a mixture of reggae and gospel music. They serve Greater Charleston's 150,000 black consumers and have been on the air for over 45 years. They have two locally-produced public affairs shows called "Open Rap" and "Wednesday's Rap." PSAs should be sent in writing or on reel-to-reel; material should be received two weeks prior to airtime. Program Director is Jaye Jackson.

WYBB FM "98 ROCK" (98.1)

59 S. Windermere Boulevard,   769-4799
Charleston, SC 29407   FAX 769-4797

This 24-hour FM station features a "classic rock" format with the best rock 'n' roll of the late '60s, the '70s, and the early '80s. PSAs may be sent in writing to Stacie Kendrick; material should be received six days prior to airtime. Ron Brandon is Program Director.

WSCI FM (89.3)

P.O. Box 801,   881-1160
Mt. Pleasant, SC 29464   FAX 849-6123

This station, broadcasting from the aircraft carrier *Yorktown* at Patriot's Point from 6 AM to 1 AM, is the local affiliate for National

Public Radio (NPR). Their format includes classical music, jazz and news. Their locally-produced public affairs show is called "Port Holes." PSAs may be sent in writing, on cassette or reel-to-reel; material should be received two weeks prior to airtime. Taylor Lewis is Program Director.

WSSX FM "95-SX" (95.1)

P.O. Box 2167,   849-9500
Mt. Pleasant, SC 29465   FAX 849-9519

This 24-hour FM station has a "hot AC" format — meaning they play a mix of adult contemporary hits from "the top 40." PSAs may be sent in writing or on cassette or reel-to-reel; material should be received one week prior to airtime. Roger Gaither is Program Director.

WTMA AM (1250)

P.O. Box 30909,   556-1250
Charleston, SC 29417   FAX 763-0304

Their 24-hour format is all news and talk. Broadcasting since 1939, the stations now features call-in shows and on-air personalities. PSAs may be sent in writing or on cassette or reel-to-reel; material should be received two weeks prior to airtime. Program Director is Dan Moon.

WXTC AM "SPORTS RADIO" (1390)

478 East Bay Street,   722-7611
Charleston, SC 29403   FAX 577-7726

This format is all sports — both of network and local origin — with some "talk" analysis and review. Sports Director is Ted Byrne. Program Director is John Quincy.

WXTC FM (97.7)

478 East Bay Street,   722-7611
Charleston, SC 29403   FAX 577-7726

This 24-hour FM format is "adult contemporary" targeting young professionals. PSAs may be sent in writing; material should be received two weeks prior to airtime. Program Director is John Quincy.

WXLY FM (102.5)

950 Houston Northcut, Suite 201   884-2534
Mt. Pleasant, SC 29464   FAX 884-1218

This 24-hour FM format plays "oldies," or music of the '50s, '60s, and '70s. They locally produce a public affairs show called "Lowcountry Close-Up." PSAs may be sent in writing or on cassette or reel-to-reel; material should be received 24 hours prior to airtime and production assistance is available. Program Director is Todd Reynolds.

WWWZ FM "Z-93" (93.3)

P.O. Box 30669,   556-9132
Charleston, SC 29417   FAX 769-0876

This 24-hour FM format is "urban contemporary," targeting affluent blacks, ages 22 to 40. Their on-air personalities appear throughout the community in local clubs and discos. Their Entertainment Hotline (766-9336) provided current details about these appearances. PSAs can be sent in writing or on cassette or reel-to-reel; material should be received one week prior to airtime. Clifford Fletcher is Program Director.

WMGL FM "COAST 101.7" (101.7)

P.O. Box 30669,   556-9132
Charleston, SC 29417   FAX 769-0876

This 24-hour FM station is the

"sister station" of Z-93. Their format is also "urban contemporary" coming directly from a satellite feed. Anthony Keith is Advertising Director. Clifford Fletcher is Program Director.

WSSP FM (94.3)

P.O. Box 1165,   824-8943
Goose Creek, SC 29445   FAX 824-8940

This is the "sister station" of 95-SX. Their format of hip-hop, rap, and rock targets 13 to 20 year-olds. PSAs may be sent in writing or on cassette or reel-to-reel; material should be received one week prior to airtime. Station Manager is Mary Russell. Roger Gaither is Program Director.

WZJY AM (1480)

P.O. Box 2188   881-2482
Mt. Pleasant, SC 29465

Broadcasting 24-hours with a gospel music format, this station also has features called "Bible Talk" and "Teen Talk," plus a public affairs program called "Community Forum." PSAs may be sent in writing or on cassette or reel-to-reel; material should be received one to two weeks prior to airtime. Program Director is Edwin Wright.

Greater Charleston
Military

Throughout our country's wars, both domestic and foreign, the strategic location of Charleston's port and the energy of the city's defenders have both played important roles. Volumes have been written on the subject, movies have been made...and there's high drama, colorful personalities, genuine courage, and no small amount of swashbuckle involved.

The greater Charleston area has served as the U.S. Navy's third largest home port and the country's largest submarine base for most of the Cold War years. North Charleston is presently home to the U.S. Air Force's 437th and 315th Military Airlift Wings (home of the new C-17 Transport planes). And the U.S. Marines, the Army, and the Coast Guard station work to underline the military's effectiveness in this area.

But how do Charlestonians *feel* about the military? The answer to that was never more evident than during the anxious days preceding Operation Desert Storm in the Gulf War. As tensions mounted in the Gulf, Charlestonians watched quietly as ship after ship from the Navy Base slid slowly past the port facilities...under the Cooper River bridges...and out into Charleston Harbor and into the pages of history.

Commuters on their way to work, tourists en route to the beaches, lovers strolling in Waterfront Park...everyone who saw them felt a pull on the heart. All those brave young people; so proud, so fine, so very American....

Such a scene is hardly a new one, here in this old port city. Generations of Charleston-based military families have watched that same heart-rending parade out into the Atlantic. And while the individual soldiers and sailors and their vessels of war do change from time to time, the deep feeling of pride in every Charlestonian (native or adopted) has not.

Historically, the importance of Charleston to the *military* defense of our country is almost impossible to calculate. On the other hand, the importance of the military to *Charleston* is a matter of clear and impressive economic record.

More than 51,800 active, civilian and contract employees have been working in the greater Charleston area making up nearly 34% of the region's total employment. The combined military payroll for the area has exceeded $1.5 billion a year, which is over one-third of

Greater Charleston's (the Trident area's) total annual payroll. And in 1990, the resulting impact of these military families on Greater Charleston's economy was estimated to be $4.5 billion.

When the military's regular and dependable engine was pulling this kind of weight in the Lowcountry's economy, the area was relatively insulated against national recessionary trends.

All that seemed to change in the spring of 1993 when on March 13th, the headlines in *The Post and Courier* shouted, "A Direct Hit!" In Washington, the Defense Base Closure and Realignment Commission had announced the names of the U.S. military installations under consideration for closure or "realignment" in response to the end of the Cold War and the government's effort to curb the nation's suffocating deficit. Starting with those words, the 200-year-long journey of Charleston and the U.S. Navy started taking a new course.

What followed was a month of controversy and campaigning with alarming daily updates speculating about the dire economic impact on Greater Charleston — should the closures indeed take place.

The entire Lowcountry seemed somber as the Trident Chamber of Commerce organized a special lobbying committee, "In Defense of Charleston," to present its case before the Base Closure Commission's final recommendation to Congress.

In May, the final hearings were held — and Charleston's case was made. Then in June, the announcement came: both the Charleston Navy Base and the Charleston Shipyard were to be cut.

The closure time line is like this:

April 1994: an Outplacement Center will open where government employees can sign up for federal job openings elsewhere — two years prior to base closure.

October 1994: Planning begins for the first layoffs scheduled for June 1995.

December 1994 - January 1995: Early outs and early retirement offers are made — pending Pentagon approval.

March 1995: First layoff notices are issued.

June 1995: First layoffs occur (3,400 job losses expected).

December 1995: Final layoff notices are issued.

April 1995: Final layoffs and operational closure. Total job loss estimates for the Greater Charleston area are 28,400.

As dark a cloud as this news was to the entire Lowcountry, there were soon early signs of a silver lining. First, Congress passed an economic growth package that, according to one official, could foster up to 132,000 jobs in South Carolina. And a large percentage of those jobs could be here in the Lowcountry.

The Base Closure Commission chose *not* to close Charleston's NAVELEX facility — but to expand it here, instead. That will bring hundreds of high-tech jobs into the area.

Then, the Defense Department announced that the Army's Maritime Prepositioned Ship Depot (MPF) would be moved to Charleston — bringing with it more than 1,000 jobs.

Most recently, the Defense Department added to the good news by naming Charleston as the site for a small civilian Defense Department payroll center — a possible precursor to larger military financial facilities.

And then, the question remains — what will become of the existing shipyard? What will become of all the facilities abandoned by the Navy? Supposedly, the Navy has indicated it wants to turn over the naval base and the shipyard to a local group of civic leaders called the "BEST Committee" by April of 1996. And various plans and proposals are afoot for converting these valuable assets into private, job-producing enterprises.

There's no question that the future of the military in Greater Charleston is insecure, at best. But it's beginning to be clear that the insecurity (for the Lowcountry's economy) may be short-lived. A staff writer for *The State*, Columbia's major daily newspaper, has estimated the economic recovery from Charleston's base closure is likely to take less than three years. His report is based on an economic impact study conducted by the University of South Carolina for the Charleston Trident Home Builders Association.

At this writing, we can only hope this is true.

Charleston Air Force Base

Charleston Air Force Base is located about sixteen miles from downtown Charleston on approximately 3,500 acres of land within the city limits of North Charleston. The base is also responsible for other property in South Carolina — including a radar site at Jedburg, SC, an airstrip at North Field near Orangeburg, SC, plus off-base housing in the North Charleston area.

Actually, Charleston Air Force Base and the 437th Military Airlift Wing are one in the same, although their stories begin at separate places and at different times. Here's a short background:

As the popularity of flying grew, air operations in Charleston began on a small field at what later became Charleston Municipal Airport. The year was 1928. During those first few years, the airfield was used primarily by commercial and private aircraft. In 1931, the City of Charleston floated bonds and sold stock for the purchase of 432 acres of land at a cost of $25,000 — establishing the area's first municipally sanctioned airport. In 1935, a WPA project was assigned the job of modernizing the existing airfield and with a $313,000 grant. A new 3,500-ft. paved runway with modern lighting was completed and another runway was started.

On (literally) the day after the Japanese attacked Pearl Harbor, the Eastern Defense Command met in New York City and made immediate plans for the defense of the eastern coast of the United

States. Those plans included the establishment of military operations at existing municipal airports up and down the coast. Thus, in December 1941, the Army Air Corps took full control of the field in Charleston for coastal operations.

In early 1942, the first flights from the newly designated Charleston Army Air Field consisted mostly of antisubmarine missions. As the year wore on, operations expanded to include training B-17 Flying Fortress and B-24 Liberator combat crews and their support crews heading for the European theater of war. At the same time, the airfield was also being used by commercial aircraft. This was an early and successful example of the "joint-use" concept which is still used here today.

Joint-use operations continued until 1946, when the military portion of the airfield was closed and officially returned to the City of Charleston. By war's end, the airfield consisted of 2,050 acres along with $12 million in improvements. Military operations were reestablished in 1952 when the City of Charleston and the Air Force agreed to establish a troop carrier base and, once again, allow joint-use of the runways.

The Troop Carrier Wing became the host unit under the Tactical Air Command. The base was transferred to the Military Air Transportation Service (MATS) on March 1, 1956. The Air Transport Wing (AT) was activated in 1954 and became the host unit until 1966.

On January 8, 1966, the Air Force revamped all MATS units and their missions. MATS became the

Military Airlift Command and the AT was discontinued.

It was the established Air Force policy, at the time, to renumber active duty units using the same numerical designations as those units showing distinguished service during World War II. And when the 437th Military Airlift Wing was activated, it was assigned to Charleston Air Force Base. Personnel and equipment formerly assigned to the 1608th AT were reassigned to the 437th MAW.

THE WING

Renaming the "new" unit in Charleston was actually the honoring of a highly respected and distinguished unit from World War II.

The 437th MAW's namesake, the original 437th Troop Carrier Group (TCG), was activated in May of 1943 at Baer Field, Indiana, and remained on active duty until November 1945. During the unit's two years of active service in World War II, its crews participated in the D-Day invasion in Normandy — primarily supporting the 82nd Airborne Division. They also participated in Operation Market Garden — sustaining extremely heavy losses while successfully completing their mission. And the 437th TCG flew the first airdrop resupply into Bastogne during the Battle of the Bulge.

In June of 1949, the 437th was reactivated in the Reserve. In 1950, it moved to Japan — flying combat airlift missions into Korea. These missions continued until June 1952 when once again the 437th MAW was placed in the Reserve.

So, Charleston's 437th MAW, reactivated in 1966, has a proud and distinguished history. Over the years, the base has supported such aircraft as the C-17, C-119, B-17, B-24, C-54, C-121, C-130 C-5, and the C-141.

The nearly 5,800 military and civilian employees of the 437th MAW today maintain and operate fifty-eight C-141 jet transport aircraft, the workhorses of the airlift fleet, in support of U.S. and world-wide humanitarian airlift missions. And as the aging C-141 is retired (after a quarter of a century of service), the C-17, MAC's newest airlift aircraft, is taking up the reins and proudly continuing the mission — flying out of Charleston Air Force Base with the 437th Military Airlift Wing.

U.S. Naval Base, Charleston

Surprisingly, the history of the Navy's presence in Charleston dates back only to 1900 when the 56th Congress of the United States authorized the establishment of a new navy yard on the west bank of the Cooper River. A site comprised of three antebellum plantations was selected approximately six miles north of the Customs House and surveying began in early 1902.

The dry dock was the first project to be completed in 1909 along with the red brick buildings and the main power plant — all still in use today. With the work force of some 300 civilians, the first ship was placed in dry dock and work began

on vessels of the fleet in 1910. By 1915, 800 civilians were employed at the yard.

During World War I, a naval training center was established and there was a considerable expansion of facilities, land area and work force. Employment reached 6,500 personnel by November 1918.

After the war, the work force was gradually reduced and only minor vessels were sent to Charleston for repairs. By 1922, the future of the Navy Yard was uncertain.

The year 1933 marked the beginning of a second upsurge at the yard. A large work load created the need for more facilities and a much larger work force. This formed the nucleus of the large group of men and women who would soon meet the demands of naval shipbuilding and repair work during World War II. This was when the Navy's facilities were further expanded to include what is now known as the "South Yard," "Naval Air Station," and the "Noisette Creek Area."

During World War II, the Navy Yard employees constructed some 200 vessels of various classes including destroyers, destroyer escorts, tank landing ships, amphibious landing ships and destroyer tenders. In addition, there was a great amount of battle damage repair work to do. Civilian employment at the yard peaked in 1943 with almost 26,000 employees working three shifts daily.

Meanwhile, the Sixth Naval District (which at the time included South Carolina, most of North Carolina and Florida, plus the states of

Alabama, Tennessee, Mississippi, Louisiana and Texas) was responsible for the protection of the sea lanes and convoy routes along 540 miles of coastline on the Eastern seaboard.

April 1943 set the record for reported submarine contacts in coastal waters off the U.S. — with 35 hostile contacts investigated. Unbeknownst to most people living in Charleston at the time, the busiest area for antisubmarine patrols was...right off the coast of Charleston!

As a result of an intensive defense strategy, only three U.S. ships were torpedoed off the Carolinas and Georgia coasts after May of 1942.

Just prior to the outbreak of World War II, the Naval Base complex had been enlarged with the establishment of the Charleston Naval Ammunition Depot. It was located 20 miles from downtown Charleston on the west bank of the Cooper River on land that had once been five plantations in the Goose Creek area of St. James Parish. All during the war, the depot was actively receiving, storing, reworking and issuing vast amounts of ammunition.

On November 30, 1945, the U.S. Naval Base, Charleston was officially established and the old Navy Yard became the Charleston Naval Shipyard, a component of the Naval Base.

The ammunition depot was placed in "partial maintenance" status in 1950 during the Korean War and that status was upgraded to "active" in 1952. Then, in 1954, an additional tract of land known as the Liberty Hall Annex was acquired for the purposes of expansion. The Marine Barracks, Charleston was established in March of 1959.

During the 1950s, the Naval Shipyard became the major overhaul facility on the East Coast for submarines as well as the outfitter for new ships constructed for the Navy in private shipyards in the district. In 1956 new piers, barracks and buildings for mine warfare ships and personnel were started. Later, Charleston became home port of combatant ships and submarines of the U.S. Atlantic fleet.

The Naval Ammunition Depot was renamed the Naval Weapons Station in 1965. By 1990, it covered 16,344 acres.

The sudden emergence of the Gulf War was an impressive test for the strategic importance and undeniable readiness of Charleston's permanent naval presence.

Greater Charleston
Airports

When newcomers need to deal with airports in the Greater Charleston area, it's good to know a few basic facts: What are the major airlines serving Charleston International Airport? Who do you call to see if a flight is on-time or not? What are some of the route and time factors involved in getting to the airport from various parts of the Tri-County area? And what about ground transportation and parking?

Here are some quick answers that will come in handy for you or your inbound friends and relatives arriving at Charleston International Airport.

The number to call if you want to check on an incoming flight — whether it's on-time or not — is 767-7009. Checking here before leaving for the airport can save you time and frustration. The Charleston International Airport's Information Desk has all the latest information that's available.

Airlines

American Airlines	722-7108
Conquest Airlines	552-2068
Delta Air Lines	577-3230
USAir	723-6107
United Airlines	1-800-241-6522

Rental Cars

Avis Rent A Car	767-7030
Budget Rent A Car	767-7051
Dollar Rent A Car	760-1112
Hertz Rent A Car	767-4552
National Car Rental	767-3078

CHARLESTON
INTERNATIONAL AIRPORT
International Blvd.   767-1100

If you're the economic development type and you need some background information on Charleston International Airport's history and present facilities, here's a quick review:

In 1928, the City of Charleston leased 782 acres for construction of a municipal airport. A year later, the new airfield was officially open for business. This facility served the greater Charleston area until 1942 when it was turned over to the U.S. Government for military use during WWII (see our Military chapter).

After the war, the City of Charleston resumed control of operations at the airfield and in 1949, the first civilian Charleston Airport Terminal was completed.

In 1952, the U.S. Government leased the airfield to begin operations at the (then) new Charleston Air Force Base. Today, Charleston is officially designated the "Southeastern Commercial Gateway" for the Military Airlift Command.

In 1970, the Charleston County Aviation Authority was created. By 1979, the Authority had assumed ownership of the airport from the City of Charleston. On March 30, 1985, the greatly expanded and modernized present terminal was dedicated — Charleston International Airport.

Today's 280,000-sq.-ft. facility has ten gates — all served by covered loading bridges. The walking distance from the terminal entrance to the most remote aircraft gate is only about 800 feet.

The International Area and Customs Service Inspection Area have 20,000 sq. ft. of space and can process international passengers quickly.

In 1992, the air carriers serving Charleston International Airport carried over 1,300,000 passengers with more than 90 flights each day.

If you're interested in business/economic opportunities at Charleston International Airport, contact the Aviation Authority Development Office at 803-767-7015.

PARKING

The terminal's parking lot can accommodate 1000 cars. Short term parking rates (for meeting incoming passengers, etc.) are $.75 per half hour. The short term parking lot (24 hours or less) is $8 per day. There's a separate long term parking lot available at $5 per day. Both parking areas are clearly marked.

ACCESS ROUTES

As a simple rule of thumb, plan on allowing at least half an hour to drive from downtown Charleston to the airport. Allow even more time during rush hour or on busy, holiday travel dates.

Take I-26 north to the Montague Ave. exit and turn left. Follow Montague Ave. till you see the green airport access sign just before the Mark Clark Expressway. This access road leads you onto International Blvd. (past the S.C. Research Authority) and right into the Terminal area.

If you are driving south on I-26 (toward Charleston from Columbia), take the Mark Clark Expressway exit. The airport exit off the Mark Clark is clearly marked, and you'll head into the Terminal area via International Blvd.

LIMOUSINE SERVICE
767-7111

Several Charleston area hotels, motels and B&Bs offer transportation service to and from the airport. Check with your reservation agent, the concierge, or your hotel for specific details.

Near the baggage carousel, you'll find a lighted "courtesy board" showing most of the area's better hotels, motels, and B&Bs. The (attached) phone offers speed dial service to those places offering airport pick-up service.

If you're left to your own resources, Airport Limousine Service is available just outside the baggage claim area at the Terminal.

Service is available 24-hours a day. Passenger pick-up is available

— with 24-hour advance notice — from your home address or from any designated hotel, motel or B&B. You can go from the airport to Kiawah, Wild Dunes, downtown or to a specific address most any time.

For round-trip service, the charge is $16. For a one-way trip into the city, it's $9. This is an extremely handy service for Insiders who manage to end up with some early departure time or some late arrival when no formal reception committee seems likely to show up to meet your plane.

TAXIS

Yellow Cab, 577-6565, is the only service in the Lowcountry area.

Private Pilot Information

Greater Charleston offers four options for private pilots — all convenient and uncongested. In addition to New Charleston at Charleston International Airport, there's East Cooper Aviation, Charleston Executive Airport and Carolina Aviation in Summerville.

NEW CHARLESTON AVIATION
6070 Perimeter Road, Charleston   744-2581
Toll Free   1-800-845-1395
Located outside Charleston AFB, off Aviation Avenue at Charles-

ton International Airport, New Charleston Aviation's FBO facility offers four long runways, nine instrument approaches and 24-hour, all-weather service. This is your best choice if you wish to land closest to downtown Charleston. Million Air also offers a wide range of services — from budget rental cars to limousines and dinner reservations with theater tickets — along with charter service, avionics repair and general maintenance.

EAST COOPER AVIATION
700 Airport Road, Mt. Pleasant   884-8837
Private pilots can access the East Cooper area (including Wild Dunes) via the East Cooper Airport in Mt. Pleasant. It has a 3,700-ft. runway and offers complete airplane detailing, tie downs, jet fuel and AV gas. Rental cars are available on the premises. The office/terminal is open from 8 AM to 6 PM in the winter months, and (after April 1) summer hours are from 8 AM to 8 PM.

CHARLESTON EXECUTIVE AIRPORT
2700 Fort Trenholm Rd,
Johns Island   559-2401
Private pilots wanting access closest to Kiawah and Seabrook will most likely choose the Executive Airport on Johns Island, 12 miles south of Charleston. Their two run-

---

International Blvd. is a notorious speed trap, so be sure to watch your speedometer closely here. Many is the traveler who, in a big hurry to catch their flight at the airport, caught a blue light and a big fine instead.

Insiders' Tip

ways (09-27 and 04-22) are both 5000 feet x 150 feet. The facility offers tie downs, jet fuel and 100 LL gas. Rental cars are available on the premises and limited limousine service to some resort hotels is offered.

CAROLINA AVIATION

890 Greyback Road,
Summerville (3 miles NW)   *851-0970*

This access for private pilots to the Summerville area and Berkeley County has a 3,700-ft. runway. They offer airplane detailing, tie downs, jet fuel and AV gas. The office/terminal is open from 8 AM to 6 PM throughout the winter, and after April 1 from 8:00 AM to 8:00 PM.

Inside
Port of Charleston

Since the first shipment of cotton was exported to England in 1748, Charleston Harbor has been the backbone of Greater Charleston's economy. Today, it's fair to say that the general health and prosperity of the entire state depends heavily on the sophisticated transportation network focused on and around the Port of Charleston.

During the past five years, the Port of Charleston has grown to become the number one containerized port on the South Atlantic and Gulf Coast — handling 45 percent of all container tonnage among competing ports. On the East Coast, only the combined ports of New York and New Jersey handle more containers than Charleston.

Four terminals comprise the Port of Charleston and together they handled 7.1 million tons of cargo in fiscal year 1993. Of this figure, over 6.4 million tons were containerized cargo and nearly 750,000 tons of breakbulk cargo. The terminals are located at Columbus Street, Union Pier, Wando and North Charleston. More than 1,500 vessels call on Charleston each year, representing service to over 120 countries all over the globe. The Port of Charleston is export-driven as well, with 60 percent of its cargo sent overseas.

The Port of Charleston's rise to international prominence is based on its status as the most efficient and productive port in the U.S. and — in world standings — second only to the port of Kobe, Japan.

Currently, the South Carolina State Ports Authority (SCSPA) employs about 406 people. The employment impact, however, means thousands of jobs statewide in businesses directly related to the port's activities. These businesses include 59 steamship lines, 38 steamship agencies and line offices, 119 trucklines, two major railroads providing intermodal and conventional services, and 38 custom house brokers and freight forwarders.

The Authority is a state agency structured as a private business and operates solely on its own revenues and earnings. The SCSPA is governed by a nine-member board appointed by the governor with the advice and consent of the Senate.

Crucial to the Port of Charleston is the connecting transportation system; the airports, highways, railroads and public transportation systems which interface with the port's services.

Airports: Charleston International Airport serves over one million civilian and military passengers every year. It is serviced by five major domestic carriers: American, Conquest, Delta, United, and USAir. In addition, six private airports are located strategically throughout the region.

Highways: The Port of Charleston has access to three interstate highways; I-26, I-95 and the nearly completed I-526. In addition, the area is serviced by four major U.S. Highways and seven state highways.

Rail Service: The Port of Charleston is served by a dedicated rail system that extends to more major cities than any other Southern Port main line railroads serving the tri-county area include the CSX System and Norfolk Southern.

Amtrak offers public rail transportation to other cities throughout the nation.

All figures presented here are courtesy of the Port of Charleston. For more information, contact the SCSPA.

SOUTH CAROLINA STATE PORTS AUTHORITY

176 Concord Street
P.O. Box 817
Charleston, SC 29402
803-723-8651
In-State WATS: 800-922-5254
Out-of-State WATS: 800-845-7106
Telex: SC PORTSAUTH 810-881-1860
FAX: 803-577-8616

ORDER FORM

Use this convenient form to place your order
for any of the Insiders' Guides® books.

Fast and Simple!

Mail to:
Insiders' Guides®, Inc.
P.O. Box 2057
Manteo, NC 27954 *or*
for VISA or Mastercard orders call
1-800-765-BOOK

Name _____

Address _____

City/State/Zip _____

Quantity	Title/Price	Shipping	
	Insiders' Guide® to the Triangle, $12.95	$2.50	
	Insiders' Guide® to Charlotte, $12.95	$2.50	
	Insiders' Guide® to Virginia Beach / Norfolk, $12.95	$2.50	
	Insiders' Guide® to the Outer Banks, $12.95	$2.50	
	Insiders' Guide® to Williamsburg, $12.95	$2.50	
	Insiders' Guide® to Richmond, $12.95	$2.50	
	Insiders' Guide® to Orlando, $12.95	$2.50	
	Insiders' Guide® to Virginia's Blue Ridge, $12.95	$2.50	
	Insiders' Guide® to The Crystal Coast of NC, $12.95	$2.50	
	Insiders' Guide® to Myrtle Beach, $12.95 (Summer '93)	$2.50	
	Insiders' Guide® to Charleston, $12.95	$2.50	
	Insiders' Guide® to Virginia's Blue Ridge, $12.95	$2.50	
	Insiders' Guide® to Civil War Sites In The Eastern Theater (Fall '93),	$2.50	
	Insiders' Guide® to Lexington, $12.95 (Spring '94)	$2.50	
	Insiders' Guide® to Wilmington, NC, $12.95 (Spring '94)	$2.50	

(N.C. residents add 6% sales tax.) GRAND TOTAL _____

*Payment in full (check, cash or money order) must accompany order
form. Please allow 2 weeks for delivery*

Index of Advertisers

Index